D0948386

BY FIRE AND AXE

BY FIRE AND AXE

The Communist Party
and the
Civil War in Greece, 1944-1949.

Evangelos Averoff-Tossizza

Translated by
Sarah Arnold Rigos

CARATZAS BROTHERS, PUBLISHERS
New Rochelle, New York
1978

First published in French under the title
Le Feu et la Hache Grece '46-'49, Histoire des
Guerres de l'apres-Guerre *in 1973* by Editions
de Breteuil, *Paris.*

First English language edition. Published by

CARATZAS BROTHERS, PUBLISHERS
246 Pelham Road
New Rochelle, New York 10805
(U.S.A.)

ISBN: 0-89241-078-7

Library of Congress Catalog
Card Number: 77-91603

PUBLISHER'S PREFACE

The last decade has seen a Greek revival of a kind in the United States: the study of *modern* Greece has begun to attract the interest of a great number of Americans.

As a result of this " Greek revival" a number of academically related organizations have been formed while many American universities are adding courses on the language, the literature and the history of modern Greece. Much of the credit for the recognition of modern Greek studies by American scholars belongs to the Modern Greek Studies Association, an organization celebrating its tenth anniversary this year; the efforts of dozens, probably hundreds, of individuals to bring Greece to the attention of the American intellectual community should also be mentioned. Finally, a number of major universities have recognized the importance of modern Greece and they have instituted programs for its study. The plans of Columbia University are perhaps the most ambitious, while Harvard has established the Seferis Chair of Modern Greek Studies and many other institutions have more limited but useful programs.

The new American interest in the Helladic area has made evident a shortage of English language material; modern Greek literature and poetry, on account of certain individuals of great stature, are to some degree known to American readers. Even so, the background and context of men like Cavafy, Kazantzakis and Seferis is largely unknown in this country, for until recently very few universities offered courses in modern Greek literature. The American public is even less familiar with modern and contemporary Greek history. Insofar as Greek history was mentioned at all it was in the context of larger European diplomatic and political movements. Monographs, some of great calibre, have appeared on specific historical problems; there remain large gaps however even in very important historical areas. One such gap is that concerning the civil war which followed Greece's liberation after the Second World War.

Many problems surrounded the writing of a history of the Greek civil war. Until recently the emotions caused by this internecine conflict were reflected in the works of otherwise competent historical writers. It is for this reason that Averoff's book is so remarkable.

It has been pointed out that the politics of Evangelos Averoff-Tossizza are widely known: he has throughout his life been a firm believer in the democratic process in a country where democracy has been a very fragile institution. He is also committed to a view of modern Greece as an integral part of what is known as the Western World. Yet despite his political commitments, or perhaps because of them, his work remains thorough and objective. (It has been praised by Markos Vafiadis, the military commander of the Greek communist forces during the civil war.)

The merit of Averoff's book lies in its even and urbane tone. Most other literature that has appeared since the war's end is polemical, even abrasive and it is difficult for an outsider not having lived through these times to understand. Averoff's book tells what happened and gives the reasons for its conclusions. It is valuable both as a historical work and as a primary source, for its author is a statesman of note (he is currently Greece's Minister of National Defense and he was for a long time Foreign Minister) as well as a historical writer. Most significantly, the American public will find in Averoff's book a sense of balance, proportion and mature judgment. It is an attractive introduction to an important period in modern Greek history as well as a chapter in postwar diplomatic history which has been largely unknown.

The publishers are proud to inaugurate their program for the publication of modern Greek historical works with this significant volume.

TABLE OF CONTENTS

ix

BY FIRE AND AXE

Chapter I

Introduction

The Essence. The struggle was local, the stakes worldwide. Now, as in the past, the Greek peninsula stands at one of the great crossroads of Europe and of the world.

Today, a crossroad of ideologies, once of religions. It is, and always has been, a crossroads of continents, of maritime routes and of the races of man.

For these reasons, throughout the ages history has left its mark on the peninsula; and for these same reasons, almost all the important crises of mankind have erupted on it.

Despite a relatively small geographical area, the Greek peninsula has influenced repeatedly, sometimes decisively, the course of human history.

This is not an exaggeration.

Over two thousand years ago the outcome of the Persian Wars prevented the Great King Darius from imposing his absolute rule on the continent of Europe and allowed instead the flowering of democratic ideals which Solon had first planted in Athens. Born then, the mature Europe of today still draws the benefits from that victory and those ideals.

Over ten centuries have gone by since Byzantium stemmed the tide of Islam and forced it to give way to Christianity. Fifty years ago during World War I, Greece's campaign on the Allied side ensured the survival of the great Serbian nation, an unhindered sea route to India via the Mediterranean, and the creation of a second front on the flank of the Kaiser's powerful armies.

Finally, a more recent crisis, as deep as any of the former, has rent the entire peninsula; its consequences are still being felt today.

At the end of World War II the Soviet Union, a great power and also standard bearer of a powerful revolutionary ideology, had trampled European territory with giant strides. In ruins, but with enthusiasm and with large reserves of manpower and resources, that nation had advanced its boundaries far beyond its prewar frontiers beyond the Dnieper and the Danube to the shores of the Adriatic.

Within the space of a few years Stalin was realizing the age-old dream which the Tsars of the Black Eagle had pursued for centuries and which their successors of the Red Star had never abandoned.

But, despite all this, Stalin, the true victor of the Yalta and Moscow conferences, could not win on all fronts. He had to renounce his claim on a Mediterranean base and to leave the Greek peninsula which he had failed to conquer in World War II, outside his sphere of influence.

So, if owing to Turkish neutrality, he was unable to seize the gates to the Black Sea, he also lost the ability to control them; the Aegean islands from which the Dardanelles can be blockaded, had escaped his grasp. As a result, he was left without a base in the eastern Mediterranean.

In regard to bases in the same area today, Moscow may not have a problem. However, in 1945 the picture was totally different and wholly negative; on the international chessboard of that period the peninsula and its islands were truly valuable. Soviet control of both would make possible a many-sided game with grave consequences: Turkey would be isolated while the new Balkan allies would be served and, at the same time, consolidated; and, above all, access to the Mediterranean and Africa would be easy. If Paris was worth one mass for Henry the Fourth, all these advantages were certainly worth one civil war for Stalin—even more so since a war would be fought by others.

Beginnings and Background. To understand how this war broke out and it was so persistently supported, it is necessary to have some idea of what preceded it. For, during forty months of guerrilla warfare, Greece suffered more destruction and greater casualties than in both World War II and the German occupation.

In every human society, undoubtedly, there have always been men who were ready to go to war, either just for the sake of fighting, love of adventure, or to satisfy an interest—love of power or material gain. However, such men can be useful; properly manipulated they can begin the most foolish adventure, and even sacrifice their lives. What they cannot do is endure. Adventure without let-up wears them out and gain that eludes them leads to despair. Coercion which can follow—and usually does—is not sufficient to see them through.

To begin a wide-ranging adventure, and to make it last, requires suitable psychological conditions. The events preceding it should be favorable and, primarily, one needs a determined—even a fanatical—"task-force."

In this case, the "task force" was the Greek Communist Party (KKE).

We will outline its history from the moment of its birth

up to the time it became actively and openly revolutionary. Its activities in this field, furthermore, will be the main topic of this book.

But, before describing that birth and the political and revolutionary activities of the KKE, it is essential to give an idea of the society into which it was born and then developed.

Those persons who are acquainted only with present-day Greece cannot picture the country at the time when the KKE began to take form, immediately after World War I. One could go so far as to say that even the territory itself was different for, although the contour of the land and the soil were the same, its development was such that it seemed an entirely different place for its inhabitants.

Covering nearly two-thirds of the country, the rugged mountains had only a poor network of roads, more fit for mules than vehicles. The low plains were plagued by malaria; irrigation was rare, means of cultivation outdated, and crops were at the mercy of both floods and drought. Even on the plains, roads were few and in a very wretched state. The single-track railway lines boasted an international width between Athens and Western Europe via Thessalonike. Maritime communications between Piraeus and the islands or ports of average importance were regular and tolerable. All others were infrequent and defective in many ways.

Large cities and great industries were non-existent. The population of the only important cities, Athens and Thessalonike together, did not exceed five hundred thousand. Moreover, industries of medium size by Western European standards, could be counted on the fingers of one hand.

The gap which separated Greece from the developed countries of the West was equally great in the social conditions.

Highway robbery on the main roads was perhaps

unusual, but certainly not unknown.

The number of illiterate people in the population most probably exceeded forty percent.

For all practical purposes a working class did not exist. Almost all those included in this category were not workers in the proper sense of the word; they belonged to the lower middle class and were employed in the very few primitive family industries.

The peasantry had just enjoyed an extensive land reform under Eleftherios Venizelos between 1918 and 1920, which reform was followed by two others still more radical—one in 1923, and the other in the early 1950's. Since then, the maximum plot of arable land which one person could own was fifty hectares, if cultivated by the owner, and twenty-five, if the owner was not a farmer. To complete the picture, it must be added that most farmers owned one to five hectares (10 to 50 stremmas), a considerable number owned five to twenty hectares and only a few had more.

The middle class or bourgeoisie was very important. Consisting only of a lower middle class, this group was deeply imbued—as were those individuals who belonged to other classes—with the ideals of Religion, Nation, Family and Property.

These classes then, for all practical purposes, formed the totality of the population. A proverbial frugality existed everywhere, while in the mountains it reached an extreme.

The upper middle class was actually of little importance. Large landowners, as mentioned, had been restricted. There were only a few hundred wealthy families. None had large fortunes except those who had acquired them abroad, and many of these enjoyed special prestige as great national benefactors. Such benefactors had founded many important institutions, schools, prisons, libraries and hospitals; these made an even greater impression on the

5

people as the country was so poor.

The country's physical and social aspect which, in a certain sense, recalled the West at the beginning of the nineteenth century, changed somewhat between the years 1920 and 1940. The Asia Minor disaster in 1922 and the subsequent arrival of 1.3 million refugees, doubled the population of the three largest cities, created a real working class proletariat, and led finally to the formation of a relatively important industry. Suddenly, the inequality of the classes began to be felt.

On the other hand, two peaceful decades with governments inspired by a reforming and creative spirit—especially that of Venizelos between 1928 and 1932—improved conditions in production, communications, industry, social insurance and education.

Nevertheless, on the eve of World War II, Greece was not very far from the point where it had found itself in the day after World War I. And it was completely different from the Greece of the decade of 1960 to 1969.

To sum up everything in a few words and with three figures, today the per capita annual income is more than 2,200 dollars, while in 1940, it was less than 150 dollars and in 1920 less than 100 dollars.

Chapter II

Historical Survey of the
Greek Communist Party (KKE)

Birth and Beginnings of the Greek Communist Party. The Greek Communist party was born in Piraeus in 1918. Then it had a different structure from the present party and was called the Socialist Labor Party. It was merely an insignificant political group restricted to its founders and a few followers, whe were mainly inspired by the socialism of the Second International. But in just two years' time it became more radically oriented.

The success of the Russian Revolution and the impetus of the Third International encouraged those who sought a bolder course and who were able after bitter arguments to impose their leadership on their comrades. During the first months of 1920 the word "communist" was added to the party's title, its participation in the Comintern was decided upon, and a dynamic young student was elected as its representative at the large international congress of the Communist International held in Moscow.

It is worth mentioning the name of this student, Demosthenis Ligdopoulos, because it was as if he were marked by fate to become a sad omen of the great adventures of the KKE. Indeed, in the beginning he succeeded in his mission.

In September of the same year, the prestigious president of the Comintern, Zinovief, announced in Moscow with open satisfaction that the Greek Communist party had been accepted unanimously as a member of the Comintern. Thus, the KKE was born and at the same time, was accepted internationally.

This glorious start for the Greek delegate had a tragic ending only a few weeks later.

A young Greek named Alexakis, who was born in Russia, was appointed as an escort to Demosthenis Ligdopoulos. Furthermore, he was named the representative of the Comintern in Athens. Both were given confidential instructions, a large amount of propagandistic material as well as five thousand gold dollars, for the first organizing expenses of their small party.

But wealth can become lost and often leads to the loss of the most powerful ideals. The two young Greek militants chartered a small ship in Odessa to cross the Black Sea. During their voyage they were both murdered and their bodies were thrown into the sea. The ship's Ukrainian crew was arrested by the Soviet authorities and executed, but that was small comfort. As ideals led to life and action, gold led to the grave.

One could make many guesses, and even some political speculation, about the human tragedy of that dark night of October 20, 1920. Undoubtedly the choice of Athens, who was crowned in Moscow, and the choice of Moscow, who was to become coordinator in Athens, acting together would have endowed the party with a strong leadership right from the beginning.

This has not been recalled just to remind one of the

importance of fate in the history of mankind, but to offer my readers certain specific facts which belong to the so-called "behind-the-scenes" history. For, otherwise, one would be too severe in judging the first leaders of the KKE.

Endowed with faith, the primary element in every great endeavour, they devoted themselves to a particularly difficult task. As we already know, Greece was not the most suitable ground in which to cultivate the seeds of Marxism-Leninism. The small political party which had decided to introduce these ideas into Greece, had undertaken an extremely difficult assignment. That is exactly the reason why its first steps did not take it very far.

Efforts toward organizing and developing the Party and the long drawn-out quarrel over whether or not obedience to the Comintern was essential—that is to say, the wish of the majority was strongly questioned by a minority—form the history of the first five years of the KKE's life. However, these years cannot be dealt with in detail in this general survey.

Nevertheless, at least one page in this history is of special interest: the activity of the Party during and after the Greek-Turkish war in Asia Minor.

During that year (1920 to 1922) the KKE conducted a widespread campaign of defeatism throughout the army in which it had converted a few hundred followers. Now, this campaign took place in an environment suitable for success because, since 1912—except for a few short intervals—the country had been at war. Although the war effort had been enormous, other factors, such as the attitude of the Great Powers and the withdrawal of the enemy deep into the interior, had not allowed the troops to expect a favorable outcome.

Propaganda was easy from the argumentation point of view, but difficult—though excellently conducted—on the organizational side. After the war the Party claimed that its propaganda was one of the principal factors contributing to the complete military disaster of 1922.

In reality, however, Communist propaganda played only a secondary role among the many very powerful factors which led to that catastrophe. In fact, in the fall of 1921 the government had taken measures against the highest echelons of the Party and many of its top propagandists were arrested or fled. But, if these measures were somewhat effective at the front, they were not particularly severe and did not eliminate the possibility of a more general activity by the small organization. This surfaced immediately after the catastrophe. Reinforced by several hundred militants who had returned from the war front, where they had been well instructed in illegal activity, all the Party cadres undertook a vigorous campaign to convert the refugees.

Convincing arguments were used: the refugees were not actually victims of a war of liberation which had failed; they were simply paying very dearly for war begun by the Greek plutocracy which mainly served the interests of British imperialism and to which French capitalism was opposed. The latter, in turn, had seen that the Turkey of Kemal Ataturk was well armed. Conveniently, the Communists had forgotten the Turkish-Soviet treaty of 1921 which, first of all, allowed the conqueror of the Dardanelles to create a regular army. But persistent propaganda did not stop at such trifles. Besides, it was easy for the propanganda effort to take advantage of many matters for its was being conducted amidst total confusion and immense misery. Arguments were easily found and all of them seemed strong.

Thus, the Party worked in a very consistent, clever and often poisonous way.[1]

Spectacular results were in the making. Suddenly, the rocky soil that had been unsuitable for seeds became fertile ground to receive them. For in one month alone in the fall of 1922, more than one million three hundred thousand refugees, naked and hungry, took shelter in an under-developed country where five million of their brothers already lived.

In order to understand better what that meant, one should imagine—without considering the differences in natural resources—that, in proportion, this would be equivalent to the arrival of thirteen million refugees in France or fifty million in the United States. It was an unique phenomenon in the history of population movements. Suddenly, in the space of a few months, Athens was joined to Piraeus through the continual addition of makeshift settlements; one city with more than a million inhabitants was formed.

On the other hand, if it were true that these people came to a country inhabited by their brothers, it was equally true that those brothers were poor, tired and disappointed, and that they received bare-footed and uprooted people, anxious and uncertain of mind, with death in their souls.

Finally, after fighting for ten years—from 1912 until 1922—the army returned home, both exhausted and humiliated, following a catastrophe absolutely without precedent. It was a defeat which caused the greatest crisis in the history of the nation since independence. Furthermore, it caused one of the most serious crises in the three thousand-year history of Hellenism because it suddenly limited the geographical area in which the Greek people had lived since antiquity and brought about very grave national, social and financial pressures.

But, out of all these difficulties, the KKE gained almost nothing. In the years which followed it was proved, as we shall see later on, that in reality, the small party had not realized any advantage.

This case is perhaps unique and, at any rate, very interesting for the political observer, as well as the historical researcher. For here historical materialism was contradicted instead of being justified, as one would expect.

The material element urged the human soul on towards revolution. The sentimental element kept to tradition. And the second won. As often happens, the non-material ideas proved to be stronger than the material necessities. It is worth mentioning the principal reason for this phenomenon: these ideas were espoused by two men beloved by the refugees.

The first was Eleftherios Venizelos who had attempted the Asia Minor campaign with the aim of uniting the Greeks of the East with those of the Motherland. He had made all Greeks, and especially the refugees, believe and dream. The dangerous enterprise had finally led to disaster. But disaster came about under the leadership of others, his opponents. The good intentions were attributed to him, the disaster to the others. Him they loved because of the hopes and beautiful dreams he had offered.

The second man who supported the "ideas" was an army officer, Nicholas Plastiras, who will reappear after twenty-five years in very critical days. Coming from a poor family, in ten years he had acquired the reputation of being a bold fighter for, in 1922, with his regiment he had valiantly covered the retreat of a part of the army. Upon his return to Athens he toppled the government, had six of its leading members tried and executed, and made himself head of a military government. Furthermore, he saw that everything possible was done to relieve the suffering of the cold and hungry refugees.

Known for his poverty, modesty, honesty and suffering of tuberculosis he had become the symbol of endurance and personal sacrifice to the refugees.

The masses are more sentimental than is usually believed. They are, in any case, more sentimental than reasonable. The only point one can make here is that for people to be led by feelings, these feelings must be concentrated and simplified and, above all, they must be expressed by the acts of certain individuals. When this happens, those people can lead the masses almost anywhere they wish—for better or worse. In history we have seen this happen many times.

In our case, Venizelos and Plastiras were that kind of people to the refugees. Both ardent nationalists, they—more than anyone else—blocked the way that had been opened to the KKE. The great majority of the refugees were loyal to them and most remained dedicated to them until their death.

*The Difficult Childhood.*Despite the great effort by the Party faithful, the first steps of the KKE were discouraging. In the early years noticeable results were not produced in any of the sectors in which a special effort was made—refugees, workers, peasants or army.

The first general elections in which the Party took part were held in 1923; the KKE garnered only about 20,000 out of a total of 800,000 votes. This caused terrible disappointment in the cadres and was, at the same time, a spectacular revelation. It spread discord among the leaders, brought the Comintern to intervene further, and caused a new effort to be made to organize the base of the Party.

Nevertheless, that which seems to have produced some meager results was the political situation in the country. The relatively sterile parliamentary government and the minor military coups which preceded and succeeded the dictatorship of General Theodoros Pangalos (June 1925—August 1926) had disenchanted part of the electorate.

Thus, in the elections of November 1926, the Party increased its following to about 42,000 votes and, owing to the system of proportional representation, won ten seats in a Parliament of 226 members. The number was not large, but it allowed a first appearance. This appearance, proved to be ephemeral.

In 1928, Eleftherios Venizelos, whom the refugees called

the "father of his country", returned to the leadership of the Liberals. In the elections of August 1928, he won an overwhelming victory. On the other hand, the KKE assembled only 14,000 votes out of over a million tallied. None of its candidates was elected.

But that was not all. Because of the illegal activities of the small party and the existence of a very grave question raised within the Party itself and to be mentioned below, Venizelos passed without delay a law permitting the prosecution of a large number of KKE members.

This law was not especially strict as far as penalties went and was similar to laws adopted by other countries after World War I. However, its importance could be attributed to the fact that the punishable act was vaguely defined so as to include any kind of activity against the established social order.

Some hard blows resulted from this piece of legislation. They were made even more effective by the fact that continued internal discord caused disunity among Party leaders for about a decade. The disputes often took on a personal character, but they continued even though the individuals involved changed or decided to compromise. For the nature of the dispute—remarkably timely even today—concerned a divergence of fundamental views:

Should there be complete obedience to the orders of the Comintern and strict submission to the Soviet Union, Motherland of Socialism and protector of the international proletariat? Or should there be relative independence and application of Marxist principles according to local conditions better known to the cadres who lived and struggled in a given country?

The struggle between these two tendencies was extremely fierce and went through many interesting phases which often obliged the Comintern to intervene. Many times it did so directly and bluntly. That is how, with occasional victories and certain compromises, the

14

"conformists"—those who held to the line of absolute obedience to Moscow—managed to prevail. But these interferences and the importance of the issue in question kept an obstinate and spirited opposition alive. For example, one of the Party leaders, Pandelis Pouliopoulos, in the summer of 1927 publicly denounced certain theories of Stalin on socialism as "anti-Marxist and anti-Leninist".

Thirty years went by and similar sharp disputes were still rocking the leadership of the Communist party during the 1960's. However, if we consider that Pouliopoulos was expelled from the Party as "an enemy of the proletariat", we are bound to believe that the cause of the great French Marxist Garaudy is not so new at that.

Seen from another angle, the predominance of the "conformists" was not only the result of the interference by the Comintern. It was also largely due to the fact that the ranks of the Party were renewed and reinforced in a decisive manner. Actually, from about 1924, the "Kutvists" and the "Hadjis" entered into this struggle. The "Kutvists" were those persons who had studied in Moscow at the Communist University of the Eastern Peoples, whose initials in Russian are KUTV. On the other hand, those who had visited Moscow on the occasion of a conference or for other reasons were called "Hadjis", a name that is used in the East for individuals who have made a pilgrimage to Jerusalem. The "Kutvists" and "Hadjis" often were better trained than the regular cadres and enjoyed a special prestige from their contacts with the "Center". They were, therefore, better prepared to undertake the struggle against strong personalities who opposed absolute discipline.

Among the devoted and skillful new agitators we must remember the name of one who soon became influential, and twenty-five years later during the guerrilla war, played one of the most important—and perhaps one of the most luckless—roles. We are speaking of Zachariadis.

15

Nicos Zachariadis was born in Asia Minor in 1902 and was one of the first students at KUTV. He studied there at a young age, when the soul and the mind are being formed. It was also at the time when Lenin—founder of the new era and of the great delusion—was still alive. It was natural for this homeless young man to want to become an apostle of communism. Endowed with a strong, magnetic personality, lively agressiveness, and speaking perfect Russian, he immediately stood out among the other candidates in Moscow.

In 1924, Zachariadis was sent to Athens where he became very active. He concentrated on the organization of the clandestine network, but without taking any special title or appearing as one of its principal organizers. It seems that he also played an important role in the Party leadership. Indicted in 1927 along with a group of activists, he defended the communist position with more courage and conviction than any of the others. After spending a year in prison followed by a stay in Moscow, he was proclaimed the chosen one.

Reports made by representatives of the Comintern, and even of certain circles within the Party, had not concealed the fact that the KKE was not making much progress and that this fact, plus the disputes between the leaders, discouraged the small, but dedicated core. On the contrary, Comintern representatives revealed these truths, often in very blunt words.

At last Moscow decided to put some order into the Greek Communist movement. The details of this intervention are not known and what is known is not particularly useful here. Anyway, it is a fact that in September of 1931, after certain advanced steps had been taken, a very important Kremlin personality, Anatole Lunacharsky, former Commissioner of Education of the Soviet Union, made a five-day visit to Athens. From that time on, the Party line changed. It became inflexible. The KKE was called upon to "Bolshevize itself", to expel any cadres that hesitated, to become more homogeneous with a new united leadership, to stop the disastrous "struggle without principles" and finally, to fight "for the right of the people to self-determination and separatism."

Nicos Zachariadis was named head of the "united leadership" and two years later, General Secretary. He became the single most powerful man in the KKE, the little Stalin of the small Greek movement, confidant of the great Stalin himself and his representative in Greece.

With dedication and dexterity, ready to use implacable harshness against any comrade who hesitated, Zachariadis tried to impose on the Party the decisions of the Comintern mentioned above. We must bear in mind two of these: the first for reasons of historical-political thought; the second because of the serious consequences it brought.

We have cited above the "period of struggle without principles". That is how the Comintern and the KKE referred to the decade from 1920 to 1930 because they believed that the cadres were inspired only by "Opportunism". They could not imagine then that, half a century later, after a world war which lasted five years and brought vast changes to the international scene, and after more than a hundred wars or revolutions of various sizes, the so-called "struggle without principles" was in reality, the struggle for or against the "principle" of total discipline which today still divides the communist world.

The second phrase to be remembered from the decisive decree of the Comintern in 1931, is much more important for it referred to self-determination and the separation of peoples. All that had occurred during the preceding ten years, left no doubt as to what was significant. The KKE was publicly invited, in spite of popular reaction, to fight for the independence of two national territories. One of these was Macedonia.

Thus, the Party was forced to ignore the main obstacle

which it had encountered on its already difficult route. But this obstacle was so important for the first steps and future progress of the KKE that it is necessary to devote a special paragraph to it.

Towards an Independent Macedonia. It is not essential to consider in detail the geographical area that should be called "Macedonia", for it varied according to the will of the conqueror, the ideas of the historian, or the needs of the polemicists. In a very general way, we can say that to the south and west this area is closed off by high mountains (Olympus, and to the west, the Pindos range and the Albanian mountains) and that it mainly includes the wave-like plain starting above Olympus and reaching beyond Skopje.

This large and most fertile region which had always been open to invasions from the north and east became, for this reason, an area of unusual ethnic composition. Isolated villages, groups of villages, towns and neighborhoods spoke different languages, or even corrupt versions of languages according to the language conditions that had prevailed after the various invasions. Even Spanish was still spoken there, a reminder of the considerable immigration of Jews from Spain in 1492.

The Greek language predominated because it was the language of the original natives, of commerce and of the Church. Then followed Turkish for it was the language of the administration, the army and many colonists. This does not mean that the other Balkan languages and local dialects had disappeared. They existed also and in many regions were unquestionably predominant.

When, in the nineteenth century, many Balkan countries won their independence, Macedonia continued to remain under the Ottoman Empire. It was natural for this unusual ethnological mixture to cause many serious crises. The reason was very simple: Every national and linguistic group pursued union with its motherland. From both sides of the border peoples dreamed of joining their "brothers".

The already intensely complicated situation became really dangerous when one of these claims was satisfied quite disproportionally, and to the disadvantage of all other claims and prospects. Having crushed Turkey in 1878, Russia created through the treaty of San Stefano a "Greater Bulgaria" which included, among other areas, the whole of Macedonia as far south as Thessalonike.

This was an ephemeral fabrication, it is true, since the Treaty of Berlin two years later gave Macedonia back to Turkey. But the evil seed of unmeasured ambition had already grown. Propaganda for a Greater Bulgaria was strong. The atmosphere became poisoned and, finally, fanatical groups of "komitadjis" (Slav-speaking guerrillas) tried "by fire and axe" to Bulgarize all this vast region, but especially the area surrounding Thessalonike. Naturally, opposing armed groups were soon formed to protect their compatriots. Terrible bloodshed followed. There were, of course, moments of peace, but the irregular and merciless war lasted for years.

The "Macedonian Question" inflamed passions in the entire Balkan peninsula, poisoned relations between the countries directly concerned and, at the turn of the century, became a serious problem for the Great Powers. The fighting was to retain its intensity almost until the advent of the Balkan Wars.

The Balkan wars of 1912 to 1913 changed the outlook completely and, in many ways, even altered the basis of the whole question.

Under the Ottoman Empire, Macedonia had acquired administrative unity through the use of force, and then was divided into three parts. Greece and Serbia dominated its largest and most fertile areas. And although the ethnological situation did not change very much (many Greeks fled from Bulgaria at that time), the administration changed completely.

19

Quite new conditions were being created in Macedonia.

However, the really radical change came after the end of World War I through the international treaties imposed on Greece, Turkey and Bulgaria and brought about an event which had never happened before: the compulsory exchange of minority populations. This meant that the ethnological mixture was altered.

The introduction of many hundreds of thousands of refugees from Asia Minor and East Thrace into Macedonia helped to populate the Greek sector in an homogeneous way. Statistics of the League of Nations at that time certified that the mother language of ninety-three percent of the population of Macedonia was Greek. Besides, it must be noted that many inhabitants included in the remaining seven percent spoke various local dialects of Slavic origin, but were bilingual. Most of them, for reasons of religion, tradition and environment, considered themselves Greek.

So, this promised land in the people's imagination since the time of Alexander the Great, who had carried the banner of Hellenism to India, this land which was an asylum for the refugees and the largest granary in Greece with a population more Greek than ever before—this the KKE was ordered to claim from Greece and to make of it an independent country and a satellite of Bulgaria.

For a long period the Macedonian problem deeply influenced the evolution of the KKE and relations between Greece, Bulgaria and Yugoslavia.

The question came up for the first time in May 1921, and in a rather unofficial way. Kolarof, leader of the Bulgarian delegation at the congress of the Third Communist International held in Moscow, brought the subject to the attention of the leader of the Greek delegation, a young lawyer named Ioannis Georgiades, who had zealously supported the line of complete submission to the

Comintern. The author had the opportunity to become acquainted with Georgiades later so that details given below derive from first-hand knowledge.

Kolarof argued as follows: if the idea of creating an independent Macedonia was supported by the Communist Party of Bulgaria, which was very weak, it would suddenly become important and would also win the votes of the Macedonians of Bulgaria who had fled to that country as refugees. On the other hand, the KKE which had few cadres in this mainly rural region, would win the votes of the minorities and all those who preferred an independent Macedonia. Finally, if the foundation of an independent Macedonian state was to be realized, the Communists thereafter would be able to write a first mortgage on the new state.

Georgiades was evasive but, after his return to Greece, he was strongly opposed to the whole idea and placed himself firmly in the camp of the non-conformists until a short time later when he was dismissed from the Party.

The Bulgarian position, though contrary to the interests and beliefs of the Communist parties of Greece and Serbia, was mentioned again and supported officially the following year in Sofia at the Balkan Communist Federation meeting. Again the Greek delegation was opposed, citing the fact that this suggestion caused dangerous problems and actually adopted the political chauvinism of the Bulgarian bourgeoisie.

But, as soon as the chief of the Greek delegation, Ioannis Petsopoulos, returned to Athens, the Party accused him of a mixture of "chauvinism" and "disrupting communism". Finally, he also was dismissed from the Party...

The KKE seemed to be veering. In fact, many of its leaders had not understood that the policy of the Communist Party of Bulgaria was that of the Comintern.

Uncertainty, however, could not last: if the whole question were to end successfully, it would very much help the spread of communism throughout the Balkan peninsula. That is why, at the end of 1923 in Moscow, the Executive Committee of the Comintern and the Executive Committee of the Balkan Communist Federation decided that the question of the independence of Macedonia was "a question of principle". This meant that all Communist parties had to follow a fixed Party line.

The Yugoslav delegates were opposed and refused to accept this decision. On the contrary, the leader of the Greek delegation accepted it—an unforeseen change of course—without being authorized by his party. This appeared to be the case from the fact that, as soon as he returned to Athens, his position became so untenable that he soon disappeared somewhere in America. He thereby demonstrated the strength of his convictions on the independence of Macedonia in a way that was hardly original, but more useful for him; leaving, he took with him the entire funds of the small party.

In the meantime, the Party continued its tactic of evasion and conveyed confused opinions to Moscow. It did not dare to assume a clear position. Anyway, this was not feasible because even among the triumvirate which was then (1924) at the head of the Party, only Maximos was in favor of complete adherence to the resolutions of the International. The KKE was then asked to send delegates to Moscow to take part in the Fifth World Congress of the Comintern.

But, in spite of everything, the leader of the Greek delegation, who was none other than the loyal conformist Maximos, changed his mind and showed great courage by placing himself in opposition to Moscow.

He was attacked along with the Yugoslavs by one of the Soviet representatives, but he refuted every argument. His main point was that seven hundred thousand refugees from Asia Minor had just settled in Macedonia—a fact nobody could deny—and that this had altered the ethnological composition of the region and prevented "Greek workers and peasants from accepting the policy of Macedonian autonomy".

Then, soon afterwards, the Greek delegation reversed itself and accepted, although it is not known under what pressure or threats. In fact, it went even further because the resolution of the Fifth World Congress called for a "unity of effort concerning the question of Macedonia and Thrace".

Towards the end of the year during a special congress, the KKE, ignoring the advice of one of its most important members, decided almost unanimously that: "As long as the division and oppression of Macedonia and Thrace continues, we cannot avoid an imperialist war. That is why we are fighting for the unification and independence of the three sections of Macedonia and Thrace".

The KKE was clearly and definitely bound; the decision was obligatory and no disagreement was permitted. From the point of view of loyalty to the "Motherland of Socialism", this was perfect. From the point of view of principles, it was grotesque and irrational. From the point of view of the Marxist movement in Greece and Yugoslavia, it was true madness.

Even so, the KKE remained loyal to the directives issuing from Moscow. It made only one concession and that only temporarily. Seeing that it had some chance of electing a few members to Parliament in the 1926 election, it did not mention the Macedonian question in its pre-electoral program. It preferred to ignore it.

That did not fool anyone. The official decisions were there in terms clearly stated, and they had never been revoked. Marxism-Leninism, which had not yet managed to put down roots in the country, now seemed burdened with national treason—a fact that seemed more disgusting because it intended to deprive the nation of its two richest regions.

23

Reaction was strong throughout all classes of the population.

Those in power took all sorts of measures, among them criminal prosecution for high treason. The best known Communists—Zachariadis, Maximos, Pouliopoulos, and others—were indicted and sentenced. It must be noted, however, that the sentences handed down were rather light.

The Greek government persecution, treated here very summarily, did not influence the persistence with which the KKE pursued its Macedonian policy. On the contrary, after its crushing defeat in the 1928 elections, and having nothing else to lose under the leadership of Zachariadis, the Party took up even bolder positions.

Thus, in December 1931, the Party proclaimed its toughest resolution on "the question". The resolution was unanimously approved by the Plenum of the Central Committee and proclaimed the following:

"Greece is an imperialist country which has conquered by force whole regions populated by other nationalities. In the name of the fundamental principles of bolshevism the KKE declares for Macedonia and Thrace the principle of self-determination which included the right to separate themselves from Greece and the Party actively sustains the revolutionary efforts of the people of these regions directed towards their own national liberation".

The crucial points of these texts are republished here for three main reasons: Firstly, because later, on certain special occasions, an effort was made to contest their existence. It is useful, therefore, to ascertain their authenticity and to mention that they are now among the official publications of the KKE from which they have been extracted word for word. Secondly, because they explain almost completely the deep and continual public reation against the KKE. Thirdly, because they prove the complete submission of the Communist party of Greece to directives originating abroad.

One could put the question this way: why did the Comintern issue these directives which were so disastrous for the KKE? A relatively complete answer would take up too much space. So, let us be content to determine the basic reasons that influenced the leaders of the Communist movement inside its international framework. These reasons seem to be the following:

The assistance given to the Communist party of Bulgaria.

The hope that certain minorities of northern Greece and southern Serbia would be attracted to Communism, which minorities, it was believed, strongly desired the foundation of an independent Macedonia.

Keeping open a question that stirred up animosities between these three small countries and which could create a local "imperialistic" war, was always useful to the movement. The hope was harbored that in a different international contingency, and with the help of the nationalistic Bulgarian organizations, a new state could be created. This state, then, would be the puppet of international communism placed among small countries with well-established nationalistic beliefs. On these conditions, the game was well worth the struggle and the sacrifices that the KKE would have to bear.

But the day came when the Comintern realized that it had chosen the wrong course. Years went by and none of the expected results was achieved. And, on top of it all, a completely unforeseen but grave question had arisen in all three Balkan countries: even the most progressive socialists did not dare to cooperate with the communist parties as they were considered treasonable and desiring the partition of their countries. It was especially disagreeable at this later date, for the era of popular fronts had begun; these groups could be adapted to the conditions of each country and were considered excellent Trojan horses.

So the failure of the effort to split Macedonia from Greece became apparent. That is why the whole matter was simply forgotten. It had been kept alive for fourteen years, from 1921 to 1935. It rose again coincidentally fourteen years later.

The separatist policy was forgotten after the first period in order to obtain a small electoral success, but remembered again after the second period to avoid a terrible disaster: total defeat in the guerilla war which began in 1946. In fact, the separatist policy was dropped in July 1935 by a resolution of the executive committee of the Party which adopted "the principle of the complete equality of minorities." This was an entirely new line.

From a more general point of view this amazing change proves how the communist world adapts its policy to circumstances without difficulty, and also, without scruples. For, let us not forget that the careers of many of the early dynamic founders of the Party had been destroyed only because they had dared to discuss the directives imposed from above before they were abandoned. But the Greek Communist party had some very special reasons for wanting to have a free hand.

Small Victories and a Great Defeat. Under the watchful leadership of Zachariadis and despite the "National Question," the KKE had made some progress. Above all, it had organized itself throughout the countryside. It had covered the whole of Greece with a network of illegal "offices" and clandestine "cells," using for the first time numerous paid employees who were devoted and well chosen. The Party had done a good propaganda job. It had mobilized new and efficient cadres and, above all, it had studied and supported all justified claims of the working classes. It had, therefore, succeded in improving its electoral position a little. In the elections of 1932 and 1933 it had won five percent of the votes, that is, 50,000, and could now justifiably hope to make that figure even higher.

For despite certain important achievements by Venizelos, who had been in power since 1928, the world economic crisis of 1930 as well as other factors had diminished the prestige of the "Father of the country," who thus lost the elections of 1932 and 1933 by a small margin. In March 1935, after the failure of a very unpopular *coup d'etat* by his friends, Venizelos left the country and sought refuge in France.[2]

It was perhaps not just a coincidence that the KKE abandoned its policy of "independence" for Macedonia just a month after the *coup d'etat*: since the *coup* had failed, new elections were expected.

The electoral gains for the Popular Front created by the Party were greater than expected: 99,000 votes, that is, ten percent of the voters! Double the votes it had won in the two previous elections!

The picture was partly deceiving when one considers that the Liberal party, to which Venizelos belonged, did not put forth a candidate. Abstention of voters had been small so it was clear that many Liberals, after losing their leader and their party, had voted for the extreme left. But that didn't matter.

What was important was the results. The Popular Front, whose name did not fool anyone, had won a considerable number of voters although about half of these until recently considered the KKE as "a party of treason." The atmosphere had changed; progress continued; the denial of the "independence" of Macedonia had brought gains The time of great expectations, perhaps even of success, seemed to have arrived.

During the second half of 1935 "a lot of water flowed under the bridges" of the small rivers of Greece.

The sad departure of the great Venizelos, the animosities he had left behind him, the fact that the new Parliament did not include Liberals, who had represented almost half of the electorate, the poor economic situation—all of these factors caused much anxiety and unhappiness.

The Republic installed in 1924 and considered definitely established for many years, was now losing its vitality. Many were those who believed that with a Crowned Democracy Greece would be in better position to face the troubled and unsteady situation and the instability aggravated by personal rivalries. This change of opinion was helped also by the personality of the dethroned king; for George II was considered a moderate, calm person suitable for the role of eventual conciliator.

Thus one sunny morning in October of 1935, the leaders of the armed forces demanded the resignation of the parliamentary government and gave the presidency to retired General George Condylis, a former republican who had also changed his ideas. He was entrusted with the assignment of carrying out a national referendum in which the people would decide the form of regime they wanted.

The people voted for a Crowned Democracy in a true plebiscite and in the last days of 1935 George II returned to Greece. He returned to his country as a true conciliator.

Condylis, a former officer, was courageous, dynamic, and astute, but loved power. He opposed certain measures of clemency that the King wished to apply at once. George II, who largely owed his throne to Condylis, offered him a beautiful walking-stick with a silver handle, thanked him for his services and then dismissed him. A university professor, Constantine Demertzis, was called in and entrusted to form a new government, to apply measures of clemency, to dissolve Parliament and to organize the elections.

Elections were held on January 26, 1936, using the simple proportional system so that all political and social trends were represented in Parliament. This time the election battle was very tough and abstention less than at any other time.

The KKE had disguised itself under the mask of a popular front, but did not manage to fool anyone. Besides, misleading the voters was even more difficult due to the fact that two small parties had been formed to take advantage of the voting system. These were led by Panayiotis Kanellopoulos, a professor of sociology, and John Sofianopoulos, a lawyer. Both of them were young, had good reputations and while one appealed to the intellectuals, the other appealed to the farmers.

The elections were well organized and conducted in a calm and orderly atmosphere. But their results did not calm the country.

The conservatives, who were curiously called Populists, won 45.5 percent of the votes, a percentage that gave them 143 seats out of 300.

The progressives, who were curiously called Liberals, won 44 percent of the votes and 144 seats. The communists under the guise of a Popular Front received 5.75 percent of the votes (73,500 votes) and 15 seats, the Unionists (Canellopoulos) no seats and the Farmers' Party one seat. These results caused an impasse.

Actually the two large parties hated each other from the time of World War I when, for a period of time, there were actually two Greek states, that of the north under the "Venizelists" and that of the south under the "Royalists." Hostility between the two parties had remained acute and their hatred had recently been revived after an attempt against Venizelos' life and the military coup of March 1935. Now the two parties had obtained equal votes so it was impossible to form a new government.

The insistent interventions of the sovereign towards securing an agreement between the two big parties, the obvious anxiety of the people, as well as certain steps taken by the leaders of the armed forces, did not help to solve the crisis. The only result was to prolong the life of the Demertzis government, but also to put a strong man in charge of the Ministry of Defense: a retired general named John Metaxas.

29

This temporary government summoned Parliament at the beginning of March 1936. Something very spectacular was going to happen. The time of the KKE had come. But the striking of its great hour sounded like the toll of a warning bell.

At the opening of Parliament the leader of the Liberals, Themistoclis Sofoulis was elected President on the second vote. He received 158 votes out of 300. Voting was secret, of course, but there was not the slightest doubt that all of the Communist members of Parliament had voted for him. No one, not even most Liberals, could understand how this had happened. They were angry and their anger was real. After much noisy hissing the Populists walked out of Parliament in protest. Public opinion was overwhelmingly enraged; it was not possible for anyone to side with "the party for the separation of Macedonia." Nevertheless, the King, wishing to respect the Constitution, asked Sofoulis to form the new Government.

Sofoulis hesitated. He suggested to the Populists that they support the existing government on the condition that the government, although of a caretaker nature owing to the origin of its members, would become political by the fact that it would be responsible to Parliament. The Populists agreed. So Professor Demertzis and his Vice-president, General Metaxas, remained in power with the blessings of almost the entire Parliament. But in this way, without realizing it, Parliament became the target of a justifiable and equally painful act of revenge.

As soon as cooperation between the two big parties was announced, the KKE published the text of an agreement, signed by its representative in Parliament, Sklavainas, and by Themistoclis Sofoulis. According to this agreement, the KKE undertook the obligation of supporting a government of Liberals under the presidency of Sofoulis. The latter incurred the obligation of abolishing the anti-communist laws enacted by Venizelos and of taking certain measures in favor of the poorer classes. These laws, however, were so demagogic in nature that they were quite inapplicable.

The first obligation gave the KKE a free hand; the second served its purposes excellently while at the same time, it exposed the Liberals.

It is easy to understand why Sofoulis hesitated to put this agreement into practice. But the KKE would not forget it. As the Party also did not forget to reveal a few days later, during a stormy argument in Parliament, that the Populists had started similar negotiations.

In this way the KKE struck a severe blow against all political parties. It believed that this was a triumph. It did not know that this was instead the threshold of the disaster. For, if a dictatorship needs a disaster in order to seize power, it also needs certain favorable conditions to open the path to power. And the best way to open this dark path is to threaten the people's calm, everyday life and to shake their confidence in politicians.

In our case, this proved even more true because oligarchic tendencies were represented by a very capable man: John Metaxas, who graduated first in his class from the Military Academy of Berlin, was only a captain when Venizelos selected him from among all his officers to negotiate the Greek-Serbian military agreements in 1912. He was just a lieutenant-colonel when, in 1915, he was offered the leadership of the Greek General Staff. These few facts are enough to indicate the abilities of the man.

During this troubled period Prime Minister Demertzis died. As was only natural, he was succeeded by Deputy Prime Minister Metaxas. But, in contrast to his predecessor, Metaxas was a very determined man. Supported by the army and helped by the loss of prestige of the political leaders, he appeared before Parliament, asked it to postpone all sessions until the 30th of October and, simultaneously, for authority to rule by decree. Sixteen members of Parliament objected, 241 agreed.

31

Parliament had dug its own grave.

The KKE did its best to bury it and to put a huge tombstone on top of it. And, as if the atmosphere was not already ominous enough, the Party quickly began to display unprecedented activity.

Besides many noisy public demonstrations and an illegal effort to create a secret organization of soldiers and noncommissioned officers, it added two especially disturbing new activities: continuous strikes and street demonstrations ending with attacks against public buildings. Between the end of April and the end of July 1936, some two hundred strikes took place.

Communist activity prepared the way for oligarchy so well that the question was raised as to whether that was not the real purpose of the KKE. Some felt that it favored the establishment of a dictatorship certain that, in the long run, this turn of events would work in its favor.

This explanation does not seem correct. On the contrary, it seems rather that the Party had made an incorrect estimate of its strength, the degree of disintegration of the State, and the abilities of its opponents. Zachariadis, a child of the Leninist era, a Stalin man and restorer of the KKE, had hoped after certain victories that with an aggressive minority he would be able to overcome a lazy, divided majority. Besides, this had happened often in other countries.

No matter what he believed, Zachariadis at that time wanted to take one more decisive step: he proclaimed a general strike for the fifth of August. It was announced but it never materialized.

On the fourth of August, Metaxas—supported by the army and with the approval of the king—suspended several articles of the Constitution.

That act spelled dictatorship.

There was no reaction against it. The KKE tried to

vanish from sight in order to survive clandestinely. It only partially succeeded in this because the new regime was quite efficient.

Metaxas was a scrupulous man who observed everything. He was impressed by the recent directives of the KKE (September 1935) which, copying the resolutions of the Comintern, specified the following: firstly, it should work towards overthrowing all non-Communist regimes, including democratic or social democratic regimes. Secondly, it should strengthen the Party by allying itself with political or syndicalist forces. Thirdly, it should transform an eventual "imperialist conflict" into a civil war!

In view of these resolutions and amidst the dark and threatening international atmosphere of 1936, Metaxas struck quickly, hard and efficiently. He had assigned the Ministry of Public Order to Stylianos Maniadakis, a devoted retired officer who, although not well known, had the necessary abilities—as was proved later—to face the cunning and endurance of a widespread illegal organization.

Within the next twenty-four hours many leaders of the KKE were arrested. Those who hid themselves were found —Zachariadis some forty days later— and were placed under strict custody. Very few were those who escaped arrest, and ever fewer those, like Siantos, who managed to get away to Moscow. So, in one sweeping move by the government, the KKE lost all of its leaders.

The KKE was about to have more bad luck. The Security Police had secured extensive information to which more was added from the secret files of the Party uncovered during the first weeks of the dictatorship. Maniadakis used this information to penetrate secretly the large underground network which had been so carefully developed in Athens, Thessalonike and elsewhere. So the government with full knowledge of the tactics and composition of the illegal cadres (directions, organization, names, specialties of persons concerned), carefully selected its agents so they would not be suspected. Their activity was assisted by certain members of the Party who, after a long imprisonment, yielded and accepted the role—inside or outside of prison—that the Security Police wished them to play. The police advanced this sly game to such a point that, in a way, it created its own Communist party. It also published its own newspaper, identical to the illegal newspaper of the real party. When this went into circulation it was artfully different as to internal arguments and directives for work.

Very quickly complete confusion reigned. Throughout the Party cadres, nobody was sure of anything anymore. Nobody knew for certain who was a real member and who an agent, who was loyal and who was betraying them. Quite often the uninitiated could not tell the real newspaper from the fake one. And, because the Security Police every now and then made a number of well-chosen arrests, many members of the Party believed their fellows had yielded and betrayed them. Sometimes suspicion even fell upon well known "comrades".

Certainly, neither did militants disappear altogether, nor illegal centers stop working. But on the whole the Party was paralyzed.

In addition to these methods, which combined craftiness and fraud, ability and force, another ruse was used. It is interesting to mention it here, mainly because certain very important activists were stigmatized by it up to the era of the armed rebellion from 1942 to 1949.

The following suggestion was made to those Communists who were in prison or exiled to islands, and to others who, due to their political beliefs had encountered difficulties in pursuing their career: if they signed and published in their home newspapers a statement renouncing communism—the so-called "statement of repentance"—they would be left in peace. This measure would not be restricted only to those who were serving a prison sentence.

The suggestion was alluring. And the longer the

dictatorship lasted and the more firmly it seemed entrenched, the more this suggestion appeared both attractive and alluring. It produced unexpected results. Certainly, there were those who refused to sign a declaration of repentance, in spite of the warnings and pressure of the regime, in spite of the pleading of their families—the greatest enemy of all political struggles. But most of them, tired and disappointed, agreed at last to sign. Finally, although it is difficult to say how many, by 1940, the number of signatures had certainly passed the 30,000 mark.

Even though all of these were not Party members, this was a large number when compared to the total number of Greek Communists. And this fact in itself brought complete confusion. A spectacular show of disloyalty and lack of cohesion had taken place. A very bad example was thus given to the young and the weak. And worst of all was the fact that among those who had signed, there were some whose activism had been remarkable. Among the latter we must mention a young graduate of the agricultural college who, after having been especially active (even among his fellow prisoners), signed a statement of repentance in 1939. His name was Athanassios Klaras, and later his nickname—Aris Velouchiotis—was to echo over the mountains and gullies of Greece.

The KKE felt this blow and fully understood its importance, for it was a blow that struck directly at the principal force of the movement—the morale of its fighters. In the prisons, the island exiles, and the outlawed centers, the loyalists began a violent campaign against those individuals who had signed, calling them unmanly, unfaithful, and accusing them of high treason. In revenge, certain cadres spread rumors to the public that this was a clever reaction by the Party: the majority of those who had signed, they said, acted under orders so that, as leftists, they would be free to help the movement. This was only an excuse given, but it was entirely false. The extremely severe attitude taken against those who had signed by Zachariadis after he was released from prison in 1945, does not leave us in any doubt about that. The regime had again exploited human weakness and the movement had paid the price.

Thus the Greek Communist party, after a difficult infancy, had rallied around brilliant leadership and had even known a period of true political power. Now, after a brief period of dictatorship, it had suffered a serious blow, as much in organization as in moral potential.

But it was not going to die. On the contrary!

Communist parties were, in those times and up to a point, always, the best attraction for all kinds of discontented people. And the Greek regime of that period, however able, did not cease being a dictatorship and, consequently, offended the freedom and dignity of the individual. However, after having benefitted from the above and having acquired a very wide base, the Greek Communist party—wounded and persecuted—came alive in another period of the nations's history: the period of the war imposed by the Italian fascists.

This war affected the evolution of events in Greece in a multitude of ways. So, it is now necessary to outline its history briefly and to mention, of course, the role of the Greek Communist party during this period.

Chapter III

The Greek-Italian War

The Preliminaries. On the 28th of October, 1940, before dawn, the Italian ambassador in Athens, Signor Grazzi, woke up Metaxas and with a worried look on his face, handed him an ultimatum. Greece was unjustly accused of allowing British warships to enter its territorial waters and of causing incidents against Albania, which was already part of the famous "Impero." For these reasons the Italian government asked for authorization to occupy the islands of Crete and Corfu, the port of Piraeus and that part of Epirus which borders on the Albanian frontier. The extent of the last two zones was not clearly defined. The whole operation would begin within three hours: thus, the utimatum did not even allow enough time for those in authority to discuss the matter and then to transmit their orders to local authorities and frontier garrisons. Conversation between the two men was painful. The memoirs of Count Grazzi, which give credit to Italian diplomacy and are based on official texts, prove that for many months the

Italian ambassador had tried to lead Rome onto a path of truth and reason. He had explained that the charges against Greece were quite untrue. He had insisted on the honorable intentions of Prime Minister Metaxas, whom he respected greatly and who—according to Grazzi—scrupulously avoided any mistakes or provocations, and even feigned not to understand certain threats in order to avoid war. And now Ambassador Grazzi was there at the home of the Greek Prime Minister, ultimatum in hand, and obliged to prove the opposite.

Metaxas tried to refute the arguments put forth in the ultimatum. But the Italian ambassador no longer had any margin for dicussing the matter. The man who had done his best to avoid war answered sadly, but firmly, "In that case, it is war". He did not know at the time that war had actually begun: two hours earlier eight Italian divisions, one of which was equipped with light and medium tanks, had crossed the frontier and were moving into Greek territory.

Mussolini, from his point of view, had good reasons to attack Greece. For a number of years he had followed a Balkan policy. In April 1939, he had conquered Albania and annexed it to the "Impero." Already World War II had continued for more than a year and during this time his Axis partner had enjoyed spectacular successes, while he had only played the role of an extra, never being asked nor even being informed of what was happening. In September 1940, German troops were stationed in Romania; King Carol had abdicated and there were rumors about a future German-Bulgarian military entente. His fortunate partner dominated the whole of Western Europe—full as it was of wealth and charm—and it seemed as if he disputed the unlucky partner even his own poor neighborhood: the Balkans. This was intolerable for the Italian dictator who had ideas of grandeur.

Mussolini felt that he must have his own success, and it

must be smashing. Greece seemed an easy prey. From all the evidence in the Palazzo Venezia, the morale factor was very much reckoned on. The Greek officers who were ousted as a result of taking part in the Venizelist coup of 1935 had not been taken back into the army, and they were both numerous and valorous. Other officers had been retired in the meantime, because they did not have the confidence of the regime. Besides, in July 1938, a small insurrection against the regime of Metaxas had taken place in Crete.

On the other hand, France, Poland, Holland and Belgium, incomparably better armed than Greece, had been crushed within a few weeks. The United States was still neutral and public opinion there, it was well known, was against any kind of participation in the war. Finally, the Soviet Union, in signing the Molotov-Ribbentrop Non-Aggression Pact of 1939, had stated that it would remain a spectator. Only England was fighting. But she had met with serious defeats and, in the autumn of 1940, seemed at the end of her strength.

Besides, the Greek armed forces were very weak. The country was still underdeveloped, its equipment was limited and the efforts of the dictatorship to furnish the army with modern arms had limited results. The Greek army had no tanks, no anti-tank guns, not even a worthwhile anti-aircraft battery. Less than one hundred fifty anti-aircraft guns were available to protect the whole country, including ports and military installations.

The regular army consisted of 70,000 men, of which 5,000 were permanent officers. These men constituted sixteen divisions, which were ready to receive reservists in case of mobilization. The navy consisted of an old armored cruiser, a small cruiser, twenty torpedo boats and destroyers, six submarines and a few minesweepers. The air force had about 150 planes, most of which could not be compared to the Italian air force either in speed or in firepower.

In addition, the land transport system was extremely poor. The army had scarcely any trucks and, in case of war, it counted on requisitioning privately-owned vehicles. The field artillery was horse-drawn. Most transportation, beyond the points the train reached, was by packmules and horses, though these too were requisitioned in wartime. Considering these conditions, to enter a war against "eight million bayonets," "the best airforce in the world," and a navy that claimed to be equal to the British fleet in the Mediterranean, was contrary to all logic. Mussolini knew this well. That is why, before starting the war, he tried the tactic of intimidation. During the last months he did everything possible to terrify his small rival. But his most violent move proved fatal for him. In the Cyclades, the Island of Tinos has an icon of the Virgin Mary which is considered to have miraculous powers. On the fifteenth of August, the feast day of the Virgin, thousands of faithful from all over Greece flock to Tinos to pay homage to the miraculous icon. Customarily, a naval vessel moored alongside the quay pays its compliments.

In 1940, perhaps because of the international tension, a cruiser—the second largest ship of the Greek navy—was sent to Tinos. During this important religious holiday, the cruiser was sunk, torpedoed by "a submarine of unknown nationality". There were many dead and wounded. At the time, no one was fooled as to the nationality of the "cowardly and impious" submarine. Besides, later, on the day war was declared, its nationality was proved beyond any doubt.

In deciding upon these acts of intimidation, Mussolini was grossly mistaken. He had judged according to his own blustering personality. Instead of frightening, he had angered a whole nation; he had strengthened its will and had gathered it around its leaders who were not particularly popular until then.

Napoleon used to say, and perhaps this was something less than the truth, that the proportion of efficiency between the morale and the equipment of an army was one to three. Mussolini tried to sap Greek morale; instead he strengthened it. And he did more: he warned his adversary and the latter hastened to prepare himself.

Metaxas and his Chief of Staff, General Papagos, had begun a very small but discreet mobilization after the occupation of Albania. Without fanfare, through "personal invitations" they had called to arms a number of reservists who had been sent to enlarge the units stationed near the Albanian frontier. When provocations multiplied, this tactic was intensified so that, the day war was declared, the three Greek divisions that guarded the Albanian border had their full complement of men; they had studied the ground and were ready for war. These three divisions managed to halt the advance of eight Italian divisions, gaining time to allow the mobilization and deployment of other reserve units.

The Military Operations. The Italian plan of attack was excellently conceived. General Visconti Prasca, if not its author, was mainly responsible for carrying it out. The plan provided for two diversionary attacks, one parallel to the Adriatic coast and the other at the end of the front towards Thessalonike. Both were important enough (one division, Sienna, and two cavalry regiments towards the coast; three divisions — Venezia, Parma, Piedmont — towards Thessalonike) so as to give the impression of being main attacks and to be able to unroll as soon as the center collapsed—this being the main target of the first phase. The plan further provided for two attacks on the center, each one in a different form.

The first, heavy and concentrated, had been entrusted to two very strong divisions, the Ferrara division and the Centaurs, which had been reinforced with plenty of artillery, good transportation units and assault tanks.

41

Upon arriving at a distance of about 35 kilometers from the border, these units had to strike straight against the strong pass of Kalpaki (Kalibaki, as the Italians called it) and, after taking it, to conquer Ioannina, the capital of Epirus, lying thirty-five kilometers to the south.

The second attack, in the center this time, would be light, bold, and sudden, through the wide Pindos mountain chain, where there were no roads, only poor footpaths. This would lead to the occupation of the town of Metsovo as soon as possible so as to cut off the only route joining Epirus with the considerable military bases of eastern Greece. This attack was entrusted to the most famous Italian alpinist division, the Julia, reinforced by similar units. A division of 12,000 men, it had 2,500 mules to use for transportation. It was completely equipped and well armed with many mortar units and seven batteries of mountain artillery.

A daring thrust seemed the easy way to begin and seemed to have a strong chance of fruitful results. Easy because only two Greek battalions, plus a third from behind, guarded the long mountain range that was considered almost impregnable owing to the land formation. Fruitful, because the occupation of the passes of Metsovo would isolate the army of Epirus from the main military bases of eastern Greece, and would also make possible a descent towards Thessaly, behind Mount Olympus, far to the south of Thessalonike.

These units of the Italian army, including Julia, had among them several Albanian batallions, beloved to the Regent King of Albania, Jacomoni, but not held in high regard by the Italian regulars. A strong air force, flying from Brindisi and from Albania, would support these four atacks, but primarily the center, and would bomb the towns in the rear as well. It would be difficult to conceive a strategic plan better adapted to the conditions of the terrain: it combined shock, suprise, and astuteness.

The distance of the objectives from the front line was short and, if they were seized quickly, defense would become extremely difficult. The leader of the Italian army in Albania, General Prasca, foresaw that he would need five to ten days for his troops to arrive at Ioannina and Metsovo. However, exactly that many days were needed for his glorious plans to be contradicted, and to lead to defeat. For those first few days were extremely critical in deciding the outcome of the war.

The most important of the two diversionary attacks, the one towards Thessalonike, on hilly ground and well guarded, advanced slightly and only served as a serious threat. The other one on the coast moved ahead better than the Italian generals had hoped. It progressed practically without difficulty. It drew only a brief artillery volley from two Greek destroyers and the firing of retreating soldiers, gendarmes, and rural police through whom the defenders were trying to give the impression of some resistance. It is true that a Greek brigade was sent there by sea, but that happened when the Italian cavalry had reached the Acheron River, or at a latitude to the south of Ioannina (see Map No. 1). This advance, however, was too late, for the battle was being decided elsewhere. Very few knew at the time, and even today it is rarely mentioned, but Metaxas and Papagos, faced with the crushing Italian military superiority and transport difficulties, had selected a final defense line which protected the most important areas of the country. Nature had designed one strong enough, but it lay to the west and well to the south of Ioannina. The two leaders had foreseen equally that the Kalpaki position, much further north, between Ioannina and the frontier, allowed some possibility of a strong resistance, but they had not resolved to make a last stand there. Anyway, they had placed there the larger part of a division consisting only of Epirotes, who fought literally "for hearth and home." The ground had been prepared in a rather rudimentary way, but it had been studied minutely. This had been done so well that every round of the artillery was adjusted in advance with complete accuracy. Thus, under the excellent leadership of General Charalambos Katsimitros, the Epirote division ceded about thirty kilometers to the enemy without much resistance. At Kalpaki it engaged in its first battle.

Obviously, from the outset this was not simply a covering battle. Resistance was stubborn, but attacks were spirited and persistent too. The Greek artillery was extremely accurate, but the Italian response was greater and heavier; offensive and counter-offensive succeeded each other night and day. The key position, a large stony hill called Charbala, was taken and retaken three times. Defense was made easier by the torrential rains that impeded the intervention of the Italian air force, but the attackers had superior fire power and more tanks which made a big impact. In those bloody days both the will and the bravery of the two sides were comparable. On the tenth day of the war, it was difficult to tell what would be the outcome of the battle in which the Italians had concentrated their main strategic forces.

One could tell much more if one knew what was happening elsewhere in the deep wooded ravines and on the steep barren mountainsides of the Pindos chain. The alpinists of the Julia division drove back the weak defense they met and made a spectacular advance. Neither the steep mountains nor the heavy rains stopped their great forward strides. On the morning of the third of November, Italian advance units at an altitude of 1,400 meters, reached a high plateau at the other end of which, after a three-hour march, they would attain their objective: the only main route through the Pindos Mountains. Their advance was so rapid that, at about midday, Italian planes, seeing infantry in the plateau, dropped packets containing handkerchiefs and chocolates to offer to the inhabitants of the

44

neighboring town of Metsovo. Unfortunately for the Julia division, these gifts went instead to some Greek soldiers. A strong cavalry unit had just arrived there and, after having left their horses in the forest, hastened forward on foot to protect the precious road.

The cavalry unit was not, however, the road's only protection. Papagos and his staff had sensed the potential danger and, from the second day of the war, had advanced all available light troops to that area. Climbing the eastern slopes of the mountain ranges, they moved forward in small groups with pack artillery, many guns and firearms, and much enthusiasm. The women and non-mobilized men of the region reprovisioned these units even as far as the most advanced and inaccessible positions.

The fine Julia division very soon found itself cut into two parts, separated by wild mountains, while a steady rain hampered all movement. Attacked day and night by an enemy who had the advantage of surprise, the men were tired, ill, and lacked provisions, for the mule trains were the favorite target of Greek marksmen.

The alpinists made some bold attacks which cost them dearly but did not alter the situation. The terrain was very rough, the supply lines very long, the assaults and ambushes numerous. In a few days, about five thousand men of the alpinists, encircled and exhausted, chose to surrender rather than be killed. This was perhaps the most critical point of the Greek-Italian war. The famed Julia division received the order to retreat with all possible speed; everything that could be saved had to be saved.

But something else had to be saved also: the number of Greek troops on the mountain range was not known and it had been ascertained that they possessed an extraordinary mobility. So, if the Greeks were numerous and if they advanced continuously towards the west and poured into the area behind Kalpaki, the stronger units of the Italian army in Albania would be encircled.

Rome, anxious almost to the point of panic, preferred a very careful tactic: it ordered a general retreat. Visconti Prasca did not want to admit defeat, and in those last critical hours, he had a remarkable idea. On the 10th of November, he telegraphed to Rome, proposing that his troops, then on the coast above Ioannina, turn toward the east and advance on the capital of Epirus and thus "open the gates of the town and cause the collapse of the whole defensive system of the enemy."

This maneuver would have created an unforeseen and serious situation for the Greek General Staff. But this bold and clever maneuver did not take place. General Soddu, deputy Minister of Defense and Supreme Commander of the forces in Albania, gave a chilly reply: Prasca should adapt himself to reality and obey orders. Prasca did not have time to obey, however; he was replaced the next day and the retreat became general.

The outcome of the Greek-Italian war had been decided. Morale, the moving power of every human effort, vanished from one side and strengthened the other. For the Italians, who thought they had one of the strongest armies in Europe and who expected an easy victory, to be put to flight by one of the smallest armies in the continent was more than shame. It gave rise to doubt as to the abilities of Italian leadership and caused a general feeling of despair and betrayal.

For the Greek side, things were quite different. The men of the army had faced the war calmly, but resolutely, because they had to protect their homes. They had to do their duty. Now they saw that they had been the first to defeat the Axis ; they were writing one of the most glorious pages of their three-thousand-year-old history. They were in a state of euphoria. Morale was so high that if the army had had the means of transport, the Italian retreat would have been turned into a rout and a large part of Albania would have been occupied in a few weeks. While this was not accomplished, the results of the Greek operations were impressive.

On November 20, in Epirus, the Greek troops were advancing towards the border after skirmishes of minor importance. The battle was very fierce at the other end of the front, on the east, where the cluster of Ivan and Morava mountains forms a huge, complicated natural fort and where the powerful diversionary attack towards Thessalonike had first shown up. There the Italians defended themselves stubbornly. From the 14th of November, the three Italian divisions came under a severe counter-attack, the intentions of which seemed at once to be very ambitious. Three Greek divisions, mainly mountain troops, had attacked them in force in an attempt to overthrow the enemy completely and to threaten from the east the whole Italian army in Albania. The Italians fought well, then withdrew to their much stronger original positions where they were reinforced by units surpassing the strength of a whole division.

The breach had been opened. Combat continued with bayonets and the local commanders reported to General Soddu who in the meantime had succeeded Prasca, that their situation had become untenable. After some hesitation and much bloodshed on both sides, especially on the 19th and 20th of November, the order for a general retreat of fifty kilometers was given on the 21st; the Italians would reorganize themselves along another strong mountain range and abandon the plain. The next day the Greek army occupied the town of Korytsa, an important base of the Italian front. A huge amount of booty, mostly sabotaged, fell into the hands of the Greek units.

Matters did not end there, however. Four elite batallions of the Greek army, supported by excellent pack artillery, were ordered to pursue the enemy into the mountains along the Yugoslav border. The operation was very risky because the Italians were numerous; the Greek army however, enjoyed another advantage in addition to high morale: the majority of the population in the area was Greek. Herdsmen living in these mountains led certain companies through paths usually accessible only to goats. Besides, a fresh snowfall had made reprovisioning of the defenders difficult and sometimes possible only by air. For the Italians, the situation was discouraging. They had made a tiring and arduous retreat to occupy safer positions only to see the enemy infiltrate them everywhere.

Nevertheless, some Italian units, mainly from the Venezia division, fought with great persistence. But they were forced to surrender after terribly bloody battles that took place between the 23rd and 26th of November. The impregnable Pogradets, near Lake Ochrida, was occupied on the 28th by the besiegers. This was a considerable advance to the north because Pogradets—at the other end of the Albanian front—lies much higher in latitude than the main port of the country, Valona (See Map No. 1).

On the rest of the front, after a very brief pause, the Greek army again took the offensive. A few local battles only served to delay its advance. The situation became more critical all the time for the Italian army in Albania and, on the 5th of December, Soddu telephoned Rome asking the government to find a political solution. This advice was not taken, and soon Soddu learned what it means to be disgraced. But neither did the situation improve at the front for the Italians.

So, in the last week of 1940, the Greek army had occupied Albanian territory to a depth of thirty to fifty kilometers, an area which included the town of Argyrokastron and the small port of Santi Quaranta. It was this port to which the Fascists, caring more for the glory of Il Duce than for religion, had given the name of the Duce's daughter, Countess Edda Ciano. It was, indeed, the fall of Porto Edda that was announced in Rome and not that of the port of Santi Quaranta. . . . .An irony of so-called "behind the scenes" history. Meanwhile, in Rome Mussolini was furious.

For political or purely personal reasons, Il Duce had not informed his Axis partner of his plans. He only did so on the 28th of October, that is, the day he put his plans into action. A special meeting was held in Florence on this matter at which time Il Duce assured Hitler that the operation, which had been exceedingly well prepared, would end in the occupation of the whole of Greece within a few weeks. Mussolini now saw himself contradicted, humiliated, ridiculed, and perhaps even in danger on the domestic front. It was his first defeat in twenty years, and it was a shocking one. He placed responsibility on his collaborators and his generals, replaced some of them, and then attended to the dispatch of reinforcements to the front.

At Mussolini's orders, the Bari division, which had embarked on ships in order to take Corfu, was sent instead straight to Albania during the first days of the invasion. However, we must not deal with only one particular case in this discussion. Aided by the dispatch of fifty German Junkers, he created a real air bridge over the Adriatic. Already by November, he had succeeded in rebuilding considerably the army of Albania, but very often he also increased the confusion that reigned in it.

Italian texts which write about Mussolini's personal reactions in the first weeks of the war describe him as a man who was at his wit's end. A typical incident indicating his moods—and perhaps also his character—lies in an intelligent comparison made by journalist Mario Cervi in his book[1] on the Greek-Italian war.

Cervi notes that Metaxas in his regularly-kept diary, in speaking of the cold and the early snow of that year, writes: "Who knows what our poor soldiers are going through at the front." On the other hand, Mussolini, when informed that it was snowing hard in Albania, said: "Excellent, this cold and snow; it favors the use of short range projectiles and it improves this mediocre Italian race."

Speaking in such a fashion, Mussolini was not only inhuman, he was an equally poor strategist. For the early, thick layer of snow and the heavy winter of 1940 saved him or, at the very least, was a godsend because it gave his army a beneficial respite. The snow, added to other factors, stopped the advance of the Greek army. Let it be noted that one of the saddest results of the heavy winter was that thousands of men on both side suffered from frostbite and many were permanently disabled.

Thus, the commander-in-chief, General Cavallero, a man of doubtful reputation, but of great intelligence, was able to organize things and prepare the army for what would follow. Looking back and evaluating the overall situation, one can say that the first two months of the war were decisive and created an atmosphere that persisted for many years. That is why the main points and some characteristic details of this early phase have been described here, although the intention of this account is to give only a brief outline of the war. However, space does not permit the same detailed description of the next phase; therefore, from here on, only the most important facts will be presented.

The Greek counter-offensive was resumed in mid-January. Enemy resistance, even greater than before, did not stop a significant advance. In less than twenty days, the enemy had been driven so far back and in such a manner that the area of Albanian territory which the Greek army occupied had been doubled. This was important, but not decisive. Firstly, because the bold attack had not been able to advance beyond the Pogradets bridge, and, secondly, because in the center the Greek army had been brought to a halt before a steep, rocky barrier. Although it had occupied some of the strongholds, the main one, Tepeleni, birthplace of the notorious Ali Pasha, had not fallen.

The strength of the Greek army in Epirus now totaled fourteen divisions and, for the first time, it had some kind of air cover. Offered by the British, this comprised four squadrons of Blenheim and Gladiator bombers of the Royal Air Force. Besides, the Greek navy safeguarded the army's sea routes and it had even sunk some large Italian troop carriers. Thus, Papagos, feeling more powerful than ever, now wanted to force through the rocky gates that closed the way, and to try and occupy Valona so as to make the reprovisioning of the enemy more difficult. It was not a question of madness, nor of glory, or grandeur. This was a necessity. There were indications that the Germans would soon interfere. Besides, it was well-known that Mussolini wanted, at any price, to achieve success before the German intervention and that he was preparing his "spring offensive" on a grand scale.

After a short respite, the Greek offensive was renewed in mid-February. The gains realized were not negligible, but they were not decisive. They constituted some improvement of positions but were not able to open the gates. The losses on both sides were very serious. In order to get some idea, let us cite the following example from the Italian side: the Julia division, which had been completely renewed in the meantime, lost in the month of February 3,700 non-commissioned officers and men and 120 officers out of a combat strength of 10,000 men and 350 officers. This example also indicates the measure of resistance met by the attack. As a result, the Greek side had to postpone its offensive for a while and, in the meantime, prepare to meet the coming Italian onslaught. It had been announced beforehand, and it would be dreadful. Mussolini wanted this time to keep the promise he had made before his first offensive. On November 17, after the first defeats, he had asserted officially that "we shall smash the backs of the Greeks."

In the first days of March 1941, Mussolini had twenty-eight divisions in Albania, all of them completely battle-ready. They were to be supported by three hundred fighters and bombers—a huge number for those times. Il Duce went to Albania himself and inspected a large part of his divisions there in order to boost the morale of the men. Rather curiously, the great enthusiasm with which he was greeted surprised even the most reserved members of his entourage. On March 9, the Italian offensive opened up on the entire front. The main objective was to create an opening in the center and, through this, to penetrate in depth with a large part of the army. At six o'clock in the morning Mussolini reached an observation post which, at an altitude of 800 meters, overlooked the crucial sector of the front. Soon after, an artillery barrage began in which during one hour and a half, 100,000 shells were fired. Then the gunners' range was lengthened and the infantry advance began, while "continuous waves of German Stukas were carrying out a fierce assault." All day Italian fighter planes covered for the Stukas. Italian infantry, especially that part of it which came under the watchful eyes of Il Duce, attacked with rare persistence and bravery. Nevertheless, this great attack failed.

It had lasted more than ten days. On some days, for instance on March 13, the attack was even more violent than that of March 9. Bombardment was carried out by three hundred canons firing along a one kilometer front and continuous waves of airplanes with perfect regularity bombing the defenders. This was again an attack against the key position of the center, the famous rocky promontory, called by the Greeks "Hillock 731," and by the Italians "Collina Monastero."

The stubborness of the defenders was equal to the boldness of the attackers. Comparable also was the blood that was shed on both sides: at the foot of the hill in some places one could see more Italian bodies than rocks. On the other side , every night fifteen hundred Greek wounded were brought to Ioannina. The hospitals of the town were so full that the wounded, before being transported elsewhere, were obliged to lie in the courtyards or the streets near the hospital, a truly atrocious sight. The battle raged for thirteen days, favoring first one side then the other, but the Greek lines were not broken anywhere.

Mussolini, continually near the front, was the first to understand that he had failed. Early in the afternoon on March 9, in the midst of general optimism, he met Francesco Pricolo, the brave leader of the Italian air force and said to him: "The attack has already failed. I have fought in the trenches and I know these things. When an attack does not succeed in the first two or three hours, it never succeeds." He left Albania discouraged on March 21 and spoke for the first time of the need to make "a detailed report on the situation for His Majesty." The assistance of King Victor Emmanuel, whom he had stripped of all powers but who had roots in the past, now seemed to him necessary. From then on, another assistance which he wished for even less, that of Hitler, seemed to him indispensable. He was already preparing himself.

The German Invasion. On the first of March, a pact had been signed between Germany and Bulgaria allowing German troops to use Bulgarian territory. The agreement went into effect without delay. It was not known then exactly how many troops entered Bulgaria, but it is known today that, at the beginning of April on the Greek-Bulgarian and Serbo-Bulgarian borders there were four Panzer divisions and eleven motorized divisions. Others threatened Yugoslavia further to the north. Finally, there were some large military units that were either moving toward the south or being held in reserve.

During the first three months of the war, Greece had refused to accept any reinforcements of British troops so as not to give Hitler the excuse for which he was looking. Besides, Great Britain's serious preoccupation with North Africa did not allow the possibility of any important assistance to Greece. Churchill wanted to help because for him it was a matter of honor: not to leave alone and unassisted the small Ally that was fighting heroically under such difficult conditions. But, for Metaxas and Papagos, no matter of honor existed: it was a tactical problem, because such a move would weaken a crucial though feeble front, that of Africa, without strengthening enough the other front in Greece.

Metaxas died on January 29, 1941. He was succeeded by one of his ministers, Alexandros Koryzis, a banker with a good reputation and an honorable man. At the same time, German war preparations showed clearly that Hitler no longer sought an excuse to interfere. The dispatch of British troops was accepted by the Greek government. Churchill made an effort greater than his nation's strength allowed but, nevertheless, it was not sufficient. At the beginning of April there were just over sixty thousand Allied troops in Greece. These were composed of four divisions, one British, two Australian and one New Zealander and a brigade of Free Poles.

These troops, well equipped and assisted by three weak Greek divisions, had to cover the northern frontier towards Bulgaria and Yugoslavia to the east of the Pindos mountain range. For the defense of the Bulgarian frontier there was also the "Metaxas Line" which consisted of a series of small forts controlling the main passes.

Concerning the plan of defense, serious disagreements occurred between Greek and British generals. Since the end of February, the British had demanded the immediate withdrawal of large Greek contingents from the Albanian front. For one week the British believed that Papagos, in the presence of King George II and Anthony Eden, then Minister of Foreign Affairs, had given his consent to such a withdrawal. Middle East headquarters wanted to organize Greece's defense on a line which would start from the Aegean, pass through Mount Olympus, and continue over the mountains of northwest Macedonia. It was along that line, undoubtedly, that the Greek army should organize a very strong defense. The powerful Italian offensive in March, however, proved that the withdrawal of Greek forces from Albania would have been disastrous, for it would have taken place during Mussolini's great "Spring Offensive."

The Greek General Staff, with Papagos at its head thought quite differently: it would undoubtedly be very difficult for anyone to put up a resistance against a heavy German attack, especially as the Germans, who were master of the air, crushed the rear columns. Secondly, if a large part of northern Greece, including Thessalonike, was abandoned, it would be a great blow to morale. Thirdly, the Albanian front, stripped of its defenders, would create serious problems on the flank of the new line of defense and would discourage the Yugoslavs who had not yet decided to put up a resistance. Finally, Yugoslavia, if it decided to fight, had a comparatively well equipped army consisting of good fighters, and so would hold out for a period of time: it was necessary to profit from that.

In reality, what the Greek General Staff wanted was to launch a general attack with maximum strength on the whole Albanian front around April 10, so as to occupy further to the north a strong line along the mountains which would cover equally the port of Valona. This would set free a number of units and would allow a more efficient defense against the Germans. To reach an understanding between the Greeks and the British was not easy; there were besides other disagreements and misunderstandings, but space does not permit us to describe in detail all that took place. The fact is there was not enough time to launch a Greek attack, nor to withdraw to the line chosen by the British.

On April 6 the Germans paralyzed Belgrade with a terrible aerial bombardment and, launching their attack from Bulgaria, charged with their armored and mechanized divisions against both Greece and Yugoslavia. Scattered along their long frontiers and swiftly crushed by the Luftwaffe, the Yugoslavs put up practically no resistance, at least in the southern parts of Yugoslavia, which was of most concern to the defense of Greece. They were attacked by two German columns. One had Skopje as its target and aimed at cutting all communications between the south and the richer and better organized north. The other column, further south, had Greece as its objective. Strong armored and mechanized units had to cross very rapidly the major part of Yugoslav Macedonia so as to enter Greece from a point that, according to Allies, was considered safe: the northeast corner of Greek Macedonia.

Four other German columns swarmed into Greece from Bulgaria. Two of them, in a kind of pincers movement, advanced towards Thessalonike and another two, towards other ports of Thrace on the Aegean. Weak Greek contingents tried desperately to defend themselves, but they were dispersed by the crushing weight of the enemy tanks. Only the small forts of the "Metaxas Line" could offer any telling resistance. Isolated, heavily bombed and under pressure from incendiary bombs and flame throwers, they did not surrender until all Thrace had been conquered. In recognition of their heroic effort, the besiegers of the Wehrmacht presented arms to the few survivors. Greece's honor had been saved. Otherwise, it was nothing more than the blitzkrieg in all its fury.

On April 9, the fourth day of the war, Thessalonike was taken and on April 10, the ports of Thrace. In the meantime, motorized units of the second German column crossed all of southern Serbia undisturbed and invaded Greece through the passes of Florina. They skirted around the Greek-British defense line of Olympus and began to cross the Pindos mountain chain from east to west. They used the only existing route, the road through Metsovo which was completely unprotected because it lay deep in the rear.

Taken on the flank and heavily bombed by the Luftwaffe, the town of Ioannina was hemmed in on the morning of April 21. This was the main reprovisioning base of the

Greek army fighting in Albania, a base that lay more than one hundred kilometers behind the lines. Thus, the victorious army, the strongest one Greece had ever put in the field, was encircled and cut off. After a few local battles, certain generals surrendered on April 22, against the orders of the King and Papagos.

North of Mount Olympus fighting continued, but it was obvious that any serious resistance was impossible. The Yugoslav army, on which the Greeks had based limited hopes, officially surrendered on April 17.

The Luftwaffe had become master of the air after having destroyed all Greek airships in a matter of days. To the rear of the lines, towns and communication points were continually bombed. After the line of the Greek-Allied front was cut, the only alternative was to withdraw as rapidly as possible. So, it can be said that, except for one serious battle during which Allied divisions made an obstinate stand on a narrow front, all other fighting simply covered the retreat.

On April 21, the Germans bypassed Olympus and, on the same day, the British General Staff decided to evacuate Greece. Owing to the exemplary composure of the troops, who knew how to avoid encirclement, as well as the daring skill of the Royal Navy, more than fifty thousand men were evacuated. As for the remainder, about ten thousand, almost all of them avoided capture as they were hidden by the population in their homes and gradually, a few at a time, they also slipped away to Egypt. On the 27th, Nazi troops occupied the capital of the country. In Athens that day, the streets were empty, all shutters shut.

The next day, after a six-month delay, but much more peacefully than Rome had foreseen, the Italian Bari division occupied Corfu. Then came the turn of the other islands and of the Peloponnesus, now easy prey. Only Crete was left; King George took refuge there.

Papagos believed that he should stay on the continental soil of his country among the men he had commanded. He was consoled to hear that Hitler had stated before the Reichstag that Greek officers and soldiers, in honor of their bravery, would not be taken as prisoners of war. Beautiful words which later did not prevent many of them from being deported to Italy or Germany. For Papagos was reserved the bitter honor of the German concentration camp of Oranienburg.

In Crete, the King was accompanied by a new government. Koryzis, a sensitive and proud patriot, had committed suicide on April 18. Tsouderos was designated by the Sovereign to succeed him. Also a banker, he was known for his ties with politicians opposed to the Metaxas regime. Without any doubt, this was a sign: George II understood that, although one of the best pages of Greek history was largely due to him and to Metaxas, this did not absolve him from the fact the he had supported a dictatorship. At this point in time he had to face a very difficult undertaking because he had resolved to continue the fight. In order to do this, only Crete was left to him.

Crete, Tomb of the Little Lions. This long island—measuring about 250 kilometers in length and 30 to 60 kilometers in width—unfortunately offered an excellent base for the Axis as it lies in the center of the eastern Mediterranean. Besides, Cretan defense was very weak. Few men had been mobilized and sent to continental Greece to fight and the old weapons, which according to tradition were kept hidden in every home, had for the most part been confiscated by the Metaxas regime. On the island itself there were only a few small British units garrisoned there since December 1940.

It is true that, during the German invasion of Greece, more than 40,000 men, especially Australians and New Zealanders, were evacuated to Crete. But most of them had been moved hurriedly and so did not remain in organized military units. They had only light arms, or no arms at all, and very few provisions. Above all, they were exhausted, defeated and had suffered from the continual bombing that revealed to them the overwhelming superiority of the German air force. They came to the island with defeat in their souls.

The Germans knew this well. If they had believed that the island would be stoutly defended, it is doubtful that they would have undertaken such a difficult operation. Anyway, in order to do the job, they deployed forces that were exceptional both in quality and in numerical strength. The German air force, which exceeded the British by a ratio of four to one according to today's estimates, used the airstrips of Greece and of the Dodecanese, which then belonged to the Italians. The British were based in Egypt and had to cover a front that started from Syria and ended in Crete and Libya. Five hundred junker bombers and many planes towing gliders ensured transportation for the German shock troops. More than two hundred Messerschmitts, Stukas and other bombers and fighters protected them and supported the operation. Immense for its time, this air fleet was commanded by the famous Richthoffen himself.

The assault troops numbered about 22,000 and were all of the elite corps. They included the only division of German parachutists, the "flower of the German army," as it was known. They included also the most famous unit of the Wehrmacht, the "First Attack Regiment," four batallions, composed of very young men, carefully selected; they were trained, educated and organized in such a way so that their fighting morale would always be very high. These men considered themselves "invincible". Until then, they were. And now they were going to Crete, obeying the orders of their Fuehrer to occupy the island in order to utilize it as an air base against the English in the eastern Mediterranean. They arrived there with victory in their souls.

Nevertheless, on the first day of the operation, victory seemed doubtful. It can be said even that, if on that day when the fate of Crete was mainly decided the command of the Allies had not met with inexplicable gaps, the island would probably not have been conquered.

At dawn on May 20th, after intense bombing of towns and critical sites, the Germans descended in parachutes and with gliders at four points on the northern coast of the island (see Map No. 3). These sites had been purposely selected to paralyze the defense. But the landings, except for local successes, shaped up very poorly. It is difficult to describe here the history of that first day in a few lines. But it may be said for sure that the losses were enormous. Several units of the invaders lost 50 percent of their total strength and almost all the commanders of the batallions and companies that led the first jumps and assaults were killed. A good number of Nazis were taken prisoner. The men of the Allied units who had come from Greece fought with the courage of despair. When the "little Nazi lions" landed near inhabited areas, they faced the entire population—even women and children—who fought them off with old weapons, axes and even with pitchforks. The landing itself was not at all easy.

In the two sectors on the eastern side (near Rethymnon and Heraklion), where the best airport of the island was located, the first hours were disastrous for the Nazis.

At Rethymnon, which was defended by Greek and Australian units, the parachutists could manage to keep only a few isolated sites where they defended themselves to the end. Most of those who landed were killed or forced to surrender. The colonel in command was taken prisoner. However, around Heraklion and Rethymnon, after three days of fierce battles, attackers and defenders assumed a curious attitude of expectancy. Thus, until the fatal dates of May 26 and 27, on the northeast coast of the island, the Allied defenders, Greek and British, were victorious, but they did not try to exploit their victory towards the West. This was even more regrettable because it was there that the battle for the island was decided.

The commander-in-chief of the Allied forces in Crete, New Zealander General Freyberg, one of the heroes of the two world wars, had correctly understood that the Germans were primarily interested in the town of Chania on the northwest coast of the island. Souda Bay, the best port in the Mediterranean, lay to the left of town and an important airport, Maleme, to its right.

The best forces of the Allies were arrayed there (New Zealanders above all, and some Greeks) but, as the situation is seen today, Freyberg broke up his forces more than was necessary. The Germans attacked the Chania area with their best troops. Here also, during the landings, losses were heavy. Some platoons lost fifty to one hundred percent of their men and found themselves isolated under very unfavorable conditions.

Perhaps this explains, without justifying, an act of unbelievable barbarism that took place on the first day and during which the "little lions" transformed themselves into "hyenas": They murdered—we cannot use the word executed—twenty patients and the doctor of a British military hospital in the countryside and forced the other patients to get out of their beds and act as their shields. Protected by these living hostages, they advanced. . .

The Nazis who managed to land fought their scattered rivals not only with courage, but also with great skill. Most of them had but one objective: the rocky positions that overlooked the airport of Maleme, and which were the key to their defense. Thus concentrated, and despite their heavy losses, the attackers were four or five times more numerous than the men of the New Zealand batallion who were defending this site. Better armed and attacking continually, by afternoon they had made the position of the beleaguered defenders extremely difficult.

The losses of the latter were enormous; for the most part all of their officers had been killed. Two neighboring batallions (New Zealanders, like the one that had suffered the main attack) did not intervene to ease the pressure on the defenders in the center, although they had repeatedly been asked to assist. In the evening the commander of the New Zealand battalion suffering the greatest pressure, judged that his position was becoming extremely dangerous and personally led a strong counter-attack. But this counter-attack failed and cost the lives of many of his men. Then, in the bloody darkness, a minor event with great consequences took place: the brave New Zealand officer thought that the two neighboring battalions had not assisted him because they had been destroyed. The heavy losses, as well as the silence of the other battalions, made this explanation reasonable. He thus took the responsibility to act contrary to orders, and withdrew during the night.

A series of other unfortunate incidents made the consequences of this mistake even graver. The morning of May 21 found the German parachutists decimated and exhausted, but in control of a good airport. This was a decisive gain for, even if the counter-attacks of the next day against the heights overlooking the airport were ferocious, they were without result. The precious valley of Maleme remained in the hands of the Nazis and large Junkers landed continually at the airport. Some of these planes were destroyed by enemy fire but others, many others, landed and took off again discharging fresh troops and provisions and carrying away the wounded.

The fact that old Albion still reigned on the sea made dominance in the air even more important for the Nazis. Harassed by the planes of von Richthoffen, at the price of great sacrifices (in three days two cruisers and four destroyers were sunk; one dreadnought, two cruisers and four destroyers badly damaged), with his men stalking the enemy day and night and provisions almost gone, the Royal Navy still was able to impede German sea transportation. Its units attacked strongly-protected convoys, sank large troop carriers and fishing boats overloaded with German alpinists, then vanished to continue the fight elsewhere.

At daybreak on the 23rd, the small fleet of destroyers of

Lord Mountbatten was attacked by waves of Junkers and Stukas. Three of his five new ships, which had a speed of thirty knots, were sunk; among them was the ship of Commander Mountbatten himself, who escaped purely by chance. In those days (May 1941) the Royal Navy maintained a high level of performance according to its best traditions. It suffered terrible blows, but lashed back without flinching. Due to its control of the sea the Wehrmacht's special mountain division, being moved up by sea to play an important role in the first days of fighting on Crete, did not arrive. Though strongly protected both by the air force and the German navy, more than five thousand men disappeared under the waves of the Aegean. Control of the sea was precious for the defense but, unfortunately, insufficient. The sea routes were no longer, as in the past, the only means of communications with an island; now, a new medium was developed, with wider possibilities: the air. There the Nazis were the masters.

Meanwhile, on the island the battle had not been decided yet. For several days it raged and seemed indecisive. Everywhere, on both sides, it was a fight to the end. Some exceptional feats of arms were enacted, such as the retaking of the town of Galatas on May 25   after a fierce counterattack by the New Zealanders who were near exhaustion.

We must also mention one more outstanding deed: the defense and reoccupation of the village of Kasteli by a Greek battalion. This battalion had been formed by a New Zealand major who had conscripted fighters where he found them and armed his men with old weapons from the Balkan wars and, for want of these, with knives. Here an atrocious act must be pointed out so that the postwar generation will know to what point of bestiality a warlike, oligarchic system can reach.

When the village of Kasteli was occupied, along with the rest of the island, the German commander declared all Greeks there to be "snipers." Such was his desire. The

Greeks from that village now would not have the right to the honors of war and could not be taken prisoner! They had only the right to die. Then all the men that defended Kasteli so honorably were executed. But that was not sufficient to calm the rage caused by the victorious resistance of poorly armed soldiers. The latter had committed the terrible crime of fighting with knives. There were also some cases of German soldiers being mutilated (an investigation later by the Germans verified five cases of mutilations), and these "atrocities" imposed a special punishment: two hundred inhabitants of Kasteli were shot in the town square on the first day of the occupation. The name of this officer, who considered himself "a civilized person", should be mentioned: it was Major Schaette.

The two feats of arms mentioned above were not the only ones. That is why, until the night of the 25th to the 26th, nobody knew who the victor was or who the vanquished. The commanders of the Allied units insisted that a vigorous counter-attack with all their forces would liberate the sector, Galata-Maleme, or at least the larger part of it. If this local success had taken place, it seems probable today—and we stress the word "probable"—that the German invasion of Crete would have failed in its entirety. Not that the Germans could not, if they perservered, bring the operation to a successful conclusion, as they had already acquired an important bridgehead. But, by now it had cost them too much. They had lost a large number of planes and many of their best troops. And these had been intended to play an important role in the imminent attack against the Soviet Union. The Germans began to doubt, not the outcome of their Cretan adventure, but its expected short duration. Unfortunately, it seems that in the highest levels of the Allied command there were doubts from the beginning as to the possibility of defending the island. So, while in the eastern sector—Rethymnon and Heraklion—the Allies were still victorious and the commanders cabled the Supreme Command to learn if they should advance to the west, to Chania and Maleme; instead of ordering this maneuver and counter-attacking, withdrawal was ordered. The key to the resistance was abandoned. This was only the beginning of the end for, unfortunately, the withdrawal took place on a line which had not been prepared, nor even studied. To the great despair of Churchill, whose advice from the start was for the use of another, and indeed better, defense tactic, the general evacuation of Crete was decided on the evening of May 27.

This evacuation was not to be easy, either by sea or land. Morale which, until then, had been high on both sides, now suddenly deserted the Allied side. In the eastern sector, where fatigue had turned to complete exhaustion, retreat became flight. In this sector, evacuation was in large part made possible due to the providential resistance of one Greek regiment. Also poorly equipped, this regiment consisted of the Army Academy students, gendarmes and Cretan volunteers. Isolated from the third or fourth day of the invasion, it was believed to have been destroyed by the Germans. In reality, it had been fighting all the time to protect the only road the retreating New Zealanders could follow to reach the southern coast. And it covered this road until the eve of total evacuation, which took place on June 1.

King George II and his government just managed to cross the mountains that separated them from the south. Constantine II, then one year old, made the dangerous journey in the arms of an officer. Making great sacrifices again, the Royal Navy managed to transport eighteen thousand men to Egypt, in the face of constant danger (see Map No. 3). The evacuation was a success. It was, unfortunately, the period of World War II when the Allied cause rejoiced over successful withdrawals.

The battle of Crete had been lost. One did not realize it then, but in a more general way, it had been brilliantly won.

On the third day of the battle the number of Germans killed was greater than their losses on all other fronts from the beginning of hostilities. Even more significant is the fact that these losses were of choice shock troops. The air force also suffered heavy losses. But, above all, what the Germans had lost in Greece, and in Crete, was time: the invasion of the Soviet Union, initially planned for May 15 took place instead on June 22nd. If the invasion of the Soviet Union had begun forty days earlier, the role of "General Winter" would have been completely different during the siege of Moscow and in the spectacular descent towards the Caucasus, a descent that threatened the oil fields of the Middle East.

The KKE and the Greek-Italian War. The first reaction of the Greek Communist Party was unforseen. On October 30, 1940, Zachariadis wrote a letter to Maniadakis from prison, where he had been for three and a half years. This letter was immediately published in all the newspapers. It contained a fine appeal for resistance, and ended as follows:

> *"Everyone in the fight, each to his post, victory belongs to Greece and its people. The workers of the world are at our side."*

It was an artful text from his point of view (victory to the people, to the workers of the world—not to dictatorship), but it was at the same time useless to the war cause. It also conformed to the attitude of all political leaders, persecuted or not, who were opposed to the dictatorship. All had declared themselves in favor of resistance to the invader.

However, the authenticity of Zachariadis' letter was questioned by the Party's underground. It was attributed to the Security Police and was declared a forgery. The latter claim was not true. With the alteration of a few words it was later recognized as authentic by Zachariadis himself and, after the liberation of the country, was included in the official publications of the Party.

It is difficult and, within the limits of this book, useless to engage in a search for motives as to why the letter was written and who doubted its authenticity and why. What must be said is that the Party, after approving of the war against Mussolini, later disapproved of it.

In another letter to Maniadakis on November 26 which was not published, Zachariadis adopted a new line. After a few days the Central Committee of the Party followed him in this new line with a manifesto that was circulated on December 7. The war, they said, was caused by a clique of the King and Metaxas, who acted according to the directives of British imperalism and had nothing to do with the defense of the country. Irrefutable proof of this was the fact that it continued after the enemy had been pushed beyond the Greek frontiers. Henceforth, the war consisted of senseless killing and the invasion of foreign territory in order to serve British plutocracy. The invasion of Albania itself was even more unjustified, as the security of Greece could have been secured through the mediation of the Soviet Union. The Soviet Union maintained good relations, the dominant power of the Axis, which had remained neutral in the Greek-Italian conflict. The Greek army was called on to refuse to fight beyond the nation's frontiers. This argumentation was propagated in pamphlets that circulated among fighters at the front.[2] The Manifesto of December 7, 1940, a more official document than the pamphlets, stated:

> We call our fighters to refuse to fight beyond the borders of our fatherland. What are we doing in Albania? The people do not want another Sangarius! When they make this decision our fighters should submit peace terms to the opponents without demanding territorial recompense or other compensation.

The pamphlets followed this line. The Security Police naturally took all precautions to see that as few as possible of these pamphlets were circulated.

One can not know why Zachariadis took this sudden

change of line or why this stand was adopted by the KKE. To this day it is difficult to explain. According to classic Leninist technique, every war was useful for the development of the Communist movement. The bloodier it was and the longer it lasted, the better. Besides, this war was between two dictatorships and brought about the defeat of the one, the native one, and strengthened the other, or foreign one, which was internationally more important.

Why did the KKE now oppose the national defense which it had initially supported? Perhaps instructions were given from abroad so that the Soviet Union would appear to the warring peoples as the protector of the peace and tranquility. Later, when the Germans attacked the Soviet Union, this position of the K K E was abandoned as were the calls to desertion; the effort was in fact made to question the authenticity of the pamphlets which were circulated in the front. After the war however, the texts were included in the official publications of the Party.

In a discussion in the Greek Parliament on February 24, 1960, this author referred to the above mentioned pamphlets and read portions of the texts (*Minutes of the Greek Parliament* of the same date). Among the EDA (Union of the Democratic Left) representatives who were present were many leading cadres of the KKE; they were publicly challenged that day to repudiate the content of the pamphlets. Their reply was only a glacial silence.

So, one can be sure that this call for desertion in time of war was authentic and expressed the Party line. Nevertheless, these pamphlets had no effect, first, because of their limited circulation and, second, because of the high patriotic spirit of the period. On the contrary, wherever they were recognized, they increased suspicion, not to say hatred, against the KKE. The Party, however, did not change its line for this reason. But, disorganized, divided, hesitant and persecuted, it could only make a feeble propaganda effort during the Greek-Italian war.

The situation changed radically toward the end of April 1941 with the occupation of Greece by the Germans.

The members of the Communist party who had cooperated in any way with the Security Police had vanished. Those who had "signed the declaration" remained in the shadows, not knowing what to do. The loyal cadres who had managed to remain active in the Party underground tried to reorganize the movement and intensify propaganda.

Many, even those highly placed, made a mistake that would be unbelievable if it were not verified by the official publications of the Party: they began to adopt a line favorable to the Axis because they believed that the Soviet Union was a friend of Germany.

The eventful 22nd of June 1941, the day Germany invaded the Soviet Union, showed the Party leadership how much it had erred and, naturally, all who had exposed themselves were discredited. But the Party as a whole was not harmed because the German alliance was of very short duration. Besides, a new and dynamic spirit was in the process of renewing the Party. Many of those who had been in prison during the dictatorship were now the leaders of this revival.

With the entry of the Germans in Greece, many detained Communists were removed by the Nazis to German concentration camps. Nicos Zachariadis was among them.

Most of the detainees—a few hundred—either escaped after the collapse of the Greek-British forces, or, without anyone knowing the reason, were set free following a special order of the Nazi Military Police. They immediately took the situation in hand but, of course, in the strictest secrecy. All of them were loyal, tough cadres toward which the Communist world had no reproach; they had not been exposed in any way, for all had suffered without flinching.

The development of events greatly facilitated their task. Just as they were beginning to get in touch with comrades scattered all over the country, the Wehrmacht forced its way over the Soviet frontier. No longer was there any hesitation as to the line to be followed. No longer did they need to make difficult contacts with Communists abroad. Nor was there any longer a need for further instructions.

Most of the elite cadres were reunited and so declared themselves to the Central Committee of the Party. At a meeting in full session they set the new objectives of the KKE. The Sixth Plenum defined among others, that the *"duty of every Greek Communist was to organize the struggle for the defense of the Soviet Union and the overthrow of the foreign Fascist yoke."* They added, at the same time, that "the Communists should explain to the people that only a popular government, consisting of workers and farmers, could liberate the country from the exploitation of foreigners."

The text was clear and official. The program of all that was to follow was stated there from the first weeks of the occupation. From then on, seeking legitimacy by use of nationalist slogans the KKE would fight for the defense of the Soviet Union and to seize power domestically. No one paid any attention to this. Neither the politicians of Greece, nor the Allied statesmen. The implementation of this program was to assume great dimensions before the world would realize what it was all about. By then, the first phase of the civil war had already begun.

Chapter IV

The First Act of the Civil War
(1943-1944)

Regrouping. After the invasion of Greece, the country was divided into three occupation zones. The Germans occupied Athens, the area of Thessalonike, the border zone towards Turkey, as well as Crete and three of the largest islands of the Aegean. These were the most sensitive points and the most densely populated places.

A fertile region separating Bulgaria from the Aegean Sea would be used as bait: this was entrusted to the Bulgarian army and, two years later, the area of this region was doubled. The rest of Greece, continental and insular, was occupied by the Italian troops.

A new experiment which was tried, proved in the end to be a great failure. The Italian occupation authorities wished to group all those who spoke a dialect with a latin base and to join them with others who did not speak it, with the idea of creating—when the war ended—a Vlach principality. This new state would form a bridge between the two latin sister states of Italy and Romania. For this purpose, the "Roman

Legion" was created which had its own "army" and helped the Italian authorities in the administration of Thessaly.

The tactics of each conqueror were suited to his mentality. The Nazis, indifferent towards everyday life, were well organized and terribly strict against any resistance, whether active or potential. The Fascists, arrogant, indulging in meanness, proved sometimes to have a faint interest in the people's fate. The Bulgarians—and later, the Roman Legion—were brutal, cruel and tyrannical in every move they made.

In addition to the traits which characterized each conqueror, all had a common specific aim which they followed with tenacity: the uncovering of hidden weapons.

When the Greek army had disbanded, more than two-thirds of the light weapons used had not been surrendered; even with poor maintenance these potentially constituted a considerable danger. This problem mainly worried the Italian troops because they guarded the mountains of Epirus, through which the men of the Greek army of Epirus had passed in order to return to their homes.

As soon as the stupor and the bitterness of the first days of occupation had passed, most of the population thought only of the need to survive. The fruit of the deserted land had to be harvested, thousands of houses—ruined or badly damaged—had to be repaired. People had to make all kinds of preparations for one of the worst winters they had ever known.

In the mountains, the situation was even more difficult, considering the closed economy that prevailed there and the austerity under which the inhabitants lived. They depended on the plains for their provisions including bread, oil and salt; communication with the plains was difficult and a scarcity of goods developed. The main concern of the population was with survival, for many it was indeed the only preoccupation.

In Athens some people had other concerns. General

Tsolakoglou, who had signed the cease-fire in Epirus, had now formed an occupation government without any popular support.

On the other hand, some young officers, employees of the Ministry of Foreign Affairs who had all—except one—refused to serve in the new government, and many others, tried to cross the Aegean Sea from island to island, escaping to Egypt through Turkey. Many departed, but very few arrived.

Inside Greece many young men organized a resistance movement. Secret organizations multiplied rapidly. Many lacked real means with which to act, and did not even have serious plans. Other resistance leaders, who were more level-headed and realistic, at times even had at their disposal a military wireless; they assembled a few people and outlined definite aims: The spreading of propaganda, the organizing of escapes to Egypt, and the transmission of military intelligence to the Allies, the relief of those in need, and the preparation of armed resistance for the Allied landing which (alas!) was forecast for the near future. In the years that followed, some of these organizations, with names such as "Alice", "Homer", "Kodros", etc., had remarkable success. Through their information large enemy cargo ships were sunk and, due to the bold actions of their members, important sabotage took place, which was punished by many executions. All classes of the population of Athens and of other large towns participated, assisted by a number of army officers, and by the clergy at the head of which was the Archbishop of Athens, Damaskinos.

None of these organizations had thought, in the beginning, of creating guerilla groups, although—this author knows from personal experience—the subject was often discussed. The results, it was estimated, would not be worth the retaliation which would be inflicted against a rural population that had already suffered enough.

None of the organizations envisaged either the creation of

a broad political or military movement under one central command. Besides, the politicians, who were capable of undertaking such an effort, did not show any activity in this direction. After five years of dictatorship, the political world had been dispersed, estranged from its surroundings and remained very much attached to the past. Many former politicians were absorbed by the secret resistance organizations, and many more were occupied with a matter of lesser importance in those critical days: the renunciation of Constitutional Monarchy and the return to Democracy. What is more, the politicians did not see and did not understand that only one party was working to achieve specific long term goals. That Party was the KKE.

The KKE was the only party which had had long experience in clandestine activity. Besides, having a leadership that was never contested, this leadership had been renewed and now offered worthy men, such as Andreas Tzimas, a young and dynamic lawyer, and George Siantos, the so-called "Old Man"—a mature, moderate, but also tenacious man of great courage.

Siantos was the main factor in the party's renewal and played an important role for many years. Born in Karditsa in 1890, a worker from the age of thirteen, a soldier and later a sergeant from 1910 until 1920, he was one of the first members of the Party, in which he held successfully many important positions. He had been arrested twice, and never had knuckled under. His last escape had taken place in September 1941, as he was being transferred from one prison to another. These experiences had made him a seasoned Party member. As soon as he came to Athens, in 1941, he began to organize the Party, which some months later elected him Secretary General of the Central Committee. In fact, he was the leader of the KKE until the return of Zachariadis to Greece in 1945.

Under Siantos' leadership the Central Committee, meeting in full session (the 8th Plenum) brilliantly adapted the

Party to the conditions of that period. Without repudiating its main principles and its final purpose, the seizing of power —this was clearly defined—the Party would now fight only for the creation of a broad national liberation front. All mention of workers and peasants would be avoided. Activity must be limited to the nation's survival *by all available means, including war,* Marxism and Leninism were temporarily forgotten and, if the Communists made an effort to undermine the dangerous bourgeois ("the reservists fought in Albania while the career officers were at their desks"), they tried equally to cooperate in a "national" framework with all the "good patriots". The line was intelligent and well suited to the atmosphere which prevailed in those days; it had only to be put into action.

The Central Committee of the KKE lost no time at all. The Party began by reorganizing throughout the country the secret cells of three to five members each. It then founded a united syndicalist front, directed by a three-member committee, of which only one member belonged to the KKE. But this member was Theos, experienced in this field and an ex-member of the Greek Parliament, where he had been distinguished for his fighting spirit. Dominated by the personality of Theos, the Workers Front made its presence felt very quickly.

The Front supported every patriotic demonstration that took place in spite of the occupation authorities' prohibitions. It took initiatives useful to the proletariat. It was openly opposed to the first forced transfer of Greek workers to Germany.

A very good job was being done. The Party won general sympathy and achieved prestige. It acquired a new political hue. The faithful went forward and, on the way, they recruited new converts; for men, striving together to relieve the oppressed, became comrades. Profiting from this state of affairs and from the inertia of the other parties, the KKE grew rapidly, engendering new groups which were conceived in the same spirit as the Workers' Front.

The most important of these groups was the one which would initiate the first guerrilla war (1943-1944) and the Revolution of December 1944, and which also later constituted the hard core of the guerrillas in the civil war between 1946 and 1949. This was the National Liberation Front, known as E A M, with its army called E L A S after the initials of its Greek name. Let us note here, as this was used as an impressive argument at first, that of these initials, the "E" stood for the word "National" (Ethnikon), the "A" for the word "Liberation" (Apeleftherosis)—terms that were alien to Marxism-Leninism, terms that were clearly bourgeois-patriotic.

The E A M was founded by the KKE in June 1941, in cooperation with two small socialist parties with a practically non-existent popular base. But these two parties constituted the facade which was to give the front an appearance of seriousness, solidarity and patriotism. And this was mainly achieved because these two parties had well-known and capable leaders, one of whom was Elias Tsirimokos. Based on active propaganda, which knew how to excite youth, and having penetrated almost every resistance cell, E A M met with great success from the very beginning.

The Armed Resistance. On the other hand, the People's National Liberation Army, ELAS, was not warmly welcomed. It was founded, according to a proclamation of EAM, on April 10, 1942. In reality it appeared in those days only in small armed groups in three mountain regions—Parnassos, Pindos, and Olympus—where the population saw neither Germans nor Italians. This, plus the fact that the mountain people led an extremely austere and difficult life, did not make it easy for them to understand the need for an armed struggle, in the course of which they could lose even what little they had.

So, even if weapons were not lacking, fighters were recruited with great difficulty, especially as the adventure of a fight—particularly attractive to youth—did not exist at that moment. Orders from headquarters were very strict; it was necessary to train themselves, impose discipline, and not to conduct the least warlike activity before being strong enough, so as to avoid useless reprisals which would provoke the enmity of the population. Both the sparkle and the glory of combat were missing. For these reasons, in the autumn of 1942, the first sector, that of Roumeli (Parnassos) could not put into the field more than about 300 men, and the other two sectors from 100 to 150 men each. The command of each group was confined to a three-member committee, responsible to the Senior Committee of the respective sector. The Senior Committee was responsible to the Central Committee based in Athens.

In these three-member committees, one member was in charge of military problems and operations, another dealt with political questions, and a third—the "chief" (Kapetanios)—was entrusted with the administration, the provisioning and the coordination of the activity of his unit. As he was usually the most powerful member of the committee, only the most able were named to this position. Usually the Kapetanios imposed his will upon the other members of the committee.

Discipline was strict; military training and lessons were given daily. Nobody talked of Marxism, of the revolution of the proletariat, of the miseries accompanying "imperialism"; the "imperialists" were at the time with the Soviet Union. Besides, it did not seem that there was any contact with the Soviets by the EAM. Only their influence was present and made itself felt, for even if the EAM/ELAS had the outward characteristics of a national coalition with socialist tendencies which included non-communist members, in reality it was controlled by the Communists.

Christopher M. Woodhouse, whom we shall mention often, quotes that the first British officers to come in contact with the groups of Roumeli, Thessaly, and Macedonia met only the KKE men in the three-member committees. All used pseudonyms. Certain ones—Markos Vafiadis among them—were the great leaders of the guerrilla war of 1946-1949. Woodhouse himself, who was sent to Athens at the beginning of 1943 to meet six representatives of the Central Committee of EAM, met only two persons, Siantos and Tzimas, who were eminent personalities of the KKE. Another common characteristic of all the EAM/ELAS leaders whom the British officers met then, was that all of them denied being Communists.

There was, however, one other exception, besides George Siantos, who also had never denied his Communist beliefs. This was a young agricultural engineer, who came from the Parnassos region and was a fervent activist of the early days, as well as one of those who signed a *Statement of Repentance* in 1939: Anthanassios Klaras. This man never concealed the fact that he was and remained a Communist by conviction. It seems certain, in spite of some "official" disputations of the fact, that he formed a group in his area and took to the mountains back in February 1942. The only name he was known by was a pseudonym: Aris Velouchiotis.

When the EAM announced the founding of the People's Army, Aris's group was the hard core of the first sector (Roumeli-Parnassos) and he himself, as a member of the Committee of Three, filled the position of military chief. But his personality soon made him the sole leader of the sector. Besides, he was the one who, at the end of 1942 on his own initiative, lit the spark that ELAS needed for its expansion.

We shall return to his personality and to the incident of November later, because first we should mention that, in the meantime, more armed groups had been formed. One of these groups—the most important one—was created soon after ELAS and played a most significant role until the end.

At the beginning of June 1942, retired colonel Napoleon Zervas, encouraged by English agents, had left Athens and had returned to Epirus, his place of origin. Theoretically, he had ties with the National Republican Hellenic League in Athens, known by its Greek initials as EDES. But in everything that concerned Epirus he was independent and, in fact, the sole leader of the movement. He took to the mountains immediately and, in less than three months, had formed a force of 200 to 250 guerrillas, quite well armed and with very good career and reserve officers with republican tendencies.

Zervas was a fearless but not flawless man. He was a card player, a *bon vivant* and was compromised by his participation in a variety of military mutinies. He was a well-loved man who outside his native land, personified the spirit of adventure. To him fell the lot of creating the spark and the leadership necessary to develop an armed resistance movement in Greece to oppose the conqueror.

Until the autumn of 1942, the Allies had not been at all interested in Greece, except to organize an information and escape network for numerous British soldiers not evacuated who had been hidden by various individuals. But, in view of the Allied offensive in North Africa, the Allied military command of the Middle East decided to make contact with the guerrillas and to ask for their help in sabotaging the railway line linking Germany with Piraeus, via Thessalonike. A large part of the supplies for General Rommel's Afrika Korps was carried on this line and then loaded on large cargo planes or ships and was transported to North Africa.

The most vulnerable point of the entire line was located at the foot of Parnassos, where three large bridges, one after the other, crossed steep precipices. All three bridges were guarded by strong Italian detachments. The Supreme Command of the Allies in the Middle East decided to blow up the longest of these, the bridge of Gorgopotamos, the "Rapid River".

A group of British and New Zealand officers, under the command of Colonel E. Myers, in October 1942 parachuted into the area near the three bridges.

The members of this mission came upon the guerrillas of ELAS, and were treated well by them. But, in spite of all their efforts, and although they had revealed the purpose of their mission, they were unable to meet anyone responsible. Aris, the leader of the guerrillas, was not to be found, for he did not wish to disobey orders from Athens. Besides he himself was not at all in favor of the operation. He was preoccupied with the setting up of his platoons, thirty men each in strength; he had no sympathy for the "imperialists" and was displeased with their unwarranted interference in his district.

After a month of waiting and of futile searching, the British, seeing that their operation risked either being delayed or not being done at all, dispatched Major C.M. Woodhouse to Zervas, who was on the west side of the Pindos Mountains. After walking more than one hundred and fifty kilometers on narrow mountain paths, Woodhouse met Zervas. The latter hastened to the site, by forced marches, bringing up a unit of his best men.

Then Aris proved that he was a born leader. The orders of the Central Committee were precise, but in this case he would not obey them. Whether or not the Gorgopotamos operation succeeded, it must not be carried out by British saboteurs and EDES; if executed in his district by others, EAM/ELAS would be discredited throughout Greece. Aris rushed up with a larger force of partisans than that of Zervas.

Much has been written since then and much fanaticism has been displayed on both sides to alter the figures in favor of one or the other. It seems, however, that an objective estimate gives a total of about 150 men for Zervas and 200 for Aris Velouchiotis.

Nevertheless, the numbers of guerrillas of the one or the other party is of little importance. The ensuing fight with the Italian garrison was so long and so tenacious that it now seems certain that the operation would not have ended well if the two groups had not taken part in it. Both guerrilla units fought very bravely and the foreign saboteurs thus had all the time they needed to do their job well. Before dawn (November 25th) the great bridge fell, all its foundations having crumbled. One of the main routes for Rommel's supplies had been interrupted, and six weeks were required to restore it.

The two armed bands had fought side by side. It was the first and the last time. From then on, they slaughtered each other.

Six weeks later British again asked for their help in blowing up another of the three bridges, that over the Asopos River. The usefulness of the operation seemed even greater for the Greeks wrongly assumed that the Allies would make a landing in Greece in the near future.

The possibilities of the guerrillas were also greater for, in the meantime, their numbers had increased; they were better organized and possessed some modern weapons, which the British had dropped to them by parachute. But this time the two organizations refused their support. The reasons behind their refusal become clear to us if we know how the situation developed.

ELAS refused, used the excuse that it had just blown up a railway tunnel which had caused the Wehrmacht a loss of 300 men. This was clearly a pretext for, in war, one does not refuse to carry out an operation because another has been performed. The particulars of the ELAS response were, according to the British, *first, no one had asked them to blow up the tunnel, an operation that cut the line for only four days; second, they had carried out the operation to counter the accusation that they were not putting up a fight against the occupation forces, but only against rival resistance groups; third, they wished to inspire the confidence of the British Military Mission so as to be able to ask for more modern weapons.*

Zervas, on the other hand, made a definite refusal declaring that the Asopos bridge was geographically situated in the center of ELAS territory and that, for him, even an attempt to reach the place would mean "suicide".

The Asopos bridge was blown up on the night of June 24, due to the daring of six British officers, mainly the New Zealander Captain Scott. Railway communications were interrupted for four months. The operation was remarkably useful, brilliant, and bold, at a position strongly guarded by the enemy and from which Greek armed resistance was absent. This absence was particularly inexcusable because on account of it the saboteurs ran a high risk of failure. Alas! As we will see, the spark of Gorgopotamos had changed everything.

Organized Resistance and Fratricide. After Gorgopotamos Zervas was welcomed back to his native province as a hero. He was becoming the glory of Epirus. His rowdy past had faded away. He was becoming a leader. Even respectable people could follow him. The British quickly sent him a mission of a few officers and began to drop weapons, clothing and gold sovereigns by parachute, so that every one of his armed men received one sovereign monthly for the needs of his family. He had the disadvantage of occupying a less important area, but he was more willing to obey the orders of Allied headquarters.

In the EAM/ELAS camp, Gorgopotamos had also caused spectacular developments, of which Aris was the principal architect. Shrewd, brave, a good organizer and a fanatic to the extreme, he lacked neither intelligence nor culture, nor—according to his point of view—a spirit of justice. That was his weakness. For, in the name of his justice, he killed with the greatest ease. It has been said, and it seems to be correct, that he sent one of his men to the execution squad for having stolen a chicken. This did not prevent him from becoming a leader. Italian General Infante, who had no reason to like him, told the author in 1945: *Among all the leaders of EAM/ELAS that I have met, and they have been many, only Aris impressed me. He was strong, he argued soundly, and he had finesse.*

From that time, thanks to Aris, the prestige of ELAS soared and the EAM Committee in Athens realized the importance of his small armed groups. The KKE realized something else: it was not sufficient for the Party to control EAM. Plans had to be made to attain the objective—of seizing power. Only the loyal could be entrusted to put the plan into action. As for the others, they had to be assigned suitable diversions. For this reason, in December 1942, an extraordinary Panhellenic Congress of the Communist Party was called in Athens. According to information from reliable sources, as well as extracts taken from statements made by leading cadres and later published in the official documents of the Party, and based on our conclusions from the events that followed, the Congress decided to adopt three basic directives:

First, to monopolize resistance thus eliminating all other guerrilla groups. Second, to infiltrate into the armed forces which had been organized by the Royal Greek Government in Egypt, and which were becoming important. Third, to undermine the authority of the King and his Government in such a manner that every opposition toward EAM/ELAS could be interpreted as anti-democratic and reactionary. These directives were put into practice with great care and persistence.

From spring until the summer of 1943, several small independent guerrilla groups, often including officers held in high esteem, were annihilated. This happened mainly in the south, in the Peloponnesus, where the nationalists—and the royalists—were predominant. EDES suffered many attacks but it managed either to resist or to withdraw and avoid being wiped out.

EKKA was the armed resistance organization that was third in importance. It had democratic tendencies and its military leader, Colonel Psaros, was a fearless soldier and was above reproach. Operating in Roumeli, Psaros's native province, the group suffered two powerful attacks (the first in March 1943) and was temporarily dissolved, but it managed to recover.

Another attack, of the same kind but in another direction, had results as unforeseen as they were beneficial for ELAS. Towards the end of 1942, career officer Major Kostopoulos organized in Western Thessaly, at the foot of Mount Pindos, a small resistance group that was well staffed with good officers. For their leader this group chose a Colonel Sarafis, a man of good military reputation but who had been retired from the army on account of his role in the 1935 Venizelist coup. Sarafis was encouraged by an emissary[1] of the Greek Government-in-exile and he accepted to lead the Thessalian group.

The author's family helped Sarafis on his perilous journey from Athens to Thessaly and thus we have a direct insight into the ideas that inspired him. He was, above all, for an all-out struggle against the army of occupation. He decided that the enemy must be struck without mercy, but also that the first place in resistance should not be given up to ELAS, which was not a national party, being controlled by the KKE, and was, therefore, dangerous to the country. He believed also that, when the war ended, there should be a referendum to determine the political system and hoped that the Constitutional Monarchy, which was unacceptable to him, would be abolished and that the Republic would be restored.

On his arrival in Thessaly, and after a warm welcome, Sarafis and his small group were encircled by the far superior forces of ELAS.

Those of his men who did not manage to escape, or did not accept enlistment with ELAS, were executed immediately. Taken prisoner, Sarafis was sent to the south, to the headquarters of Aris, where he remained imprisoned for some days under humiliating conditions. He left prison to announce that he had accepted the proposition made to him, viz to become the Military Commander of ELAS.

It does not seem that fear led him to this decision. His few days of command with the Kostopoulos group, the massacre of his men, his trip and his sojourn close to Aris Velouchiotis had persuaded him that his ideas were out of date; from now on: one must either die, or fight with ELAS. Sarafis opted for the second solution. He gave ELAS what it lacked, a good staff officer, a name that was respected by a large part of the regular army, a front that would give the impression that EAM/ELAS did not necessarily mean KKE.

The Central Committee in Athens did not lose the opportunity. One of its own, one of its best, Andreas Tzimas, a trained member of the KKE, left for the mountains. In May 1943, ELAS was directed by a committee of three, all first-rate: Sarafis, military leader; Aris, kapetanios; Tzimas, political commissar.

The results were soon apparent. In a few months the armed groups became an organized army and their aggressiveness increased. Rival groups either disappeared, or confined their activities to smaller districts. The excuse used to attack them was mainly that they had collaborated with the enemy, or that they had been the first to attack. This was sometimes the case. Generally, the excuse was false, for, neither the valor nor the patriotism of the others, ascertained over a period of years, nor reports of foreign officers that were there, allows one to believe these accusations.

It is necessary to note here that the small group of Gorgopotamos saboteurs had been reinforced by several officers, who already formed the British Military Mission. This organization was in regular contact by radio with the Supreme Allied Headquarters for the Middle East and acted as its representative. Most of its members were detached as liaison officers with the largest guerrilla units. They were able thus to see first hand what was happening. One of their main missions now was to prevent fratricidal fighting and, if possible, to reconcile the three principal organizations: EAM/ELAS, EDES and EKKA. The Allies succeeded in doing this only occasionally and partially. Once, however, on July 26, 1943, they managed to get an agreement of cooperation signed.

The Allies succeeded because Middle East Headquarters was asking the Greek guerrillas to do as much as they could. Their headquarters in the Middle East did not explain the reason for this, so everyone believed that the landing on Greece was imminent. This was not quite true, but they wanted the Germans to believe it for the Allied Command was preparing for the Italian campaign. In fact, they managed to fool the Germans thanks to the intensity of Greek resistance and to the Asopos operation. This was, perhaps, the greatest specific service offered to the Allies by the Greek resistance groups, for shortly before the Allied landing in Sicily two strong Wehrmacht divisions were transferred to Greece where four other divisions were already assigned.

But every coin has two sides. EAM/ELAS had also believed that British troops would soon liberate the country so it had to eliminate its rivals in time. That is how officers of the British Military Mission explained the renewal of ELAS aggressiveness against the nationalist groups during this period. This was also the explanation given by all Greek sources, except those of the extreme left.

After the landing in Italy it became clear that the liberation of the country was postponed. From the other side, the bloody fratricide had been costly, had not brought any decisive results and had not affected morale of EDES and EKKA. These were the main factors that enabled the British Military Mission to bring about an agreement between the three groups on July 26, 1943.

According to this agreement, the three organizations were placed under the orders of a Joint General Headquarters, even though they retained a high degree of independence. The British Military Mission would participate in this body, whose seat would be the headquarters of ELAS. The location was at Pertouli, a beautiful small village, isolated among dense forests of fir trees in mountainous west Thessaly.

The three groups were now stronger, better organized and functioned well. ELAS had about 18,000 fighters; EDES had 5,000, as well as a number of men to handle supplies and other services. EKKA, though weaker (about 1,000 fighters), had the advantage of having the best and most respected leadership. Kartalis, a young and brilliant politician, was its political leader; Psaros, the military commander. The three guerrilla organizations did everything they could to form small but effective armies.

In the meantime, great international events radically affected the general outlook and changed the plans of EAM/ELAS for the immediate future. The second half of 1942 was a period of success for the Western Allies: the battle of El Alamein, the campaign in North Africa, the landing at Casablanca with American participation. The first six months of 1943 was a period of success for the Soviet Union; the disaster of von Paulus' army at Stalingrad, the opening of the Leningrad pincers, the successful counter-attack against the dangerous push towards the Caucasus, the springboard leading to the Persian Gulf and the Middle East.

On the other hand, in the Greek arena, leftists had penetrated government units in Egypt Among all its divisions, only one had remained inaccessible: that was the Sacred Regiment that consisted exclusively of officers who fought as ordinary soldiers, and which was continually in the vanguard of Montgomery's army during the advance in North Africa.

The other units of the army gave cause for anxiety. In March 1943, two brigades had mutineed and committees of young officers and non-commissioned officers had temporarily taken command. The mutiny did not result in bloodshed, but two hundred officers of the "Old Regime" were removed. Discipline was shaken. Several ministers, among them Deputy Prime Minister Panayiotis Cannellopoulos, were obliged to resign. The position of the King was weakened.

In the light of all these events we must judge the efforts of ELAS to eliminate EDES and EKKA in the first part of 1943. EAM had to gain time, which explains better the honeymoon of Pertouli. But that did not last. In August and in October the clouds gathered and darkened under the influence of two unforeseen events, and then the storm broke.

On August 9 representatives of the General Headquarters of the Resistance took off from a small temporary airport in the mountains. They were headed for Egypt. The Allied headquarters in the Middle East wanted to achieve some cooperation between the resistance forces and the Royal Government abroad.

The discussions were not easy but, nevertheless, the delegation of the resistance forces made various proposals for discussion. There was, unfortunately, no time for this, as the delegation that represented EAM/ELAS (composed of four individuals, all belonging to the KKE, with Siantos and Tzimas at their head) surprised all parties by submitting propositions that concerned only their own organization.

The ELAS proposals were: that it must be recognized as being part of the Greek armed forces, officers who served in the regular army abroad had to be replaced with officers serving ELAS mountain units and EAM had to be represented in the Royal Government-in-exile with three ministers. In the atmosphere of distrust and suspicion the talks failed to produce results, and the representatives of the extreme Left departed.

The attitude of the British towards EAM/ELAS continued to remain the same in part because, according to British sources, certain officers in the Allied Headquarters in the Middle East favored the guerrillas of the extreme left. In addition, the British Military Mission, which now saw the EAM intentions clearly, was still in favor of continuing support of ELAS.

From the point of view of the British Military Mission ELAS was by far the strongest guerrilla movement in Greece and it operated in the region that was militarily most important. Also, the British always hoped to be able to influence ELAS, for it continued to call for British material aid and maintained a semblance of good relations with the British Military Mission. Then, requests for assistance diminished, indeed practically ceased altogether. This signalled the beginning of the Civil War which lasted until 1949.

Equilibrium is upset, Civil War begins. On September 8, 1943 Italy capitulated. The Italian troops were in flight, and were disarmed wherever they were found, or as in Cephalonia, massacred by the Germans.

Only the Pinerolo division, which occupied central Thessaly, definitely lined up with the Allies. Reinforced by other Italian units, it had about 18,000 men with modern armament at its disposal, including twenty pieces of mountain artillery. Its morale was low, but discipline remained good and its commander, General Infante, was an officer of stature.

Anticipating what was going to happen, the Italian general had already contacted the British Military Mission. On the day of the capitulation he asked to place his troops under British orders. The BMM did not accept this right away, but it did propose to mediate in negotiations with the General Headquarters of the resistance, in which it also participated. Thus, on September 11, an agreement was signed, according to which the Pinerolo division, divided into small units would cooperate with the guerrillas in operations against the Germans. Later, under certain conditions, a special sector would be entrusted to it. The agreement was signed by Sarafis, Infante, and Woodhouse (who, in the meantime, had been promoted to colonel and Chief of Mission), and by a representative of Resistance Head-quarters.

After the failure of an almost impossible operation that had been assigned to the Italians (occupation of the large Larissa airport), they were distributed in small detach-ments in various villages which were strongly guarded by ELAS. The men of the Italian division were encircled and disarmed and they were sent to work camps in the moun-tains. General Infante was taken prisoner and sent to Pertouli. On orders from the General Allied Headquarters for the Middle East he was transferred to Albania and, from there, via submarine to Italy. ELAS thus inherited armaments which heretofore had been undreamed of.

In the midst of all this, another important development was taking place in Greece. A large number of German troops were moving towards the north. This movement was explained by the Greeks as the beginning of the German evacuation of the country. We now know that this is exactly what the Germans wanted them to believe. Knowing well the local animosities, they wanted the guerrillas to profit from their "retreat" and begin killing each other, so that they could attack them more easily. The Germans had just lost the assistance of numerous Italian garrisons and, seeing that the guerrillas now constituted a grave danger to their communications, they had decided to strike the guerrillas and crush them, or at least neutralize them for some time.

The Wehrmacht concerned itself as much with ELAS as with EDES. The Germans believed the latter to be impor-tant because, though EDES was the weaker of the two resistance groups, its men fought well and it controlled one of the two evacuation routes from Greece which ended at the Albanian port of Valona on the Adriatic Sea. This road was the most secure for the Germans because it by-passed Yugoslavia, dominated by Tito's strong partisans.

As a beginning, the Wehrmacht now decided on a strong attack against the forces of EDES, master of Epirus. On October 16 the attack was launched with five columns to the east of Arta and to the southeast of Ioannina, and aimed to cut the enemy lines and to surround them. For ten days EDES, with Zervas himself at the head, drove back the assault and inflicted heavy losses on the Nazis. It was the first time that EDES had engaged in a real battle, so different from ambushes and hasty skirmishes, and it was successful.

But ten days later five battalions of the Edelweiss alpine division, transported to the front in great haste, reinforced the aggressors, and the German offensive took on renewed vigor. It was also sustained by a large number of mortars and several guns of the mountain artillery. Zervas then realized that this time the Wehrmacht intended to destroy him completely. So he withdrew to the east only to find himself face to face with an imposing concentration of ELAS units.

What Zervas did not know was that, in the meantime, his representative at Pertouli had been arrested and that Aris, at the head of a new division armed with the Italian weapons, was crossing the mountain range to crush him. He was also unaware that Siantos and Sarafis followed this operation at close quarters (from Messochora and then from Pachtouri)—an operation which would deliver them from their greatest rival.

The forces of Zervas now had to fight on two fronts: to the east against their brothers, to the west against the Germans. For four days the battle raged, to culminate on October 30 in fierce combat on some high rocky ridges where all able-bodied men, officers and guerrillas, fought a final battle of despair.

But, with the coming of night, the remaining EDES guerrillas disappeared. Divided into groups of ten to thirty men each, they marched until dawn, taking to the steep cliffs which were beyond the reach of the enemy. Zervas had arranged a rendezvous for six weeks later in another mountain spot south of Ioannina.

The troops of ELAS withdrew and remained intact. Other units had, in the meantime, crushed some small resistance groups. Two or three of these only carried the name for, parallel to the true resistance effort, bands of brigands and small armed groups of secret enemy collaborators also existed.

The Nazis themselves wasted no time either. They struck everywhere, in the mountains of central Greece and in the north. They crushed all resistance, but almost always the guerrillas refused to engage in battle. However, this resulted in frustration for the Germans who fell upon the guerrillas' supporters. Many hostages were executed and more than two hundred villages were burned to the ground and completely destroyed. At inaccessible Pertouli, ELAS headquarters, only one house was left standing, perhaps to remind future generations that German officers had slept there, while their men razed this charming village.

This time protests were not raised against the Nazis: they were raised against ELAS. These protests were all the more resounding as, for the first time, the Allies were the accusers. The BBC, through its Greek program which was secretly listened to throughout the country, had greatly favored the formation of ELAS; in always giving it warm praise, the British had helped to give ELAS authority and thus enabled it to recruit to its ranks thousands of noncommunist partisans. Now the BBC changed its tone; it was speaking of bands of brigands, revealing that Aris Velouchiotis had attacked and arrested members of the Allied Military Mission.[2] That is to say, it accused Aris of being a war criminal. Churchill himself denounced these deeds in Parliament, citing details, and revealing that a British officer had been assassinated. But there was more than this on the other side of the coin for ELAS and for the general situation.

The Germans in the meanwhile continued to exert pressure, not only on EDES but also on ELAS. Their operations continued until the middle of winter. The ELAS groups, though they avoided large-scale engagements, suffered terrible hardships, as much from losses resulting from lack of organization as from actual combat. Furthermore, ELAS had to face another enemy, which had developed in reaction to its extremist activities: the Security Battalions. The occupation government (headed by Tsolakoglou, Logothetopoulos, Rallis) had formed battalions in order to face the incursions of ELAS. But, having been created by such a government and with the material assistance of the Germans, it was not possible for them to be supported by the populace. Nevertheless, the people accepted them when ELAS openly launched an intense civil war. What is more, the Security Battalions included some brilliant officers who had managed to escape when their armed resistance groups had been crushed by ELAS. Later, the Security Battalions lost their authority completely and brought on the people's hatred because the Nazis used some of them, especially in Athens, to round up Greeks to be sent to Germany as forced laborers.

At the beginning of the fratricidal war, however, things were different. The men of the Security Battalions considered themselves the protectors of an already exhausted population. They felt they had the people's support. They had capable leadership, were well armed, and were aggressive. ELAS had paid dearly for its existence, especially in Attica and in the Peloponnesus.

Eventually, the beginning of the true civil war had another unfavorable aspect for the People's Army. The fear and hatred that reigned in the country were reinforced by doubt and bitterness, even within ELAS itself. There was a profound uneasiness, caused by the divergent views of the two strong men holding the key positions. Since autumn Siantos had been in the mountains taking the place of Tzimas, who had gone on a special mission to Tito. Thus,

Siantos was political commissar at the General headquarters of ELAS, Aris was kapetanios, and Sarafis military leader. Siantos favored slow development and methodical preparation to enable EAM/ELAS to become stronger, and, in the meantime, to collaborate up to a certain point with the Allied Military Mission. Aris took the opposite view. For him, the settling of matters must be prompt and also radical, or else they would be playing the game of the native monarcho-fascists and the foreign imperialists.

The turn of events that followed rather justified Siantos, a fact that Aris's stubborness did not allow him to accept. The "Old Man" had never yielded, whereas the captain had once been a "declarationist". This was Aris's great handicap. It was also perhaps his greatest weakness and the subconscious reason for his cruelty.

Agreements and Rebellions. The results of the Nazi campaign and of the fratricidal struggle became taxing due to the play of other factors. The liberation of the country it was clear was not imminent. Winter came again, a harsh winter, like the terrible one of 1941-42, because the Germans, who had run out of provisions, confiscated food, animals, machines, and tools. The Bulgarians, extending their occupation of Greek territory, tried to "bulgarize" the area. Hundreds of people were executed and it was estimated that more than 50,000 Greeks were deported to Bulgaria.

Terror, anxiety, famine, and cold again gripped the naturally poor country, now torn to pieces. These circumstances accomplished indirectly what Greek brotherhood and the intelligence of the British officers had failed to do: to restore the peace between the three large resistance organizations.

This temporary peace was established tacitly and was used by the three organizations to reorganize themselves and to augment their forces. The Allied Military Mission also profited very cleverly from the situation; it sent representatives to Plaka in Epirus where on February 29, 1944, a new agreement was signed between ELAS, EDES and EKKA.

The Plaka accord formed the oasis of all the agreements that later enabled the Government-in-exile to return to Greece. At that time it guaranteed a respite from the internecine fighting, and assured supplies by the Allies to all resistance fighters.

Upon signing the Plaka accord the resistance organizations undertook the obligation not to fight among themselves, to stay within the area occupied by each one respectively at that date, and to combat the enemy separately or together. The agreement also included other conditions of lesser importance. It carried the signatures of the three organizations, as well as its chief instigator, "Chris"—that is, Colonel Woodhouse—and his American adjutant, G.K. Wines. Of these last, the first signed "for the Greek High Command and the Allied Military Mission", the second "for the Allied Military Mission—with the participation of the United States.

So much muddy water—and so much blood—had flowed under the bridge that this time no one could afford illusions. Nevertheless, as everyone had something to gain by the Plaka accord, all of the parties to it, without being sure of anything, cherished hopes. When events are judged in retrospect there is a tendency to be overly critical of the principal actors. Persons who have held responsibility during historically crucial periods know how unjust this criticism is. After the event all seems simple and clear. Evolution is no longer possible, the evolutionary process is completed. The impression is given that an action was clearly justified so that those who judge retroactively ask themselves how the actors did not understand the true meaning of the events. To the contrary, at the time of the action, all seems unclear and complicated, the future is uncertain. This happens especially when one of the major principals in an action thinks in complicated ways. It is then very difficult to understand his intentions; one begins to understand later, as a consequence of the first result of that act, by which time it is often too late.

At the beginning of March 1944, on the Greek scene, this principal was EAM/ELAS, strong with its material strength, its peculiar mystique, its freedom in selecting methods of action—strong through its secret planning and highly centralized leadership. Finally, those "initiated" members of EAM were strong from another point of view: they had one single task—to serve their ideology.

On the other hand, the other resistance groups, without abandoning their credos, were at the same time clinging to conceptions and quarrels outdated long ago. They did not realize that something completely new was happening. Besides, their tactics were so much more difficult than those of EAM, that is to say, of the KKE that controlled it, for EAM, in the beginning, was as clever as it was ambiguous. Just the same, only a few weeks were necessary for one to understand that the temporary breathing space would be succeeded by a terrible confrontation.

On March 26, 1944, the creation of a Political Committee of National Liberation (PEEA) took place in the mountains. One of the EKKA leaders, Colonel Bakirdjis, renounced his organization to become its president. Some progressive personalities of repute (such as Svolos, professor of constitutional law) joined the organization as members or as officers of the new administration.

People had the impression that, from then on, there would be a "Government of the Mountains". Many asked themselves if this was the beginning of a political solution to the great drama which threatened, or if the plot was thickening. Was the KKE yielding and cooperating with persons of authority, or was it setting a trap? Hopes were stronger than doubts. However, two days later, the Tass Agency and Moscow Radio attacked the Government-in-exile, declaring that it did not represent anyone; until then, the Soviet Union had supported it. Tito also officially recognized the PEEA. This was already a bad sign. Those that followed were much worse.

On March 31, in Egypt, officers of the army, navy and air force asked Prime Minister Emmanuel Tsouderos to resign, which he did at once. He remained in his position, however, until a government had been formed that would be acceptable to the armed forces. This move was made by republican and leftist officers who had not understood anything and who, often without wishing to, got involved in a true army and navy mutiny. Some days later several officers were arrested by their soldiers, or were thrown into the sea by their sailors. Surprised by this flare-up, Tsouderos and Sophocles Venizelos (son of Eleftherios) cabled PEEA and demanded its intervention. George II returned from London in a hurry and repeated that, after the liberation of the country, the people would decide on the system of government they preferred.

On April 13, Venizelos was instructed to form a new government. Tsouderos did not participate. Persons opposed to the Metaxas dictatorship predominated in it. Admiral Voulgaris, an old republican, and a strong and irreproachable man, took command of the navy. Finally, on the 17th, Venizelos announced that deputies of the three resistance organizations were coming to Cairo to have talks concerning the forming of a government of national unity. There was no time even to hope. Conflict resumed again worse than ever. The political atmosphere was far from being one of national unity.

On the same day that Venizelos announced the arrival of the resistance deputies, strong ELAS forces surrounded "the perfect and fearless soldier", Colonel Psaros; after a ferocious five-day battle they annihilated EKKA. Psaros himself and some of his officers, caught in a ravine, were slaughtered with knives. Some of the officers, miraculously saved and mad with rage, hastened to enlist in the Security

Battalions. To make up for this, the skirmishes that took place those same days against Zervas's groups did not have much success, for EDES was much stronger and better entrenched than Psaros. At the same time, in Egypt the mutiny spread. Several units of the army and of the navy were already commanded by committees of non-commissioned officers, of soldiers and of sailors.

On the night of the 22nd, Admiral Voulgaris led groups of officers in a boarding assault on the ships. It succeeded, leaving many dead and wounded of both sides on the decks and in the holds of the ships anchored there. On the 24th, English troops encircled and disarmed one whole Greek brigade, while another was placed under supervision.

Positions were becoming defined, hatred profound. In this tense atmosphere the representatives from the Greek mountains arrived in Egypt. Among them was the young and brilliant George Kartalis, the political leader of EKKA. Another politician had arrived a little earlier; twice as old as Kartalis, three times as astute, four times a better orator: George Papandreou. Not even among the Venizelists—democrats, republicans from among whose ranks he came—did Papandreou inspire great confidence because he had often changed sides. But he was a newcomer, not compromised by the quarrels, and he was a skillful negotiator. So to him went the presidency of a conference that took place in Lebanon, which hoped to impose—despite all that had happened—some kind of national unity.

The KKE had insisted that the Party, EAM/ELAS and PEEA be represented separately in the Lebanon conference, and this was accepted out of weakness. But in this way, all of the delegates—some of whom were not Communists—found themselves all together in the dock of the accused. Kartalis was ferocious, quoting evidence as dramatic as it was irrefutable, concerning the execution of the exceptional man who had been military leader of EKKA, Colonel

Psaros. None of the participants at the conference showed any pity towards the representatives of the Left. Men like Athens University professors, Alexandros Svolos and Angelos Angelopoulos, members of PEEA, realized for the first time exactly where they stood.

However, after four days (May 17-20) of impassioned discussions and with some reservations by the representatives of the extreme left, the "Lebanon Agreement" was accepted by all. It was, in fact, a repetition of the Plaka agreement for the guerrilla organizations, but resemblance did not stop there: it cited the "reign of terror" that existed in Greece; it spoke of the military effort in Egypt, as well as of the political and military conditions *for the liberation of Greece . . . by a Government of National Unity.*

On the 24th the Papandreou government was formed. Some of those who participated in the conference of Lebanon became part of it with five posts remaining vacant to be occupied by members of the extreme left. The latter, in order to enter the government, first wanted to get "the consent of the mountains", where Sarafis and a member of the KKE (Miltiades Porfyrogenis) had been sent to report on what had happened and the terms of the agreement.

Again a political imbroglio ensued. The mountains of Greece once more doubted the logic and the sincerity of the Middle East. The latter responded in the same tone. It is useless to mention here the details concerning this sad game which lasted two months and which was one of wiliness, treachery, and occasionally of blood; nothing new was added to the atmosphere previously described.

A major new development, however, must be mentioned: a series of unfortunate events and of ambiguous information placed in doubt the sincerity of the British and of the Greek Government-in-exile. According to certain indications, it seems that EAM/ELAS had grounds for suspecting that both governments wanted to exterminate it.

This, however, was not true. First, because this was practically impossible and secondly, because all the cases to which ELAS had made allusions could be explained. For instance, the most serious case referred to by EAM/ELAS was that in July, i.e. after the Lebanon conference; Zervas had attacked the 24th Regiment of ELAS and had forced it to abandon its position without the Allied Military Mission intervening. Based on evidence produced by local AMM and EDES officers, the answer was that this regiment of ELAS had crossed the "frontiers" set by the Plaka Agreement and that, therefore, it obstructed all operations EDES was carrying out on the main route towards the port of Valona.

But all of this—allegations or truths—did not get to the heart of the matter. The main point was that, while spectacular changes were taking place on the Russian and Italian fronts, as well as in the interior of the Balkan countries, the complicated Greek political situation remained at an impasse. The only important change took place in the military sphere, and it had a more general significance, because it strengthened the prestige of the Papandreou government. In fact, two squadrons of Greek planes were fighting in Italy and a mountain brigade was ready to enter the Italian front. The shake up of the Greek armed forces had indeed recreated "Free Greece" overseas.

From the Magic Wand to the Tragic Uprising. During this period neither the prestige of the new government, warmly supported by all the Allies—except the Soviet Union—nor the efforts of the Allied Military Mission, were able to bring the Greek political impasse to an end. Then, a "magic wand" solved the problem in a few days and without further discussion.

On the evening of July 25, 1944, a Russian airplane asked for authorization from the commander of an Anglo-American base in Italy to take off for a night training flight. Later the same night, this airplane landed at Tito's headquarters: ten Russian officers were aboard under the command of a colonel named Popov. Two of the men were dropped in Macedonia by parachute and, at dawn, the airplane landed at the mountain airstrip of ELAS in west Thessaly.

We must mention parenthetically some events that surrounded the arrival of the Popov mission: readers not acquainted with these facts would be unable to understand the sequence of events, especially those of the winter of 1944-45. In May and June of 1944, in London and Washington an exchange of views took place between the British, the Americans and the Russians: in order to achieve a final victory, the first would have a free hand in Greece and the last in Romania. Despite some hesitation by the Americans and also by the Russians, they reached a kind of agreement, very secret and not clearly defined, "on a trial basis for three months". The agreement was completed on a higher level about three months later.

On the European chessboard, things took a decisive turn: in September Russian troops had entered Romania, Bulgaria, and Yugoslavia ; Churchill wanted to clear matters up and realized that he did not have any time to lose. He knew equally well that if the Allies pledged action, even of a provisory nature, this did not compromise the future less.

On October 9, 1944, in Moscow, after having settled certain other matters with Stalin, Churchill faced the question directly. But let us allow him to narrate the scene himself, an astonishing one from many points of view.

". . . I stated: 'Let us settle about our affairs in the Balkans. Your armies are in Romania and Bulgaria. We have interests, missions, and agents there. Don't let us get at cross-purposes in small ways. So far as Britain and Russia are concerned, how would it do for you to have ninety percent of predominance in Romania, for us to have ninety percent of the say in Greece, and go fifty-fifty about Yugoslavia?' While this was being translated I wrote out on a half-sheet of paper:*

Romania
Russia _____ 90%
The others _____ 10%
Greece
Great Britain _____ 90%
    (in accord with the U.S.A.)
Russia _____ 10%
Yugoslavia _____ 50-50%
Hungary _____ 50-50%
Bulgaria
Russia _____ 75%
The others _____ 25%

*I pushed this across to Stalin, who had by then heard the
translation. There was a slight pause. Then he took his blue
pencil and made a large tick upon it, and passed it back to us.
It was all settled in no more time than it takes to set down.*

*After this there was a long silence. The pencilled paper lay
in the centre of the table. At length I said, 'Might it not be
thought rather cynical if it seemed we had disposed of these
issues, so fateful to millions of people, in such an offhand
manner? Let us burn the paper.' 'No, you keep it,' said Stalin.*

All this was not known then—not even well after the
Allied victory—to the leaders of the KKE. There are some
indications that at a precisely-defined date the Russians let
Siantos vaguely understand that the British had been
given a privileged position in Greece. But even this is not
certain. In any case, neither he nor the other leaders of the
Party knew what was happening, nor did they suspect that
the KKE had been abandoned by the 'Motherland of Socialism', which it supported and defended with such devotion
and sacrifice. If they had known, would they have followed
another line?

It is difficult to answer. Those who have followed the rise
of Communism know that, for certain militants, Moscow
was always right, come what may. Since Stalin's time, Com-

munists like Tito have been very few. Even so one must ask: why had Stalin yielded so easily? Most certainly, the answer cannot be categorical, but one would not be far from the truth to think as follows: Stalin had had his way on several important questions (Poland, the Baltic countries, etc.), though agreement was not definitively finalized. At the same time he was in the process of infiltrating everywhere in the Balkans, where he had obtained most of what he wished—a free hand in Bulgaria, an outpost which dominated the Bosporus and the Dardanelles. So, he had to give up something if he wished to remain on good terms with the Allies, who were still very useful to him. Greece seems to have been used as bait by Stalin at that time, or one could say, as small change that could buy much in view of Churchill's interest in the country. To illustrate this idea, and to see how Stalin made use of it, let us recall here a detail from the Yalta Conference: on that occasion, when Stalin had asked that the three Great Powers support the political leaders who had taken part in the struggle against the invaders, he had hastened to reassure Churchill about Greece. There, he had said, "it would be very dangerous for the Prime Minister to allow other than British forces to enter the country". Therefore, it was a question of minor concessions to obtain much greater ones. Besides, he had not said that he would really give these! According to his logic and his mentality, he was making them for as long as circumstances made it necessary. Did Stalin not say to Tito, who persistently refused to bring back young King Peter: "It is not necessary for you to restore him for good. Take him back temporarily and, at the first opportunity, knife him quietly in the back".[3]

Thus, the purpose of Popov's mission to the Greek mountains seems to have been to inform Stalin on the exact situation, as it was there. It was reasonable for him to want to know: Was he acting well in starting to yield? How far should he advance? Could he, and when, "knife in the back" those who had already ceded, or were on the point of ceding?

Before closing this parenthesis, it must be said that the British were shocked and uneasy over the Soviet visit. It was completely unforeseen. They had not been informed. A subterfuge was used to organize it, and it was outside the framework of the Anglo-Russian agreement. Finally, perhaps by pure coincidence, it took place when the chiefs of the Allied Military Mission were away in Cairo. The British did not know what all this meant.

In return, the KKE was overjoyed. Until then, it had not been in touch with Moscow, except through Tito's Headquarters—a difficult contact and humiliating to the Greek Communists. Now eight Russian officers under the command of a colonel made a difficult journey to visit them. The KKE believed that its time had come: at last it would get the Soviet help that it had often asked for in vain. None of this happened. In the end, the British were pleased and the Communists disappointed.

EAM/ELAS were given the cold shoulder by all members of the Soviet mission and did not receive any promise of material aid. On the contrary, they were only given advice, probably not what they expected. And the advice was given in such a way that it could not even be discussed, for the main points of it were told only to Siantos, who had a long confidential conversation with Popov.

It seems that the Russians had expected to find a Red Army of the size and style of Tito's. They were disappointed. Now it seem certain that their account spoke—however unjustly—"of a group of armed men scarcely worth assisting."

It is not known what was said in the mountains, nor what were the consequences of these talks. The fact is that on August 2, that is, only one week after the arrival of Colonel Popov, the representatives of EAM/ELAS on their own initiative resumed contact with the Papandreou government. The latter had talks with them, but did not alter its program which was based on the Lebanon accord.

After some disagreement and quarreling, on September 2 six representatives of EAM/ELAS were sworn in as members of the Government of National Unity. Two of them, one of whom was Yannis Zevgos known as "the Calm One", were the only members of the KKE in the Papandreou government. But terrorism in Greece did not decrease much. On the contrary, it became more oppressive in the countryside and more threatening in Athens. In the capital everyone was convinced that ELAS was preparing for the takeover of the city as soon as the Germans left, and that mass executions were probable. Such mass executions had already taken place in the countryside and especially in the Peloponnesus, a region known to be loyal to the King.

Nevertheless, the Papandreou government remained calm both in Egypt and, later, in Italy where it had been transferred. Its authority had been greatly strengthened by two favorable occurrences. One was the good conduct of the Greek Mountain Brigade on the Italian front where it saw continuous front-line action against the Germans. The other was the signing of the Treaty of Caserta (September 26, 1944) between the Supreme Allied Command (General Wilson, Minister Resident H. Macmillan) and ELAS and EDES (Sarafis, Zervas).

According to the Caserta Treaty, all the guerrilla forces, as well as the regular forces which would land in Greece, agreed to place themselves under the orders of General Scobie, representative of the Supreme Allied Command. It was further agreed that any act opposed to the orders of General Scobie would be considered a crime. The Security Battalions were strictly condemned and a formal obligation was undertaken to harass the retreating German troops. Sarafis and Zervas were to impose order in their respective regions, but Attica and certain other small districts would remain under the jurisdiction of General Spiliotopoulos, acting jointly with the British Command.

All this was too good to be true. Nobody expected that this agreement—even though it was official and clearly spelled out—would be respected. Not only had ELAS never felt bound by its agreements, but it had also caused terrible sufferings directly or indirectly.[4] Despite the above, the situation in some regions had in fact worsened. This was particularly so in Peloponnesus where, in the beginning of the summer, the General Headquarters of ELAS sent Aris with an elite unit, the "Mavroskoufides", or Black-caps.

In the Peloponnesus the Security Battalions, well led and supported by the population, had managed to control the towns, certain villages and the main transportation centers. It was the only region besides Epirus which had escaped total control by ELAS. Aris now turned against the Peloponnesus to wipe out the Security Battalions and to restore the prestige and power of his comrades. He took his time so as to become organized and, from September 2 until the end of that month—when the Government of National Unity was being formed in Egypt—he attacked the towns and large villages of the southwest Peloponnesus, Calamata, Pylos, Meligalas, Gargalianoi and other towns were the sites of cruel battles and even more cruel "punishments".

The massacres were without precedent. The largest of all took place in Meligalas between September 12 and 16: 1,450 men, women and children, and about fifty officers of the Security Battalions were executed and thrown into a large well that was afterwards filled in.[5] Nothing seemed to stop this new wave of terrorism. The representatives of the Allied Military Mission were powerless onlookers, and did no more than mention the events to the Supreme Allied Command in the Middle East.

Finally, the Government of National Unity under the premiership of G. Papandreou and still based in Caserta, decided to make a try. It dispatched one of its most eminent members to be on the spot. On the afternoon of September

27, a day when many executions had taken place in the area, Panagiotis Canellopoulos landed at Calamata. Aris was absent because he was preparing the siege of Tripolis in the center of the Peloponnesus. P. Canellopoulos hastened to meet him at his command post. He arrived just in time to save the town from a massacre. And the bloodshed would have been great because, on one side, Aris and the "Mavroskoufides" wanted to take Tripolis at any price, but, on the other side, the population of the town and the Security Battalions which also had artillery, had resolved to fight until the bitter end.

Calling on the Caserta Treaty, which had been broadcast by the BBC, Canellopoulos persuaded the Security Battalions to lay down their arms and depart for an island. Appearing in the town by the side of Aris—something which later cost him many unjustified accusations—he managed to avoid what might have been the greatest massacre of the fratricidal war.

Due to the Caserta Treaty, the killing in Athens was equally limited, which enabled the Government in exile to land in Attica twenty days later. The emissary of the government for this operation was a brilliant young law professor, Themistoclis Tsatsos. He landed in Thessaly at the beginning of October with Yannis Zevgos, one of the most influential members of the KKE. After a trip on muleback lasting many days, he arrived in Athens on the tenth of the month.

The atmosphere of hatred and terror which reigned there made his mission extremely delicate. Nevertheless, addressing himself to ELAS through Zevgos, and to the ardent patriots of the resistance in Athens through the Archbishop, to General Spiliotopoulos or to police commander Evert, who were both highly esteemed, and sometimes addressing himself directly to the entire population, Themistoclis Tsatsos managed to bring some calm to the capital—as much as was possible at the time. His was an exercise in preparation as difficult as it was precious.

Thus, nothing had changed for the immediate future, as everything depended on a balance of power. The Caserta Treaty had considerably altered the situation for the moment: it had restricted the terrible fratricidal war and it had finally allowed the landing of a national government, accompanied by Greek and Allied troops. Given the fact that ELAS was actually in control of nearly all the country, this was an enormous success for the national democratic forces.

Chapter V

The Second Act of the Civil War
(End of 1944)

Prelude to the Storm. On October 17, 1944, in a delirious atmosphere of enthusiasm and confusion, the national government returned to Athens. The implacable line of Aris Velouchiotis seemed to have been abandoned. But it soon became clear that this was just temporary and constituted only the end of the "first round". The second one would begin a few weeks later and would be much bloodier.

The return of the government resolved only one question, one which admittedly created great controversy though it was of secondary importance at the time. The Greek government-in-exile had committed itself to return with the King and to hold an immediate plebiscite on the future of the monarchy. Instead, King George had been persuaded to remain in London to await the results of a plebiscite to be held at a later date.

Obviously, this course would not offer any solutions to the substantial problems which faced Greece. And even though "the liberation without bloodshed" was an undoubted success, all the burning problems remained to threaten the future.

First of all, the Commander-in-Chief, General Scobie, had under his command a very limited number of men. For the whole of continental Greece he had only 20,000 men by mid-November. For the area of Attica, including all its military and port installations, he had no more than two British brigades.

Some Greek units existed more in theory than in practice —a concession by Papandreou to certain ministers of the old PEEA. The prestigious mountain unit, named the "Rimini Brigade" because it had liberated Rimini after tough combat against the Germans, had only light arms and instead of occupying key positions was restricted to barracks. The renowned "Sacred Battalion" was scattered among the islands. A mechanized gendarmerie battalion was travelling by ship somewhere in the Adriatic. General Scobie could still count on some Greek battleships, on two Greek air force squadrons, and on three squadrons of the RAF.

The British commander's weakness was made all the more real by the fact that his troops were dispersed throughout the country and were assigned to unusual jobs; his army was distributing food to the population and building temporary bridges.

Winter was near and the country was devastated and isolated. Food and medicine, shoes and clothing—all were scarce. The main ports—Piraeus among them—had suffered serious damage; most of the bridges on roads and rail lines had been blown up; transportation in the interior of the country was deplorable. For instance, as the Corinth Canal was closed, one had to go around the Peloponnese in order to travel from the west coast to the east coast by sea.

For this reason, long before the founding of UNRRA, the British and Americans delegated to a special organization— known by its initials as M L (Military Liaison)—the job of relieving the misery which prevailed. Military Liaison did

110

wonders: by the end of November it had distributed more than 100,000 tons of food to the most remote corners of the country. This was possible only because Scobie's men buckled down to the task.

The country was actually controlled by ELAS. EDES was also strong enough, but was restricted to Epirus; and it felt its role had ended: its men had been prepared to start demobilizing.

Since the war had not ended, the mission of ELAS and of EDES was to weaken the German troops who were leaving to fight on other fronts. The two organizations more or less fulfilled their mission, but their intentions now differed.

The men of EDES believed that they had done their duty; they had fought and now that liberation was at hand, they wanted to return to their villages to look after their families and their fields. The men of ELAS, however, were prepared for something quite different: as soon as Greece was delivered from the foreign invader, it would be necessary to shake off the yoke of those Greeks who exploited their country economically. This fundamental difference in outlook was not understood well then, nor even later. In addition, ELAS felt itself greatly strengthened in terms of material.

Actually, ELAS occupied the most important regions of the country, and especially the large military centers, such as Athens, Larissa, and Thessalonike. Even if it was not true that ELAS then sought mainly to capture arms and munitions—as some foreign authors believed—it was natural for it to get the lion's share of the war materiel left behind by the fleeing German divisions. The combination of strengthened morale and additional materiel was, perhaps, what made EAM/ELAS bolder at the end of the autumn in 1944.

Papandreou answered this boldness by temporising. Sometimes he resisted, but more often he gave in. He pretended not to understand certain events that others con-

111

sidered very dangerous. This tactic was certainly justified up to a point. For, not only did the government lack power, but also, the British Command often had doubts as to what should be done, despite General Scobie's strong personality.

After the liberation of the country, the Allied Military Mission had been dissolved. This organization had acquired great experience, knew people of all factions and the methods they used. But it was not around any longer to give its advice. The experience it had acquired was useless: experience cannot be transferred, it is gained each time individually. Some British officers were in the process of acquiring it then. So it was natural that they had doubts about the meaning or the importance of certain incidents; over the weight of a promise, or the validity of excuses advanced by certain persons. However, we would need many pages to take only a brief look at everything that led to the events of December 1944. Let us cite only those that are certain and those which resulted directly in the revolution in which so much blood was shed.

On November 22, General Scobie met Sarafis and Zervas and asked them to demobilize their units. Zervas accepted at once for he had been told beforehand that if he refused or even hesitated, he would give ELAS the pretext it was looking for not to comply. But Sarafis, who was much stronger then, dodged this request by demanding an order from the government signed by all the ministers including those of PEEA.

A most difficult political impasse was created as this was a repudiation of the Caserta accord. Prime Minister Papandreou then turned to his non-Communist ministers, who were members of PEEA, to help him. They accepted, and in cooperation with Zevgos, "the Calm One" and the British military authorities, they managed to sign a new agreement after tough negotiations. The agreement was handed to Papandreou on November 27 by Professors

Svolos, Tsirimokos (both ex-members of PEEA) and Zevgos. The next day, with some difficulty, Papandreou secured its acceptance by his Cabinet and announced through the press what had been decided.

The essential points of the agreement were: a national army would be formed of which the first unit would be a division consisting of two brigades "each of equal strength." One would include the Rimini Brigade, the Sacred Battalion, certain units of EDES and some recruits. The other would be composed exclusively of ELAS units. Later on, two more divisions would be formed with officers and men that had served in ELAS. All other guerrillas from all organizations would be disarmed and disbanded.

This was clearly a strengthening of the Left's position. Nevertheless, on the afternoon of the 28th, there was a sudden unexpected change. Zevgos demanded that the Rimini Brigade and the Sacred Battalion be disbanded and that the disarming of guerrillas be stopped. What had happened? Who, or what, had caused this radical change within twenty-four hours? It was so sudden and so dangerous that Professor Svolos termed it the next day *unexpected and inexplicable.*

Several explanations have been given. Secret advice from Moscow which, while remaining neutral, would gladly see its game being played by another? This explanation seems very unlikely because everything indicated that at that time Stalin sincerely considered Greece as an exchange. Had the hardcore of the Party taken the "upper hand"? This is a more probable explanation, but not completely convincing, as there had been negotiations before the agreement and everyone had agreed on the text submitted to Papandreou. Finally, a third explanation has had support: faced with Soviet neutrality the "tough" members of the KKE had asked for the advice and support of Tito, making known to him at the same time that the British forces in Greece were weaker and much smaller than had been expected. Tito had

113

answered late in the evening of the 27th, that they should occupy the capital and that he would offer his moral support to the KKE. It is difficult for one to say which explanation is correct. Perhaps the truth will never be known.

In any case, it is certain that a new development, during the night of November 27-28, changed the minds of the KKE's leaders. It made them reject an agreement reached with difficulty and seek a confrontation instead.

The government could only reject Zevgos's conditions. Acceptance would have meant complete surrender. On the evening of the 29th Papandreou's Cabinet met without inviting the PEEA members. The next day the EAM gendarmerie refused to act upon a government decision, broadcast on the 24th concerning its replacement by the National Guard: this had just been formed and included reservists of the class of 1936 who had fought in Albania.

The same day ELAS units, very well armed with German weapons, surrounded the capital. Howitzers and cannons were placed on the hills around the city. Zevgos published an article in the Communist newspaper saying that "the time for negotiations has passed" and that "only arms could settle their differences."

On December 2, the ministers who were members of the PEEA resigned their posts and, in their absence, the government signed a decree by which all guerrilla organizations were dissolved. All officers of the regular army were obliged to present themselves immediately to the War Ministry: those serving with ELAS must also obey. Whoever possessed any weapons or ammunition of any kind must surrender them to the authorities without delay.

Pretending to confuse EAM with PEEA, the KKE answered by calling the people to a mass meeting in the center of the capital on December 3 and ordering the workers to conduct a general strike on December 4. Confrontation was inevitable.

The demonstration took place on December 3, in spite of a

government ban. Shots were exchanged between demonstrators and police. There were dead and wounded on both sides. According to the Left, the police fired first to disperse the crowd; according to the Right and the authorities, the demonstrators fired first either to break through the police barrier, or simply to provoke the authorities. As the situation stood, the truth on this matter is of little importance. Actually, even if there were no firing that day, another serious incident would have taken place. The Revolution had been set in motion before December 3.

The Revolution of December 1944. On December 4, ELAS patrols in uniform entered the outlying districts of Athens and of Piraeus.

The weak British forces avoided any conflict, but in the evening of the same day, General Scobie ordered ELAS to withdraw all its detachments before midnight of December 6.

The next morning, from London, Churchill ordered Scobie to occupy the capital. His cable was short, but clear:

> *Without bloodshed, if possible, but with bloodshed if inevitable. Do not hesitate to act as if you were in an occupied town and a local revolt was being launched.* (From Churchill's *Memoirs*)

The British troops sided with the government and General Scobie ordered his forces—busy repairing roads and distributing food in the countryside—to assemble in Athens, Thessalonike or Volos in Thessaly, though this was practically impossible for many of them.

On the same evening, Scobie held a press conference to explain his position: The army had intervened in order to obtain a political solution, as the ELAS forces had rebelled; he had been named Military Commander by common consent so he had the right and the duty to restore order.

The engagements of December 5 were uncertain in the beginning, decisive towards evening. It could not have been otherwise: a division from Parnassos reinforced the ELAS troops in Attica, in the Athens sector, while a division from Peloponnesus arrived to the Piraeus sector.

After having been repulsed at various points in Athens and at the headquarters of the Greek-British General Staff for the Navy at Piraeus, ELAS was victorious by nightfall: one could catch a glimpse of its detachments in the streets near the center of the capital; they occupied nearly all of the police stations whose officers and subordinates had been executed. During that same night the headquarters of the Navy's General Staff fell into their hands. By dawn they controlled all of the road from Piraeus to Athens; thus they had separated one part of the British troops from their commander and cut him off from his supply base. Papandreou, one of the principal authors of the "liberation without bloodshed," sick and overcome with discouragement, resigned; for the sake of form, he was forced to remain in his post. The Greek Government, in fact, no longer existed.

Scobie commanded only the small government forces, an indefinite number of snipers and an organization called "X" under Colonel George Grivas (the future leader of the guerrillas in Cyprus) who put up a resistance at the temple of Theseus, to the west of the Acropolis. Still resisting east of the Acropolis was a gendarmerie regiment: this had a more general significance, for the complex of buildings concerned dominated the road towards Phaliron and the sea. Completely isolated, tightly encircled, bombarded by artillery and mortars, pressed day and night by daring operations, the regiment held on. The shooting that was heard from that direction did not signify only that resistance was continuing, it also boosted the morale of the many beaten and subdued, and of the few who were still free.

Thus, Greece existed only in the center of Athens in an area of about four square kilometers; in the shadow of a phantom government it was governed by General Scobie, though one has to say that the beseiged General at that time was not governing, but rather directing a very uneven battle.

Indeed, Attica was flooded with bands of ELAS snipers. In this war of the streets, with its idiosyncratic nature, where numbers play a most important role, ELAS had several advantages. It had the initiative everywhere; it could put up barricades here, attack there; it blew up houses at intersections to block important crossroads; it took large buildings by assault encircling them with overwhelming fire-power. *The men of ELAS fought with a tenacity few of them had shown against the Germans.*

The other side fought with equal persistence and often counter-attacked; the result was that the defenders remained free within their few square kilometers. In all other districts of the city terror reigned: executions by the hundreds, thousands more were imprisoned or deported to the mountains around Athens.

The situation in the rest of the country was not much better, but there the Revolution was felt less. Isolated and far away, Epirus remained free, but half of its army was demobilized and morale was low. Some islands held by the British—Phaliron, Patras, the airport near Athens—were also free. Finally, at Thessalonike where the British garrison was substantial, the coolness of the ELAS Military Chief and of its captain, Markos Vafiadis—a name to remember—was such that, though some executions took place, for example that of the brilliant young industrialist, Vaggos Glavanis, it was not in any way a revolution.

In the rest of the country, ELAS did not have to fight. Little by little, nearly all of its units were concentrated in Attica or in Epirus. ELAS dominated in such a way with nothing but its paramilitary and civil organizations (EP, OPLA=EAM security forces) that no one could challenge it. Those who dared were executed. From the general point of view, the rest of the country was of little interest. Everything was happening in Athens, the seat of both Greek and British civil and military power.

117

In Athens, the situation was critical. General Scobie, while resisting coolly, reported to his superiors and informed them that, without adequate reinforcements, nothing could be done.

On December 11, Field-Marshal Alexander came to Athens in person to examine the situation on the spot. The armored car that carried him from the airport to the Hotel Grande-Bretagne, "the capital of the capital", was hit by enemy fire.

Alexander saw matters clearly, approved of Scobie's decision to assemble all of his units in Athens, and ordered the diversion to Attica of an entire British division enroute at the time from Egypt to the Italian front. The division was to land near Athens with a specific aim: to relieve the port of Piraeus and to clear the road that connected it with the capital. Field-Marshal Alexander fixed as the general objective of the first phase the clearing of Attica, a huge operation if we bear in mind that this was a densely populated area of about sixty square kilometers.

Having been informed of the Field Marshal's visit, ELAS reacted in a curious way, perhaps because it wanted him to believe that the war could end peacefully. On December 12, an ELAS envoy asked Scobie under what conditions he would sign a cease-fire agreement. The answer of the British general was laconic: evacuate Attica. An answer from ELAS was not expected.

The same day, some hours later, an impulsive attack allowed ELAS to occupy other buildings. The British-Greek "free zone" shrank appreciably. It now comprised even less than three square kilometers. The next day the attack was wider and tougher. Numerous mortars and about fifty pieces of artillery, as well as various types of sabotage, were put into action.

All tactical units of ELAS, without waiting for reinforcements that were on the way, went on the offensive. But they did not make much progress because all buildings at

118

crossroads were furiously defended by the nationalists. This day, however, had seen the hottest fighting since hostilities began. It was the same kind of fighting as in Patras and Piraeus.

In Patras, the British had been attacked by forces much stronger than their own which, however, they repulsed. In Piraeus, the British had made a counter-attack and had managed to re-occupy the headquarters of the navy command and a small part of the port. But still, the main part of the port and the road that linked it with Athens had not been liberated. Four squadrons of the R A F had bombed and raked the men of ELAS with machine guns. (Papandreou had forbidden Greek planes to intervene), but neither did this allow the clearing of the important road. Then, suddenly, for a few days there was a remarkable period of calm. Some shots were fired, some small skirmishes, some mortar hits, but there were no major engagements.

The lull in the fighting was inexplicable. If it had not come, if the attack had continued in the same spirit without relief, it is not known whether the weak "free zone"—so feeble then—would have been able to resist any longer. The period of calm was even more difficult to explain as "the battle of Athens" was directed by General Mantakas, a former career officer who was known as a very aggressive leader. So this was probably a suspension of large scale operations imposed by ELAS' political arm. The rest was salutory for the government, but unfavorable, not to say disastrous, for the rebels.

Perhaps ELAS' political leaders had preferred to wait for the reserves that were rushing in from all directions, even from towns as far away as Thessalonike. Often they arrived with lorries taken from the British: in Volos alone, which had been evacuated by the British, ELAS forces found 100 lorries, slightly sabotaged, which they easily repaired.

119

In the meantime, important reinforcements flowed in also for General Hawkesworth who, under Scobie's orders, directed the operations. They arrived from the interior (from Volos and elsewhere) or landed at Piraeus. The entire division which Alexander had promised was going to enter the war.

The political leaders of ELAS did not know this perhaps, for they tried another maneuver: on December 13, the day of the fiercest battles, General Plastiras, "the poor, modest and brave soldier", who had dethroned George II in 1923 and had declared a Republic, arrived in Athens from France where he had been living in self-exile. This was a new factor and, in these times, it carried weight. By a curious coincidence, the same thing that happened after the arrival of Field-Marshal Alexander was repeated at the arrival of Plastiras: ELAS sent an envoy to Scobie telling him that it agreed to evacuate Athens, under certain conditions.

Scobie refused to discuss these conditions exactly because he had his back against the wall. The battle resumed with greater force both in the north and in Athens. In the north, Zervas, much weaker now, was still master of Epirus. It would have been better for EAM/ELAS to ignore him and to concentrate all its forces in Athens. But it did not do so.

On December 18, about fifteen thousand of ELAS' best fighters with Aris and Sarafis at their head, attacked EDES from the south and east, and secondly, from the north through Albania. For ten days Zervas could only conduct some rear-guard action, which cost him dearly, before withdrawing to Corfu. In this way he saved what was left of his army and, clever as he was, he saved the lives of his friends who had stayed behind: he took with him to Corfu as hostages five hundred of the most outstanding leftists of Ioannina and then spread the rumour that he would execute ten for each one of his partisans who lost his life.

In Athens, the struggle began again on all sides. The first day, the 18th, an attack against an RAF airstrip fifteen kilometers to the north of Athens, at Tatoi-Dhekelia, was repulsed, but on the following day the strip fell; British reinforcements which were rushed there only managed to liberate 100 of the 350 RAF men taken prisoner.

On the same day, among the buildings attacked was the Averoff Prison, where government forces had barricaded themselves and where were detained some important Leftists and some collaborators including the last prime minister. The attack was driven back, but on the next day some walls of the prison were mined, blown up and the buildings set afire. Most of the defenders and 650 prisoners managed to get away, but others were killed, or taken prisoner.

The lot of the prisoners constituted another drama. Taken in mid-winter to quite primitive concentration camps in the neighboring mountains along with thousands of hostages, these men and women were selected, above all, because they were royalists. For the most part, they were executed. Executions also took place in the suburbs of Athens. In the meantime, the British forces were able to begin a serious counter-offensive. Scobie announced it beforehand on December 20 and warned the public to take to shelters.

General Hawkesworth threw all his troops into the counter-attack keeping practically no reserves. Consisting of Greek and British forces, plus the newly-arrived division, his troops were supported by RAF planes, artillery, mortars and some tanks. For five days there was tough house-to-house fighting; certain ELAS detachments fought till the last man, but others gave up. Mantakas tried to fill the gaps with his new reinforcements, but to no avail.

Blood ran in the streets and the government area was perceptibly expanded. ELAS continued to fight, but gradually withdrew. The morale of the insurgents was shaken due to the great losses sustained, including some desertions, and by the force of the counter-offensive. Their morale was also affected by what was happening on the political scene. This had not been the case in the first weeks of the Revolution.

During this "Red December" of Athens the policy of the British government was harshly criticized by the parliamentary opposition, certain large daily newspapers of international stature and wide circulation, by its Allies and even by the American Secretary of State Stettinius.

The opinion was heard that this was a struggle between monarcho-fascists and democrats. The idea of a deadly coup through which a small armed minority wished to abolish democracy and to impose its own despotic regime on the large majority was rejected without discussion by many good democrats around the world.

Churchill was only applauded much later when the meaning of the conflict became clear and, mainly, when undeniable evidence of the horrible massacres became known. Proof of them came from a report of a workers' delegation under the presidency of Sir Walter Citrine, a man known for his integrity, who had no liking for Churchill, and who made a detailed inquest on the spot. The report, though not wholly favorable to the British government, spoke of a large number of executions and mutilations perpetrated against civilians among whom were women, old people and outstanding intellectuals. But all this became known later, when peace was restored to the capital.

In December, Churchill was fighting a personal battle on many fronts. He mainly faced the charge that war with Germany had not ended, that all British troops were needed for the war and that, besides all this, some British troops were interfering in a civil war that tore an Allied country apart. The Greek affair had to end soon and with good results.

Accompanied by Anthony Eden, Minister Resident Harold Macmillan, and Field Marshal Alexander, Churchill came to the burning capital on December 24.

Here we must insert a small parenthesis to describe a controversial event that was in all ways sensational. It was said later, and many serious writers believed it, that without knowing it, Churchill had caused the defeat of ELAS by nothing more than his visit. ELAS, they said, had mined the Hotel Grande Bretagne, the seat of military and civil government, and was going to blow it up on Christmas day. It would then attack and easily occupy the center of the city paralyzed by the loss of its leaders. But the beautiful hotel was not blown up, they asserted, because Churchill was staying there and he had agreed to receive a delegation of the revolutionaries.

There is some truth in all this, but the most important fact is false. Indeed, on December 26, a British patrol chanced to open an iron manhole cover, near the hotel, which led to a central sewer. There the soldiers saw a small box and heard footsteps disappearing hurriedly towards the west side of town (towards Omonia Square) which was occupied by ELAS. The English soldiers immediately climbed down into the manhole and, following the sewer in the opposite direction, found many small boxes with explosives at a distance of about 150 meters and under one of the main entrances of the hotel. They quickly brought them out through the nearest exit and the hotel's director, one of the few people who had been informed of the matter, counted sixty boxes of explosives.

The above facts and other details lead to the conclusion that ELAS was in the act of mining the hotel, having entered the sewer at a point (near Omonia Square) that was about one kilometer away. Bearing in mind the great depth of the sewer, the importance of the building, and especially the fact that the difficult transportation of explosives was still going on, it seems certain that on December 26, the dynamite that had been amassed there was not considered sufficient to do the job. So, the men of ELAS did not believe the time had come yet to set fire to the dynamite. Probably they would have done it the same evening or on the following day. If it had been thought of earlier, and if they had been ready, they would not have waited for Christmas, a day when the military situation did not allow them to take complete advantage of the explosion.

Most certainly, in this case, ELAS lost an exceptional opportunity. But not because of the British prime minister's visit. The opportunity was lost because the guerrillas were not prepared, and because at the last minute, completely by chance, their terrible and daring preparations were discovered.[1]

Churchill's visit affected ELAS, but in a quite different way. First, it directly affected morale on both sides: it was bad for the one and excellent for the other. Second, in addition to the orders Churchill gave to the British forces, he wished to give a decisive turn to the political situation. For this purpose, on December 26, he organized a meeting under the presidency of Archbishop Damaskinos, in which Greek politicians representing all parties took part. Among them were three deputies of EAM/ELAS: the "Old Man" (Siantos), Mantakas and Partsalidis. Churchill and the officials accompanying him, the American ambassador, General Scobie and Colonel Popov, also participated in the meeting.

Churchill skillfully began by stating that President Roosevelt and Field Marshal Stalin were informed of his visit to Athens and approved of it. After having made a strong plea to serve his purposes, he posed the problem. In a moving appeal he called on the Greeks to solve their problems by themselves. And then, taking all of the foreigners there with him, he departed.

The Greek leaders remained alone but they did not know how to proceed because their passions were too strong: the mind is never clear when the soul is on fire.

There were many long and passionate discussions of the past, to which some politicians remained attached in spite of everything: they even went so far back—while Greece was collapsing and Athens burning—as to discuss who was responsible for the Metaxas dictatorship. Agreement was reached on only one point—and that with some reservations: the need of setting up a Regency under Archbishop Damaskinos who had acquired great prestige during the German occupation and who also presided over this meeting. There was no other progress. Only sharp arguments concerning the past and the present.

Finally, the "Old Man" (Siantos) suggested a solution to pacify the country, but his conditions were so oppressive that we must indeed ask ourselves if he knew that they were unacceptable or if he formulated them in order to justify himself against many leftists who had accused him of being too compromising. His conditions were as follows: half of the new government would be members of EAM, and they must include the ministries of Justice, of Interior Affairs (in which was incorporated the Police, the Gendarmerie and Security), as well as the deputy ministries of War and Foreign Affairs. All government forces, including the National Guard and the Gendarmerie, would be demobilized. In April, parliamentary elections would be held.

By way of reply, the political leaders of the Right immediately left the meeting. Plastiras refused to discuss these conditions, but he was constructive in his own way. Siantos had been particularly aggressive, often menacing, occasionally even impudent. Plastiras got even with him. Carrying it to an extreme, he spoke at times in vulgar language with contempt, with vigour, and even with hatred. At one point, he who was called the "Black rider," banged his fist on the table and said to the "Old Man," who was originally from the same town of Karditsa: "Death, cur! If you don't shut up, I'll break your ribs!"[2]

No stinging words remain without a suitable reply and until the last minute, the discussion was explosive. This may, eventually, appear secondary, but the sharp tongue of Plastiras was upsetting to the deputies of the extreme left. This was not the language used against them by the royalists, the politicians, or the foreigners. It was the language of the people. The Conference did not end in any decisions being made, but it had decisive consequences.

King George II was opposed to the establishment of a Regency because it made his return more difficult. He was even more opposed to Plastiras, who had dethroned the king twenty years ago and had executed six distinguished royalists. Nevertheless, the king listened to Churchill's persistent advice and, on December 30, accepted the Regency and announced that he would return to Greece only *after* a plebiscite was held, if it favoured restoration of a constitutional monarchy.

The next day, the Archbishop was sworn in as Regent, Papandreou resigned and Plastiras formed a government with a republican majority. General Hawkesworth's attack, meanwhile, had made great progress. The morale of ELAS was collapsing, reinforcements from the provinces were not enough to fill the gaps, and ammunition was lacking, either because it was wasted or was lost to the enemy.

On the 29th, the last important battle took place. Greek-British forces opposed an entire ELAS division that had come from Mount Parnassos. After a two day struggle, the rebels were forced to abandon all their positions. On January 1, 1945, Aris was summoned urgently to Athens where, doubly strong after Zervas's defeat he was asked to give all of his fighting spirit once more for ELAS. He began

126

with his usual fervor, but it was too late. In spite of his zeal, in spite of the executions of deserters in front of their comrades, Aris managed to do no more than to delay a rout.

On January 6, another conquering hero of the faraway and almost useless battle against Zervas arrived; this was Sarafis, who came only in time to ascertain defeat. By January 5 one could communicate freely with Phaliron and Piraeus and the Greek-British vanguards had reached a distance of more than forty kilometers to the north of the capital. ELAS had begun a withdrawal and some of its units were in full flight.

In the meantime, Scobie had received an EAM delegation headed by Zevgos, who offered more favourable proposals for a cease-fire. The British general not only rejected them, but also withdrew his earlier conditions of mid-December; he justified this attitude by referring to EAM's lack of respect for all laws of war, above all those concerning civilian hostages—about 20,000 in all—many of whom were executed.

Nevertheless, following the advice of the Regent, General Scobie invited delegates of ELAS to meet with him on January 8 and again on the 11th, after which meetings an agreement was signed with Zevgos. A cease-fire was agreed on to begin on January 15 while certain details were to be clarified on January 21. As per the conditions of the cease-fire agreement the ELAS forces had to be 150 kilometers from the capital while Thessalonike, the Peloponnese, and all the islands were to be evacuated. These conditions had no more than theoretical value.

Although some guerrilla units, and above all their leaders, had lost none of their will to continue fighting, ELAS was no longer the terrible power that had conquered the whole country. Lack of discipline reigned, bitterness and disappointment permeated their souls. Their spirits were tormented as a result of Moscow's abandonment of their

127

cause, and there was something else: Men who until then, had been the masters, now felt the hatred of the people. They stumbled at every step and were forced to hide. For four years the population had suffered all kinds of evils but now, according to a universal rule, they remembered especially the recent disasters.

Under these conditions, reestablishment of the movement to its previous position was impossible. The leaders understood this and accepted a compromise which came to be known as the Agreement of Varkiza, which was signed on February 12, 1945. But, before concluding peace, they prepared themselves for the future: a large operation had already started on January 10 in the provinces where ELAS was strongest. As secretly as possible and with the help of only the most loyal men, carefully selected weapons and provisions were sent up to the mountains in large quantities. Smeared with oil and concealed in boxes and barrels, they were placed in caves or other hiding places and covered with care. Neither the eyes of man nor inclement weather must reach these precious packets.

If the later discovery of many of these hiding places or the official evidence produced are not sufficient proof of this operation, the author himself can note here that in four key towns—Lamia, Larissa, Trikkala, and Ioannina—he knew people of unquestioned integrity who were eye witnesses. They themselves had seen the shipments without knowing, of course, their destination.

Besides, the whole affair had not passed unnoticed. At that time nobody had thought it important. There were many who had doubts as to the extent of these shipments because ELAS had surrendered a larger number of weapons than was called for in the Varkiza agreement: 40,000 rifles, some 2,000 machine guns and sub-machine guns, 160 mortars and dozens of field guns had been delivered. The "third round" had to begin before the size of the secret shipments to mountain hiding places could be estimated.

Nevertheless, although some were already thinking of the "third round", which was to be the fiercest of all, the "second round", as they called it, had ended and had been a complete loss.

Some Remarks and Afterthoughts. EAM/ELAS had thus totally failed in one of its two reasons for existence: the seizing of power. Several writers, many well-known politicians like George Papandreou, and a multitude of other people who lived during those tragic years maintained that this was the sole reason for the existence of EAM and of ELAS. This view, which was very widespread, had serious and manifold consequences for the evolution of Greek affairs and must be discussed here briefly.

First, it is not precise. A distinction must be made. EAM/ELAS was dominated and controlled by the KKE, but it had other members too. Thousands of people who had no ties with the KKE had joined them. They had done so because they wanted to put up a resistance against the invader and EAM was both the most widespread and best known resistance organization. They had done so also, because many of them were in isolated areas occupied by ELAS, and they could not do otherwise. Of course, many of these people—for one reason or the other—stayed with ELAS until the end; but most of them left, either during the various crises that shocked them or, above all, in the first days of "Red December." So, one part of EAM/ELAS was for resistance against the Germans and nothing more.

As far as the heart and brains of the organization, the KKE, is concerned, beyond doubt its main aim was to seize power. This was proved by the cruel extermination of all other resistance organizations—even the most effective ones—by many official statements and documents of Party leaders, and by the Party's own basic political theory. However, it would be inexact not to add that resistance against the invader was also one of the aims of the KKE.

The KKE had always considered the Soviet Union as a sort of "Motherland" and had remained loyal to it. The Party never disagreed with it. Disagreement came only for certain elements of the Party much later, between 1960-1970, at a time when huge centrifugal forces had developed in the Communist world. Resistance during the Occupation was useful to the Soviet Union; so resistance was then necessarily one of the aims of the KKE.

The difficulty for the KKE was that its two aims were, for the most part, contradictory: Its followers had to resist the conqueror but, in order to seize power, they had to annihilate all other resistance groups. Thus, EAM/ELAS wasted its strength in a fratricidal struggle and, by revealing publicly its true intentions, caused a deep reaction. Nevertheless, later on, this development had a logical continuity: the more the fortune of arms favored the Allies, the more the "motherland of socialism" seemed out of danger, the more the fratricidal struggle took precedence over resistance to the conquerors.

In spite of everything, viewing matters from hindsight, it is difficult to understand why the KKE failed so completely to fulfill its fundamental purpose. Towards the end of the "first round" (1942-44) EAM/ELAS had been, or easily could have become, the sole master of the entire country without any compromise. During the "second round" (December 1944) again, it could have totally dominated the country from the first days, perhaps between December 14 and 18, particularly if it had not undertaken the large operation against EDES, five hundred kilometers from the main battlefield.

The fact that the KKE was a minority and that its rivals were brave and persistent does not invalidate these considerations: all successful armed revolutions have been led by active minorities who knew how to take advantage of the situation.

A parenthesis is necessary here also.

Why did the operation against EDES take place, and why did some of the elite units and the best leaders of ELAS take part in it? Three theories have been put forward. The third one is the most valid as well as the most interesting. According to the first theory, ELAS wanted to get rid of EDES in order to safeguard its rear and not run the risk of having Zervas advance on Athens. This view is not convincing. Weak and with no ammunition, EDES was far away. It could only reach Athens by sea, a difficult operation at the time. Besides, if EDES used this approach it had the flexibility to withdraw to an island, if attacked.

The second theory is that Siantos did not want to share the triumph of the occupation of Athens with Sarafis and, above all, with Aris. This explanation is even less convincing: the "Old Man" had never placed his personal interest—if he had any—before the interest of the cause and of the Party. The third theory is something more than a theory, as Captain Orestis (nickname of Andreas Moundrikas), commander of the second ELAS division brought back some information which makes the explanation appear reasonable.

Captain Orestis confided to an American writer of Greek origin that he had vainly opposed the operation against EDES. He had believed that EDES was harmless, isolated as it was, that they should not lose time with it because whoever controlled Athens would be master of the whole country. According to Captain Orestis, Siantos told him, after the Varkiza Agreement, why he had not followed this advice. He had reasons to believe, he had said, that Tito would intervene in Northern Greece with strong units of Yugoslav partisans under the leadership of one of his best comrades, by the name of Tempo (real name was Svetesar Vukmanovic), with the excuse of exterminating EDES, ELAS' most dangerous rival. This explanation, if it is exact, is completely logical and is very edifying concerning the lack of unity between the Communist movements in different countries.

Here we must close the parenthesis and mention another opportunity that the KKE lost in those days.

The Party could actually, *by renouncing the tragic uprising of December 1944*, have gained a preponderant and perhaps dominating place in the political life of the country. At the end of 1944, it had already entered the government. It had developed ties among all classes of the population. Many of these allies, even if they still had doubts concerning the Party, were already so exposed that they would necessarily remain its followers. Besides, the KKE had infiltrated everywhere and its rivals were weak and divided. Political life offered it clear, certain, and perhaps later, decisive advantages. It is difficult to understand how the KKE allowed all these excellent opportunities to go to waste.

Very probably it is because the KKE followed two completely contradictory lines; it could not decide to follow either the one or the other. It vacillated between struggle and compromise, between force and politics. It used war and force only in the "third round". If it had followed one course earlier, it is possible that the disastrous "third round" would not have taken place.

Siantos, the "Old Man", was considered the protagonist of the political line up to a point. After his death he was accused by the Party of being a "traitor", "an agent of the English", "author of the strategy of capitulation to the British . . . of the strategy which restored the feudal-bourgeois regime."

However, this son of a proletarian, a proletarian himself from the age of thirteen, a persistent fighter at sixteen, was one of the most faithful, the most disciplined, and the most daring members of the KKE. He was always in the vanguard, always risking his life before the others, and continued the war in its "third round" as general secretary of the Central Committee until May 20, 1947, when he died under rather mysterious circumstances. This was the sad end for such loyalty, perserverance, struggle and suffering.

Aris Velouchiotis was, without doubt, the protagonist of the hard line. And he was not punished less for this. He was so sure that he was right that he did not accept the Varkiza Agreement. When it was signed, he and a number of his loyal followers crossed the wild mountains between Athens and Albania on horseback. He was going there to prepare a new guerrilla revolt. It is interesting, from several points of view, to illustrate this man's thoughts, as revealed in a heretofore unknown incident.

The night before the end of his long journey, he passed by a village, lost in the forest, near the pass of Metsovo—a place which had been burned two times by the Nazis during the occupation. This village is called Milia. Aris chose for his lodging a hut near the ruins of the church. In the evening by the fireside, a young student of the village, who is today a lawyer in Athens, asked him the reason why EAM/ELAS had been defeated.

—"It is because we did not kill enough," he answered. "The English were interested in this crossroad which is called Greece. If we had not left any of their friends alive they would not have been able to land anywhere. But the others called me a killer; this is where they brought us. How many people in your village?"—"Twelve hundred," said the young man. —"We should have killed six hundred. The calf dies when its head swims in blood. Revolutions succeed when the rivers redden with blood. And it is worth shedding it in this way, when the reward is the perfection of society."

These were the motivations of Aris Velouchiotis, and his illusions. His fellow-believers had not followed him united, but they would do so after two years. But this did not prevent the KKE in the meantime from delivering him to his rivals and reserving for him a tragic death. Life is cheap during revolutions. This will be seen in the next pages, in

133

which I shall outline the history of the guerrilla war in Greece during the years 1946-49.

Postscript. At the end of this first part we must add a postscript that chronologically belongs to the second part. And this, because the reader would rather know beforehand how Aris Velouchiotis died. Aris went to Albania because he refused to believe that Moscow had abandoned EAM/ELAS. He wanted to clear up the matter and to return and organize a new revolutionary army. What he did in Albania is not known. We do know that Aris returned to Greece four months later at the end of spring 1945—the exact date is unknown—at the head of an important enough band of guerrillas. He remained in the Pindus mountains, slowly advancing to the south. He was not being pursued.

Then, unexpectedly, on June 18, the government announced that strong forces of the National Guard had pursued Aris and that, on the 16th in mountainous West Thessaly, they surrounded his men and forced them into a battle which lasted over six hours. There were some dead, among whom were Aris and his lieutenant Tzavelas; the heads of both men were put on display in the main square of Trikkala, so as not to leave the slightest doubt that they had actually been killed. Aris's band was comprised of eight men and two women who had, besides personal weapons, fourteen heavy machine guns, two mortars and a wireless.

This was the official version and on several points it is exact. But the man who had caused so much bloodshed was not fated to die with a gun in his hand. Aris and his lieutenant were betrayed by an old comrade in whose house they had spent the night. At dawn going out on horseback on a reconnaissance mission, they fell into an ambush laid by a former captain of EDES, who had been notified by their host. Many members of EDES know who this chief was. It was he who delivered the two heads to the gendarmerie. The rest of Aris's guerrillas were pursued

134

the next two days by the National Guard and the gendarmerie. Finally, they dispersed thus leaving only a few dead and six prisoners.

Such was the end of the founder and true chief of the KKE army of ELAS, which controlled all of Greece for more than a year.

If one of his old comrades dared to betray him, it is very probably because, two months earlier, in April 1945, the supreme authority of the Party, the Politburo   had publicly accused him of being a deviationist. The word is not new. Neither are its sinister consequences.

Chapter VI

The Curtain Rises

The Alarm Sounds Far Off. At the time of the Varkiza Agreement, the Second World War had not yet ended. Victory could be seen ahead, but many were still being killed. No one knew when the guns would stop firing, especially in the Pacific theater, where the Japanese made the American effort pay dearly for every victory. The favorable, yet truly frightening, telegram Truman received at Potsdam, "the baby's successfully born", had not yet been sent. The atom bomb was still not perfected.

The Grand Alliance was bound by very strong ties; collaboration, in spite of some deep differences of opinion and some even greater deceptions, was good in principle.

At Yalta (February 4 to 11, 1945), where most people believed that all the postwar problems had been solved, no final solutions had been reached. To the contrary, the illness and weakness of Roosevelt on the one hand, and the strong position, the lack of scruples, and cleverness of Stalin, on the other, had created enormous problems.

However, in finding a "formula" which would satisfy a powerful and cunning man and which, besides, would save face for the others, serious discord was avoided and everyone even seemed happy. It was the happiness of a realist for Stalin, the euphoria of a dying idealist for Roosevelt, and a very dubious satisfaction for Churchill. Stalin knew that he had won on nearly all points: at the price of nominal concessions he had won his case in Poland for whose independence this incredible war had begun; which had fought so hard, had shed so much blood, and which had 170,000 men fighting on the side of the Allies. In addition, Stalin was participating in the "Occupation zones" of Germany, the prelude to the dismemberment of the Reich. He made sure that Allied troops—especially the Americans—withdrew from large areas that had been liberated. Finally, he acquired major concessions in the Far East, as much on the continent of Asia as in the archipelago to the west and north of Japan, against which he had not yet declared war; he did so later after the atomic bomb of Hiroshima. Roosevelt believed that he was the inspirer and the arbiter of a new period of peace and fraternity. As he was dying, others let him believe this and they took advantage of his kindness. Churchill, on the other hand, understood the situation and that is why he fought with all the force of his character and with the whole of his penetrating mind. But he knew, more than anyone else, that although his country still appeared to be a great power, in fact it was not. Unable to react, he yielded and was fully aware of what he was doing. With the exception of Greece where he had won, he knew that elsewhere he had achieved no more than to keep up appearances, or he had gained points of secondary importance, and many of these only temporarily. In spite of his official statements at the time his memoirs concerning that period reveal that such was his state of mind. Churchill was uneasy. He became more uneasy within the next months because of the turn of events in

Europe where the Soviet troops were advancing. Nevertheless, now he had someone to whom he could speak and explain his fears.

On April 12, 1945, Roosevelt died. He was succeeded by his vice-president, a haberdasher who had distinguished himself in politics by putting some order into purely domestic matters during his career as U.S. Senator. He had no experience whatsoever in international affairs. Yet he had common sense and a strong character. His name was Harry Truman. All of Truman's chief advisers, who were almost entirely those of Roosevelt, made him feel apprehensive of Soviet expansion from his first days in office.

Churchill seconded these thoughts on several occasions in his flamboyant, precise style. It is worth citing in this context his message of May 12 for which, much later, he indicated a particular liking. An expression henceforth known universally was then used for the first time.

> *"An iron curtain," he telegraphed to President Truman, "is drawn down upon their front. We do not know what is going on behind. There seems little doubt that the whole of the regions east of the line Lubeck-Trieste-Corfu will soon be completely in their hands. To this must be added the further enormous area conquered by the American armies between Eisenach and the Elbe, which will, I suppose, in a few weeks be occupied when the Americans retreat, by the Russian power.... and it will be open to the Russians in a very short time to advance if they choose to the waters of the North Sea and the Atlantic....Surely it is vital now to come to an understanding with Russia, or see where we are with her, before we weaken our armies mortally or retire to the zones of occupation...."*

Churchill was addressing himself to a standard-bearer who could continue his policy. Not only did he lack the means to implement it, but two months later he had lost his premiership. During the Potsdam Conference, Churchill lost the first postwar elections and was replaced by Attlee, leader of the Labour party.

But Harry Truman raised again the Churchill banner in another style because he had many more means. In addition to its immense resources, the United States had radically altered warfare through the use of a new weapon. In two disastrous blows (Hiroshima on August 6, 1945 and Nagasaki on August 9) the atomic bomb brought an end to the war with Japan.

Disputes between Washington and Moscow were numerous and often concerned basic questions. Among the most serious we must cite that of Austria where Stalin seemed to want control, particularly of Vienna. It was the same for the region and the city of Trieste which was of chief importance for the supplying of the numerous Allied garrisons in Central Europe. Tito de-italianised and practically annexed it. These two questions caused much trouble and the second one, in particular, led to a serious concentration of American troops near the city in question. Nevertheless, amiable solutions were finally reached.

Thus, already in the Potsdam era, one can say that the spirit of the Grand Alliance no longer existed. Nevertheless, there had been no rupture in diplomatic relations in spite of the various disagreements; there had been agreement on some secondary matters and on the functioning of the United Nations. One could not speak yet of a "cold war". The first indications of this war became apparent some months later. They appeared in the south, in Iran and in Turkey.

It is very useful to retrace briefly this bit of history here for these two questions occupied international politics for several months. At the end of 1941, British and Soviet troops had occupied Iran; the two governments declared then that their troops would be withdrawn within six months after the end of the war. This declaration was reiterated by the three Great Powers when they met in Teheran. The war ended and the six months ran out. In the meantime, Moscow, which had strongly supported various separatist movements, withdrew its troops from Teheran but not from the rest of the country, although the final date for complete evacuation was fixed for March 2, 1946. Twice the Iranian government had laid the matter before the Security Council as being a threat to international peace, but the Council could not resolve the problem. The situation deteriorated; riotous strikes, extensive activity by the separatists and their secret and official protection by Moscow, the threats by the latter to obtain oil exploitation concessions, the imposing concentration of Russian troops on the frontier—all this caused an atmosphere of chaos. At that period Iran seemed to be a powder keg which was already smoking. In addition, the language which Washington was using to address Moscow had become less and less diplomatic; it had become almost bellicose in tone.

On the other hand, in London, even if with the forming of the Labour government "an empty taxi stopped outside 10 Downing Street and the man who got out of it was Attlee", and if, "Attlee was a sheep dressed in sheep's clothing" (Churchill's description, according to Chastenet), he had as his Minister of Foreign Affairs the son of a policeman, a former dockhand, Ernest Bevin. This inveterate socialist could better understand the haberdasher than the tsar of socialism. In the summer of 1946, he went into action; after some local incidents he dispatched British troops to the Iranian coast opposite the large Anglo-Iranian petroleum installations at Abadan. If the texts of the communications did not mention an armed intervention, their tone and events left little doubt as to the possibility of such a move by the Anglo-American bloc. Fortunately, this was not necessary. By winter, Iranian troops, though very weak, easily repulsed the separatists who fled across the border where strong Soviet forces were stationed. Iran was evacuated and

Moscow abandoned its demands for petroleum concessions. The following summer after general elections, a parliament with a clear anti-Soviet majority was formed. The Soviet Union, in spite of its threats and military preparations near the frontier, did not make a move. But though war had been avoided—perhaps owing to the Anglo-American mono-poly of the atomic weapon—the portent was of another kind of war which would come to be called the "Cold War".

As far as "portents" are concerned, we could use the plural even if one bore in mind only the most important events. Indeed, very soon after, Moscow's attitude toward Ankara caused further uneasiness. For centuries, relations between the empire of the tsars and the empire of the sultans had been very bad and had provoked many wars. The deepest reason, although not the only one, was that the Russian empire of the north needed free access to the warm seas which washed the coast of the Turkish empire of the south.

The two empires changed radically between 1917 and 1922, and the new master of the north was the first to help the new master of the south in establishing his power. So, relations between the two countries became excellent under the protagonists, Lenin and Ataturk, and under their succes-sors, Stalin and Inonu.

The problem of a warm water outlet for Russia, which became of interest to other nations with the development of maritime communications, after a preliminary bilateral a-greement was finally resolved in 1936. After long study and extended negotiations in many capitals a multilateral agree-ment was signed in Montreux which provided: in time of peace the Bosporus and the Dardanelles would be free for all cargo ships, as well as the warships of all the countries bordering on the Black Sea. Turkey, master of the straits, could forbid the passage of warships in time of war or the threat of war.

Relations between the two countries began to cool off after the Ribbentrop-Molotov agreement and there were several incidents of rather minor importance during the Second World War. In spite of the various mutual assistance agreements signed by Turkey, Inonu very prudently kept his country a "non-belligerent", and he altered this position very slowly according to the progress of the operations. This was even more discreet.

But caution mattered little to Stalin. As soon as he felt his position was very much stronger, he also changed his attitude towards Turkey. To consider only the essentials, in Moscow, when the agreement took place concerning the allocation of spheres of influence in the Balkans, Stalin again brought up the question of the Dardanelles: the agreement of Montreux had to be revised. The question was raised again in Yalta.

Four months later, in the course of direct talks with the Turkish government, Moscow suggested a revision of the statute of Montreux, establishment of a Soviet base in the Dardanelles, and the restitution to Russia of three regions occupied by Turkey since the First World War. The alarm had sounded again. It sounded more clearly when the Georgian commander-in-chief of all Russia spoke again about the Dardanelles at the highest summit meeting of the alliance, Potsdam: under no circumstances would Turkey have the right to close the straits, and the Soviet Union should have a permanent base in the Aegean. To Churchill he designated that this base must be the port of Alexandroupolis (he mentioned the Turkish name, "Dedeagh") the last city on Greek territory near the Greek-Turkish frontier in Thrace. Nobody yielded. But Stalin returned to his demands; persisting in various arguments, he ignored the compromising proposals of Washington and eventually deployed Soviet troops along the Turkish frontier. A crisis seemed imminent in August 1946.

The convention of Montreux foresaw that after ten years it would be tacitly renewed, if none of the parties thereto asked for its revocation. So, the Soviet Union asked for its revision in due time and notified Washington and London of its demands. At the same time Moscow accepted a compromise that had been proposed by the Americans and until then had remained unanswered, adding to it, however, a somewhat imprecise clause though most clear in intention: the defense of the Dardanelles would be guaranteed by Turkey and the Soviet Union in common.

Washington did not delay in officially backing the Turkish view in unequivocal terms. So as to leave the least possible doubt as to the outcome, Truman dispatched a strong naval squadron including one of the largest aircraft carriers to escort the only American battleship that was then in the Mediterranean. In London and Paris Truman's daring act was strongly supported and Stalin stood fast. Everyone understood that in all probability the monopoly of the atom bomb had again played a role. But everyone understood also that the alarm had sounded again in that summer of 1946. Within a year it had rung in Alexandroupolis, Teheran, Istanbul. When contemplating the Greek guerrilla war, one must bear in mind the events worldwide, for while it was being planned for a whole year, it began in 1946, the year the alarm sounded from the Caspian Sea to the Aegean. That year, when pressures and military preparations elsewhere would have had the same results the Greek guerilla war would have had, had it been successful, in another part of the world, a military clash between the world's strongest powers was avoided. The Greek guerilla war was not avoided, and that could not have been a coincidence.

Varkiza, the New Rule. One would believe that after the complete military, political and moral defeat of EAM/ELAS, the agreement of Varkiza would have been easily concluded. This, however, did not happen. About ten days were needed

143

for Siantos's conditions concerning the calling of the meeting to be accepted and more than ten days for the agreement to be reached. This was natural, for the deputies of EAM did not take the attitude of the defeated, but rather that of equal with equal; they became arrogant claiming that they were being unjustly treated. Siantos demanded the participation of the KKE in the government and a general amnesty. A bargaining position perhaps, but considering the conditions of the period, this demonstrated the line the Party would follow. Such a line had brought the Party excellent returns.

The text of the agreement is comprised of about fifteen hundred words divided into nine chapters that concern the following: the restoration of individual liberties, the abolition of martial law, amnesty, hostages, the national army, demobilization of ELAS, purging of the security forces and the referendum on the form of regime and elections. As to the latter, it was agreed that they would be held after the referendum.

According to the terms of this agreement, the KKE made certain concessions. A fundamental one was the preliminary condition to the whole agreement: the demobilization of ELAS and the surrender of arms "according to the specified conditions of the protocol established by a committee of experts." (In fact, as mentioned before, more weapons were turned in than was anticipated.) Another unavoidable concession, but, in part, one rather advantageous to the Party, was that the KKE recognized as necessary the formation of a "national army"; the social and political views of the citizens serving in the army would be respected. A third concession is both shameful and inexplicable, for the Party seems to have desired the persecution of many active Communists: indeed, the agreement foresaw that in Athens and Piraeus a warrant would be needed in order to arrest civilians, while in the rest of the country, until "the reestablishment of the administrative authorities, judicial and military", such arrests could take place without a warrant. It was mainly in the provinces where the population sought revenge, for it

144

was there that tensions were magnified because of the smallness of the communities. As a result of the agreement, therefore, those needing more protection received less.

Along the same line of thought, we must mention the amnesty clause which, in the atmosphere of that period, allowed disastrous interpretations to be made by all those who were not at the head of EAM/ELAS. Excluded from the amnesty were all those who had committed violations of penal law...."that were not absolutely necessary for the accomplishment of the political crime." Here also it was not easy to say whether this was a concession or an excellent way to allow the persecution of elements of the extreme Left by elements of the extreme Right. Nevertheless, concession or not, a nasty trick or a careless mistake, the fact remains that, as a whole, the agreement reached at Varkiza was an unexpected success for the KKE.

The Party had suffered disaster on all fronts, and the weapons it was making every effort to conceal could not be of use to it at that moment. Certainly, the loyal, the true followers, did not disavow the Party, but almost all of them were in hiding and more than three thousand of them took refuge beyond the frontier, mainly in Yugoslavia (a larger number of former guerrillas followed them after the first arrests were made). But, apart from the faithful, all of the others disappeared, remained silent, or spoke against them. The overwhelming majority of the population declared itself against the Party and a part of them—primarily relatives of those who had been executed—demanded strict punishment or even took revenge without awaiting any kind of trial. With rare exceptions the politicians were all against EAM/ELAS because they realized better than anyone else that the final aim of the organization was the abolition of democracy. The leader of the Center Party, the octagenarian Sofoulis, author of the pact with the extreme Left in 1936, was one of the sharpest critics of EAM/ELAS. Finally, the authorities were in the main carried along by the general hostility of the public. In a few words, during the first weeks of 1945, if someone was a former member of EAM/ELAS, it would have been difficult for him to live in a village or a small town. He had to lose himself in the anonymity of a city.

Nevertheless, while the situation was such, the Varkiza Agreement conferred on the KKE the status of a legal political party and thus allowed its newspapers to circulate freely, its members to be accepted in the armed forces and security forces (if they were covered by the amnesty), while the government undertook the obligation "to safeguard...individual liberties, such as the right of assembly, of association, freedom of the press...and more particularly, the complete restoration of the freedom to organize trade unions".

Seldom in history had the vanquished achieved so quickly such a complete reinstatement in spite of the prevailing climate of hatred and violence. The reasons for this are diverse. The first, and undoubtedly the most important one, was the strong pressure exerted by the British—in charge of all the nation's supplies—on the Regent, on the members of the government, and on the military. This was not at all surprising: the British had been accused of fighting in the streets of the capital of a friendly country and of taking sides in a civil war while the Allied troops faced a German thrust in the Ardennes. The retort to these accusations was not easy, and it was not enough just to reply. The British had to prove that if they were the only ones among the Allies to involve themselves in an area apart from the war's main front, they did so to safeguard democratic liberties in a friendly country. And this was all the more important, as the Varkiza Agreement preceded Yalta by a few days. For this reason the pressure exercised by the British ambassador, and especially by General Scobie, who had great prestige in Athens, was strong and persistent.

All other reasons were secondary: the Archbishop, as a man of the Church, was obliged to be less severe than the

146

politicians. Plastiras, absent from the country for twenty years—with some rare intervals—listened to the advice of old friends who, in the meantime, had formed ties with EAM; Sarafis, a military expert on Varkiza, was an old and dear friend of his. The Minister of Foreign Affairs, leader of the government delegation at Varkiza, and a very intelligent man, Sofianopoulos, had ties with the extreme left since 1936, ties which later on—we will see—were revealed in a spectacular way. Finally, though many Greeks sought revenge, those who were more numerous, seeing the defeat of ELAS, attributed no importance to the concessions which were made to it and only wished the negotiations to end as soon as possible.

This was how, after a revolution that cost so much blood and after such a total defeat, the KKE was fully and legally reinstated. In order to reestablish its good name, it pulled the first and greatest hat trick. On the evening of February 11— the Yalta meeting was still going on—Siantos told foreign correspondents: "From the moment the Allies decided that it was useful for British troops to remain in Greece, it then became a good thing"....and attributed the conflict between the ELAS and the British forces to a misunderstanding that should be forgotten. Certainly a great deal of courage and discipline was needed for this man, who had been accused of following a soft line, to dare speak in such a way. But, let us repeat, the meeting in Yalta was still going on and General Popov was still in Athens. Stalin had apostles at his disposal and he knew how to use them. Besides, Siantos, outside of his personal position, should have been happy at the reinstatement of the Party. Nevertheless, the provisions of the Varkiza Agreement and the intentions of those who were then the rulers of Greece were one thing, but the implementation of those intentions was something quite different. This, exactly, was one of the greatest difficulties and, with other factors of a different nature, deeply influenced the development of the situation in the years that followed.

Difficult Recovery, Impossible Entente. For the whole of Europe, 1945 was an especially difficult year. But, very probably in no other country, except Germany perhaps, was it as difficult as in Greece. There were shortages of everything: food, clothing, medicine, domestic animals, machines, and means of communication. A large segment of the population did not even have roofs over their heads for, without mentioning places bombed, about one-fourth of the villages had been burnt. Without the precious help of UNRRA and the private organized assistance of Greeks overseas, 1945 would have been a year of famine. It was instead a year of great misery.

Many writers ignore the actual situation when describing the preliminaries of the guerrilla war, when they accuse governments of ineffectiveness, or point out the lack of discipline of the people, the appetite of black marketeers and speculators, or strikes caused by the Communists. All these were not at all the causes, but the results, which after the Revolution, became only secondary causes. These same writers often forget a simple but basic truth: that human societies are not made up of angels or of robots. They forget that they comprise men whose driving force is the instinctive will to survive and to satisfy their passions, good or bad. Thus, the situation in Greece in 1945 was such that survival was very difficult. Passions and hatreds were excited. Weaknesses were inevitable and good administration impossible.

Added to the shortage of goods was a disastrous financial and monetary situation. Naturally, the coffers were empty and the receipts minimal. Money—after the issue of bank notes during the occupation, each one of which represented millions, then billions—had been abolished; with it disappeared the obligations that were expressed through it. A new drachma had been created, but it was also rapidly losing value, because money is always and everywhere the reflection of a national economy and forecasts one can make on it. Recovery, therefore, was greatly impeded.

148

Strikes organized regularly by the KKE did not help the situation, of course, but they did not come as a surprise either. The working class suffered from unemployment, from all kinds of hardships, and from depreciation of wages.

Certainly, the KKE could, if it wished, reduce strikes appreciably. But it did not want to, for another element entered the game: passion. Throughout the year 1945, passions had scarcely abated. In addition to hardships, other factors stirred them up. Undoubtedly, all those who had belonged to ELAS were then the object of numerous and varied persecutions, legal or illegal, justified or not. The persecutors were often individuals or private organizations, sometimes of questionable intentions, such as the Mandakas group in the Peloponnesus and the Sourlas in Thessaly; persecutions were also carried out by lower functionaries of the government. These persecutions did not seem to displease the Party leadership because they played into its hands more than anything else; they fanaticized its members, regrouped around them a certain number of fellow travellers who filled the prisons, those universities of Communism; finally, they offered perfect arguments for counter-attacks.

The counter-attack tactics of the Party were very diversified. The Party took advantage of the bad economic situation in every way possible, even by making it worse. On the other hand, the KKE did its utmost to regroup the syndicalist forces in a wide labor front, where it pulled the strings but kept out of sight. This was the great secret of the labor union movement which was usually ignored by the governments: the Party attempted to gain influence over the leadership of the labor unions by seemingly yielding on many union demands; for it is the leadership that determines the course a labor union will take, not its membership.

Then, again the KKE continually accused its enemies, often unjustifiably, of collaboration with the enemy. The law recently enacted concerning this carried a strict penalty for collaborators of all types. The Party also reported and publicly condemned every violation of the Varkiza Agreement. It has already been mentioned that such violations were frequent; but we must add that KKE newspapers multiplied them tenfold and presented an altered and exaggerated account of them. In March 1945, the representatives of EAM presented a long list of complaints of this nature to Harold Macmillan himself, then Resident Minister for the Mediterranean. Finally, to cite only the general line of the Party: the tone was neither one of prudence nor of caution; rather it was characterized by arrogance and provocation. By provoking others, they could hide their weakness better and encourage those who hesitated.

Certainly, all this did not bear the desired fruit because the audience had changed drastically: the Party was now the least valuable speaker. The great majority of the people had simplified things to the point of exaggeration. If one had once belonged to EAM, even without being a member of the Party, he was automatically suspect. In contrast, collaboration with the enemy, provided that it had not been on a high level or for large returns, was easily forgiven.

The hierarchy of values had been upset. Simplification and generalization were the new rules for the establishment of this hierarchy. Suffering, tears, privations, and fear of the Iron Curtain had made the KKE public enemy No. One in the common mind. Party sympathizers were an evil, their adversaries represented the spirit of good.

Churchill and Foreign Minister Eden, passing through Athens on their return from Yalta, received, together with General Scobie, a welcome that the Greek capital had never known before. George II was again becoming popular as a symbol of order. The pressure of public opinion was so strong that even the allies of the KKE, former members of EAM, kept their distance and, under the leadership of Professor Svolos and Tsirimokos, they formed a new party in April of that year, the Popular Democratic Union (ELD), without however acquiring serious popular support.

The Communist leaders did not consider themselves beaten. Besides the somewhat chaotic conditions already described, the political situation was of help to them too. For, although the Archbishop-Regent was gaining prestige and was considered a dynamic and useful arbiter, Plastiras proved, to say the least, a very weak prime minister.

A wonderful campaigner, Plastiras was not a commander at a time when one was desperately needed; he could not solve the great problems he had to face and often made them worse. He did great damage to his popular prestige by using some of his old friends who, in the meantime, had either belonged to EAM or had been tainted by collaboration with the Germans. A minor collaborator could be pardoned, but he was not to be tolerated in a key administrative post. Finally, Plastiras committed the worst offense possible with an act that was typical of the general confusion in which the government found itself: at the United Nations in San Francisco, Minister of Foreign Affairs Sofiano-poulos voted against the admission of Argentina, a country friendly towards Greece; this admission was supported by the United States and Great Britain, but opposed by the Soviet Union!

Thus, when a compromising letter which Plastiras had written in 1941 to the Greek envoy in Vichy was published in the Athens newspapers,[1] the Regent took advantage of the situation and replaced him with Admiral Voulgaris, a strong man, as anti-royalist as he was anti-communist.

The Right was not satisfied; the extreme Left even less. However, Voulgaris formed a much better government, including many "technocrats", as they would be called today, and retaining the best ministers in the Plastiras cabinet. The difficult atmosphere did not change, of course, but there was a better government.

The KKE which had fought fiercely against Plastiras, now attacked the Regent because he had sent him away and replaced him with Voulgaris. The new government, in spite of some small domestic successes, also came up against many difficulties and was unable to survive longer than five months. Certain large problems became more complicated and others were added to them. One of these, of an international nature, caused a strong reaction by the population, above all, by the extreme Right, which controlled many newspapers and certain very active organizations.

When Trieste was lost to the Eastern Bloc and the frontiers between Yugoslavia, Albania and Bulgaria were permanently defined, these three neighboring countries seemed to turn against Greece. The main objects of their covetousness seemed to be Thessalonike and the ports of Thrace, which had remained in Bulgarian hands for three years.

In the summer of 1945, the newspapers of Belgrade, Sofia and Tirana simultaneously launched an attack against the Greek government saying that the Albanian-Moslems of Epirus and the Slav-speaking Macedonians were the victims of persecution and atrocities. On July 8, Tito himself made a speech more than stern in tone. It was the language one would use when preparing for an invasion. The KKE echoed these accusations through its newspapers and the speeches of its leaders. Other Greek newspapers answered, accusing the three neighboring countries of having exterminated the Greek minorities formerly flourishing in their lands. The extreme Right through its newspapers demanded the direct occupation of Northern Epirus and certain Bulgarian provinces. The state of the Greek armed forces made this demand a ridiculous pretension, but this sort of policy was scarcely designed to calm things down. Tito and his little Albanian disciple, Hodja, seemed offended and sent the Greek government very stern notes that clearly gave the impression of preparing their people for an invasion of Greece. It is not known how or why—perhaps because of international mediation and the firm, but calm, attitude of Athens—this disaster was avoided. The atmosphere, however, remained heavy.

Domestically, in addition to the above-mentioned difficulties, the political situation gave cause for much concern. Members of the government suffered continuous attacks for one reason or another. By the end of September many ministers—and certain outstanding ones among them—had resigned. Some party chiefs considered elections indispensable to set things right, but elections were practically impossible; conditions in the country did not seem to permit them. Furthermore, the electoral lists had not been revised since 1936. The clearly democratic parties demanded the formation of a coalition government representing all parties except the extreme Left. Finally, there was the one big question: Should the referendum on the form of regime take place first, *or* should elections precede the referendum? The agreement worked out at Varkiza had, of course, solved the problem. However, the democrats realized that, if the referendum took place first—as the accord clearly stated—George II would win a big majority, not for his person or type of regime, but as a symbol of anti-communism. On the contrary, the democrats believed, elections coming first would allow a choice among all political tendencies and, once this was over, the electors would then be less influenced by anti-communism. Besides, they believed that the referendum would be considered more valid if it were organized by a parliamentary government. The KKE inclined towards this view but was opposed to any thought of elections before order was completely restored, perhaps because it was certain that the Party would get only a small percentage of the votes or because it was preparing itself for something else.

Unable to face this general confusion and an intensifying inflation, Voulgaris resigned on October 9. After an

153

interlude under Panayiotis Canellopoulos, which lasted from November 2 to 20, further deep disagreement led to the Regent's resignation, which was later retracted. Then, after strong British intervention, the leader of the Liberals, Sofoulis—85 years old, but still active—formed a government. It included representatives of all the parties up to the left of center and had Sofianopoulos as its Minister of Foreign Affairs.

The KKE, Ardent and Aggressive. In order to describe the development of the internal political situation we have sacrificed chronological continuity. For, meanwhile, some remarkable events had taken place in the Communist camp.

We have seen that the Communists had borne their great defeat well and had quickly become active again. Ardor had somehow decreased during the spring, however, because it became known that Zachariadis, who was believed to have died in Dachau, was still alive. So the leaders did not want to expose themselves without knowing what line would be followed by Stalin's man, who would soon take the reins of the Party in hand again.

Then, on May 30, 1945, a plane of the R.A.F. landed at the Eleusis airport with the former leader, now crowned with the glory of long suffering and completely free of responsibility for the failure of December 1944. The first statements of Zachariadis, published in the Communist newspapers, included some careful reservations but did not leave any doubt as to the line he would follow:

"We shall return to a regime similar to, but stricter, than the monarcho-fascist dictatorship", he said, "or the struggle of EAM for national liberation will be crowned by the establishment in Greece of a People's Democracy". The text was concise, but tough and clear: there was to be no intermediate situation, no understanding nor compromise.

No one paid any attention to Zachariadis' speech however. The centrists, and especially the Right, often have the

154

unbelievable fault of not even reading the texts of the Communists. They busy themselves with their own writing and their own quarrels. Usually they discover the actions of the other when it is much too late.

The actions of the Communists were moderated in the beginning, exhibiting both prudence and daring. Here is an example of a prudent act which took place before the arrival of Zachariadis: the 11th Plenum of the Central Committee of the KKE (beginning of April 1945), in order to prove its peaceful intentions, did not hesitate to condemn Aris Velouchiotis as a "deviationist"—the man who, in reality, was the soul of the Party's armed struggle. The reason given was that he had not accepted the Varkiza Agreement. He was condemned to death and this sentence was soon carried out, as previously mentioned.

Similar examples concern Zachariadis himself. At the 12th Plenum (end of June), the first after Zachariadis' return, and after taking uncompromising positions on several questions, the leftist leader suddenly declared that, owing to the importance of the Mediterranean for the British Empire, the foreign policy of Greece must be realistic and move between a European-Balkan axis with its center in the Soviet Union and a Mediterranean axis with its center in England. In addition, under the leadership of Zachariadis the Party took a position in favor of Greece's annexation of Cyprus, the Dodecanese islands and, with serious reservations since the territory belonged to Albania, a "Peoples' Democracy", of northern Epirus. But these were all very cautious concessions for tactical reasons. Taken as a whole, the activity of the KKE was an unchanging intense political struggle.

Aside from propaganda, which used every means to attain its ends, we may distinguish three principle lines of Communist activity, the last of which had international repercussions.

The first line, assiduously followed, concerned trade

unions. By way of a brief explanation, one must say that it was, in the beginning, very difficult and that it never met with real success. Nevertheless, the effort was so persistent and so adroitly led that, by the beginning of 1946, the executive committee, elected by the unions to administer the General Confederation of Labor, had included among its members some Communists and the General Secretary was a member of the Party. It is true that for entirely valid reasons of procedure the government at that time annulled these elections and appointed a provisional administration to precede to new elections. It is also true that no strike or demonstration organized by the leftist unions (Workers' Anti-Fascist League—ERGAS) met with success. But, anyway, the outcome of the annulled elections—an outcome obtained after a general defeat—demonstrates that a popular front policy had been followed with dexterity among the working classes.

The second line followed by the Party was more daring. It was the logical outcome of regular and continuous condemnation—and exaggeration—of the persecutions suffered by "democratic civilians from the monarcho-fascists." For soon, the newspapers and cadres of the Left began to speak about the need of organizing persecuted civilians throughout the country into self-defense groups. The Party adopted this "demand" and, with defense as a cover, such groups were set up in many villages and in every district of the larger cities. In spite of their name, which was always emphasized, they became more aggressive in their writings and discussions.

Articles in leftist newspapers, as well as statements of leftist leaders soon began to speak about the necessity of "an active defense". In August 1945, Zachariadis, during a speech in Thessalonike, mentioned reprisals using the slogans of 1943-44. "If it is necessary," he said, "the glorious march, 'Onward ELAS for Greece!' (song of the guerrillas), will resound again in the ravines and on to the mountaintops!" This was hardly mincing words, and this was scarcely the attitude Zachariadis's rivals would have observed if he had been the winner and was governing. But few people paid any attention to these indications, and even fewer were worried. In general, it was thought that all these were merely the boastings of a defeated man.

The third line barely appeared on the horizon in the beginning, but made itself clear very quickly and became bold: it aimed at the complete withdrawal of the British forces. These troops were not numerous, but they had cardinal importance for the KKE; they constituted tangible proof of the interest Great Britain continued to show in Greece. Indirectly, they encouraged by their presence alone the rightist fanatics. Finally, and perhaps mainly, parallel with the various British missions, they contributed significantly to the training of the new Greek armed forces.

The Greek army in those days could not be compared with the formidable organization that had fought against the Axis at the height of its power, the army that in 1941 had exceeded a total of 500,000 men. At any rate, although the Greek army numbered only 30,000 men the day after the Varkiza Agreement was signed, this figure had doubled to 70,000 by the end of 1945. It was rather poorly supplied by the English, but it was trained; just as the gendarmerie, under their continuous control, it started to become a force not at all negligible. For all these reasons, the aim of the KKE was to get the English out of the country. The early counterpart of "Yankee, go home!" was heard ever louder, and was becoming a familiar slogan.

In July 1945, a decision of the Politbureau of the Party spoke for the first time of the "British Occupation Authorities". In October, at the 7th Congress of the Party, in which 300 deputies from all over Greece participated, many speakers condemned the "British occupation". It was the same conference that officially reiterated that the final aim of the

Party was "the victory in Greece of the people's democracy ...and the establishment of a socialist-communist society". In December, Zachariadis himself expressed his opinion in an article published in the official newspaper of the Party. He was especially virulent. Here are some passages of the text: "...the first national demand at this moment is for the English to leave. The British occupation has been the sole obstacle to the rehabilitation of the country during the past year. In the last ten years the Greek people have faced so many storms and made so many sacrifices for liberty that they will not lay down their arms until they are assured of peace and the future of their country in the way that the people desire". To use such language surely meant something. That meaning became obvious one month later.

At the United Nations. On January 21, 1946, two acts different in form but alike in substance took place in two different places, a coincidence that from all evidence was not a coincidence. On that day the Central Committee of the KKE in Athens published a manifesto including a list of charges against the "British occupation troops" and stating that the accused were considered responsible more than anything else for the condition of the country. The manifesto demanded their immediate recall from Greece and concluded by declaring that a corps of democratic volunteers must be formed "to rid the country of the monarcho-fascist filth and to eliminate this *threat to the peace.*" On the same day the Soviet Union asked the Security Council of the United Nations to take up the "Greek question". The Russian representative explained that there was no reason any longer which could justify British troops in Greece and maintained that their presence in the country constituted "a danger to world peace." We understand now that the "Yankee, go home" of that epoch was not a local slogan: it was uttered in other capitals and echoed in Athens.

Perhaps for the first time since December 1944, one truly had the impression of danger throughout the country. Public opinion was troubled; the extreme Right saw its position reinforced and so became noisier; the government—the third formed by the democrats—had increased difficulties and pressure to proceed to elections as soon as possible was mounting. Aggressiveness increased in the Communist camp. During the days which followed not only was a systematic propaganda campaign undertaken by the leftist press, but steps were also taken in the United Nations and advances made towards the ambassadors of the three Great Powers demanding, in the name of the Greek people, the immediate and complete withdrawal of British forces from their country.

The international aspect of the subject was being discussed in Lancaster House in London because the United Nations had not yet settled into its trim glass palace in New York. The meeting lasted six whole days. The Russian delegate, Andrei Vishinsky, upheld the Soviet position. He did not present any new facts, but he showed all the passion and dexterity he had exhibited during the famous Moscow trials, as a result of which many leading Communists had lost their lives. He also carried, above all, the weight of the power he represented. In addition to the arguments of the KKE already cited, which Vishinsky presented with vigour and competence, he maintained that not only the KKE, but the entire Greek National Liberation Front had protested: "In the name of the Soviet government, the Soviet delegation insisted on the motion it had made, that is to say, the immediate withdrawal of British troops".

The answer given by the old docker of the Thames was not less forceful, far from that. The Security Council, said Bevin, must first of all decide if the weak British forces garrisoned in Greece constituted a real danger for peace. "We are there as allies and guarantors because the government of the country invited us. If the Greek government does not want us, we are not going to impose ourselves on it." It was an argument and, at the same time, a commitment. Another argument used by Bevin made an allusion that must have been a nightmare for Vishinsky. Here it is in all its severity: at the time of the country's liberation..."a government of all the parties was formed. It was agreed that, as there was no police, no army, nor even a civil administration, British troops and civilian employees must go to Greece with the consent of Field Marshal Stalin." Then, to conclude, Bevin made a counter-attack. Yes! There was a threat to world peace: it consisted of the continual propaganda spread by Moscow and all the Communist parties to defame the people and the government of Great Britain.

The tone of the meeting concerned the Greek side exclusively. The old Athenian democrat Sofoulis, had sent to London as his minister of foreign affairs, Sofianopoulos, to verify that all post-war Greek governments including his own, as well as the great majority of the Greek people, considered the presence of the British soldiers in Greece a guarantee for the maintenance of order. Now, being a Popular Front man before the Metaxas dictatorship, Sofianopoulos, when he arrived in London, refused to carry out the instructions which he had received on departing for his post! He insisted on adding that Greece had considered as an indispensable condition of every decision concerning her the unreserved and unanimous agreement of all her allies. Without hesitation, and while the Security Council was in session, the old politician presiding over the government in Athens abandoned his young minister of foreign affairs!

The Greek position was presented by the Greek ambassador in London, Thanassis Agnidis, the former undersecretary of the League of Nations: the presence of the British troops in Greece, Agnidis said, was based legally and politically on the Caserta Agreement of September 26, 1944, which had been accepted by all political parties including the KKE. Being both brief and concise, Agnidis explained why all the charges made were completely groundless.

160

The Security Council decision went against the U.S.S.R. The Council simply bore in mind the discussions without even mentioning the English promise of withdrawing troops as soon as their duty in Greece had been fulfilled.

From the United Nations' point of view, this was among the first matters with which the Security Council dealt. The outcome was satisfactory: an appeal aiming at something different from what it called for had been set aside, the members of the Council had all taken a stand, there had been no veto, and there had been no quibbling about procedure to impede its work.

In Greece, the result of the Soviet appeal was important for the majority of the people, and not very satisfying to the KKE. A democratic government with left of center tendencies had been obliged to take a stand against the Communist Party before international public opinion. The Right was justified; the Greek public had been sharply warned. The alert had sounded in several capitals. In London, the socialists reacted against the slanderers and Stettinius, the U.S. Secretary of State, was obliged to support the British position, abandoning an unfriendly neutrality toward the events of December 1944.

Perhaps it was Stalin more than anyone else who personally felt the weight of this failure. One must say "perhaps" because nobody can be sure of his reactions. In any case, it is a fact that a few days after that meeting of the Security Council, he made his sensational speech that could be considered the first declaration of the Cold War. In fact, on February 9, 1946, in Moscow, after professing the impossibility of attaining peaceful international development "under the present state of the capitalist economy", he urged his people to develop their country into one of the world's most important military and industrial powers. The repercussions of this speech throughout the entire world were momentous indeed.

In the U.S. government, alerted by a lucid and prophetic

warning from the counsellor of their embassy in Moscow,[2] the realization dawned—perhaps for the first time—that "stemming" the multiple Soviet infiltrations was a question of life or death for the free world.

In Athens, three days after Stalin's speech, on February 12, the first anniversary of the signing of the Varkiza accord, the Central Committee of the KKE sat in plenum and decided "to organize an armed struggle against the monarcho-fascist orgy". This date is considered by Greek Communists as the beginning of the third round. It must be noted that the KKE had one more special reason not to postpone making this decision: it was already quite clear that elections would take place under the supervision of foreign observers. The KKE knew that it had no hope of making a good showing, and it did not wish now to participate in the elections. But the Party also knew that a government based on the will of the people, in spite of the weaknesses of parliamentary government, would have much greater authority to block its way. So it was necessary to weaken that government from its birth, and to prepare itself in time.

Elections After Ten Years of Dictatorship and War. The Sofoulis government did not have an easier time than its predecessors. Quite the contrary, but still it had succeeded. It had to face certain new problems; yet it was able to make some progress and, finally, to restore the democratic way of life to a country that had been in a chaotic state. Several factors contributed to this, but without any doubt one of the most important ones was the personality of the Prime Minister. As we shall meet Sofoulis again during the most critical hours of the guerrilla war, it is necessary to draw a portrait of him now in a few words.

With a pipe in his mouth and a smile on his lips, always pleasant and witty, though a mediocre orator, Sofoulis had some simple but fundamental virtues: he was extremely calm, very courageous, full of common sense, though not lacking in astuteness. He never lost himself in details which, besides, did not agree with his proverbial laziness. Perhaps, because of that, he always discerned, in the midst of confusion, the essence of larger problems. Fervent patriot, anti-royalist, leaning slightly to the left of center in politics, he was one of those who had remained loyal to Eleftherios Venizelos. Now, at the age of 85, he was the patriarch of the "Venizelists", the leader of the Liberals.

Sofoulis began by improving the economic situtation. He had as his two principal ministers for economic questions, Tsouderos, who now leaned to the right, and Kartalis, who was inclined towards the left. Due to a stricter distribution of UNRRA shipments, to loans obtained in England and in the United States, as well as to a stock of gold pounds provided by Great Britain and sold at their new official price (20,000 drachmas each, against 180,000 previously), Sofoulis's government somehow managed to control inflation and to inspire confidence again.

Next, with the collaboration of the World Federation of Trade Unions he put the syndicalist movement in order. Of course, he provoked loud protests by the extreme Right, as the former secretary general of the Confederation of Workers, a member of the KKE, was reelected to that post. Considering that which preceded and all that was being prepared, he took great risks, but the old politician, unperturbed, wanted to weaken the arguments of the leftist trade unionists, and he wished above all—since he had to organize elections—not to seem partial and unjust.

In order to lessen hatreds and persecutions, he declared a broad amnesty and was at the same time strict—as far as the fanaticism of his subordinates permitted—in the pursuit of excesses, including those of the Right. For instance, when on January 19, 1946, the town of Kalamata in the Peloponnese, which had suffered terribly from the atrocities of ELAS, was occupied by the Mandakas band reputedly belonging to the organization "X", he proclaimed martial

163

law, made an attack on all organizations and generally took such strict measures that order in the Kalamata district was restored within three days.

Finally, he resisted all pressure aimed at postponing elections and at the end of January, he announced they would be held on March 31. Nearly all of the parties had agreed on elections preceding the referendum. Altering of this clause in the Varkiza agreement had been facilitated by a step taken in this direction by the governments of the United States, England and France, on British initiative. The Labourites in England, who did their utmost to interfere as little as possible in Greek affairs, were in a curious position: to vote on the referendum first, according to the Varkiza Agreement, was contrary to the wishes of the democrats and favored the return of George II. But refusing to intervene in order to postpone the referendum meant indirect intervention in favor of the King, a very unpleasant charge against the Labour party. So, as it was expressed with wit, "the policy of non-intervention obliged the Labourites to make a last intervention", and to use their influence with the other two governments so as to persuade the Regent and the Prime Minister that elections must be held first. Even more wittily, the idea was expressed in the House of Commons that "non-intervention was a metaphysical term that could not be separated from intervention".

This matter was easily solved, but others could not be so readily resolved and gave rise to strong reaction. The electoral lists had been imperfectly renewed and dated from 1936. The parties did not have sufficient time to reorganize themselves and to select new candidates. There was still much hatred and sometimes even violence. All of the parties, except the Populists—the royalist right—demanded the postponement of the elections. Some threatened not to participate. Since the beginning of March, ten of Sofoulis's ministers had resigned and, among those, deputy prime minister Sophocles Venizelos left the Liberals to form a party of his own.

The old man did not, however, knuckle under. It is true that besides his wish to finish with this matter and to reestablish constitutional order in the country, he had another serious reason to be persistent. The Voulgaris government, from its formation, invoking the Yalta declaration according to which the three Great Powers would aid their allies in restoring democratic regimes, had invited their respective governments and the French government to send observers for the elections. The Soviet Union had declined the invitation. From all the evidence, it appears that it did not wish to attest to the defeat of the Left, nor, primarily, to create a bad precedent for other countries of the Eastern Bloc. The other governments, however, had accepted and in December 1945, their representatives arrived in Athens by the hundreds to form the Allied Mission for Observing the Greek Elections, commonly known by its initials in English as AMFOGE. In January they were all there—about 1,200 of them—and the three governments warned that the observers must depart no later than mid-April. Some politicians maintained that it would be better for the elections to be prepared and held in an atmosphere of calm, than to have foreign observers. But the crafty old Prime Minister, in order to convince the world of the regularity of the elections, considered that it was, above all, necessary that they take place under the eyes of a large number of foreign observers. So, afraid that he would lose the observers, he carried on, hoping to avoid abstention by another ruse. The Right wanted elections held under the majority system so as to get together and crush all parties of the center and left. Sofoulis, with some excuses, imposed proportional representation which favored the small parties, his own included; for with the departure of Venizelos his party had weakened considerably because many believed that his government was partial to the Left.

The KKE remained until the end firmly in favor of abstention. One important point must be decided concerning these elections. On this depended the proportion in which legality was reestablished, as well as the representative character of the new parliament: what exactly was the true extent of abstention? The extreme Left maintained, in Greece and abroad, that about fifty percent of the voters abstained. This is absolutely false. Before citing the conclusions of AMFOGE, some events must be described and figures mentioned.

With the registration of new voters as they came of age, the electoral catalogues had been altered. But they had been very superficially revised. Thus, most of the voters who had died between 1936 and 1945 were still listed. Under the conditions which existed then, this was unavoidable; however, this did not ensure a true expression of the people's will.

So, there were 1,850,000 registered voters (women did not vote then) from which 100,000 must be subtracted for the military and police (out of 130,000) who could not vote according to the laws of those days because they were not living in their electoral district. Out of 1,750,000 voters, a figure that included for the most part those who had died in the past ten years, some 1,122,000 persons voted.

A figure of fifty percent abstentions is thus flagrantly untrue. Besides, even if the death rate of the years 1936-45 was the usual one (and unfortunately, it was not) very simple calculations prove that political and natural abstentions (sickness, absence, etc.) could not have exceeded twenty-five percent. AMFOGE, after a detailed investigation of the electoral lists, announced that 78% had been validly registered, 13% were invalid (dead), the remaining 9% were in doubt. It was estimated that abstention for political reasons was "between 10 and 20% at the maximum, with a probability of 15%".

In addition, we must also mention that a small amount of abstention was due to the fact that on the eve of the elections, the Communists terrorized a large number of villagers, especially those who did not vote at their own village but at a neighboring one. Some small groups of guerrillas had already appeared and threatened those who were going to vote in a nearby village. To make the threat greater a group of guerrillas occupied Littochoron at the foot of Mount Olympus on March 30, the eve of elections. In other places groups of bandits, who claimed kinship with the Left, therefore supported abstention. Such was the case, for example, of the Zaralis band in the Pindos mountains.

It must also be pointed out that the majority of the "abstentionists" belonged to the extreme Left, but not entirely. In fact, certain small parties and some independent ones also did not participate in the elections. To be more precise, Kartalis, Svolos, Tsirimokos, Tsouderos—a former colleague of Eleftherios Venizelos, George Kafandaris, and others. Thus, in that which concerns political abstention, and particularly by the KKE, it was nearer 10% rather than the 20% maximum cited by the foreign observers.

As far as the elections themselves are concerned, it is better to refer to the AMFOGE's conclusions. It would really be absurd to believe that such a large number of observers coming from three different countries, where there had been a campaign against Greek "monarcho-fascism", would consent to serve it by concealing the truth. AMFOGE, it may be noted, did a methodical and detailed job during and after the elections. Every electoral district was inspected by about six "groups of observers", who checked samples of the electoral lists, examined them for validity and were on hand on March 31 to observe polling stations.

Here is the final conclusion AMFOGE arrived at and which it submitted to the three governments:

"Consequently, the mission has concluded that, in spite of the intensity of political feeling in Greece, conditions were such as to guarantee good elections. That the electoral proceedings were, on the

167

whole, free and just, that the general result represented a true and valid decision by the Greek people."

Thus, even elementary objectivity forces us to recognize—and this is an important point in judging all that followed—that on March 31, 1946, there was in Greece a popular mandate freely and properly expressed.

The results of the election, as foreseen, were favorable to the Right, and went as follows:

PARTIES	VOTES	%	SEATS
Nationalists' United Front *(Coalition of the Right)*	611,000	55.2	204
National Political Union *(Center-Center Right)*	214,000	19.3	70
Liberals *(Center-Center Left)*	159,500	14.4	42
National Party of Greece *(Right)*	66,000	6.0	17
Various Parties and Independent Candidates	58,000	5.1	11
TOTAL	1,108,500		344

The governments originating from the new Parliament, distributed as shown above, were faced with guerrilla warfare until the end of 1949. Thus, it is now useful to comment on the parties which were represented in this parliament. Beginning with the bottom of the list, we may ignore the last category. It was small, consisting mainly of members of the extreme Right, which played no role in the Parliament except that of making an incoherent noise. The National Party, under Zervas, the well-known leader of the resistance, was a local one; in the elections it swept Epirus. Also well known were the Liberals, and their leader, Sofoulis, who in March 1946, had the honor, under difficult conditions, to hold free elections and to lose them. The National

Political Union (EPE) consisted of three parties under the leadership of Sophocles Venizelos (36 MPs), George Papandreou (28 MPs), and Panayiotis Canellopoulos (6 MPs). On the day after the elections EPE dissolved and the three small parties conceded their role as "principal opposition" to the Liberals. The great winners of the elections were, in fact, the Populists, who held 171 seats out of the 204 of their coalition. The Populist Party was under the leadership of a committee, but after the elections one of its members, Constantinos Tsaldaris, immediately took the leading role and was elected party leader in mid-April. Nephew of a former prime minister of the same name, a good, honest man of simple tastes, but a poor orator, he had had an insignificant political career and did not seem destined to become the leader of a large party. But among all the other known politicians, he was the only one who had not renounced his principles, the only one who had not expressed reservations as to the restoration of the constitutional monarchy and the return of George II. This attitude, in 1946, was his best asset, in the eyes of the people. All the efforts of the democrats towards the carrying out of elections before the referendum played against them.

For the masses, especially in the countryside, Communism was scarcely an ideology or a political movement. It was crime, violence, and blood. An irony of history is that Aris Velouchiotis, one of the most idealistic members of the Communist movement, had contributed, more than any other, to this conviction. So, as the King symbolized anti-communism and the restoration of order, the majority of voters during the parliamentary elections chose mainly those candidates who were in favor of the King's return. Such was the case of the Populist Party, of its allies from the party of Zervas, and of about half of the deputies of the National Political Union. If the referendum for the return of King George II had preceded elections, the results would have been quite different. Satisfied and reassured as to the important issues, voters would then have felt free to select among parties and candidates. But voters thought differently. Things were such—Vishinsky and Sofiano-poulos had done their best to put them in relief—so that the choice was simplified. One had to choose between Communism and anti-communism, between the Soviet Union and the Western Allies, between order and disorder, between law and terror. From all the evidence, George II had become the symbol of Good.

Just or unjust, it was so; to such a degree that certain candidates, tainted from collaboration with the Germans, were elected deputies only through their recent affiliation with the extreme Right. Only in this way could the Right manage to secure such a large majority. And in this way, Tsaldaris, whose royalist feelings had never been doubted, was elected leader of the Populists and became the first prime minister in ten years to come to office by the will of the people![3] Although Tsaldaris did not have all the qualities of a leader, we shall see later that he had a deep sense of honor and self-denial—necessary virtues for a politician.

Chapter VII

By Fire and Axe

Guerrilla War Begins. The 12th of February 1946, as mentioned earlier in this book, is considered by Greek Communists as the day the guerrilla war was declared. On that day a mere formality was fulfilled. In reality, other dates are more important because they concern key matters.

The most important decisions perhaps, were taken on December 15, 1945. On that day, in the Bulgarian town of Petric, near the Greek-Bulgarian border, a meeting took place between the Central Committee of the KKE and Yugoslav and Bulgarian officers, representing the army general staffs of the two countries. There a decision was made to reorganize the Greek partisans under the name of the "Democratic Army" "in order to fight against the Greek government in power". The Yugoslavs promised all sorts of assistance in many fields and asked that their efforts be coordinated.

Reorganization began with the former officers of ELAS from the towns of Naoussa (Macedonia) and Volos

(Thessaly), towns which had the largest percentages of leftist militants. Others, originating elsewhere, joined them gradually and soon these first initiates restored throughout all of northern Greece the supply corps of ELAS, known by its Greek initials as ETA. Very secretly, during the first half of 1946, this new ETA compiled lists of all arms and ammunition stocks, saw to their safekeeping and, for greater security, transported to foreign territory those that were near the frontier. Supply centers were set up just beyond the Greek frontiers, and a large camp to the north of Belgrade, at Bulkes, which was already sheltering thousands of ELAS refugees in Yugoslavia, was used for the training of the "Democratic Army".

In March 1946, Zachariadis himself visited for the first time the camp at Bulkes. While there, he made a long speech addressed to his future soldiers who were all veterans of the battles of 1943-44.

The date on which effective operations began was March 30, 1946, when Littochoron was occupied. People often spoke about small Communist armed groups being active before then. But this is not exact. Such activities existed, but there is no proof that the principal aim of these bands was political: it just offered a wonderful alibi. In that period, when prosecution of violators of the law was difficult and there was a shortage of everything, robbery flourished. However, it helped for the brigands to claim that they were attached to one or another of the political extremes. We could mention a number of this kind of "archbrigands". On the contrary, the attack against Littochoron on March 30 took place under such conditions that we can see in it the first indications of the guerrilla war. Besides, it was not the only such assault, with the difference that for a few months it was not repeated in exactly the same manner.

In the central provinces and in the north of the country, during spring and especially in summer, there were many incidents on the main highways. Small groups of former

172

members of ELAS, rather poorly armed, halted buses, distributed propaganda, and threatened people. They took food if they could find any, but otherwise they did not do any looting; sometimes they treated travellers badly, but they never killed. The same slogans were always used: *"We took to the mountains to protect ourselves from the monarchofascists. We are fighting back. We must save the people from oppression, from fascism which has reinstalled itself in Greece. The third round is starting. Pay attention! Follow us and this time we are sure to win!"* One could speak already of serious disturbances of the peace, not of a true and widespread guerrilla war.

One could really speak of a guerrilla war, however, after the referendum (September 1, 1946) which returned George II to the Greek throne. This was probably the KKE's way of answering this expression of the people's will, because the incident at Littochoron was thereafter repeated with a marked rhythm. Everywhere the tactic was the same: simultaneous attacks in small groups from various directions; coordinated efforts against gendarmerie stations and the extermination of personnel, followed by mutilation of the head of each station if he fell into their hands; execution of some important citizens known to be rightists; and, finally, the carrying off of food. On September 14, the village of Aliakmon in the northern part of the country was attacked. On the 19th, Pyrsoyianni, near the Albanian frontier—an attack in which the chief of the station, deputy captain Kourkoulas, nicknamed "the lion", was beheaded after putting up a ferocious resistance. On the 20th, an attack against the village of Sourvena near the Yugoslav frontier.

The most serious attack was that of September 24 against Deskati, a large village not far from the border on the administrative demarcation line between Thessaly and Macedonia. This time it was a true military operation, directed by Captain Ypsilantis (pseudonym), and in which participated—perhaps because there were not enough local forces—the band of the brigand Zaralis and, according to Athens newspapers, a band of Albanians. On the preceding night, seven small villages around Deskati were taken over, their gendarmes wiped out and their telephone and telegraph destroyed. Thus isolated, the village was attacked at dawn from all directions. It was defended by its gendarmes and a weak army company.[1] The engagement lasted until 9 PM; the garrison, which risked extermination, launched a massive counter-attack on a point, broke through the enemy lines and withdrew to the neighboring heights. In addition to the wounded, the defenders lost forty-seven men, among which the bodies of two officers were found mutilated; several men were carried as "missing". The army rushed reinforcements up the next morning, but they only managed to make contact with the aggressors as they withdrew after having emptied the UNRRA storehouses and taken with them all the food available in private homes. Their losses seem to have been serious. They are not mentioned here because the details are not certain. For psychological reasons the guerrillas tried never to leave behind dead and wounded on the field of battle.

This operation took place on September 24 (King George II was returning on the 27th). This was not the only ominous "fireworks" the Democratic Army was preparing with which to welcome him. There was another—much bigger this time—on the night of October 1. On this occasion, the guerrillas attacked the small industrial town of Naoussa in Macedonia, at a considerable distance from the Yugoslav frontier. The official communiques concerning the operation differed considerably from the newspaper accounts, but we will not be far from the truth in giving the following account of what happened: at 23:00 hours on October 1, a "fifth column" composed of workers from the town's factories, cut telephone and telegraph lines. They then set fire to the houses of outstanding citizens after sprinkling them with benzine; anyone who came out was gunned down. At about the same time a bridge linking the town with the capital of the province was blown up; guerrilla bands surrounded an army regiment camped on the outskirts and other bands infiltrated the town. The most important ones immediately attacked the gendarmerie station using machine guns, grenades, and mortars.

On the following day Athenian newspapers described the events under the headline, "A Night of Terror". But this night was an unlucky one for the gerrillas. The stronger-than-usual gendarmerie station put up a successful defense and the encircled regiment managed to break through enemy lines and fight with unforeseen fury. In the early hours of October 2, as the regiment was entering Naoussa, the gendarmes left their position and made a counter-attack. After some skirmishes in the streets, the guerrillas and the "fifth column" hastily departed for the nearby hills. They were pursued without being overtaken by forces of the army which arrived at break of day. The "fifth column" numbered about one hundred men and the guerrillas were, according to the authorities, "superior in number" to the soldiers and gendarmes. According to the newspaper accounts, they totalled nearly one thousand men and belonged to "groups" from four mountains nearby.

Although from one point of view Naoussa was a defeat for the assailants, and though they did not get much "loot", from another point of view it was quite a success: they had dared to attack a town and had caused serious damage there. The consequences of these events were many and so obvious that they do not need to be specifically pointed out. However, let us mention one that may not come to mind: all of the small towns terrorized began to insist on government forces being garrisoned in them. Nearly all of the members of parliament of continental Greece, especially from the north, were bombarded with such requests; naturally, it was impossible to fulfill them. The guerrilla war had begun.

The attacks continued—sometimes here, sometimes there—although it must be said that for some months no engagement was as important as that of Deskati or of Naoussa. No one knew at the time how all this was organized and coordinated. The general public was worried but, owing to the fact that the government tried to minimize what was going on, it knew no more than the most important events. The officials responsible for public order were well informed on everything, of course, but they lacked true information as to the direction and co-ordination of the guerrilla operations. At that time they only knew what they saw or were told by prisoners; that is to say: the bands were small. They consisted of five to ten men in the beginning, thirty to eighty later on, rarely more. They were almost always former members of ELAS and had as leaders those guerrillas who had proven themselves. Their arms were in excellent condition, but light: some rifles, light machine guns and grenades. By autumn they also had some mortars of small caliber and heavy machine guns. Each band usually had its own small area and lived at the expense of the inhabitants from raids which it made. People generally believed that these were their sole source of supply.

These small groups followed "hit and run" tactics. But, light as they were, they could unite and constitute a force capable of undertaking more serious operations. As soon as these were completed the force dispersed again into small scattered units. The lack of uniforms made their appearance and disappearance easier. This tactic was excellent, and its application too; it was intensified, and improved. Certainly, it was not all clear sailing, but until autumn, nobody knew exactly who attacked and how. The facts only came out some months later, and now are finally known in every detail.

In August 1946, the Central Committee of the KKE had

appointed a military chief and had given him broad authority in all questions concerning the "Democratic Army". The name of this leader was Markos Vafiadis. Born in Asia Minor in 1906, Vafiadis took refuge in Constantinople in 1923, and then went to Thessalonike. He was a militant of the KKE from the time of his arrival in Greece and was also for some years a tobacco worker at Kavalla in Thrace (northern Greece). Arrested many times, he escaped each time and was always in the first ranks of the Party faithful. During the occupation he was the political commissar of ELAS for Macedonia. But he took to military affairs and devoted himself solely to these, participating personally in the operations. The career officers of ELAS headquarters in Macedonia who, in a way, were his tutors in the art of war, spoke of "his military genius".

With Aris dead, the career officers formerly in ELAS did not inspire confidence as leaders and probably also did not wish to get involved in the fighting. Thus, Markos Vafiadis seems to have been easily chosen as the most suitable person to lead the new bands of insurgents. Known henceforth as "General Markos", he proved at once to be a true military leader. As soon as he was appointed to this position, he left for Yugoslavia to establish himself in Bulkes. His first preoccupation was to organize liaison with all of his armed bands and to put them under his control. At the same time, he organized supplies for his partisans—locally or across the frontier—and formed an information network. He imposed doctrinal and tactical training on all his men, but especially his leaders. Finally, he developed methods for his troops to cross the border in both directions easily, either to secure supplies and rest, or to save themselves in case of great danger.

One can understand better now how and by whom the operations of Deskati and Naoussa were organized—operations that were extremely bold for scattered guerrilla groups. Besides, it seems that if these two assaults pleased the Communist leadership in Athens as a welcome to the King, they were equally pleasing to the leader of Bulkes for a different reason, that is, to test his tactics on a larger scale.

In order to continue to expand his operation, Markos needed both to improve and to organize his troops. In this he was promptly assisted by three neighboring communist countries, especially Yugoslavia. Considerable help came from Bulgaria also, but only after the dynamic Dimitrov had fully established his rule. These three countries not only allowed the guerrillas to freely cross over their frontiers which were impossible for Greece to guard because of their length, but they also assisted them in many other ways. Centers for training supply were formed; small bases were set up near the frontiers and means of transport were given to the Greek revolutionists. Map No. 4 shows the most important of these bases.

There was nothing peculiar about this at all. Yugoslavia, Bulgaria and Albania had a common ideology and were on excellent terms with each other, and with the Soviet Union; they had every reason to want a communist country as their neighbor to the south. For them, it was primarily a matter of security to gain an outlet to the Mediterranean. This most probably involved annexation, according to old theories of the KKE of certain border areas. The three countries were perfectly consistent in their thinking and in their machinations considering that Greece was extremely weak and also had a "fifth column" resolved to put up a fight.

Nevertheless, "General Markos"—though determined to fight and inspired by a deep personal respect for Tito—had some reservations. From what has become known today it seems almost certain that he did not wish to depend exclusively on bases beyond the frontiers of Greece. He asked himself whether events taking place elsewhere, such as the Trieste affair, for example, or those of more general interest, or even foreign intervention, would not one day deprive him of those bases. That is why, without abandoning them, he made use of the facilities granted to him and also did all he could to establish some important bases on Greek territory as well, plus many other secondary ones. This gave him greater mobility.

The undertaking was successful. Before winter arrived, the stores of food, ammunition and weapons which he had in the mountains, especially those near the border, were sufficient to maintain a much larger army than his for many months. The big difficulty lay elsewhere. His "army" was small. When he took command, he had only 3,000 to 4,000 men. After two months he had no more than 6,000 and, by the end of December, 8,000 without counting those in the auxiliary services which had begun to form. The numbers do not seem impressive, but they constituted 100 to 200 groups of thirty to eighty guerrillas which, with the tactics he applied, could throw the whole country into confusion. But this was not the aim. The adversary must be harrassed all the time so as to lead to some sort of capitulation. That is why a larger guerrilla army was needed.

However, recruitment limped along. Without the former members of ELAS who took refuge at Bulkes and their comrades in Greece, who were in danger of being arrested, there would not have been any effective increase in the "Democratic Army". True volunteers were rare. The defeat of January 1945 was recent, the memory of Moscow's abandonment smarting, and lastly, it was not known or believed by most people that a serious organization existed in the mountains. Under these conditions even the loyal hesitated to commit themselves. Even less likely were those that lived in towns for there they were less pursued and they saw that the state was beginning to assert its authority.

Thus, Markos increased his efforts in all directions. In October, a short while after Naoussa, he announced the creation of a headquarters in Greece. Probably it consisted of the regional commands that he had just created, some liaison officers and certain chiefs of auxiliary services and was called headquarters for reasons of prestige. He himself was often away at Bulkes and it would be difficult for one to speak of the existence in Greece of a headquarters of the Democratic Army. But the announcement sounded good. Then, without abandoning attacks in the central and northern areas, Markos did his utmost to organize revolutionary bands in the Peloponnesus. There, at the southern end of the country, every activity, even though limited, was precious for two reasons; first, it refuted the thesis of the government that the guerrilla war was organized and supplied from abroad. Secondly, it persuaded those who hesitated that the revolution was general and extended throughout the country. In the Peloponnesus, the cause did not advance as well and as rapidly as elsewhere. Nevertheless, before the end of 1946, in the mountains of the Peloponnesus but especially in Taygetos, there were about fifteen small armed groups, numbering three hundred men all told, which by sudden attacks verified the presence of the Democratic Army.

This was enough activity for the "General" in the isolated Peloponnesus. Elsewhere he wished to appear in a more favorable light in order to gain recognition. To do this, he had to prove that he was strong and well enough organized to be able to survive the harsh winter in the mountains. This approach was very useful to him in order to put into action another plan: the recruitment of guerrillas, if not by force, at least against their will. In fact, during the last months of 1946, when the partisans occupied a village for a few hours, they did not restrict themselves to the carrying off of food and the execution of a few villagers, they threatened the former members of ELAS and they obliged some of them to follow them, especially the younger ones. The isolated mountain villages of Epirus and Western Macedonia suffered more than other areas from these raids of the new army of the KKE, which in December had been rebaptized "Democratic Army of Greece". Such was the approximate situation from the point of view of the revolution at the end of 1946.

Before we conclude this section on the birth and the beginnings of the Democratic Army of Greece—this reincarnation of ELAS—it is of interest to mention one of the last military operations of 1946, perhaps of secondary importance, but nevertheless typical in many respects.

At the southernmost point between Epirus and Macedonia there is a long mountainous valley with a sharp slope and some dense forests which includes seven villages, two of which are of some importance. Isolated thus, the valley did not then have a passable road. None of the villages in the valley had gendarmes or soldiers. A famous former chief of ELAS, "Captain" Vassilaras, had occupied the valley at the end of summer with around thirty guerrillas and lived there as absolute master.

So as to dispute every inch of ground and to strengthen the morale of the population the authorities sent a platoon of elite troops to the area, made up of men who knew the countryside well. They had a good commander, were well armed and challenged the enemy, but were always refused combat. The valley thus lived in agony under a sort of condominium. A young member of parliament who visited the seven villages in October, escorted by friends armed to the teeth, met the government platoon many times but never saw any trace of armed Communists. Just before Christmas the platoon was temporarily sent elsewhere. The next day the commander of the nearest gendarmerie post at Metsovo, Lieutenant Mourgás, nicknamed the "Wolf", was informed by "a reliable source" that Vassilaras had been left with only twenty men, that he was not taking any security measures after the platoon's departure, and that he was indulging in amusements.

The "Wolf" was renowned for his courage and his relentlessness in pursuing Communist bands. On the outskirts of Metsovo he had hunted down one of them; in the ensuing fight three were wounded, including himself, but he had killed four guerrillas and taken two prisoners. At news of the weakness of his principal adversary, he did not hesitate a moment. He took his ten gendarmes and twenty national guardsmen who had been placed under his orders and, after a forced march, they arrived on the same night at the first houses of the village that had been named as the enemy hideout. His plan was to make arrangements with the Rightist villagers whom he knew well, and then to attack at dawn. He had time to meet with only one villager. Vassilaras did not have only twenty men. He had more than one hundred, all determined to fight and well armed. They attacked the "Wolf" from all sides. Some national guardsmen hid themselves. At mid-day, the survivors of the small government force, including its wounded leader, were taken prisoner. They were then obliged to parade nude through three of the villages, where the population was ordered to throw stones at them and insult them. In the third village, the national guardsmen were set free, the gendarmes were shot, and the "Wolf" was beheaded. As a supreme insult maintained by tradition throughout the centuries, from the time of Antigone of Sophocles, the bodies were not buried.

To complete this drama and characteristic of this incident, a speech was made by Captain Vassilaras to the people of the three villages who had been ordered to come and listen to him. The democratic forces of the country, he said to them, had punished the monarcho-fascists who tyrannized the people. No one would get away this time. Even so, he had decided not to touch any democrat, if he were reasonable. A proof of this was that the soldiers who were children of the people and had been subject to compulsory mobilization had not been touched. Another proof: the young member of parliament during his visit had not been attacked because in the referendum, he had voted for the Republic. It was an intelligent speech supported by evidence. However, what was not mentioned his listeners learned at the end of the guerrilla war: for three days captain Vassilaras lay in ambush waiting for the young MP along the way he was expected to pass; but he did not go that way for, under the seal of secrecy, he had been warned by a shepherd loyal to him, and so had escaped harm.

On the Other Side. To the Tsaldaris government fell the task of facing this extremely difficult and complicated situation. In the beginning neither the majority of the people nor the government itself seemed to have any understanding of what was really happening. Their bourgeois mentality did not allow them to conceive that after five years of terrible suffering, with the country still in ruins and full of new graves, and legality just re-established, that a new revolution could be starting. Most people believed that the guerrillas were nothing more than small bands of brigands —creatures of misery to whom were added some former partisans—creatures of passion and fear. That was all; it could not last. From this general impression came the popular, and later official, names of "communist bandit" and of "bandit war". But though it took some months to speak of war or of guerrilla, it took much longer for people to comprehend that the conflict was not due to the despair of a few passionate men.

That is the reason why, in the beginning, the Tsaldaris government which undoubtedly wished to do its duty, could not put "first things first". The return of King George II was one of its most pressing preoccupatons. The referendum, not on the regime any longer but on the return of the King, was announced during the opening of parliament on May 13 in the speech of the Regent. It was set for the first of September. The results showed clearly that the people favored the King's return to the throne, with 68.6 percent of the voters opting for him. Against the King were 11.3 percent of the voters, while 20 percent left their ballots blank. This last group were not in favor of a constitutional monarchy but, following the lead of the republicans, had voted in this way so as to distinguish themselves from the followers of the KKE and fellow travellers who voted against.

The popular verdict was clearly unfavorable to the King in Crete and in the cities of Piraeus and Thessalonike, while it was particularly favorable in the provinces and regions which had suffered most from the civil war during the occupation. In those areas the members of parliament who dared to support the Republic were rejected by a large number of their friends.

It is true that the genuineness of the results was contested by some. But they did so without much enthusiasm, because, even if polling had been ideal—and it was far from it—again the results would not have been very different. Thus, George II returned to Athens on September 27, rightfully and legally.

Another serious preoccupation of the government was the matter of national claims, ancestral aspirations which had been excited during the Greek-Italian war of 1941 in the Dodecanese islands, Northern Epirus and Cyprus. It was quite normal for the majority of the people to believe that, having fought to the end against the Axis while all of Europe was subjugated and England humbled, while the United States and the Soviet Union remained neutral, their claims should be satisfied, especially as they were based on the principle of nationalities. Unfortunately, the people could not imagine that international justice does not exist. On this issue Tsaldaris and his collaborators were not so lucky. They were able to incorporate within Greece only the Dodecanese islands which had been occupied until then by the Italians. But, as for the other claims, they could not obtain even a vague promise. This was a deep disappointment to the people.

In other more urgent matters, the efforts of the government did not bring the results expected. At the opening of parliament the government had promised "financial stability and economic progress", but the realization of this promise was too slow to be visible and sometimes did not occur at all. In spite of diligent efforts by the people and an exceptionally good wheat harvest, according to UNRRA and FAO reports, 1946 agricultural production had only slightly exceeded 90 percent of pre-war production, while industrial production lagged at only 45 percent of pre-war figures. The balance of payments was disastrous, government receipts very small, and deposits of the issuing bank absurdly low. The only way for the value of the money to be strengthened was to sell gold sovereigns at the official price. Certainly the government was not responsible for all this, but, whether responsible or not, it was the government which paid the price for the financial depression.

In the re-establishment of order the Tsaldaris government failed completely. It could not even eliminate the factors which reinforced the rebellion or which gave arguments to it, good for the East, but valid also in the West. Not that it did not want to do so. Its intentions were good and it demonstrated them with acts that were considered daring for a Rightist government. Such, for example, was the closing of all provincial offices of the organization "X" and the arrest of Mandakas, unfortunately known for his occupation of Calamata in January 1946. But because of a lack of prestige or of strength, of shrewdness and of a spirit of continuity, the government could not impose its initial impartiality on all the officers of the administration, still less on the lower ones. Thus, to the fierce animosity which a large part of the population nourished against the extreme Left, was added a certain partiality in the application of the law.

The situation became so much more dangerous that in June, the government had submitted to parliament a very severe law entitled "Special Measures for Public Order", which had been passed by parliament, although the Liberals had abstained. According to this law, certain offenses, directly or indirectly linked to the organization of rebel bands, carried the death penalty or other severe punishment. The police were allowed additionally to conduct searches of private homes by day or night with the purpose of uncovering war material or persons under warrant for arrest. On the other hand, revision of a former decree authorized a committee, formed by the monarch of each province and two judges, which could exile any person suspected of activity "against the order, tranquility and security of the country". This law, though useful in view of the storm that was brewing, was at the same time dangerous because of the fanaticism reigning in the lower echelons of governmental administration. Although in a general way the law was objectively applied, some unjust cases caused strong protests and were largely used by "anti-monarchofascist" propaganda. Besides, certain cases concerning well-known people gave the impression that the government persecuted the Left without reason. University professors and high level civil servants, formerly associated with ELAS, were discharged. Sarafis, Bakirdjis and about a hundred former officers were exiled to various islands. It was not known then that the security police had received information—albeit unverified—to the effect that these people were to leave the capital to join the guerrillas.

Intervention in the trade union movement—intervention based on the law, but always in favor of some elements of the Right—was another source of domestic friction and also caused suspicion abroad. However, the reaction of a large part of the working class against the Communists was so strong that none of the strikes called had had any success. Thus, with more coolheadedness and reason, it would have been possible to secure less radical, but more effective solutions.

The worst fault of the Tsaldaris government was that it often contradicted itself. This was conveyed by many details, but most significantly in two cases concerning public order. For a few months, almost until the return of the King, the authorities minimized the importance of what was happening in the mountains so as not to worry the people. But under these conditions, many people of good faith and especially many former members of ELAS, asked themselves whether the "inexplicable" strictness was not due exclusively to vengeance and a spirit of partiality. As a matter of fact, if nothing serious was happening, then why was such severity shown? Another fault of the government lasted a long time and increased confusion and reaction in certain circles: while the government seemed strict toward and often treated the lower Party cadres severely, those at the top, who organized and directed the budding war, were permitted complete freedom of action. During the whole of 1946 and many months thereafter, Zachariadis worked freely as head of the Politburo of the Central Committee, ran its two newspapers and its illegal network under the protection of the authorities. This was done as offering proof of respect for the rules of democracy, a proof that was especially useful abroad; but it was, at the same time, irrational and contradictory to the rest of governmental activity. And this policy made some of the Party faithful, who feared persecution, take to the mountains.

Certainly, one does not find here the cause of the guerrilla war; it would have taken place anyway because its causes were much deeper. But it is also obvious that this first parliamentary government, at least up to the time of the referendum, was not equal to the task at hand. George II, who received in Athens a very warm popular reception, tried immediately to improve the political situation. He accepted Tsaldaris's resignation, submitted as a matter of form, and entrusted him as leader of the majority to form a new government under the condition that he would widen its base. In the meantime, Sofoulis, who had put up a bitter opposition in the name of "persecuted democratic citizens,"

187

flatly refused any collaboration. The leaders of the three parties of the National Political Union (Venizelos, Papandreou, Canellopoulos) asked for the Ministries of Foreign Affairs, of Economic Coordination and of Defense. The winner of the elections would have been deprived of all power.

So, the government's base was not widened and Tsaldaris formed a new Populist cabinet. But one month later the King, to whom Tsaldaris was very faithful, asked him once more to resign. This time George II intervened in the negotiations himself, but a liberalization of the government was again impossible. Tsaldaris came to power by himself again, or rather with his ally, Gonatas, who added nothing to his prestige nor to the government's effectiveness. Not only did the prestige of the government suffer from the guerrilla war, the development of which was now obvious to everyone, but also by the evident wish of the King to replace it with a coalition government. This was certainly not good for a struggle against revolutionaries who were experienced, resolved and disciplined under a very centralized command.

Nevertheless, this government, in spite of its very mediocre Minister of National Defense—advantageously replaced in January 1947—realized towards the end of summer that military strategy against the rebel bands would have to change. The brunt of the struggle had been shouldered by the gendarmerie, which was weak in numbers and scattered among many isolated stations which succumbed one after the other. The gendarmerie was assisted by the national guard, equally weak, poorly armed, poorly trained, and with few officers. It became clear that the "Communist guerrillas", or "Communist bandits"—a name of doubtful taste for propaganda purposes—were much more significant than mere bandits and that the rising tide had to be faced in a different way. So, it was decided that the national army would have to be used.

The British Mission, which had undertaken to organize

the Greek army, did not agree with this; the army was still weak, not well enough armed or sufficiently trained. The British commander, General Rawlings, was of the opinion that it should not enter into a guerrilla war, the tactics of which were completely different from regular army tactics. Nevertheless, with the steady deterioration of the situation, there was no other alternative, and the British Mission was forced to yield. Thus, the decision to use the national army was taken in August and, at the beginning of autumn, it went into action. The army entered the struggle very apprehensively because, though the people and their representatives had illusions, the army command itself had none. First, on the insistence of the British, who supplied all war material to the Greek army, only about half of the troops were equipped for mountain warfare. The other half was motorized. For a classical war that was good. For a guerrilla war in a country with many mountains and a limited road network, this was disadvantageous.

In addition, the army was then 92,000 men strong. This seemed a large figure to the uninitiated person who thought that they would have to face only a few thousand guerrillas; but it was very few to a strategist who knew that not only did the frontiers (about one thousand kilometers in length) have to be guarded, but also the towns, as well as all kinds of installations and depots, communication centers and main bridges. On top of all these, the main job of the army would be to track down and crush the guerrillas. This was an impossible task; the whole of Greece was becoming a "front", if it was not one already. During a high level meeting held at this time, the leaders of the army did not conceal their fears. Some of them asked for a general mobilization, "because guerrilla warfare can only be waged by a flooding of troops". Material means were lacking so it was decided that the army would be increased to a total strength of 200,000 men. This decision was entirely formal. The leader of the British Mission finally accepted a figure of

135,000 men, which for several months existed only on paper. In November 1946, it was necessary for General Rawlings himself to escort the chief of the Greek high command to London so that General Montgomery could authorize equipment for another 3,000 men. We repeat, the number was three thousand! The army profited from this to create shock troops of the commando type, known by the initials of their name as LOK. Actually, this was of very little assistance in the huge job the army was undertaking, but like it or not, it had to fight with what it had.

The national army, endowed with some first class officers did its best. In the Peloponnesus, there were about 300 guerrillas who caused no small embarrassment, but did not present any real danger. So the general staff, in spite of very strong and very understandable political pressure, withdrew all of the army from the Peloponnesus; the entire area was turned over to the gendarmerie. In addition, the already well-trained units in the vicinity of Athens were withdrawn and sent to Thessaly. The mission of these units was to better protect the fertile plain surrounded as it is by wide mountain ranges. From there—the geographical center of Greece—they could rush to the assistance of places attacked and pursue the aggressors.

Another important decision was made in October 1946. It concerned the forming of "units of rural self-defense", the MAY. In each village men who were loyal to national traditions would be armed and placed under officers or non-commissioned officers of the reserves who lived in the district and would be mobilized for this reason. The men would keep their weapons in their homes, would be trained on Sundays, and would have to be at the disposal of their commanders for any operation, day or night. Instead of payment they would receive small gratuities in kind. The plan was a good one and was accepted with enthusiasm by the rural population although, in the months which followed, certain isolated MAY groups paid very dearly for their activities. The greatest difficulty to overcome in the formation of these units was that of supplying them with weapons and ammunition. The British supplied only the regular army and the country did not have the foreign exchange with which to buy war material abroad. Nevertheless, by gathering all the old material which could be used, as well as by purchasing a certain number of weapons, many MAY groups were formed. Their high morale made them at once an appreciated auxiliary force and many groups even fought by the side of the regular forces.

So, although the guerrillas had the initiative everywhere and had the advantage from many points of view, a resistance was being organized. This resistance was not always sufficiently strong to last until reinforcements arrived, as in Deskati, Pyrsoyianni, and elsewhere; but it constituted a defence and often, as in Naoussa, the attackers were forced to flee leaving their job unfinished. What is more, while fulfilling this mission the army was preparing itself to undertake more serious operations in the spring. For, even though both sides were wary and were "exploring the ground", they were no less determined to fight fiercely, steadily, with hate in their souls.

The new war cry of the "Popular Democratic Army" already resounded in the air: "By Fire and Axe!" On the other side of the deep ravine, the national army echoed the slogan of the struggle for Greek independence in 1821: "Freedom or Death!" In these two war cries were contained both the nature and the reason for this fratricidal struggle. For the one, it was the fervour of the attack and the destruction that seems indispensable to the builder of the totalitarian state. For the other, it was the stubborness of defense and the quintessence of human life. A deep ditch had been dug between the two ideologies. Quoting Aris Velouchiotis, "the river must run red", for one of the two ideologies to prevail. It would run red for three years.

Local Conflict, World Conflict. The last months of 1946

were to reveal the true dimensions of this local war sustained by a small irregular army.

At the United Nations, Stalin, who had demanded one seat for every "Republic" of the Soviet Union, finally succeeded in getting three seats: one each for the Soviet Union, Belorussia and the Ukraine. Thus, these two regions became members of the United Nations' Organization. Then, the Ukraine affirmed this great, and perhaps only, proof of her independence by submitting an appeal against Greece to the Security Council on August 24, 1946. As is the rule in these cases, there are two discussions: one on the admissibility of the appeal, and the other, after it is accepted, on its contents. Soviet representative Andrei Gromyko was the first to support the acceptance of the Ukranian appeal with arguments varying from terrifying to ridiculous. If the Council did not take the appropriate measures, he said, the development of relationships between Greece and Albania, Bulgaria and Yugoslavia would threaten peace in the Balkans and even general security: great wars had started with incidents that, at the beginning, seemed insignificant. The internal situation in Greece, together with the foreign policy of the government in Athens, had already been described as expansionist, and with incidents on the frontier as well as other provocations against Albania, influenced the international atmosphere in a dangerous way. The internal situation which the United Nations, according to its charter, was not allowed to consider "was not internal as long as it caused international difficulties and threatened peace and security". (Today this theory is believed to be entirely new . . .)

Before and after the acceptance (to which the Americans gave their support) Gromyko maintained that the "irresponsible" actions of the Greek authorities could transform the Balkans into a training ground for a new war. Finally, he called the presence of the British troops, "a decisive encouragement for the crushing of democracy and for aggression against neighboring countries", proof of the abolition of Greek sovereignty. Each paragraph of his two long speeches always ended with the same stereotype: "the question was very serious".

The Ukranian deputy, Dimitri Manouilsky, did not put himself out to take up again the arguments of the man who was then his comrade, not his master. He limited himself to modifying it a little, by exaggerating it. He developed the ludicrous side of it. In fact, Gromyko had maintained that the Ukraine was interested in the matter because it bordered on the Balkans!! Manouilsky completed the argument by adding that the Ukraine had suffered four invasions within thirty years and this fact alone was reason for the appeal! Small omission, he was forgetting that these invasions had not come from the Balkans and that in those days the Balkan countries, save Greece, which was weak and situated on the far side of the peninsula, were all the Ukraine's own allies.

Let us include one more official and even more ridiculous example, because these details show much more generalized tactics when the ludicrous side of the argument reached its zenith some days later during another meeting. Molotov himself compared the validity of the referendum in Bulgaria—which had been held on September 8—to the validity of the referendum held in Greece. The first, in which the result came close to the total number of voters, was valid; the second, "because of conditions in Greece, could only be a falsification of the people's will." It was difficult to go further under these circumstances. But the ludicrous in that epoch did not cause laughter. On the contrary, it showed that the fire no longer smouldered, but it burned seemingly out of control.

The answers remind one of an indictment. Those of Greek representative Dendramis were calm, controlled, very detailed and refuted point by point all the accusations. Those of the representatives for Great Britain (Cadogan)

193

and the United States (Hershel Johnson) briefly refuted the accusations and rejected all the allegations. Their tone was harsh and rather disdainful..(.."the argument is not far from the absurd"..), heavy with implications, (.."all the world knows of other sinister cases of territorial claims at the expense of allies or of enemies"..), rather sarcastic, (.."frivolous question, frivolously presented"..).

The discussion was interrupted on December 11, so the representatives could consult with their governments. Talks resumed again on the 16th. In the beginning, it was believed that agreement could easily be reached because, at the opening of the meeting, the Australian delegate proposed an absolutely inoffensive way out: a draft resolution, according to which the Council after listening to the various views, "passed to the next question." But this colorless suggestion did not succeed as the Westerners had hoped. Gromyko submitted his own draft resolution, according to which the Security Council considered Greece guilty of all accusations formulated by the Ukraine and demanded among other things that the Greek government "cease persecution of national minorities in Greece...and the activities "of aggressive monarcho-fascist elements". The Council had to state that it would retain the menacing question on the list of matters to be discussed "as long as the Greek government did not obey the recommendations of the Council".

One can well understand that this proposition, after the categorical rejection of the accusations by the United States, provoked the latter and placed it in a very delicate position. That is why, after the speeches of several delegates—the Greek one among them—the American delegate took the counter-offensive two days later. Following the instructions of his government, he said, he would vote against the Soviet draft. He said there had been the Council border incidents and some cases of bad treatment of minorities, but the United States did not believe that Greece was responsible and, further, these incidents could be due to "the problem of the border's definition". He suggested that the Council concern itself with the "border difficulties" and with the problem of minorities in those regions. The implications of this were great. The discussion was passionate and neither side minced words. Gromyko even spoke of the etiquette of "liberty" under which slavery was veiled so as to serve the oil interests. Johnson went so far as to mention Bulgarian claims on Thrace and of the desire of Yugoslavia "to protect the unfortunate Macedonians" by the incorporation of Bulgarian and Greek Macedonia into that federation.

On the next day the American counter-offensive became stronger and took a more concrete form: that of a draft resolution according to which the Security Council would form a committee of three, selected for their objectivity by the Secretary General—a committee which would search for the truth then and there, so that the Council could decide what had to be done. Gromyko defended his views with passion and dexterity. The vote on the American resolution, which took place first, ended in a large affirmative majority; seven votes for, one abstention, and one against. But this dissenting vote was that of the Soviet Union, one of the "Great Powers" whose negative vote in the Security Council equaled an irrevocable veto. The Americans had been blocked.

Nevertheless, those twenty days of struggle in the Security Council were revealing. They demonstrated more than ever that Markos's small army interested Moscow keenly, that although its fight was local its consequences were worldwide, and, finally, that Truman seemed resolved to relieve the British in the protection of Greece.

The repercussions of this diplomatic struggle on international public opinion and on the Allied governments were important, but they are outside the scope of this book. However, one of these is closely connected to our subject and was of fundamental importance. The American tactics used during the struggle at the Security Council suggested to Greek diplomats the way in which to follow up. During October and November the Greek delegation at the United Nations submitted to the Secretary General of the organization six consecutive memoranda concerning the incidents which had taken place on the northern frontiers of the country. On November 26, after consultations between Athens, Washington and London, the Greek delegation officially informed the Secretary General—through four letters sent the same day—of all of these incidents, adding others and making specific accusations. Finally, on December 3, the interim leader of the Greek delegation, Aghnides, submitted to the Security Council a request for an on-the-spot investigation of the disputes between Greece and its neighbors. The latter were accused of assisting the guerrillas, which was a blow both to public order and to the integrity of the country. There was proof, it was maintained, that the guerrilla war had the official support of Yugoslavia. The situation could endanger international peace and security.

The debate on the appeal took place from the 10th to the 19th of December, and was almost a repetition of the discussion on the Ukranian appeal. This time the Greek position was maintained by Prime Minister Tsaldaris, who had suffered strong personal attacks as the leader of the "fascist" government, cause of all the evil. But this time, after the oratorical duels primarily between Greeks and Yugoslavs, the result of the debate was entirely different from the preceding one. The American delegate, H.V. Johnson, again proposed the forming of a Committee of investigation on both sides of the frontier. His intervention was strong, his tone more reserved and the proposal was modified by the fact that it asked for the members to be elected by the Security Council, not chosen by the Secretary General as before.

The next day, the 19th, Andrei Gromyko, after a long and

harsh indictment, accepted that a commission of the Council "examine the facts and study the situation" on the territory of the four interested countries. The only hint he made to justify his change of attitude was that the discussion had proved that the Americans and British were interested for the time being in the procedure and were not ready to uphold the position of the Greek government. This was then one of the greatest successes of the Tsaldaris government in the matter concerning the diplomatic handling of this struggle against the rebels. It had not been won due to the Greek appeal, nor to the steps of the Greek government or to Greek diplomacy. The Greeks, to their credit, had conceived of the appeal and had handled it well. But it is certain that this success, which had such important consequences, had been realized thanks to an understanding among the Great Powers.

Why did the Soviet Union accept the commission, this international investigation—unique to this day—on territory belonging to three members of its bloc? The reason will perhaps never be known. Many and various explanations were given in an attempt to discover what benefit Moscow could receive in adopting this position:

—Prevention or at least suspension, of an immediate Anglo-American intervention considered as probable.
—Eventual enlargement of the powers of the Commission so that this question, of particular interest to Moscow, could be raised in the Security Council over a long period of time.
—Fear that it would be accused of impeding the functioning of the United Nations after about ten votes in one year.
—Simply moving pieces in a larger game that aimed at greater gains in other areas: the Soviet Union was then preoccupied by very major economic problems.

All these reasons are, perhaps, valid; there is no need to discuss them further here.

What is important is that the Soviet Union, probably without consulting her small allies which were directly involved, and certainly without consulting the KKE, which was paying in blood, made a decision in many ways against the rebellion, which had scarcely begun. The movements of the guerrillas were restricted; the neighboring socialist countries were exposed to grave suspicion when they refused to permit the visits of the U.N. observers. A body of eleven international officials would be there to examine and to confirm each proof furnished by the Greek authorities, proof which otherwise would have been contested. Some time later it became obvious that the Soviet concession played indirectly an even more important role in crushing the revolution. The establishment of the UN observers helped President Truman to get his policy of aid to Greece and Turkey accepted by the American people. The Kremlin was not infallible.

Chapter VIII

The Rising Tide

After the First Wave. Markos had not only succeeded in establishing his authority before winter, but he was in a position to apply his tactics during winter without respite. In spite of various misfortunes, he had really accomplished a great feat.

It is now known that towards the end of the year 1946, the "General", in order to attain his final aim, wished to have at his disposal an army of 50,000 men. This is the number of combatants that he judged would be necessary to neutralize all of the nationalist armed forces. The two principal difficulties were the supplying and, mainly, the recruiting of such a large number of fighters. Moscow, to which he had made overtures, had been evasive and had only sent a few officers as silent observers and they remained mostly beyond the Greek frontier.

A visit that Markos paid to the Balkan capitals improved the situation noticeably. In fact, he was given more materiel and greater facilities. In exchange, it seems that he made some written promises concerning "corrections of the frontiers" and the "status of the minorities of northern Greece"—promises which, according to certain foreign writers, were made on his own responsibility without the consent of the KKE. It was a business that would be settled later on. For the time being, he received an indispensable payment on account; a true network of camps, bases and roads was created beyond the border for the supplying of the "Democratic Army of Greece" (see Map Number 4).

But in order to augment the revolutionary army, a much greater problem had to be solved; that was recruitment, which did not depend on foreigners. Within the first six months, the "Democratic Army" began to face the problem of deserters. By the end of 1946, more than 600 guerrillas had abandoned their comrades and surrendered to government forces. They were mainly young men who had been recruited more or less by force. Little by little, a certain number of former members of ELAS, even some well-known "captains", deserted. Nothing strange about that: it is easy to imagine the advantages of a guerrilla war, but no one thinks much about the difficulties of those who actually carry it out; the guerrilla who must change lodging frequently, who succeeds in some raids but is always pursued, who, nearly dead from fatigue and chilled from cold, must flee quickly. He gives up more easily if he is guaranteed amnesty and the freedom to return to his home. The DAG had to face these difficulties during its entire existence, though, from the very beginning, Markos did everything possible to overcome them. Regular indoctrination was administered, both oral and written, under a just but strict discipline. The guerrillas were fed well and in general, treated well. A deserter, if caught, was always executed. In engagements, the new recruits, led by one of the old ones, fought in the front line. Loyal volunteers fought behind them. Security measures were indispensable, for semi-forcible recruitment was largely applied. From all their forays, nearly without exception, the guerrilla bands returned to their quarters with a large number of so-called "recruits". "Enlistment" was simple: in the terrorized and often burning villages all those who had any ties with the Left were gathered together. The guerrillas spoke to them about the aims of the struggle and of certain victory; if need be, they threatened them. Like it or not, some followed. If they did not manage to desert in the first days, they were trapped because by returning home they knew that they exposed themselves to persecution.

Official documents give the proportion as 30% volunteers and 70% "mobilized by force". This, however, is highly improbable. Such a tenacious struggle could not have been carried on for three years if the majority of the fighters did not have faith in the cause.

In any case, this admixture of soldiers, of those ready to sacrifice themselves and those not so enthusiastic, enabled Markos to intensify guerrilla operations during the first three months of 1947. On New Year's Eve, a large town in Epirus was attacked, as was Ypati in central Greece. On January 3 there were several movements of guerrilla bands towards Thessaly and towards the south. On January 4, the mountain village of Vovoussa was occupied for several hours. The same day, Varflarion in Thessaly and Messochori, south of Lamia, were also occupied. There were, of course, executions and forced recruitment. On January 6, the movement south was accentuated, and penetration into Thessaly continued. It became clear that the arrival of the UN observers provoked this movement away from the frontiers. From January 7 through 10, two villages in Thessaly were attacked and provisionally occupied, nine in Macedonia and Thrace, and three bridges in Thessaly destroyed.

From the 11th to the 15th, two villages in Thessaly and four in Macedonia were occupied, and a fairly important

201

bridge was blown up. Everywhere the tactics were the same with this difference, that during the last attacks the guerrillas also carried off animals belonging to the villagers. From then on, this would happen regularly. The stolen animals were entrusted to villagers who lived in isolated areas to keep for the rebels. In return, the villagers received payment in kind. In this way, the guerrillas solved the important problem of the most perishable commodity, meat, so necessary for the army.

On the 17th, another tactic was initiated. In Thrace, near the Bulgarian border just before dawn, guerrillas in superior numbers simultaneously attacked the camps of two companies of the national army. The commanders, other officers, as well as many soldiers, were killed, and assorted plunder fell into the hands of the aggressors. As we can see, taking the enemy by surprise nearly always brought results. From that day until January 31, that is, for fourteen days, there were forty skirmishes between guerrilla bands and government forces. About half of these were caused by late pursuits of the army against rebels who had occupied various villages for a few hours.

The pace accelerated in February. There were attacks against more than 75 villages in the central and northern regions of the country. Hundreds of dead and wounded were counted and many villagers were taken prisoner or executed. Also, ten bridges and sections of railway lines were blown up, and two attacks were made on army troops camping near large villages.

Certain attacks differed from those of January. For instance, in the attack of February 12 on a village in Macedonia, near Ardea, the guerrillas set fire to 48 houses. They executed twelve men, six women, and two babies and seriously wounded twelve villagers. This village had not responded to the recruiting call and punishment was, for the first time, extremely severe. Such, also, was the daring attack against the little town of Sparta, in the south of the country on the 18th. Nearly all the guerrilla bands of the Peloponnesus had cooperated in this operation of short duration and limited purpose: to penetrate into the town and liberate all prisoners. Recruitment for this was easy. Another variation, finally, was a massive simultaneous attack on five large villages of Thessaly on February 9. All together, 600 guerrillas took part in this operation.

One can see that the leaders of the movement did not lack imagination. Tactics were not always the same; there were variations, and these were dangerous for the enemy.

But something else was even more dangerous and also a novelty: the mining of roads. The guerrillas began to utilize this in 1947. They blew up the means of transportaion on the main highways, whatever trucks or buses happened to be there. In those days the condition of the roads, full of holes, gravel or mud, prevented drivers from seeing the mines. Henceforth, this was one of the most effective weapons used by the DAG.

And the pattern repeated itself month after month. It repeated itself so regularly that, from now on, we shall only mention here the most important event. Nevertheless, the details mentioned for January and February 1947 reveal how much the life of the country had been affected. They reveal, too, how well Markos had organized his army, how he was able to coordinate military attacks so as to attain their objectives and, at the same time, be useful from a political point of view.

In those days (end of February 1947), Markos Vafiadis had about 13,000 fighting men under his command. The bands which, at first, were small and were referred to as "groups", now consisted of 70 to 100 men and had the more important name of "Military Formations". Every group henceforth had, in addition to its leader, a political commissar, or "captain".

Finally, toward March, what had seemed in the beginning only propaganda materialized; a General Headquarters was formed with Markos himself at the head of it. Seven commands came under him. Each was responsible for one of the following regions: Thrace, eastern Macedonia, Epirus, Thessaly, Roumeli and Peloponnesus. These commands had to execute the orders of General Headquarters, particularly those concerning military operations. But on their own initiative, they also had to organize intelligence and all the other services which the headquarters of large military units require.

The seat of the seven commands was not always fixed. Bases were transferred if operations demanded it, and then the commissariat took precautions to hide materiel well or even to transport it to a depot. This last case was rather rare, and even more rarely did the guerrillas lose their reserves of food and ammunition. Such was, however, the case of Kikitsas, one of the best subordinates of the "General". On February 9, after a sixteen-hour battle, Kikitsas left behind twenty dead, as well as important stores.

To make up for that, a permanent headquarters for Markos was decided upon at the northwest corner of the country, near the lake of Prespa on this side of the Greek-Albanian and Greek-Yugoslav borders. There the mountains of Grammos and Vitsi form a natural fortress with narrow, denuded passages surrounded on all sides by forests. The army had not ventured into this wild region which, in addition, was very near the supply bases on foreign soil. There Markos had his headquarters, though he himself was often elsewhere.

All this organization and the astonishing activity which derived from it are even more remarkable considering that the leadership of the KKE did not particularly favor a rapid development of DAG. The clandestine organization of the Party had not been put at the disposal of its army. For about a year, the leaders—especially Zachariadis—chose another tactic: organizing themselves in the mountains for restricted activity and for the future. For the time being, the struggle of the proletariat in the towns predominated. Intensified activity in the mountains could, in the form of reprisals, prove disastrous for the struggle in the towns.

If we believe what Markos Vafiadis maintained officially when, much later, he renounced the past (October 1957, letter to the Central Committee), then during 1946 and in the first months of 1947 the towns restricted the development of DAG.

In any case, with or without the support of the towns, the DAG—due above all, to the talents of its chief—could in a few months deploy an activity which convulsed the whole country. Of course, this did not happen without causing a serious military reaction. As a rule, after each raid the guerrillas were counterattacked by the army and, in order to avoid battle, were forced to flee. Very often they sustained losses which they could not conceal by carrying their dead with them, as they had been ordered to do. Finally, hundreds of the country's crucial points— towns, communication centers, etc.—were relatively well protected. In view of the circumstances, this was invaluable, but at the same time insufficient; the guerrillas were becoming stronger all the time. So the army now decided to strike a severe blow against the DAG. The Greek general staff was fully aware of the special conditions of the struggle and of its insufficient means. But it judged, nevertheless, that for the sake of the morale of the population and of the armed forces as well as for reasons of international policy, the army could not remain on the defensive.

However, before writing about this first general counter-offensive of the national army, which began on April 10, we must return to the beginning of the year to note other political and military events which influenced overall developments.

To Stem the Flood. The state in which the country found itself during the winter of 1946-47 could only create a very bad economic and financial situation. Even if administration had been ideal—and it was not—even if the rich and the profiteers had perfect morality—which they had not—the economic and financial picture would have been gloomy. In the autumn of 1946, when the guerrilla war was in full swing, it became evident that not even a minimum of economic stability could be attained by the play of the usual internal factors. And certainly nobody could speak of progress.

Since 1946, London, which furnished, in addition to the precious contribution of UNRRA, indispensable aid to this devastated country, had begun to inform Washington that it could not carry the Greek burden any longer because of its own difficulties. The American government had officially been informed besides, by the Greek prime minister and a group of politicians belonging to the opposition under the leadership of Sophocles Venizelos, of the insurmountable economic difficulties which menaced the country. Greece risked losing in the economic field that which it had struggled to save on the battlefield.

Meanwhile, the Americans and the British had indicated to the government of Athens, and to its parliamentary opposition, that a broader based government was necessary so that international public opinion would be convinced that it was not only the Right which governed.

In January 1947, a new government was formed. It kept many of the old faces of the preceding one (Tsaldaris in foreign affairs, Zervas in security) and it was presided over by a modest and respectable banker, Maximos. Also included: Venizelos, Papandreou and Canellopoulos who were the leaders of three small parties of the center, whose seventy members represented one-fifth of the parliament. Thus, at the beginning of the New Year, when the guerrilla war was revealed as extremely dangerous, the political conditions inside the country facilitated subsequent action by the United States.

Certain events may be considered as having caused the Truman Doctrine to take shape. But the decisive event, fundamentally and formally, was the step taken by the British ambassador in Washington on February 21. The State Department had already been officially informed that the British troops garrisoned in Greece would be reduced to one brigade, retained only for symbolic reasons, given the presence of Soviet troops in Bulgaria. On February 21, British warnings became persistent in two diplomatic dispatches that were handed to the American Secretary of State. In one, the British government recalled the similarity of views of the two governments on the need for preserving Greek independence. In the other was an account of the country's economic plight which stressed that it would be impossible for a solution to be found if the Greek government did not eliminate the guerrilla bands. During 1947, it stated, Greece would need aid amounting to from 240 to 280 million dollars in foreign exchange. The British government hoped that, after April 1, this economic and military assistance would be given by the United States.

These two dispatches and the messages exchanged on the same day between Secretary of State George Marshall and Ernest Bevin overcame an inertia which very probably only awaited such a moment. As one foreign writer observed, "this sudden spark started a train of action that within fifteen weeks laid the basis for a complete change in American foreign policy." The great protagonists of this change were Truman, Marshall, Under-Secretary of State Acheson, as well as the powerful Senator Arthur Vandenberg, formerly a fanatical isolationist and now a fervent internationalist.

After careful preparation by the State Department, and the Army and Navy, and after contacts with Congress where the Democrats were in the minority, President Truman was able to present to the people on March 11 the law which was named the Truman Doctrine. In explaining this law to the nation he declared that throughout the world two political systems are in conflict: one is based on the will of the majority and is distinguished by free institutions, and the other relies upon terror, oppression and the suppression of personal freedoms. "I believe," he affirmed, "that the United States must uphold the free people who are resisting attempted subjugation by armed minorities." (It was the end of 1947 and he spoke, of course, of the democratic Greece of those days.) Both the House of Representatives and the Senate passed this proposal by a large majority. The plan foresaw a first installment of 250 million dollars for Greece and 150 million for Turkey.

From an international point of view, the Truman Doctrine was of enormous importance; with it a true campaign to stop the Soviet Union was launched. This campaign was to be greatly enlarged a few months later with the inauguration of the Marshall Plan, through which a devastated Europe could be reconstructed in less than ten years. Nevertheless, these developments accentuated more than ever the division of Europe into two opposing blocs.

For the first time in history, the frontiers of national democracy were extended by the United States to encompass a horizon of world democracy. This extension was realized by practical means which made it even more effective. The Soviet Union, by definition enemy of democratic ideas, found this impossible to accept. Even less so as the Marshall Plan was greeted with enthusiasm by those countries where Russian domination was beginning to assert itself. Also, the negotiations that Molotov himself led with a view to accepting it naturally ended in an impasse. On July 2, there followed a fierce condemnation of the acceptance of the Marshall Plan which, according to Molotov, "would lead the countries of Europe to lose their national and economic independence". Before mid-July, by one method or another, the Plan was rejected by Albania, Bulgaria,

Finland, Hungary, Poland, Czechoslovakia and Yugoslavia. On October 5, the Cominform was created. Europe was divided in a decisive and dangerous manner. This division placed in relief the true basis of the struggle going on in Greece and persuaded every man of good faith that the excesses of the Right were not at all the cause of the local struggle.

It is obvious that the cause of the government was greatly served by the Truman Doctrine on the moral, political and financial levels. At the same time the situation was influenced by another favorable factor: the UN Commission of Observers. The Commission met for the first time in Athens on January 30, 1977, under the presidency of its general secretary, a Norwegian, Colonel Lount. It consisted of a representative for each member of the Security Council, that is, from Austria, Belgium, Brazil, China, Colombia, the United States, France, Great Britain, Poland, Syria, and the Soviet Union. This Commission of eleven members was in touch with four "liaison officers", representing Albania, Bulgaria, Yugoslavia, and Greece and often invited them to its meetings. Those who accompanied the liaison officers were sometimes more numerous than those who accompanied the members of the Commission. The Bulgarian delegation, for instance, numbered ten without counting its leader, who was Vice President of the Republic and of the National Assembly.

The first meetings were tumultous because the three Balkan representatives passionately maintained their slanderous attacks against Greece. Politicians and Greek resistance leaders were accused of having been agents of the Gestapo. The Greek "monarcho-fascists" were charged with imposing tyranny on "democratic citizens, defenders of the peace." All post war governments sustained by the British occupation forces were "fascist" and did not represent the Greek people.

This tactic provoked a reaction for which the three delegates had scarcely bargained; the facts were opposed to them and the Yugoslav representative, the most ardent of the three, was accused of doing everything possible to conceal the truth from the Commission. An effective lesson was also administered to them by old Soufoulis, the advocate of the "persecuted democratic citizens", who was the relentless adversary of the Right. It was a good lesson in democratic behavior and so is worth mentioning here:

"An on-the-spot inquiry by the Security Council," stated Soufoulis on February 8, *"is indispensable to learn if it is true that armed bands come from neighboring countries and to what extent this information is exact. The difference of opinion as to the way to face the armed rebellion falls within the province of internal politics, is a manifestation of the normal functioning of our democratic institutions and cannot justify any intervention, verbal or active, on the part of our neighbors."*

Finally, the Commission was able to get to work. It had difficult situations to surmount, especially when reliable testimony proved the existence of foreign intervention. But it was able to listen freely to representatives of the Left, active "captains" of DAG, and deserters, among whom were two or three "captains" of note. It was also able to examine war materiel and printed documents from Yugoslavia which had been found in the hands of guerrillas. Later, when its base was moved to Thessalonike, it could move freely near the frontier.

Both the authorities and the people strove to facilitate the inquest. This attitude went to the extreme, however, when on March 3, 1947, in Aghoriani (Thessaly) the Commission, after having a talk with four of the most famous "captains", attended a parade of DAG forces! In fact, that day, a company of guerrillas with two companies of cavalry marched past the Commission of the United Nations. All of the men were armed with rifles or machine-guns, wore uniforms, and had among them a number of very young recruits.

At the departure of the Commission from Aghoriani a guard of honor, consisting of 150 mounted men, accompanied them until the bend of the road. The scene was somewhat ridiculous but at the same time tragic.

In a period of two months the Commission had only one incident which, however, was made into an issue by the Soviet delegate to the Security Council: in a refugee camp, stones and insults were hurled at the envoys of Russia, Poland, Albania, Bulgaria and Yugoslavia, who were heading for the mountains to meet Markos.

The Commission finally departed from Greece and after brief stays in Albania, Bulgaria and Yugoslavia, met in Geneva where it submitted its report on May 23. The report was made up of two parts, the first dealing with recommendations, the second with conclusions. The first had been accepted by nine votes against two (Russia, Poland), the second by eight votes against two with France abstaining. Of the recommendations we must keep in mind the one that advised the setting up for two years an International Commission of Observers which would report to the Security Council every three months. (This was decided upon by the Security Council after long discussions.) Of the conclusions, we must particularly retain the positive attestation that "the three neighboring countries to the North, and especially Yugoslavia, trained the guerrillas, supplied them with arms and ammunition, offered them asylum and facilitated their passage across the frontiers". The Left, of course, contested the truth of these conclusions, but without result. International public opinion had been widely and responsibly enlightened.

To this factor, favorable to the somewhat shaken morale of non-communist Greece, something else important was added: nearly all of the Greek politicians took a common stand to protect the democratic principles of freedom and human dignity. Although nobody could speak yet of true solidarity. The Liberals, under the control of Soufoulis, led

211

an especially sharp, and sometimes venomous, opposition. But from this animosity issued the strong solidarity which, we have seen, showed itself in the gravest hours.

The same solidarity did not exist on the side of the Left. There, discipline was complete, because it could not be otherwise; under the surface however, dissension existed about which we know much more today.

Markos, the military leader—strong from the success of the DAG—had acquired an independence, not of form but of fact, which created discontent within the leadership of the KKE. This discontent was both personal and doctrinal. Zachariadis and those loyal to him, although they naturally supported the guerrillas, believed more in the orthodox social revolution of Lenin and Stalin, which emanates from the towns. They did not believe in the new kind of revolution, that of Mao Tse Tung, which proceeds from the rural areas towards the cities. Besides, Siantos—the respected "Old Man"—began to have doubts as to the outcome of the revolution itself, when it became evident that the United States was offering political and material aid to the enemy. The arguments he set forth, clearly and without passion, had an undisputed realism: America's entry into the picture made it almost impossible to gain power through arms. The Party could provide incidents but it could not conquer. So, something had to be done before American assistance arrived in Greece. The Party was legal, it enjoyed certain facilities, but all this would cease one day. There was still time for the Party to be saved by a good compromise negotiated from a position of power. This would make the political struggle a bit slower, but surer. This tactic must be studied.

But Zachariadis did not wish to hear any of these views. Some of his friends later attributed this revolutionary zeal to a combination of an inferiority complex—a result of circumstances—and a superiority complex—a result of his state of mind, which conditioned all his behavior. He was the chosen one of Moscow and of "his" people. Some considered him a kind of Messiah and that is how he imagined himself. Then, all the others had staged a revolution in December 1944. They had failed on their first attempt to get Greece into the large socialist family under the control of the respected leader, Stalin. Other comrades in other countries had fought and had succeeded. He himself, the Stalin of Greece, was the only one who had not taken part in a revolution. Now that it had actually begun, had met with its first success and was supported by three neighboring countries, now that he himself was its supreme leader, the revolution must continue and succeed. It would re-establish his good name. Certainly, this is not the first time that historical events were swayed by such psychological complexes. Nevertheless, the arguments of the "Old Man" were far from groundless and carried some weight.

When the U.N. Commission of Observers transferred its base to Thessalonike, Zachariadis went there too. It is certain today that after a few days he had long talks with the Soviet and Polish delegations, and with those of Albania, Bulgaria and Yugoslavia. His main idea was that, after the launching of the Truman Doctrine, the KKE must be supported quickly, morally as well as materially. The response was satisfying, but what is particularly interesting is what was said by the Russian, Graouer, and the Pole, Kraumvack, to the leader of the KKE.

The Commission had responded to the desire of Markos to appear before it and had sent a sub-commission, under Belgian Lieutenant-Colonel Delvoie, to the mountains. This sub-commission had followed in its itinerary the instructions transmitted to it by the headquarters of the DAG. But after wandering about for six days from one guerrilla band to another, it did not manage to overtake the "General". After this, it had decided by seven votes to two that it must return to Thessalonike. Only the two who had voted against returning to Thessalonike, that is, the Russian and the Pole, accompanied by liaison officers, remained in the mountains. Then, by chance, they met Markos at Chryssomilia (Golden Apple), a tiny village lost in a large forest, northwest of Meteora (Kalabaka).

Zachariadis conversed with Graouer and Kraumvack on March 23, the day after their return. They were both enthusiastic. They told him that they had been very much impressed by all that they had seen and that they believed that victory was quite probable. They promised to mention in their report that the DAG must receive unreserved support. They said that things seemed ripe for the Party to adopt the armed struggle officially and that the leadership of the Party must take a definite position. It must abandon the towns leaving behind only small groups which would make use, as much as possible, of the advantages of legality. Finally, they asserted some thing very important, although it is not known if they spoke in the names of their governments or, indeed, if they were carried away by enthusiasm. *If the DAG*, they said, *could dominate a small region and form a provisional government there, this government would be recognized immediately by all the socialist countries.* Then, commercial agreements could be signed with this government and the socialist countries would be able officially to offer all the material assistance needed.

Zachariadis also had a long personal talk with Lavritchev, the chief of the Soviet delegation in the Commission of Observers. This was not to discourage the KKE leader, nor to stifle his ambition, but rather to make him change tactics.

He did so explicitly before the Party's higher Thessalonike cadres, whom he had invited the same evening to the Hotel Astoria where he resided. Moreover, his freedom of action was greatly facilitated by two deaths which occurred at an opportune moment. On March 20,

Zevgos, the "Calm One" was assassinated in Thessalonike by a disaffected member of ELAS just returned from Bulkes. The KKE and EAM naturally attributed Zevgos's death to the "monarcho-fascists" and deplored his loss. His death influenced the Party for he was a serious man and was respected by all. Two months later on May 20, Siantos, under treatment for several days in the clinic of Professor Kokalis, also died. No one knew that he was even ill. Professor Kokalis, an eminent surgeon, had been a member of the government of the mountains in 1944. Seven months after Siantos' death, he became Minister of Social Welfare and Health in the "Free Democratic Government" under Markos Vafiadis. Zevgos and Siantos had been perhaps the two most respected leaders of the Party. Their sudden elimination left the path clear for the others. Moreover, KKE members were now in the presence of a new personality, Markos Vafiadis, who was becoming stronger all the time and was much talked about during this period.

The Flood Seeps Through The Dikes. All these events, favorable to the government cause, did not prevent the military situation from deteriorating. On the contrary, two events, the presence of the UN observers and the announcement of the Truman Doctrine, intensified guerrilla activities. March of 1947 was a terrible month. Not a day went by without blood running unchecked in all parts of the country. Without mentioning minor incidents (raids for food on small villages, incidents on the highways, destruction of bridges, etc.) between March 1 and April 10 there were 91 raids similar to those already described. The behavior of the guerrilla bands was much more cruel than before. Now they executed presidents of municipalities, if they were nationalists, as well as priests, civil servants, and distinguished civilians. They set private homes and state buildings on fire, including welfare institutions.

Sometimes the raids had a limited aim: For instance, the

215

blowing up of the central power plant of a town (Verroia) in Macedonia, or the destruction of important bridges or railway lines. The raids were sometimes led with such savagery that all the inhabitants of a group of villages, terrified, took refuge in a neighboring town. This was the case of some villages around Grevena, a small town in southwest Macedonia where, in March, all the priests of the region were executed. Such was the case of the large village of Velvendos: in the beginning of April, after seeing their schools, post office, gendarme station and forty houses (where six women were burnt alive) set afire, its inhabitants took refuge in nearby Kozani. A schoolmaster of the region described it: "to live in despair under the conditions of hell".

Now a new problem was added to the others, that of refugees. Some foreign writers believed that this situation had been created by the army; it wished, they said, to leave the guerrillas in the middle of a deserted country. That was only true later, in 1948. Those who saw things firsthand knew that at least for one year, the situation was scarcely thus. Villagers, on their own initiative, abandoned their homes because terror reigned there night and day.

With this flow of refugees, first in the northern provinces, and second in central Greece, the size of certain towns doubled or trebled. In March 1947, the number of refugees totalled approximately 400,000. This proved disadvantageous for the rebel bands; they lost their centers of supply and recruitment which were already insufficient. On the other hand, the refugees constituted an enormous problem for the government, which had to provide housing, food, and medical care for these people who carried with them only their despair. The miserably over-populated towns were almost always military bases, a fact which did not help the morale of the troops. In addition, the army was harassed. Due to the intensity of the guerrilla war, it had to be continually on the alert in order to pursue

216

the rebels, who usually struck quickly and then disappeared. Moreover, the army now had an additional reason to increase its efforts; the Truman Doctrine had been announced but it had not yet been put into effect. So, the army had to act in a way that would not discourage those who could potentially fill their ranks.

There was still another thing; since the beginning of February the fighting had become more deadly. For reasons of prestige abroad, or to strengthen their own morale, the guerrillas sometimes shifted from their "hit and run" tactic to one of resistance before giving ground. This happened even in certain cases where they were not superior in number. For instance, at the end of February, an offensive led by three rebel bands against the large village of Saint George of Phokis, in which was stored a considerable quantity of food, ended after a battle that lasted sixteen hours. Similarly, the pursuit into the Vardoussia mountains (Roumeli, end of March) of 1,300 guerrillas left about 200 dead. Among the military casualties resulting from this action was the M.P. Dedoussis, a former officer of Psaros, who had left Parliament and had enlisted as a volunteer. Finally, there was the fight in Lidoriki (Roumeli, beginning of April) where 103 dead guerrillas were counted.

These blood-lettings were perhaps easier to bear during the first three months of 1947. DAG volunteers were more numerous and DAG activity had increased during the winter. The impression that the State could not possibly take the lead was bearing fruit. In April 1947, the number of guerrillas exceeded 16,000. There were also some thousands of men in the auxiliary services, thousands of liaison, informers, and contributors to various secret funds, without speaking of thousands of men and women "sympathizers." Henceforth, it was a military and paramilitary power of some note.

In this period reaction against the persecutions of the

217

extreme Right enlarged the rebel bands in certain regions. These activities had never disappeared completely. Nevertheless, the public's disapproval of them, as well as governmental measures and accusations in Parliament, had restricted them tolerably. However, in the spring of 1947 they were revived with more intensity in the district of Sparta. In those days, the vendetta was still quite common in Greece. In Laconia and Crete, it was closely associated with the sense of honor of a man, or of his entire family. The Spartans were the most conservative Greeks and a majority always belonged, and still belong, to the nationalistic Right. These tendencies were accentuated, due to the fact that the rebel bands of the Peloponnesus were in the mountains of Lacedemonia most of the time and caused serious incidents. We have already mentioned the attack that ended in the liberation of those detained in a prison of Sparta. The Right reacted strongly, but this only made matters worse. In this atmosphere on the night of March 21, two respectable men, considered to belong to the leadership of the extreme Right, fell into an ambush outside Sparta and were killed. On the following night rightist groups entered the small town of Gythion, the port of Sparta, opened the prison and killed thirty detained communists. They also killed eight leftist citizens. On the 25th in a neighboring village, they killed fourteen, and on the 30th in another village farther away, nineteen more, all known for their leftist connections.

The government had proclaimed martial law from the 22nd, in the whole of Laconia, but members of the Right were enraged and continued their reprisals. They intended to reduce terror through the use of terror. They thought that they were crushing the enemy, but, in reality, they were playing his game. All of this resulted principally in facilitating recruitment of guerrillas and in exposing the government to harmful accusations. It was necessary, therefore, to dispatch troops against these extremists in the Peloponnesus and elsewhere, at a time when the army was already weak for the fight against the rebels. At the end of April many arrests were made and all the organizations of the Right were dissolved and declared illegal. Papandreou (Prime Minister in 1964), then Minister of the Interior, and Zervas, Minister of Security, were the protagonists in the application of these decisions that finally crushed the organizations of the extreme Right. They acted in time. The horizon, already dim, was to darken more and more, to become finally completely black. It was not to light up again before two years had passed.

Chapter IX

Freedom or Death

Operation "Terminus". Affairs had reached such a state that the only alternative was to fight, and each of the adversaries did so in a totally different manner. The strategic objective of the rebels was to make daily life for the others as difficult as possible in order to force them to beg for mercy. The strategic aim of the nationalists was to search out the enemy and crush him. That was much more difficult.

Nevertheless, the army's General Staff—for reasons previously mentioned—had to try to attain its objectives. At the very least, it had to strike a strong enough blow against its rival to decrease its aggressiveness. While preparing and evaluating this operation, headquarters formed the impression that the high morale of the troops and the fighting spirit of the officers would permit them to achieve significant results. Thus, plans were made first to encircle, and then to annihilate, a large part of the rebel forces. Certain disagreements as to tactics postponed putting the plan into action until mid-April. So, operation "Terminus", as it was known, officially began on April 5 with the shifting of some small national units—composed of soldiers, gendarmes and MAY. They were sent to occupy the most critical passes and bridges to the north, and especially to the south, of the main mountain chain traversing central Greece. After this was done, at dawn on April 9, all available airplanes were used to drop thousands of leaflets over the guerrilla positions. These tracts called on them to surrender and to take advantage of the amnesty that had been announced.

Then, three columns of strong reserve units rushed towards the mountains. They started from different points and converged on the same region, making at the same time various pincer movements of local importance. One of the columns started from the south (Lamia via Karpenissi, at an altitude of about 1,000 meters) and advanced northwards. The second column set out from Epirus, following the Acheloos River and its tributaries, and advanced eastwards. The third set out from the opposite direction, from Thessaly, and advanced towards the West.

These columns totalled 16,000 combatants and were supported by pack artillery, some mortars, and squadrons of airplanes—among which were Spitfires and C-47's— which would bomb or strafe the enemy.

The guerrillas were taken by surprise. Matters became worse for them on the third day when bad weather set in. A thick blanket of snow covered the mountains and the temperature fell below zero. They believed that the army, used to defensive tactics and pursuits which ended quickly, would not continue its offensive under weather conditions that made air force intervention impossible and operations generally difficult. That is why the rebel units did not disperse in time.

The offensive continued night and day, however,

without respite, even during a snowstorm. For a whole night the operations continued high in the mountains although the temperature was well below zero. Towards the end, they continued in spite of torrential rain. Engagements were numerous and bloody. The guerrilla bands always managed to escape, but almost always after having been obliged to give battle. This difficult pursuit lasted for eleven days.

Then, between the 20th and the 24th, by a swift large-scale maneuver, a large part of the fighting units successfully carried out similar operations in Khassia—a branch of the Pindos towards the southeast—and in Mount Olympus. Another part of the army, with less success, tried to encircle the enemy on Othrys, a mountain near Lamia.

On April 30, operation "Terminus" was stopped and the troops returned to barracks. They were exhausted with many hundreds sick, but they had not sustained heavy losses: 120 officers and soldiers killed or seriously wounded. In return, the army had inflicted heavy losses on the enemy: 647 dead of which 100 were found frozen, about 100 wounded and 412 prisoners. The guerrillas had certainly had many more wounded; when pursued in the middle of a snowstorm, troops do not easily carry away their dead, but more easily retrieve the wounded that can walk.

The blow had been severe. The weakening of certain DAG "commands" was considerable. The guerrillas' morale had been shaken: the figures and the accounts of the prisoners proved it. Nevertheless, the overall result of operation "Terminus" was not satisfactory; the majority of the guerrilla bands had escaped while the aim of the operation had been to encircle them. This was a fact and it had grave consequences. The influence it had on the army's morale which until then had been excellent, was debilitating. For the time being, nothing could be done:

the forces had been insufficient to the task.

According to a foreign military observer, "*if the cordon of troops had been better placed, if more troops had been used and more transport had been available, if operations had been followed rapidly by others of the same kind before the end of winter in the mountains, the hard core of General Markos's army would have been blown to bits and the rest would have been demoralized and dispersed. An opportunity had been lost.*"

This is true; but troops were insufficient. Besides, they could not all be utilized because Markos did not only have his men in the mountains of central Greece. They were everywhere with their fingers on the trigger. Actually, during the twenty days operation "Terminus" lasted, rebel raids continued almost everywhere. Some of these had rich populous villages as their targets. One of them (Mount Parnon in the Peloponnesus, April 23) completely wiped out a gendarmerie company of 93 men. There were also some attacks on large Aegean islands.

Crete, rather calm until then, was not spared. In those days, recruits of questionable loyalty were sent there. Then, at the end of April, more than fifty of them suddenly joined the small guerrilla groups in the mountains. An insignificant number, but enough to disrupt the calm of the island if the guerrillas wanted to and if they knew how to wage a guerrilla war. And, alas!, they knew how to do just that.

So, national army units had to operate throughout the country, even in the regions where they had just fought for twenty days and had barely had time to rest.

Some Lightning before two Thunderbolts. During the months of May and June, the same type of guerrilla activity continued in all parts of the country. Some attacks were unusually extensive. For instance, let us take the case of Florina. Isolated among high hills near the Yugoslav border, it suffered raids on the 19th, the 29th and 31st of May. The second and third times, more than 1,000 guerrillas made the assault and only bloody combat could repulse them. Among the dead guerrillas was a well-known captain, Tzoumerkiotis, whose true name was Constantine Maltezos, a former regular army officer.

On those same nights of the 29th and 30th, 400 guerrillas penetrated into the little village of Kilkis near the Yugoslav-Bulgarian frontier and were pushed back after a battle that ended at dawn. On June 25, there was a similar raid against a large village at the northeastern corner of Greece near the Bulgarian frontier. Attacks like these seemed to be, in some degree, a change of tactics. A more serious interpretation was given to them when the proceedings on June 25 at Strasbourg became known.

Zachariadis had left Greece immediately after his talks in Thessalonike with Party cadres and had visited Belgrade, Prague and Moscow. On June 25, escorted by a leading officer of the KKE, Porfyroghenis, he showed up at the annual conference of the French Communist Party in Strasbourg. At the meeting he was thunderously applauded when he announced that henceforth "all of the political, military and international conditions existed for the creation of a Free Government in Greece", and he demanded the support of all the Communist parties in order to win a final victory.

On the government side, it seemed that this official proclamation, made after a visit to the Eastern Bloc capitals, signified that Moscow now believed in a DAG victory, that authorization had been given to create a Free Government and, finally, that all this was imminent. This was hardly an unreasonable interpretation. Thus, every large-scale operation, if it took place in northern Greece, now assumed another meaning: the intent was to occupy an area where a "Free Government" would be established.

One of the first alerts was in mid-July. It was one of the most serious during this period for certain individuals in authority lost their heads. On the night of July 13, 1947, eight batallions of well-armed DAG units, each 450 men strong, crossed the Albanian frontier. They swept the key position at the Bourazani bridge, which we will note again later on, and then divided into two columns.

The one, with a thousand men or the strength of two batallions, attacked without success the little town of Konitsa near the frontier in the northwestern corner of Epirus (the 16th and 17th). The other, reinforced by rebel bands that had come down from the Pindos mountains, advanced towards Ioannina. The capital of Epirus, though the headquarters of a division, had no troops and the population became anxious. Worry increased when it became known that the division's auxiliary services had been ordered to leave the town and to burn what they could not take with them. The mere idea of a massive attack from Albania, aiming at the occupation of unprotected Epirus so as to establish a KKE government there, was more effective than anything the guerrillas could have done. Facts revealed that the whole idea was erroneous. Minister of Security Zervas hastened to Ioannina himself to boost morale; some officers were sent from Athens to take the situation in hand, as well as four battalions of the regular army to stop the guerrillas' advance.

The way was blocked at a point 22 kilometers from Ioannina, but it was evident that the guerrillas had not planned to attack the town. After an engagement which lasted several hours (the 17th) and which left on the field 107 dead and wounded guerrillas and some prisoners, all DAG forces disappeared into the Pindos mountains. The whole affair had merely concerned the transfer of newly-formed troops that would be used in another operation beyond the town and the rebels had profited from this transfer to frighten Epirus. Perhaps they also wanted to see what resistance would be met, or what they could achieve without too great a sacrifice.

The Greek government did not allow this action to pass

without placing the matter before the Security Council. It sent an urgent appeal during the invasion, and a few days later, it reported events in detail. Proof in hand, it accused Albania of violating Greek territory.

However, one cannot stop the march of resolved and armed men with mere pieces of paper, no matter how well they are written.

Meanwhile, the guerrillas who had vanished from Epirus were marching in another direction; they were crossing the Pindos mountains towards the East in order to attack the small town of Grevena (6,000 inhabitants and 8,000 refugees), a provincial capital located in a small isolated valley up in the mountains.

It is worth describing this operation in some detail because it was the only operation of the guerrilla war for which the plan of action fell into the hands of the army. Found on a captain (Katsonis) who was killed during the battle, it demonstrated that besides the "hit and run" tactic, DAG could plan large-scale operations very well. The plan, moreover, was signed by General Kikitsas, a former reserve of the regular army known for his activities as an ELAS captain. He was now Military Commandant for DAG in central Macedonia.

The conduct of the battle was confided to Captain Yannoulis, Brigadier of DAG and a lawyer by profession, considered one of its most capable captains. Designated as his command post was a small church on a hill three kilometers from the town. Eleven battalions were assigned to him, all commanded by famous captains. Each battalion had 400 fighting men and fifty that carried machine guns and mortars of various calibers. (Perhaps it should be noted here that machine-guns were then very rare among the regular forces, a fact that often placed them in a disadvantageous position. The guerrillas with their heavy machine-guns could fire against their enemy before the latter could return the fire—a tactical drawback which also influenced army morale.)

226

Five battalions were to occupy the positions set for them late on the night of July 24; these were well chosen positions on all the highways that linked Grevena with the rest of the country. There, the roads could be mined and, in certain cases, destroyed while the fire of the combatants would help to block the approach of reinforcements. Telephone and telegraph lines would be cut before midnight.

At 3:30 a.m. on the 25th, the five battalions would attack the town from all sides, while another battalion would take up a position somewhere on its outskirts. Any idea of withdrawal was excluded. In case of resistance being offered at the town's advance posts, it would be bypassed and each group would advance toward its clearly-defined objective. These were the following: command posts of the national guard and the gendarmerie, the prisons, the food stores and the State treasury, the banks, the post office, the high school and the pharmacies. All buildings defended by their adversaries must be destroyed. At 4:30 a.m. the reserve battalion would enter the town and assist where necessary in accomplishing this last task. All resistance had to be crushed before 6 a.m. so that the airplanes would find a completely occupied town and would be unable to spot the attackers.

The plan had certainly been well conceived and had anticipated the forces that would defend Grevena: 500 officers and men of the army, 100 gendarmes, and 50 MAY or country militia who had machine guns, some mortars and two light tanks.

So, the town garrison had only one-fourth of the assailants' strength—one-seventh if we also consider those forces used to cover them. Another disadvantage of the small garrison was its distance from other important garrisons in the towns of Trikkala and Kozani. However, it had a great advantage in having as its commander a competent officer, Lieutenant Colonel Costas Pantazis of the infantry, who had been successfully tested on the battle-fields of Asia Minor and Albania. Suspecting that something was being prepared, Pantazis took the necessary precautions. He even went so far as to conceal one of his best companies of 120 men outside of the town every night after curfew.

The commander had been warned of the impending attack half an hour before it began, so the precious element of surprise was lacking. At each entrance to the town the rebels were caught in a crossfire coming from men barricaded in the houses. Only one breach opened up after an hour of fighting, but was quickly closed by reserves that hastened to the spot. Then, at 5:00 a.m. two companies of defenders came out of the town and, surprisingly, launched an attack from the flank against a battalion of guerrillas (some 850 men) who, finding themselves uncovered, withdrew in disorder leaving behind 87 dead and 47 wounded. Only then did the commander of the Grevena garrison manage to contact his division, based in Trikkala about eighty kilometers away by wireless. He reported what had happened and announced that he was starting a general counterattack. At an agreed-upon signal all the defenders emerged from their hiding places around 5:20 a.m.; the company concealed under an old bridge and the reserves of the command post, with their lieutenant-colonel leading them, took up the chase.

Now surprise played a role in favor of the defenders. At 6:00 a.m. two more DAG battalions hastily withdrew from the battle. Soon after the guerrillas were strafed by planes taking off from Larissa.

By ten o'clock all combat had ceased and the guerrillas withdrew towards the mountains. Though unfortunate in their offensive, they were fortunate in their retreat: as soon as they began withdrawing, the sky clouded up and air force intervention could not continue. Besides this, in the afternoon an intermittent, but heavy, rain began which lasted for a week. Thus, the reinforcements which arrived from various directions could not make contact with the assailants.

DAG left behind on the outskirts of the town 197 dead, among which were one captain, three company commanders and eight plattoon commanders. It also left about 200 seriously wounded men, 300 prisoners, 65 automatic guns and 150 rifles. The losses of the garrison are not known although the official count (12 dead and 22 wounded) seems quite unlikely. This had been a hard lesson for the DAG.

Today, it is known that the morale of the entire organization was shaken, that the commanders of the battalions were severely criticized and that punishments were imposed. It is also known that the Yugoslavs, who had been assured that the town would be conquered, criticized the tactics used and "expressed some doubt as to the possibility of the establishment of a Free Government in Greece".

But, the DAG was not discouraged by that. It continued its attacks without respite against isolated villages and, in some cases, undertook operations much larger in scope.

During the night of July 30, simultaneous raids were made on five large villages in Thrace. On the next night, the guerrillas attacked Alexandroupolis probably intending only to cause fear. On August 6, the rebels occupied Arachova near the archaeological site of Delphi on the side of Mt. Parnassos for one night. During the night of August 18, supported by a "fifth column", DAG attacked in force the industrial town of Naoussa, in Western Macedonia. On the 25th, it was the turn of the little Macedonian town of Nigrita, which had suffered a strong attack on July 21. In all these cases, as well as in many others of minor importance, the behavior of DAG forces was harder and more cruel than previously: they executed more leading citizens, they did not spare the women, and they set fire to many public and private buildings.

The repulse of the enemy at Grevena had not paid for the government. On the contrary, guerrilla warfare was intensified. The nationalists did not know then that it had not even discouraged them from carrying out more important operations and that two major battles would take place before the end of the year.

General Situation before the Squall. The fact that the army did its duty and that its morale remained good did not improve matters.

The uneasiness of the people—or rather, their anxiety—increased. And their suffering also. Under these conditions it was difficult to govern the country. In addition to the numerous attacks aimed at the government may be added another criticism which came, primarily, from abroad and was aimed at Zervas. In July, more than 3,000 persons had been arrested in Athens, Thessalonike and three other towns, among whom were many former leaders of EAM. Zervas maintained that the clandestine mechanism of the KKE would be reactivated after Zachariades' appeal from Strasbourg, and that this must be avoided at all costs. Abroad, even in friendly countries, he was accused of being a fascist because he had exiled 20,000 persons to the islands, and made other arrests by the thousands. These allegations were exaggerated, but insistent.

Discouraged, Maximos resigned towards the end of August; this was the end of the Center-Right coalition. The Populists immediately formed a government by themselves, but no one had any illusions; while the country was burning, a serious political crisis was breaking. It was then that Constantine Tsaldaris knew "his finest hour".

He controlled an absolute majority in Parliament and he had had some very important successes (the Truman Doctrine, the U.N. Commission). He had suffered no spectacular defeats, so he could now be obstinate and

230

remain in power, especially as Sofoulis had put up an extremely tough and sometimes unjust opposition. The Right now called the grand old man an "Eamobulgar".[1]

Then, at the first sign by King Paul to Tsaldaris—George had died on April 1—the latter offered the Presidency of the Council to Sofoulis, who controlled only 46 out of the 354 seats in Parliament.

Sofoulis accepted; Tsaldaris became his vice-president and also retained the Ministry of Foreign Affairs. Some members of the old populist team—13 ministers out of 24 —retained their portfolios, but new blood changed the aspect and the effectiveness of the government which was formed. The most profound change—besides that of the prime minister—took place in the ministries of Public Order and Justice, which went to two notorious "Eamobulgars", Rentis and Ladas.

Part of the Center—the group including Venizelos, Papandreou and Canellopoulos—and of the extreme right —Zervas—did not participate in this government, but the structure of it was such that one could already speak of a kind of Grand Alliance, as it included members of both the right and the left wings of the center party. It could now maintain to the people and abroad that a clear majority, representing all sides, had united to fight against a small minority that wished to gain power "by fire and axe".

This was what was best for morale inside the country. It was also good for the West and the United States, where often a spiritual donquixotism supported, in the name of Democracy, those who wished to abolish democratic principles, even at the cost of death and destruction.

Sofoulis's government was sworn in on September 8, 1947. It had to treat, among many others, a delicate and important question which must be mentioned here in a few words. The lack of results in the military sphere, certain animosities between high-ranking officers, leftovers of previous manifestos or rebellions in the Middle East and

231

still other reasons created an unstable situation in the top echelons of the army. The unwarranted interference by the British and American missions, instead of helping, only complicated matters. The chiefs of the two missions were members without a vote—but their opinion certainly carried weight—of the various military councils, even of those which decided upon promotions and appointments.

None of the military chiefs managed to assert his authority over the others. What was worse, there was rivalry between them. The only one who could have imposed his will—even on the allied generals—Alexander Papagos, did not accept to reassume the post of commander-in-chief. He had set conditions that concerned, among others, the size and structure of the army; but these conditions could not be satisfied. Thus, while discipline in the entire army was excellent, cohesion among its leaders was not always the best. This was a problem which had varied and dangerous consequences.

The Sofoulis government, for diverse reasons that are not within the scope of this book, was not always particularly happy with its interventions in the top echelons of the army; but, at least, these interventions were made by a government of a very wide coalition. This was the great power of the Sofoulis government. It represented the nation.

The KKE was not impressed by that. It is true that there were some gestures of reconciliation. The most important one came about in a particularly strange way: *The London Times* of September 10, 1947 published extracts from a letter that Markos addressed to that newspaper, declaring that he believed in parliamentary democracy and the inviolability of frontiers. He asked for a general reconciliation mentioning at the same time various conditions. He suggested further a cease-fire, the forming of a government that would include EAM and also requested that DAG's position be presented to the United Nations. At the same time, EAM—stressing that it had nothing to do with DAG—sent a note proposing negotiations for an agreement, under the condition that ample measures would be taken for clemency and that the MAY, referred to as "bandits of the Right", would be disarmed.

Sofoulis would listen to none of this and defined his position very clearly: it was not possible for negotiations to take place between a government based on a popular majority and a minority that intended to seize power by fire and blood. He noted that all of Markos's demands, and much more, had been included in the program the new government had announced. This program had pledged the government to invite U.N. observers as soon as peace was restored, to observe the application of "measures of reconciliation". Consequently, the Sofoulis government refused any talks with the guerrillas.

Sofoulis agreed only to prolong for two more months the amnesty which had just ended and which concerned anyone who wished to abandon the guerrilla war or illegality. As the old politician of the center-left inspired wide respect, many people believed then that the amnesty would bring results. Almost nothing came of it, however.

The KKE for its part adopted a much harder line which was revealed on October 8 by two texts published in the official newspaper of the Party, *Rizospastis*. One text announced certain decisions of the Third Plenum of the Central Committee assembled in Athens between September 12 and 15; the KKE which, until then, had not officially recognized its link with DAG, now began supporting its armed fight unreservedly. The second was an article by Zachariadis, which had been sent from abroad where he still resided. It was published in *Rizospastis* on October 8, 1947, under the title, "For Home and Hearth". In this article Zachariadis called on the faithful to support the armed struggle, stressing that "our struggle for home and hearth is a struggle for Greece and for the people so it cannot but triumph".

Under these conditions, legality for the Party was no longer conceivable. Between October 15 and the end of the year a series of government measures excluded the KKE from the Greek political scene. Its newspapers were not allowed to circulate, its offices were shut down; all officers found were arrested and the Party was declared illegal. Banished by the overwhelming majority represented by the government of the "Eamobulgarian", the Party went underground and reappeared in the mountains. This time it was war to the bitter end. It was not known then that the war would change somewhat in form and it is not known yet today why it happened. Perhaps we should look at the involvement of foreign military more closely.

Actually, the agreements signed by Markos in 1946 were renegotiated in Bled during the summer of 1947 between himself and representatives of the Albanian and Yugoslav General Staffs. Some Soviet officers were also present at these negotiations. The aid given to the Greek rebels, it was decided, would be increased, and in addition, they would receive more effective military equipment (artillery of all types, trucks, wireless stations, etc.) in order to improve training conditions. They also agreed that more allied troops be stationed near the frontiers in case DAG was encircled or pursued outside Greek territory.

In exchange, the Greek Communists placed themselves, in a way, under the protection of the Yugoslavs, for the latter would have control over the Greeks' army. In fact, a Joint Balkan Headquarters was created and the DAG came under it to such an extent that high-ranking officers could not receive a new assignment without the consent of the joint command. Obviously, such interference, especially by the Yugoslavs who dominated the command, caused some clashes with Markos. The latter did not always agree

234

with the tactics, or even the plans, of his Balkan protectors, who were headed by a Yugoslav general named Popovic.[2] Little is known of these disagreements. Nevertheless, it seems certain that Markos did not give in easily, but that—especially in the beginning—he was obliged to yield on important questions. Moreover, as we shall see further along, he often disagreed with Zachariadis and other leaders of the KKE on military matters. At any rate, whatever the reasons were, toward the end of 1947 the DAG, without abandoning its former tactics, adopted a new one that will be described in the following pages.

From the government's point of view, after the decisions of the Third Plenum of KKE's Central Committee, new developments were expected; but no one believed that serious incidents were imminent. The conclusions of a large meeting of the military leadership, which took place in Volos under the presidency of King Paul with the participation of foreign military missions, are extremely interesting in this connection. Here are these conclusions: the rebel bands still had the initiative. The tactics they followed were very profitable for them so they had no reason to change them. Winter would reduce their great mobility, however. Undoubtedly, they needed an area in which to establish their "government" but they should know that this territory could not be defended. Being easier to defend, the mountain range of Grammos and Vitsi was beginning to be fortified by DAG, but had only very small villages whose miniscule size made them unsuitable for a seat of government. Consequently, the great danger continued to be guerrilla warfare as it had been carried out until then. The government must take advantage of the relative calm of winter to increase the total strength of the army in order for it to take the offensive in the spring.

This is what was decided. The army's effective strength of 92,000 would be increased to 132,000 which would enable it to carry on a more active pursuit of rebel bands. The auxiliary forces (national guard and MAY) would be considerably reinforced and would play a larger role in the protection of population centers. Finally, General Ventiris, a good organizer and an aggressive soldier, would take over immediately the leadership of all troops in the northern districts.

The First Battle. This conference took place between the 16th and the 20th of October 1947. However, in order for these decisions to be put into practice, the weapons offered by the United States had to arrive in Greece. This could not happen very soon. Besides, forecasts as to the relative calm of the winter months were incorrect.

Actually, during the Volos summit meeting, curious information reached the Greek General Staff. In the Pindos—that large mountain range that divides Greece into two parts from north to south—frequent movements of guerrilla bands were observed. Many of these forces escorted to the Pindos the families of guerrillas who then proceeded northward on foot or on muleback. This march by a number of such groups had started in the first days of October.

On the government side, it was believed that this could mean but one thing: the abduction of children had already taken place to a limited degree. On the other hand, many families of guerrillas continued to live in the villages of central Greece. However, this was bad for the fighters' morale because this area was exposed to attack by the army. So the DAG wanted to safeguard these families, as well as the abducted children, and the most suitable places for this purpose were Albania and the northwest refuges which could be easily supplied. That must be the explanation of the tragic procession and the security measures that were taken.

This was the truth, but there was something else too. During the fascist offensive of 1940, the Italian field

236

marshal , through a daring advance of alpinists, tried to occupy the national road—the sole route crossing the Pindos mountains through the narrow passes of Metsovo. Thus, he would have isolated Epirus. That is exactly what the DAG wished to do in October 1947. The precious road was not guarded on the eastern slopes for a distance of fifty kilometers because the terrain there is more accessible; so, if the need arose, it could be easily defended by strong garrisons located in Thessaly. The route was well guarded on the western slopes on its most dangerous sector beyond a hill 1,700 meters high which crowns the deep ravines. There, a brigade of 1,300 men was stationed, reinforced with mortars, four pieces of artillery, and two light tanks. Cannons, tanks, and an entire battalion protected a large bridge on the western end of this dangerous part of the road.

Infantry battalion No. 584, the army's strongest, occupied the wooded slopes of Karakoli, whose summit reaches to 1,500 meters and below which, at an altitude of 1,050 to 1,280 meters, lies the town of Metsovo; it is separated by a deep gully from the village of Anilio (meaning *without sun*), surrounded by forests, and is an important pass and road junction.

The commander of the brigade (Colonel Dovas who, twenty years later, in December 1967, organized the unsuccessful military coup of King Constantine) had set up his command post at the mid-point of the dangerous sector. A third battalion under his command was deployed in the surrounding hills. Colonel Dovas had realized that an extensive operation was being prepared against him and had insisted that reinforcements be dispatched. An entire battalion was sent on from Larissa by truck—a luxurious means of transport for the Greek army in 1947. A regular battalion in those days had a strength of 700 men, if newly formed or reorganized, and 350 to 450 if they had been tried. That battalion consisted of about 500 men and, in the afternoon of October 18, it took up a position around Dovas's command post. They had arrived just in time. At 22:00 hours on the 18th, in the silence and darkness of a rainy night, all the positions of the brigade were strongly assaulted. Two other extensive operations supported this local offensive. One had as its objective to mine, sabotage, and occupy the routes that government reinforcements must follow. The other had as its objective to draw the garrisons elsewhere, especially the strongest one in Thessaly, by minor or major raids in the nearby regions. These raids were numerous and sometimes extensive.

From about midnight, it had become evident that Dovas's brigade was facing much stronger forces. Later, it was learned that 5,000 guerrillas made the assault, that 3,000 guarded the passes, and well over 1,000 carried out smaller diversionary attacks.

The offensive lasted, with brief intervals, for nine days and nights, from the 19th to the 27th of October. Its main characteristics were the following: the strongest attack took place at dawn of the 19th with a force of three battalions and two companies against the positions of Battalion 584. The battle raged unremittingly for ten hours, slackening slightly in the afternoon, without the assailants being able to overrun the positions of the defenders who fought resolutely and bravely. During the battle another battalion of the DAG, under cover of fog, went around Battalion 584 from the east and occupied the village of Anilion, to the southwest of Metsovo. From there, the guerrillas advanced towards the lower part of Metsovo, which was unguarded, and thus occupied about half of the town without difficulty.

On the night of the 19th to the 20th, the attacks were repeated with greater force against the positions of Battalion 584 on the hills of Karakoli and Tsouma, with mortar, machine guns, field guns and hand grenades. The battle was fierce and lasted for five hours. However, in the early morning hours the attackers were forced to withdraw.

Typical of the high morale and determination of the surrounded battalion, which knew it was defending positions of great importance, was the message sent by its commander to the Eighth Division headquarters on the 20th of July: "Our men and I will fall till the last man, but Metsovo will not become Markos's capital."

On the night of the 20th to the 21st, the poignant column of guerrilla families coming from the south passed through the broken line of the brigade and the rebel bands that were with it joined the attackers. So, from the 21st on, pressure became stronger. A battalion of the brigade which included leftist elements, as was learned later, abandoned its positions twice and retreated in disorder. It was saved and a dangerous breach avoided due to counter-attacks by neighboring companies and redeployed on stronger positions.

At Karakoli, the besieged found themselves in an extremely critical situation as ammunition and food were almost exhausted and they were under continuous and very strong pressure. Clearing weather permitted the planes to drop supplies on the 23rd and 24th, although many of the drops fell into the hands of the assailants, owing to the mountainous terrain. However, through an intelligent maneuver and daring attack, Dovas succeeded in liberating the dense forests to the north of Karakoli. This enabled men on foot or on mules to bring reinforcements to the defenders.

The town of Metsovo had been taken and evacuated twice, being struck from Anilion and attacked from lower and higher ground. The inhabitants, who initially had helped the battalion, had seen their homes pillaged, their schools set afire and their mayor (Vasilios Zaoussis) commit suicide at the moment of his arrest. They had hidden in basements or fled to the heights held by the battalion

239

where they lived in the forest or among the brush, often in the rain. The army had to assist them, which certainly did not help their defense.

The nine-day ordeal was a series of attacks and counter-attacks which usually took place during the night; several actions were launched, from both sides, by almost impassable routes. During the day there was often a heavy exchange of fire. Such was, in general, the way the battle went until evening of the ninth day. On the next day, the 28th, pressure diminished. Several difficulties, among others a very dense fog covering the eastern slopes of the mountain range for forty-eight hours, had delayed the advance of reinforcements which converged from Epirus (West) and especially from Thessaly (East). But on the 28th, supported by pack artillery and mortars, these troops made a strong attack against DAG forces defending the approaches to Metsovo. Tenacious at the beginning, the resistance of the guerrillas slackened toward evening and, on the next day, turned into a rearguard action. The rebels hastened to withdraw. On the 30th of October, the anniversary of the region's liberation from the Turks in 1912, the last shots were fired. Markos's men retired, pursued but without stopping to engage in any serious fighting, and disappeared beyond the frontiers for a rest.

The resistance of the Dovas brigade, particularly that of the battalion assigned to the key position of Karakoli, was of great importance. If it had yielded, the general situation would have been gravely imperiled. The narrow valley of Metsovo—let us rather call it a wide ravine—is surrounded by steep crests or ridges having an elevation of over 1,600 meters, with their summits reaching 2,300 meters. The ground is now very steep, now densely wooded with an early, heavy winter—ideal conditions for the defenders. If the guerrilla forces attacking Dovas's brigade could have ended their operation successfully in two or three days, they then would have been free to join forces with those defending the approaches to the valley, thus making its recapture extremely difficult. Now, if the valley, with winter assisting, had remained in the hands of the guerrillas, the KKE would have had the territory it needed in which to establish a provisional government for some months. Thus, they would have accomplished much more than to cut the main route to Epirus. Disappointment within DAG went deep. As was revealed later from the monthly magazine, *Democratic Army of Greece* (April 1948 issue), the battalion commanders were accused of "lacking imagination and initiative". "For this reason", the critics wrote, "they could not meet the requirements of combat".

The DAG had lost the first real battle of the guerrilla war. The first as seen by the importance of its objectives, its duration, and the number of men who had participated. Including the fighting for the passes, it had lasted altogether twelve days. The total number of men who had taken part were: in the main theater of operations, 7,000 at the beginning, and 8,500 to 9,000 after the second day; on the periphery, towards the end, more than 15,000 without counting those who, elsewhere, made or repulsed diversionary raids.

The regular army had every reason to be satisfied, especially as morale again had proved to be excellent, and under particularly difficult conditions. The slogan, "Freedom or Death", had perhaps a touch of despair, but it had, above all, the flame of conviction and of stubborness that derives from it.

The Second Battle. Before describing the second and most important battle, which took place two months later, we must note a fact which touches on the first one. This is necessary because this fact is very probably closely linked with the launching by the DAG of the two battles which were, to say the least, approved of by the United Balkan General Staff.

After secret meetings and conferences for over a year,

241

and in spite of the hesitation of some Communist parties, Stalin managed to resurrect the Comintern. He had dissolved it in 1943 in order to calm the suspicions of his allies in those days, and he reconstituted it now as an answer to the grouping of states that was created automatically by the beneficiaries of the Marshall Plan.

This reappearance in the beginning was modest: "Common information office" of the nine Communist party founders, or "Cominform"; its name differed only slightly from Comintern. The date of birth was October 5, 1947; its sponsors were Russians, Yugoslavs, Poles, Romanians, Hungarians, Czechoslovaks, Bulgarians, French and Italians.

Other Communist parties were not invited to take part, neither in the difficult preparatory, or the final phase. And this applied to both the Chinese and the Greek Communists who, though neighbors of many of the sponsors, were at that time generously shedding their blood for the common cause. On the other hand, a dominant role was given to the Communist Party of Yugoslavia, a fact which for various reasons caused the hostility of certain brother Communists, but especially of the Communist Parties of France and Italy. The crowning favor, on formal instructions from Stalin, Belgrade became the seat of the Cominform.

Today, one can realize—as Andre Fontaine[3] so brilliantly explained—that "Moscow had urged the Yugoslavs to be the leaders in order to isolate them from the rest of the movement and to make the others hate them". In those days, this was not yet understood. On the contrary, many saw in this distinction a sign of confidence and favor. Nevertheless, it seems certain that the Yugoslavs, sensitive and experienced in Stalinist tactics, did not take long to realize the true intentions of the master of the Kremlin. Besides, Tito and his comrades had already picked up various minor indications that had aroused their suspicions.

242

Unfortunately, as long as the Yugoslav authorities maintain their official attitude from years past, according to which their country did not directly intervene in the Greek guerrilla war, we will not know how the development of the Moscow-Belgrade relationship influenced what was happening in Greece.

In any case, the change in military tactics and—as we shall see—certain political directives of the KKE coincided with the first difficulties in Tito's relations with Moscow. It now seems very probable that Tito tried, through the United Balkan General Staff, to give the Greek matter a decisive turn in order to feel more secure on his southern flank; this is most probably the reason behind the first two battles of the Greek guerrilla war.

Be that as it may, guerrilla activity was in full swing throughout Greece and kept the country in constant upheaval. But now this war took another form. The first large-scale battle at Metsovo was not the only indication. By mid-November, the rebel forces of the Epirus Command, numbering 5 to 6,000, were spread along the Pindos range in an area which extended from the passes of Metsovo to the foothills south of Grammos. It was expected that they would remain there for the winter and continue raiding in one direction or another. Towards the end of November, it became evident that they had other intentions. In the first place, they were reinforced suddenly by around 1,000 fighters from other commands and by 2,500 Slav-speakers of the Macedonian Command under Ypsilantis.[4] Then, under cover of a thick fog, all these forces left the chain of high mountains and, in two wide columns, descended into Epirus between Ioannina and the Albanian border.

As the guerrillas advanced, small army garrisons—each with one or two companies—withdrew to Ioannina, seat of the Eighth Division. Markos's rebel forces easily took Kalpaki, as well as other naturally strong positions. Their objective seemed to be to cut Epirus in half—not from north to south this time, but from east to west.

However, tis sizeable force advanced much more to the west toward the region formed between the frontier, the Adriatic, and the route linking Ioannina to Igoumenitsa, opposite Corfu. Here the rebels established themselves, but mainly on Mourghana—a wild, very long, and arid mountain that extends lengthwise over the Greek-Albanian frontier. Being very sparsely populated, this region was not suitable for worthwhile guerrilla operations. Besides Mourghana, forming as it does a kind of bridge to Greece's northern neighbor, is strewn with small, poor villages, completely inadequate for so many men to spend the winter.

All indications now led to the prediction that the DAG was preparing itself for a winter campaign from Albania via Mourghana, in order to threaten all of Epirus, even Ioannina itself, and to set up a Provisional Government somewhere. Besides, the Greek General Staff had good information that the three neighbors to the north—according to other sources, only Tito—had become impatient and were pressing for a Communist government to be established as soon as possible.

The threat seemed serious enough and the Eighth Division had to be ready to act in time. This division was made up of five brigades, each one with a strength of 1,700 to 2,000 men. Two brigades covered the road to Metsovo along its entire length. Another—that of Dovas —reinforced by the 582nd Battalion, was at Konitsa, a small village near the Albanian border in the northwest corner of Epirus. Two others guarded positions of strategic importance or formed the reserves of the division. Six of the ten battalions of these last two brigades, reinforced by some groups of gendarmes, were sent west in the middle of December, and above all, against Mourghana. But that is exactly how Markos had wanted his enemy to react. On the 24th of December, Porfyroghenis, Zachariadis's comrade in Strasbourg, spoke from the DAG radio station, located then in Albania. He announced the great news: a Provisional Democratic Government of Free Greece had been formed under the presidency of Markos Vafiadis, who was also Minister of Defense. Six members of the Central Committee of the KKE took the other portfolios (Vice-president, Foreign Affairs, Justice, Agriculture, Finance, National Economy). The distinguished surgeon, Professor Kokkalis, Siantos's last doctor, became Minister of Health, Education and Social Welfare. He was the only one who did not belong to the Central Committee because he was not even a Party member.

According to the proclamation, the principal aim of the Provisional Democratic Government was "to mobilize all the popular forces in order: a) to liberate the country promptly from the yoke of foreign imperialists and their local lackeys; b) to assure national sovereignty; c) to defend national integrity from all foreign imperialistic claims; d) to assure the victory of Democracy, recognizing complete equality for all national minorities and their right of free national development; e) to create a strong people's army, navy and air force belonging to a strong Greece, able to defend its national sovereignty, its independence and integrity against all foreign imperialistic claims, in close brotherly cooperation with all friendly neighboring countries".

In the same manifesto the Provisional Government promised the nationalization of heavy industry and of all foreign property in Greece, agricultural reforms, the reconciliation of Greeks, and friendly relations with all democratic countries.

All the players and the plan were there. Only the chessboard was missing.

As to the chessboard, the Greek government correctly

thought of Epirus, but it had given the DAG more credit than it sought. Although the Greek army imagined that Ioannina was the target, DAG had limited itself to Konitsa, a town with only 5,000 inhabitants, which, however, had the advantage of being near the Albanian frontier.

Konitsa, lying on a slight slope, is fenced in on the east and the south by very wild mountains. To the north, almost at the outskirts of the town, a long rocky hill separates it fron the brush country which, after a few kilometers, continues into Albania. To the west, at the bottom of the slope and near the last houses, stretches the small plain of Aoos (Voyoussa), a river that crosses Albania and empties into the Adriatic near Valona.

From this direction, against which there is no natural protection, Markos's men launched their surprise attack. It took place before dawn on Christmas Day, just three hours after midnight mass.

The guerrillas managed to advance unnoticed to within a few hundred meters of the first houses, but the guards sounded the alarm in time and well-directed fire coming from most of the houses prevented the rebel forces from penetrating into the narrow streets.

The element of surprise lost, tactics changed immediately. The offensive became general; an impressive number of mortars of all calibers began to hit the town and for the first time, well-directed artillery fell upon the defender's strong points.

In the plain towards the west, two strong companies reinforced by gendarmes and MAY, who under a capable commander, Captain Theodoros Vitos, guarded the Bourazani bridge, a key point for communications with Albania, had no time to defend themselves. They were annihilated by a concentrated fire of all types which lasted two hours. Not a single officer escaped, but a fair number of men managed to make it to the surrounding hills.

To the north of the town, a company of Battalion 582,

246

which was near the border, was forced to withdraw in haste. A second company of the same battalion a little further back, was obliged to follow it after a minor engagement. They were faced, keeping all proportions in mind, with a flood of guerrillas.

All other points were putting up an effective resistance, but pressure was very strong. The encirclement was so tight and the perimeter of the besieged positions was henceforth so reduced, that if a breach opened up, all could end in an hour or two. Then, to crown their difficulties, towards noon, Dovas, who was going around by jeep to inspect the most threatened positions, hit a mine and was seriously wounded.

No one could doubt that this was a large-scale offensive, well-directed, and led by strong detachments which fought bravely.

Later on, it became known that the battle was directed by Markos himself, with his headquarters at Kastaniani, some twenty kilometers to the northeast of Konitsa.

The plan of action had many points in common with the battle of Metsovo, including that of misleading the enemy. By a sudden turnabout of his forces from Mourghana and with other guerrillas rushed in from elsewhere, Markos had occupied the area around Konitsa in depth, especially to the south for about forty kilometers towards Ioannina. All strategic points in the area were occupied by strong forces with Kalpaki as pivot of the barrage. More than 10,000 fighters were blocking the routes leading to the scene of battle. For this encounter Markos had chosen two of his best and strongest brigades—the 16th and the 32nd—totalling 7,000 men. He had also used two companies of saboteurs, two batteries of 75 and 105 mm. pack artillery, a large number of mortars and, for the first time, anti-aircraft guns.

After a respite on the evening of the 25th, the desperate battle resumed with fierce fighting, broken only by short intervals, continuing until the morning of the 31st. On the whole, it seemed indecisive, the defenders ceding ground at several points.

Towards the plain, a bold thrust by the guerrillas allowed them to occupy the lower section of the town, which the defenders were unable to reoccupy. Nevertheless, they managed to check the rebel advance with a line of defense improvised in the labyrinth of narrow, winding streets.

To the north, battalions 582 (except for the companies at the Bourazani Bridge) and 584, under the defender of Metsovo, Lieutenant Colonel G. Palantas, pulled back slightly, shortening their lines, and so covered the town and its outskirts by holding the whole of the long rocky hill of Profitis Elias. This was the last rampart of the town; if it fell, further defense would become impossible. The defenders of the hill put up a fierce resistance, conscious of their mission. Their commander,[5] Major Peridis—one of the best EDES captains during the German occupation —was there to remind them of the importance of the struggle.

Perhaps it would be interesting for the reader to know that, exactly twenty years later in December 1967, Dovas organized the royal coup and Peridis was its main protagonist, being then commander of the strong Third Army Corps that defended Thrace and Eastern Macedonia. The two men had collaborated for a long time, but their star was not as lucky after twenty years.

In December 1947, in spite of the unbelievable pressure on this bloody Christmas, the star of Konitsa still shone, only its light was often unsteady. Nobody could really say if the besieged town would continue to resist until reinforcements arrived. The garrison, however, did not fight on alone for the inhabitants of the town—men, women and children—were at its side, either with gun in hand, or to offer any kind of service. And, when the weather cleared, parachute drops of food and ammunition aided the besieged, as well as low-flying planes which strafed the enemy.

All Greece followed this first great battle in agony and many were skeptical of the outcome. On the 28th, the governments of some friendly countries became quite anxious. On the 29th, the Balkan Committee of the U.N.[6] sent an official warning to the governments of Greece's three neighbors: "A recognition, even de facto", said the warning, "of the Provisional Government would constitute a violation of international law, of the peace treaties and the UN charter, and would create a serious threat to the maintenance of peace and international security." The text was urgent. Anxiety made it so.

Even though the garrison still resisted, at several points the situation appeared desperate. On the night of December 30, everyone thought that it was all over. Inside the town, though, the defenders were holding well. The little stone houses were turned into small forts which could resist. But on the denuded hillside the situation became unbearable. The fire from the guns and the mortars was not the worst of all, for the ruggedness of the rocks offered good enough protection for the defenders, but the men were exhausted and had to defend themselves continually against assaults by enemy forces that were often rested and refreshed.

At 21:00 hours on the 30th, a fierce attack was repulsed. Around midnight, a second one—fiercer and extremely unyielding—succeeded in taking about one-quarter of the long hill, its southeastern end; but the company defending it withdrew and joined the other two. A little before dawn of the 31st, the guerrillas attacked again from all directions. In some phases the battle was savage hand-to-hand combat, but at daybreak, the attackers withdrew.

Then, there was almost complete silence, except for some exchanges of fire here and there. The men asked themselves if it were the calm before the storm. But it was not. Rather, it was the first wavering of the enemy; reinforcements which had converged towards the steel ring around Konitsa had begun to break it.

Two days earlier, Kalpaki had fallen. It had been taken by the cadets of the Reserve Officers' School of Corfu, units of LOK, and men of the Eighth Division. With Kalpaki clear, the regular forces covered themselves lightly and advanced along the dirt road knocking down all resistance. The engineers followed, setting up temporary bridges on the foundations of old ones that had been blown up.

In the meantime, on the 30th, two companies under Major George Lygerakis, one of the former EDES chiefs, entered Konitsa. These units had crossed steep mountains by the wildest footpaths imaginable; they had marched through streams and had entered the besieged town by routes considered impassable. They did not waste any time for they wanted to get there before a group of the LOK, who were attempting the same feat from another direction. The LOK entered the town early on the morning of the 31st and joined the defense before the arrival of the main reinforcements. Morale again played a role. Konitsa was saved. At this time there was not to be a seat for the "Provisional Government of Free Greece".

And, if this was not enough, the saviors and defenders of Konitsa were ordered to attack the enemy and pursue him. This pursuit did take place, but was not carried out in great depth. It was not felt to be worth the sacrifice since the frontier was very near and the guerrillas could avoid encirclement. Once repulsed, it was easy for them to get to a safe place where they could rest and reorganize themselves. For the government troops this was one of the great disadvantages.

Moreover, if certain units of DAG withdrew in disorder, others fought with persistence. The passes toward

Kastaniani, Markos's base, were fiercely defended with the guerrillas' artillery and mortars in full action all the time. The objective of the pursuit was to completely free Konitsa and the surrounding area. This was achieved in one week, and by the 7th of January, firing had ceased completely. On the battlefield were found 240 dead and 77 seriously wounded guerrillas. Nevertheless, their total losses were heavy; according to the accounts of several prisoners, these were calculated at about 1,300 men, while those of the regular army amounted to 513 dead, wounded, and missing in action.

This was the second large-scale battle, but it had been much more dangerous for the Nationalists than the first because of its proximity to the border and the weaponry that had been used. As for the number of troops involved, over 30,000 were engaged on the spot and in the surrounding area. During the final phase, the government side had thrown into the battle about 10,000 officers and men, 5,000 national guard, and about 1,000 gendarmes and MAY: that is, a total of 16,000 without counting Dovas's brigade.

There were several conclusions to draw from both sides. We will see some of them in the next chapter. Perhaps the most important was that the morale and the stubbornness of the defenders was revealed, to say the least, to be equal to that of the aggressors. The guerrillas had been assured that on the other side of the barricade, lay "corruption in the service of imperialism and foreign capitalism." Now they realized after eighteen months, that the others fought resolutely against all difficulties, and even sacrificed their lives—something which in our time does not happen when serving others, but only when serving one's own convictions.

As for the defenders, they saw the real difficulties of the struggle, but their morale rose because of them. The spirit of the Army of Albania was reborn in the postwar national army. It was not necessary to be sure of victory to fight unto death. The ancestral cry "Freedom or Death" had once again assumed all its meaning.

251

To end this chapter, we must mention a gesture that had certain repercussions and was mentioned in many texts. King Paul had proved to be a great sovereign who combined kindness, common sense, and authority. His absence was felt on the battlefields. No publicity had been given to the fact that he was ill with typhus. Now, in his place, immediately after the battle, Queen Frederica flew to Ioannina. She ignored the objections of the military and, escorted by only one jeep, arrived in Konitsa at dawn on January 7. She had covered seventy-five kilometers on a road that was far from safe and was, thus, one of the first personalities, and the first woman, to visit this small town which had suffered so much. This gesture, which engendered a great deal of enthusiasm, was followed by considerable personal activity on behalf of refugee children, who had particularly suffered under the hellish conditions of those difficult days.

So, in a spirit of brotherhood, eminently Hellenic, Queen Frederica then managed to become, within a short period of time, the most popular person in Greece. Unfortunately, later on, with an obstinacy typically Prussian, the Queen managed to squander all this capital of popularity by intervening in politics and offending all those who, by the will of the people, were elected to lead, to defend, and to reconstruct the country in the postwar era.

Chapter X

1948: A Year of Suffering

The Military Events. For the two adversaries, 1948 was a year of great sacrifice, vain hopes, and bitter disappointment. In the Communist camp, the outcome of the battles at Metsovo and Konitsa caused a strong reaction. A turning point, they marked the beginning of conflict between the political and military leadership of the rebels.

The political leadership wanted a real army that would be able to face the national army, win battles, and occupy regions, including at least one town. The aim was to seize power. It was now necessary that DAG organization and tactics be adapted to this objective.

The military leadership held the opposite view; DAG had obtained spectacular results against a much stronger adversary. Whenever the guerrillas had tried to fight real battles, they had known bloody failure; therefore, it was necessary to continue their old tactics. The hour of change would come when the national army would become discouraged, when the country would realize that DAG could not be defeated.

Zachariadis supported the first view, Markos the second. From all the evidence available in that era, the latter was correct. But Markos could not win this argument and the disagreement was finally settled by a compromise. The political leadership prevailed as concerned the reorganization of DAG which then numbered about 24,000 men, not including the auxiliary services and party organizers.

DAG's Regional Commands would be abolished and the guerrilla bands would be amalgamated into divisions, each comprising three brigades. Each brigade would be made up of three battalions with a strength of 430 men. Each battalion would have three infantry companies and a weapons company. The battalion, furthermore, would be equipped with hand grenades, six mortars, four heavy machine-guns, 25 light machine-guns, 60 automatic rifles and a variety of other weapons. Also it would have field telephones, a wireless set and 40 mules for transportation. Special arms, such as artillery and anti-aircraft guns, bazookas and mines, would be available to the division. It must be noted that the effective strength of the battalions was often inferior to that mentioned above. Brigades, which should thus have included at least 1,400 men, often did not put into the field more than a thousand.

Another innovation imposed by the political leadership concerned the commissars; henceforth, they would form a special corps, under a Supreme Council, and would play an important role in all units from the division to the platoon. These changes were made because the leadership was not satisfied with the loyalty and discipline of those guerrillas who had not volunteered. Both, it was thought, would improve with better organization of the political commissars, as the proportion of volunteers was not considered satisfactory.

Perhaps this is the reason why the number of women among the ranks of the combatants continually increased.

In 1948 and 1949, women occupied a remarkable position within DAG itself. Their numbers were not negligible (10 to 25 percent, according to the band and the season). They were fanatic, they fought well, and their exemplary behavior had another very important effect: it stimulated aggressiveness and stubbornness among the men who fought at their side .

The new structure of DAG, which ressembled that of the regular army, was not appropriate for guerrilla bands. But the political leadership had its way as to the tactics that were to be followed. On this point it finally compromised; the guerrillas would not fight battles, they would only make raids. These would usually take place at night and would aim at bringing the maximum returns in supplies and demoralisation of the enemy. DAG bases would multiply with a view to increasing the mobility of the units, but no large base would be formed, except those that were in the mountains astride the frontier. These base areas would also be fortified. Finally, aggressiveness would increase and "the country would be treated as an enemy country", the economy would be paralyzed, and the enemy's morale would be seriously weakened.

On the government side, a change of tactics was being decided upon. Up to the end of 1947, with the exception of operation "Terminus", the army had followed purely defensive tactics, which had proved harmful. For each operation—whether planned or not—a time limit varying between two and six days, had been set. Afterwards, the forces had to return to camp so that the towns would not remain for a long time without protection. This was logical, considering the fact that troops were insufficient, but, on the other hand, it interrupted operations and permitted the guerrilla bands to disappear easily. So, it was decided to no longer limit pursuit, but to continue it until the bands were exterminated and the hideouts occupied. In order to accomplish this, national guard battalions were increased and better armed. In the summer of 1948, they totalled 97, each one with a strength of 500 men. Of course, the guard battalions could not be compared with those of the national army in terms of officers, weapons and men (the guard having men belonging to older age groups), but their distribution (23 in Macedonia, 14 in Thessaly, 9 in Epirus, etc.) and their cooperation with the MAY homeguard, freed the army from its defense commitments.

The army became much stronger, and reached its full strength during 1948. Although the actual size of the army remained the same (about 135,000 men), armament and organization were significantly improved. The army's main handicap was that it undertook reorganization and training in the use of new American materiel, while, at the same time, it had to fight the enemy unceasingly. For Markos did not allow it any respite.

Almost everywhere, and especially in Macedonia, Thessaly, Epirus, and central Greece, from the beginning of the year guerrilla raids were at their height. They were of the same type as those described in previous chapters, with one difference—they were led with more enthusiasm and cruelty. Not one day went by without three or four such attacks. Sometimes they were against important centers.

On the night of February 5, one of these—though of minor importance—was very bold and thus had a considerable psychological effect. A group of about 100 guerrillas attacked and occupied for a few hours the village of Pyli, at the foot of Mt. Parnis in Attica not far from the outskirts of Athens. On the night of February 10, two bands of 500 guerrillas each advanced from different directions towards Thessalonike but did not enter the city, content to barrage it with artillery fire. Once again Markos had attained his goal because these two operations, though not pushed further, clearly had psychological objectives: first, to demonstrate to the population that DAG could reach the outskirts of the largest cities and, second, to influence the leftists who were hiding there. As in the past, the army pursued the rebels, but obtained only meager results. Its morale was weakened, and, at the beginning of March, it received another kind of blow.

The army General Staff was preparing a large-scale operation for the summer: the occupation of the main base of DAG, that on Mt. Grammos, a veritable fortress astride the Albanian frontier on the northwest end of the Pindos range. In order to cover the left flank of the troops that would undertake this operation, the Greek General Staff first wanted to clear out Mourghana, a very long rocky ridge that starts in Albania and stretches into Epirus. The border intersects the mountain approximately at its midpoint. It was known to be fortified and defended by 1,300 to 2,000 men easily supplied from Albania.

Under the code name of "Pergamos" this operation was assigned to seven battalions of the Eighth Division, a company of volunteers, two squads of field artillery, and one battalion of raiding forces (LOK). The operation began on February 28 and ended on March 6 in failure; it was the first time that DAG had come out victorious in a confrontation with the national army. For five days the battle was indecisive, but on the night of March 4, a surprise-attack led by forces including a company of the "Democratic Youth", overthrew a whole battalion of the regular army. The ground had been very well chosen, the breach was dangerous, and other assaults followed immediately. The units of the Eighth Division were forced to withdraw.

A new operation was set for March 30 against the fortified positions on Mourghana, under the code name of "Falcon", in spite of the objections of Eighth Division officers, who were opposed to any offensive near the border. But other officers held the opposite view and they were strongly supported by the chief of the American Mission, General Van Fleet, a good soldier, who had distinguished himself in World War II. Van Fleet believed that the Mourghana retreat had to be cleared out *at any price* and, naturally, his opinion carried weight.

Operation "Falcon" brought some minimal results but was suspended on April 5. The reason for the stalemate was that the artillery had not seriously damaged the pillboxes which covered all the passes, which were also amply mined.

Questioned by journalists after this last setback, General Van Fleet sang the praises of the Eighth Division and declared that Mourghana, divided as it is by the Greek-Albanian frontier, posed a political problem which must be solved by the United Nations and the Greek government and which the army could not resolve by force.

Operations "Pergamos" and "Falcon" had cost the army dearly. Besides the fact that morale had suffered, 596 officers and soldiers had been killed or wounded and 178 were missing.[1] DAG "confirmed" losses were 87 prisoners and 312 men out of action. But real losses, it was estimated, were about double this.

Ten days later another operation, more serious and better justified, was undertaken in Roumeli, in central Greece. After operation "Terminus" (April 1947) DAG controlled the mountains of Roumeli which extend from southwest of Parnassos to the southernmost tips of the Pindos range. The strategic importance of these mountains of central Greece was considerable, for they constituted a threat to the communication links between Athens and Thessalonike. In such rugged terrain, with summits sometimes exceeding 1,500 meters, the operation was not an easy one, since the territory involved was roughly 350 square kilometers. The entire area was held by only 3,800 fighters, nearly all of them ex-guerrillas of ELAS. They were supported by 2,000 men of the auxiliary "self-defense" organization, responsible mainly for supply and transport. Though non-combat in theory, these men were also lightly armed because Markos believed that an un-

258

armed man was useless in a guerrilla war. Because of the importance of the region, Roumeli was the object of DAG attention during the winter, 1947-1948. The area had been well organized and, at certain points, somewhat fortified.

The Greek General Staff planned the clearing out of the whole area. For this purpose it concentrated considerable forces: three divisions, two battalions of raiding forces (LOK), four squadrons of armored cars, four battalions of the gendarmerie and national guard and a large number of mortars and field guns.

The offensive would be led from all sides, except from the south where there was the sea. Ships of the navy would patrol the coast to prevent any rebels from escaping to the Peloponnesus and, if necessary, would bombard mountain positions (See Map No. 5). Nearly all the available airplanes would participate in this operation, whose code name was "Dawn". The plan foresaw a campaign of two weeks minimum and three weeks maximum, at the end of which the army seriously hoped that this important region would be completely cleared.

Strategy had been well worked out, the troops were numerous and spirited, but nevertheless, forecasts were only partially realized. Only after forty days of combat accompanied by exhaustive pursuits—from April 15 to May 26—were acceptable results obtained: 610 dead guerrillas were counted, plus 310 wounded and 995 self-defense personnel taken as prisoners. Also many depots of war material and food were found as well as herds of cattle and dairies. In addition, several installations of all types were destroyed.

This was not at all negligible: the blow to morale and loss of material had been hard for the rebels, and communications between the capital and the north had been reestablished, at least for some time. These last words, "for some time", speak for themselves of the true liability of this vast operation. Most of the Roumeli guerrillas—disorganized and hidden, perhaps demoralized—were still there and the army did not have enough men to occupy these mountains on a permanent basis; the guerrillas would again become the masters there.

Two other operations, of the same type but on a smaller scale, took place between May 25 and June 5 to clear out two other mountains north of Roumeli: Othrys and Agrafa. In these three operations the army lost 202 officers and men, either dead or wounded, and 27 were missing. Considering the number of troops involved, these losses were not heavy and this meant that DAG forces refused battle when possible. More importantly, however, something else had been lost: the illusion that it was possible to control the situation easily by force of arms. The guerrilla war had already lasted two years. The army, becoming stronger all the time, had done its duty night and day and it had been victorious almost everywhere. But matters did not improve. On the contrary, the situation could be said to be worsening. There had been no break in discipline, but doubt—not to say pessimism—had appeared among the troops in the field. Sometimes it was confided to Members of Parliament visiting army camps preparing for battle, that the possibility of a "political solution" should be examined. Besides, these military operations which gave rise to skepticism were not the only reason for it.

Threatening Interlude. Actually, in this same period, other kinds of threats reached full proportions. The abduction of children by the Communists had not really been considered serious when it first began in 1947. Such a monstrous act, it was believed, could only be limited in extent due, perhaps, to special circumstances, such as personal vengeance. Nevertheless, the cases multiplied, and even seemed somehow organized. Finally, on March 11, 1948, the "abduction of children" was officially announced by the Provisional Government of Markos Vafiadis. The announcement was made by Radio Belgrade. The Provisional

Government stated that it had decided to send children from the regions it occupied to friendly countries which would accept them; this decision had been made, he declared, because of the many dangers Greek children faced from malnutrition, cruel bombing by the monarcho-fascist air force, looting in the villages, and assassination of people by the fascists. The young Greek children would remain abroad until conditions in Greece changed. This announcement coincided with a period when the round-up of children from three to fourteen years of age had reached its peak.

Tragic scenes were enacted in many villages. Mothers, mad with despair, attacked the guerrillas, cursing them. Others clung to their dear ones until they fell under the blows of a rifle butt. In the happier cases—I know three of these—parents and children ran away before the guerrillas could catch them. The gods were thirsty for human tragedy and the thirst of the gods was not easy to quench.

At the end of March, the Albanian capital announced that it had just received 300 Greek children, the Yugoslav capital 400 and the Bulgarian 600. By 1949, these figures would reach a total of 28,000. The matter naturally provoked a strong reaction. The extreme Left made every effort to justify itself internationally, saying that the parents of these children had asked for their expatriation. This was true only for a limited number of children coming from families that had already taken refuge in the Grammos base. Otherwise, hundreds of cases were verified that did not leave a shadow of doubt: it was clearly abduction. Besides, the Balkan Commission of the U.N. visited several villages, heard the parents' complaints and in a long report, ascertained that a large number of children had been abducted and had crossed the northern frontiers in groups. The Greek government also referred the case to the U.N., basing its appeal on many concrete examples. This aroused worldwide indignation.

In the country itself, "Children's Towns" were set up in safe areas. Refugees arriving from villages of the north, could send their children to one of them if they wished. And thousands of women volunteers, directed by the Queen, transformed these Children's Towns into true families. But the inhuman operation still continued.

Why had it taken place? And why did it continue after causing so much reaction? The two explanations which prevailed at that time were the following: 1) the KKE wished to have, in the near future, a considerable number of young militants, fanatic and well indoctrinated, 2) DAG profited from them in order to terrorize and more easily subjugate the rural population by shattering their morale.

In fact, this last objective played against DAG because, simultaneously, the army decided on a policy of evacuating all villages near the regions controlled by the guerrillas. It aimed to create an empty space around them, thus depriving the rebels of information gleaned from the peasants and all the other facilities they had found in the nearby villages. Therefore, nothing assisted this difficult and thankless task of dislodging the villagers from their homes more than the abduction of the children.

Alas! That in turn, created many other problems; in the spring of 1948, the rural population that had taken refuge in towns exceeded 700,000. This was very serious from many points of view. First of all, the humanitarian aspect, for these uprooted people, far from their homes, often in makeshift shanties, lived on the food rations distributed to them in towns that had suddenly become overpopulated. Then, there was the economic aspect; these men, formerly contributing to the nation's productivity, mainly by cultivating the land, now lived at the expense of the government whose financial means were limited. Finally, we must note the immediate and harmful influence that these facts had on the morale of the town's citizens and on the morale of the army. To give just one example: the town of Ioannina, one of the most important military centers, normally had 25,000 inhabitants, a figure which increased to 80,000 within a few months. The majority of these refugees lived in huts hastily constructed, and a number of them in tents. One can easily imagine how difficult everyday life was in these improvised homes, deprived of every comfort. One can also understand how the army's morale would be affected, seeing all this and realizing that it was the result of two years of struggle and sacrifice.

At about the same time, another factor upset life in the provinces even more: the mining of the roads that joined provincial towns. This practice was widely applied. By the summer of 1948, in certain districts communications had become extremely dangerous. Buses and trucks were blown up at such a rate that no one dared use the roads that joined the prefecture capitals in the northern, and even in the central, provinces. People did not travel unless assured of a place in a military convoy. Picture two or three mine-sweeping cars in front with open trucks full of soldiers armed with machine-guns scattered throughout the column. This convoy usually crawled at a speed of ten to fifteen kilometers per hour, the whole trip an unending agony.

In the spring of that year, an isolated but tragic event made the atmosphere even heavier. On the Saturday before Easter, May 1, 1948 at 22:00 hours, at the entrance to the Athens church of Saint George Karytsi, Minister of Justice Christos Ladas was assassinated. (He has no connection with Colonel Ladas of the military regime imposed on April 21, 1967.) A brilliant lawyer, he belonged to the left wing of the Center Party. When apprehended, the young assassin stated that his name was Stratis Moutsoyiannis and that he had acted on orders from the KKE. On the same night at 22:30 hours, the DAG radio station recently installed in Belgrade, had praised the murderer, a loyal fighter of the December 1944 revolution in Athens. The praise ended with an appeal to the members of the

263

KKE who were in Athens: it called on them to help DAG by murdering Prime Minister Sofoulis, Minister of Foreign Affairs Tsaldaris and Minister of Public Order Rentis. In the capital the news spread immediately.

And so it happened that Easter 1948, which is the most important Greek holiday, was for the capital of the country a day of grief and indignation, infused with a spirit of vengeance. The government had to react strongly; it declared that it was resolved to keep up the struggle to the bitter end and many preventive arrests were made within forty-eight hours. On May 4, the harshest counter-measure possible followed: the execution of certain Communists who had been sentenced to death and were in prison for a long time.

Within a few days, the Soviet government made a strong protest and asked the Greek government to stop these executions at once. The censure of Greece did not take long to expand to the West where severe criticism was also pronounced.

The government, unperturbed, made some explanations a week later. In an interview to a Reuters reporter in Athens on May 7, 1948, Prime Minister Sofoulis declared the following: *"The government decided to clear out the files of all those sentenced to death long before the murder of Christos Ladas. It was also decided that all the files on which proceedings had ended, including rejections of appeals for pardon, be forwarded to the public prosecutor to order the execution of the sentenced, according to the law. No change has been made in these proceedings."*

On the same day, Constantine Rentis—Minister of Public Order and temporarily, of Justice—denied rumors of mass executions in retaliation and told the Reuters reporter that "among 2,961 Greeks who had been sentenced to death for crimes committed before and after the December revolution of 1944, 157 persons had been executed before May 1 of the current year. Between the 4th and the 7th of May, 24 more were executed in Athens and today, 19 others in Aegina". "It is ridiculous to speak of mass executions," continued the minister, adding that 1,100 appeals for grace had been submitted, 500 of which had been rejected. Those individuals who were executed had killed at least one person in cold blood, not during an engagment. Among the first 157 executed, many had killed more than one person and one had slain 27.[2] Now the executions were temporarily postponed, but that did not pledge the government to anything. In fact, on June 28, the government announced the execution of six other young militants recently condemned to death.

At about that time, a story began to circulate abroad that a compromise solution would be formulated to solve the Greek crisis, similar to the Varkiza Agreement. Upon being informed of these press reports, Sofoulis made the following statement on May 14: "Regardless of what happens on the international level, the situation in Greece itself will be cleared up either by the unconditional surrender of the guerrillas, or by their complete defeat." Eighty-eight years did not weigh heavily on the shoulders of the leader of the center-left, the "Eamobulgarian". However, a few days later another tragic incident occurred which heightened the crisis and distressed the "Old Man".

On May 9, an American journalist, George Polk, correspondent of CBS, disappeared from his hotel in Thessalonike. It was learned that, through friends belonging to the extreme left, he had obtained an audience with Markos. Then, on the 17th, his body was discovered on a beach near the city.

The affair caused quite a commotion, particularly since no clues to the mystery could be found. The situation became more confusing when a close relative of the prime minister, a leftist and a friend of Polk's was suspected of conniving with KKE terrorist groups. Finally, after a thorough inquest and an irreproachable trial, the court ruled that the unfortunate journalist had been a victim of a secret communist organization which aimed to have his death appear the work of both the Right and to the Center government which had opposed his visit to Markos.

Wide international publicity given to the inquest and the trial somehow lessened the reaction to this murder abroad, but did not erase it completely. In the United States nothing harmed the Greek cause more during this period than the Polk case. American public opinion, though used to dark and murderous intrigues, could not see why the criminals were not tracked down immediately. Fortunately, the American missions in Greece were of a different opinion; they were sure that the Greek government had done its duty. At this point, another clarification seems necessary. At that time, and even later on, certain foreign journalists maintained that Greece was governed by Americans and that its army was under the command of American officers. This was completely untrue.

After the declaration of the Truman Doctrine, two important American missions were set up in Greece: one economic and the other, military. The first one, in collaboration with the Greek government, managed the economic and financial aid offered by the United States to Greece and gave advice on the policy to be followed in matters relating to it. Distributed by the appropriate Greek authorities, this aid was also administered by the latter; but, close to them, in the higher echelons, members of the American Mission had the right of inspection and of advice. Néver did the Americans administer or decide alone. Most certainly, as the members of the American Mission could influence the allocation of money or goods by their reports, their opinion carried weight. Whenever their Greek counterpart was of a different opinion— something that was not unusual—an unpleasant situation was possible. But, in general, the Americans restricted themselves to their role of observers and advisers, and collaboration was satisfactory.

What had been said about the economic mission applies also to the military mission, which was more important and had a more difficult role to play. In the summer of 1948 it consisted of 250 officers, some of whom were instructors in training camps. More than fifty were attached to the Greek General Staff. Never, in any case, did American officers command Greek units, large or small, and they never imposed their views on commanders of units. That they were there was entirely natural, as their country offered a profusion of up-to-date materiel to an armed forces whose number in its entirety (army, navy, air force) now amounted to 167,000 men.

The collaboration of officers of different nationalities is always a delicate matter, especially at the top, where the most important decisions are made. And so it was in Greece during the guerrilla war. However, understanding between Greek, American, and British officers—for a small British mission was maintained—was excellent. Neither reverses on the battlefield, the lack of decisive results, nor even the Polk case, weakened this understanding. As to the Polk case, other events of much wider significance soon pushed it into the background.

The Belgrade-Moscow Rupture and its Direct Consequences. From Belgrade on May 31, 1948, the Provisional Government of Markos Vafiadis launched a call for a ceasefire with startling suddenness. Its tone was very aggressive against "the foreign imperialists and the Greek traitors", but its conciliatory position was clearly spelled out; DAG did not believe in exclusive power imposed by force. It proposed that fighting cease immediately and promised to help Greece regain peace and a completely democratic way of life. The next day, in the same tone, Zachariadis declared that the proposals of the Provisional Government were sincere.

In many capitals people tried to interpret this spectacular

267

gesture. For the Left, this was the grand gesture, "the one that Van Fleet had rejected." For many people it was a sign of weakness, or an astute maneuver in order to place the Greek government in a difficult position, since everyone yearned for peace. For others, according to information from Belgrade, it was the result of a meeting that had taken place there at the end of March, between members of the Cominform Bureau, Zachariadis, and the three principal ministers of the Provisional Government.

Through this information the Cominform had confirmed that, henceforth, DAG could not come to power by force. Such an attitude by the Cominform was probable, according to Djilas, knowing that Stalin had had the following conversation with the Yugoslav delegates:

Stalin: Do you believe that the revolution in Greece can succeed?

Kardelj: Yes, if foreign powers do not interfere and if no political or military mistakes are made.

Stalin: Always "ifs" and "buts". No! There is no chance of success. Do you believe that Great Britain and the United States—the most powerful country in the world, will allow us to cut their lines of communication in the Mediterranean? Nonsense! And, besides, we don't have a navy. The revolution must be stopped as soon as possible.[3]

Moreover, it should be noted that the Markos-Zachariadis proposals were announced about five months after this conversation and three months after the meeting of Zachariadis with members of the Cominform Bureau in Belgrade. If he were obeying orders, there could not have been such a delay. So it seems that the causes of these spectacular proposals should be sought elsewhere.

Relations between Stalin and Tito worsened from one day to the next. Those who were in the know realized this. The position of the KKE and its army was most delicate for the quarrel was between the uncontested and authoritarian master of the "Movement" and the one who was giving the actual unstinted support to the rebels. And it is thus quite probable that, seeing the approaching storm, the leaders of the rebellion sought a compromise settlement.

For one or two days the Sofoulis government did not deign to reply. But, on June 3, by telegram to the governments of Albania, Bulgaria, Czechoslovakia, Hungary, Poland, Yugoslavia and the General Secretary of the U.N., the Greek government demanded the repatriation of all the children who had been abducted and were in those countries.

Speaking of the telegram on June 4, Prime Minister Sofoulis said, "*This is official proof of the peaceful intentions of Greece. Secondly, it is a certain way of learning the intentions of the Soviet Union's satellites, as well as of testing the sincerity of Markos's proposals. If the various governments reject the Greek demand, or indeed, do not reply at all, that will mean that they did not sincerely intend to restore their relations with Greece and that Markos's proposals are nothing more than propaganda tricks without any meaning.*" This was a clever maneuver. On June 10, the governments of Hungary and Poland rejected the Greek government demand.

Markos's new overtures had not lasted long. They had, besides, reduced the intensity of the guerrilla war to a minimum—that war which shed so much blood and paralyzed the country from the Peloponnesus to Thrace, from the Aegean to the Adriatic. To give a precise report of it one would have to make a long list of all the villages that had been looted and burned and to enumerate the executions which did not cease. There would be nothing to add to what has already been written in previous chapters, except perhaps for a small variation; more than ever the guerrillas looted the hospitals and the pharmacies for the wounded and the sick were numerous, while medicines and sanitary equipment were insufficient. Supplies of these precious items were also scarce among the neighbors to the north. In a few words, the destruction was extensive; with the exception of a few islands, Greece was burning from one end to the other.

Nevertheless, two important events renewed hope. The first was the grand offensive launched by the National Army in mid-June. This event, purely military, will be the object further on of a special section. The second event was of a completely different nature, which perhaps, explains the peace proposals of May 31. On the other hand, its consequences go far beyond the local scene. On June 28, the Free World learned for the first time that there was a serious conflict within the Communist world. In fact, a resolution of the Cominform meeting in Bucharest violently attacked the Communist Party of Yugoslavia; the spoiled child was now hated, for it had dared to resist.

A militant of the Party from the age of sixteen and a prisoner of the Russians in World War I, Walter (assumed name of Josip Broz-Tito before the war) had enrolled in the Russian Red Guard, had fought via the underground the regime of Alexander Karageorgevitch and had become General Secretary of the Communist Party of Yugoslavia. He had approved of the Molotov-Ribbentrop Agreement and, when the "Motherland of Socialism" was in danger, he had launched and marvelously waged a guerrilla war without precedent. Now this faithful one among the faithful had lifted his head against the supreme leader of international Communism. On the international political scene it was a sensational turn of events.

The causes for it were many. Perhaps the real reason was unique; domineering to the extreme—or raving mad—Stalin was convinced of the need for his personal supremacy and could not bear that any other personality dare to measure up to him. No other leader in the Communist world, including Dimitrov and Gomulka, had the personality of Tito and of certain members of his brilliant team. Besides, the latter took liberties in their words and deeds, which not only irritated Stalin, but also worried him. From his monolithic, domineering point of view,he was right; today one can see how far Titoism had gone. For Titoism was on the move and beginning to make headway in 1944.

In the very edifying book of Dedijer that Tito points to as reporting faithfully his conversations with the author,[4] one sees that from the first visit of Tito to Stalin (September 1944) friction between the two men had already begun. But that was not all. Later on, the Yugoslavs maintained that they themselves had liberated their country. Stalin, openly rejecting this view, deemed that the Balkans had been liberated by his troops and thought that for this reason, everything must be forgiven them, including pillage and rape. Milovan Djilas, a first-rate militant, was disgraced simply because he dared to ask a question.

Then came the more serious questions: the claim for recovery of Trieste from Italy, of South Carinthia from Austria, and Macedonia from Greece and Bulgaria. These claims were persistently mentioned by Tito without having come to terms with Stalin beforehand. The indirect but firm control of Albania by Tito was also irritating to him. Likewise, the attempt of Belgrade to make Bulgaria a member of the federation of Yugoslav States, while Moscow wished a Balkan federation in which Bulgaria and Yugoslavia would be members with equal rights.

All this was certainly enough to enrage a person, even if he were not Stalin the Terrible. Besides, Tito's group—whose members I had the advantage of knowing well—though brilliant, had the weakness of believing that they could do as they pleased. Moscow's reactions were numerous and varied, and continued to intensify until the final break.

Unfortunately, the extremely interesting history of that break between Belgrade and Moscow cannot be fully described here. The reader nevertheless, would be interested to know the main events of this history, as well as

271

some characteristic details which are very little known outside Yugoslavia.

In February 1948, Moscow's reactions seemed to endanger the economic recovery of Yugoslavia. In fact, after fruitless contacts for the establishment of a Bulgaro-Yugoslav federation, Moscow brusquely cancelled very important commercial negotiations between the two countries that were scheduled for April. Since the bulk of Yugoslavia's imports and exports were with the Soviet Union, the threat was grave. The Yugoslavs had the courage to accept the challenge. At the beginnng of March, the Central Committee of the Communist Party of Yugoslavia, by a resolution drafted in a very clear style, interpreted the cancellation of the negotiations as "inadmissible pressure" and flatly refused to comply with Soviet directives for the creation of the federation.

On March 18, the chief of the Soviet Military Mission in Yugoslavia announced to the chief of the Yugoslav General Staff, Koca, Popovitch (later a distinguished minister of foreign affairs of his country), that he had received orders to leave the country with all the members of the mission, because they were surrounded by ill will and treated with hostility. The next day, the charge d'affaires of the Soviet Embassy announced this decision to Tito personally, and it was carried out the same day.

Without delay Tito wrote a letter to Molotov. In it he stated his good intentions, but his tone was firm and his conclusion hard. "It is clear," he concluded, "that the reasons you have put forward are not true. We warn you against information you have received from non-official sources. It is not necessarily objective, precise or well intentioned."

The answer to this letter was dated March 27   and carried the signatures of Stalin and Molotov. It was handed over to Tito by the Soviet ambassador and the charge d'affaires in a meeting during which the two Soviet diplomats were obliged to stand. In the eight typewritten pages the form and substance of this letter were brutally frank. It began with the following phrase: "We consider your letter as untrue and for this reason, utterly inadmissible." There followed two types of accusations. One concerned the treatment of Soviet officers in Yugoslavia, the other was much more serious: the Yugoslav leaders were accused of ideological deviationism because they had imposed on the Party a dictatorship of a small group. So as not to leave any doubt, Stalin and Molotov attacked individually some of Tito's principal collaborators—the ministers of propaganda, defense, economy and interior. They wrote: "It is absurd to listen to stories spread about here and there concerning the Soviet Communist Party, by doubtful marxists such as Djilas, Vukmanovitch, Kidritch, Rankovitch and others." The following phrase, which ended the letter, was a terrible threat: "We consider that the political career of Trotsky is a good enough lesson."

Tito drafted the answer himself within two hours after he received this lecture from Stalin and Molotov. It was a firm, but moderate, refutation of all charges, a fervent profession of faith in communism and of friendship with the Soviet Union. But also it was a statement of independence and sovereignty. Tito's reply, with a few slight alterations, was approved of by the Central Committee of the Communist Party of Yugoslavia after long discussion. Only two members of the committee—Zugovitch ferociously and Hebrang, weakly—declared themselves "against this dangerous attitude towards the Soviet Union and its Communist Party." The reply was delivered by Vladimir Popovitch, the Yugoslav ambassador in Moscow, to Molotov at the Soviet ministry of foreign affairs "in the presence of a secretary who took notes in shorthand. Molotov was very nervous."

His nervousness was justified. He and his master had clearly lost the first round. It was the era when a gesture from Stalin determined the fate of his subjects throughout the entire world. Now here, his reiterated curses had brought no result; they had not even affected the calm and dignity of his small adversary.

Stalin then sent a copy of his letter of March 27 to all members of the Cominform and demanded that they take sides in his disagreement with a former disciple. They did so in a clearly partial, and often outrageous, way.

Tito did not fail to answer in the same vein. Nevertheless, he made sure to underline his loyalty towards marxism and his friendship for the Soviet Union. Stalin was furious. The affair could no longer remain within the Communist inner circle.

During the great May Day parade that took place in Belgrade only one member of the Yugoslav Communist Party's Central Committee was absent from the reviewing stand. He was in the parade itself with the people and proudly passed in front of the official stand. It was Zugovitch who had strongly opposed the negative reply to Stalin and Molotov. The challenge soon became known. The warning was serious. But it would not end there.

On May 5, a letter of the Soviet Communist Party's Central Committee was handed to the Yugoslav leaders. Again it carried the signatures of Stalin and Molotov. In twenty-five typewritten sheets Stalin accumulated the gravest accusations and the basest insults possible, like an enraged Tsar who thought that he could crush his enemy with his curses. These charges and flagrant insults went from the assertion that "the ambassador of the United States in Belgrade behaved in Yugoslavia as if he were the master of the country", up to the total denial of the role the Yugoslav people had played in the liberation of their country. Anathemas against its leaders kept pace with the rest of the text. In conclusion, the letter rejected the Yugoslav proposal that a Soviet delegation be sent to make an investigation on the spot and, furthermore, it demanded that the matter be put before the Cominform.

The Central Committee of the C.P.Y. however, refused the interference of the Cominform in this quarrel. Zugovitch and Hebrang were expelled from the Central Committee and from the Party. After a few days they were arrested and an investigation was opened against them for high treason.

Stalin was losing the second round as well. His worst threats, his gravest warnings did not make his former disciple waver at all, while his trusted men were placed behind bars. There remained for him the third round, which would be played publicly in common with his allies. He was going to lose that one also in a spectacular manner.

After many efforts to get Tito to participate personally in the Cominform meeting, which was to initially take place in the Ukraine (where the personal safety of Tito could not be assured), the international Communist summit met without the Yugoslavs in Bucharest on June 20. On the 28th, a unanimous resolution of the Cominform was given for publication in the news media; it exploded like a bomb on the entire world which had not gotten wind of anything. The C.P.Y. was accused of following an erroneous line, of abandoning Marxism-Leninism, of slandering the Soviet Union, of abolishing "democracy" in the affairs of the party, of deserting the family of Communist parties by following leaders imbued with nationalist and revisionist ideas. The "healthy elements" of the Party must oblige their leaders to return to the right road and, if they refused, they must be replaced.

Considering the mentality of that era, and with the control exercised by the Soviet Union over the Communist world, this was equivalent to a death sentence. All Communist parties were in agreement with this condemnation. One after the other, they denounced the deviation of Titoism in very strong terms.

Nevertheless, that did not bother Tito and his colleagues.

They organized the only reaction possible, which was again that of the entire Party and the people. First of all, they published the letters that had been exchanged between Tito and the Soviet Communist Party. In this way, they provoked a reaction from a proud people who had sacrificed so much for national independence. Immediately after that, they organized a large congress of the Communist Party of Yugoslavia with 2,344 delegates participating (who were elected from all the regions of the country by a secret ballot among the 468,000 members of the Party). Among the delegates only six were not from the ranks of Tito's guerrillas. The congress lasted for six days and the discussions were broadcast on the Yugoslav radio network. At the close, there was unanimous approval of the positions taken by the Party leadership. What is more, this gathering unleashed a surge of enthusiasm for Tito and of national pride in him as a great leader. Thus, a pro-Soviet military coup organized a few days later by a group of officers, among whom were three generals, was quickly discovered. Most of the organizers were arrested while trying to cross the border and were summarily executed. The Field Marshall and his friends were professionals. They knew how to protect themselves.

But there was also the Eastern Bloc and the Communist Parties throughout the world. The Red Tsar of all the Russians roused his followers against the incredible and dangerous heresy of Belgrade. In the next few years no means of pressure and of defamation were spared. Those years were particularly hard for Tito and his friends, but they would not lose their composure. Certain of their position in their own country, they sought with calmness and dignity, avoiding all provocation, to persuade the "Peoples' Republics" that Yugoslavia was and wished to be part of the family.

This completely reasonable tactic must have been one of the factors that influenced Tito to continue his support of the Greek guerrillas as before. A change of attitude would have weakened his position in the communist world.

Thus, aid did not decrease by one bullet and, in autumn, at the U.N. General Assembly (see below) the Yugoslav representatives, cut off from their former friends and allies and completely isolated, were the most fervent pleaders for Markos's cause. (Kardelj, chief of the Yugoslav delegation and a very ponderous man, even went so far—Vishinsky was present—as to make a long speech in Russian on November 29, 1948.)

Besides, there was another factor which militated in favor of the continuation of aid to DAG. During the second half of 1948, the KKE avoided committing itself in the conflict between Moscow and Belgrade. It was perhaps, the only communist party in the whole world that took this position. And it had a serious reason for doing so. To condemn Tito meant to deprive themselves of the main source of arms, ammunition and food, plus the loss of their bases and free crossing of the Yugoslav border in both directions. From one month to the next, these things could not be replaced. On the other hand, to condemn Stalin meant the same losses on the Albanian and Bulgarian side and, what is more, isolation from the whole communist world. The situation of the KKE leaders, engaged in a mortal struggle, was most delicate. Whatever their sympathies and their convictions were, they must remain silent.

Under these circumstances, Tito, by continuing his assistance to DAG, wished to prove his loyalty to the international movement. Encircled by hostile communist parties, he tried to attach himself to the KKE, that is, Greece, if they were victorious. In case of victory, at least one door would remain open to him. Besides, he did not ignore that if, among the Greek Communist leaders there were some disciples of Moscow with Zachariadis at their head, there were others, like Markos, who had great respect for him. That is why, during the first months after the rupture between Belgrade and Moscow, Yugoslav material and moral assistance did not decrease at all. This was a painful disappointment to the West, especially to the Greeks.

The behavior of Yugoslavia towards DAG changed completely when two significant developments occurred almost simultaneously in the first months of 1949. First, as we will see further on, the fortunes of war were changing and it soon became clear that DAG was going to lose the game. Second, a few months after the break with Moscow, a compromise between Yugoslavia and the Free World became indispensable for that nation to survive.

Actually, from one month to the next, the foreign commerce of Yugoslavia was deteriorating. Purchases of goods and sales by countries governed by "brother parties"—until then practically Yugoslavia's sole trading partners—were clearly going downhill. In the spring of 1949, the deliveries of goods essential to the nation's reconstruction and to everyday life, such as tools and machines, fuel and medicine, fell practically to zero.

Stalin was putting Tito against the wall; he would either capitulate, the score would then be settled and his country made secure, or he would have to approach the West, turn bourgeois or, at least, be accused of bourgeois deviationism. As it turned out, the daring Yugoslav leader had to bring about a reasonable and dignified rapprochemet with the West. To do this, he had to change his attitude towards certain serious matters, and especially the Greek guerrilla war.

Tito began to diminish his assistance and facilities to DAG from the last weeks of 1948; but he did it in stages, so the decrease was not perceptible until the beginning of spring 1949. By June, it can be said, he no longer supported the civil war in Greece. Finally, on July 10th, in a speech the Yugoslav premier made at Pola in Dalmatia, he announced that the Greek-Yugoslav frontier would be progressively closed. He did this, he said, "because of numerous incidents, because of the deaths of several Yugoslavs during these incidents, and finally, because of the false news broadcast by DAG, according to which the Greek army had been authorized to cross the border to attack the enemy." From that time, the direct interference of Yugoslavia in the Greek civil war ended completely.

On the Greek side, however, future developments were not influenced decisively by the new Yugoslav position. However, it constituted an unfavorable factor for the KKE because it hurt the morale of its followers and, during the very first months of the year, it complicated foreign assistance.

In Europe, in truth worldwide, the whole affair had been extremely unfavorable for Stalinism. When Stalin began his campaign against Tito, "certain that it would be enough for him to move his little finger to crush him," he did not have the least suspicion that he would suffer the most spectacular defeat of his life. He was not concerned that the Yugoslavs—strong, proud men and very attached to their land—would recognize, irrespective of their political tendencies, that Tito and his partisans not only had put up an unequalled resistance during the German occupation, but had managed to save the dignity and independence of their country as well against the all powerful Kremlin. Stalin did not know that young militant Walter, revolutionist Tito, now head of State, would not become bourgeois by drawing nearer to the West. He did not imagine, furthermore, that Marshall Tito would create a socialism, difficult to define in a few words, but which has always remained within the communist constellation as a peculiar type of socialism. Lastly, he had no idea that one day Tito would even appeal to countries outside the communist sphere and establish a Third World Movement.

Returning to that bloody conflict, the Greek civil war, which was reducing the country to ruins, our account picks up again at the beginning of summer in 1948 when Tito was giving considerable assistance to DAG. The doubts of government officials as to the possibility of a quick and decisive victory continued, and increased. Thus, from every point of view, the hour for the great offensive the army had long been preparing had come.

The Great Carnage: Operation "Coronis". Up to that time, nobody had dared venture into the large mountain region known as Grammos. Now the Greek army would do just that. In army circles, as well as among politicians who knew what was happening on the battlefield, agreement was not unanimous. Many doubted that such an operation should be undertaken. But other generals, mainly General Van Fleet, believed both that it was necessary, and that it would be successful.

Planned for months before, the operation under the code name "Coronis", was launched on June 14. It was the largest, the most difficult, the longest, and the most deadly battle of the entire war.

The terrain where the drama would unfold was very rough. Grammos is a series of ridges of 1,500 to 2,500 meters with slopes that are rather steep and rocky or covered with dense forests. Seen on a horizontal plane, this mountain block forms a trapezoid of which three sides are about one hundred kilometers long. A fourth side to the north, is only fifty kilometers, and is on the Albanian border. At that time this trapezoid did not even have a single dirt road on Greek soil, but to the north, on Albanian territory, there was an old road running along its entire length which had been widened and repaired by the Italians. It was an ideal location for one of the guerrilla's main bases as it could be supplied through Albania and was completely isolated from the rest of Greece.

To complete the picture, the general aspect of the land there is wild. Small rivers, which for six months of the year become tumultuous torrents, rend the narrow valleys.

High mountains stand tall on all sides. Towards the south, lies the Pindos mountain range; to the north, the Albanian mountains (see Map no. 6).

The Supreme Military Council of the Provisional Government had its seat at Aetomilitsa (Little apple tree of the eagles), a village at an altitude of 1,400 meters. DAG had resolved that the Grammos fort would be defended inch by inch.[5] For this purpose, two lines of fortifications had been prepared, each one a few kilometers in depth. The first one, or the "outer defense" was to block the passes that led into the mountain through deep ravines. The second one, the "inner defense" line, prevented access to the center of the region. These fortified lines consisted, primarily, of machine-gun emplacements which were usually covered over with six to seven rows of logs and a thick layer of earth. These positions were perfectly camouflaged, their resistance to bombing and shelling good, and their positions carefully selected so they could cover each other with their fire. The approaches to the fortified lines were protected by minefields. DAG alluded to these mountains in writing and in song, as the "impregnable fort."

Markos realized in time that the army was preparing for an attack against his main base. That is why he entrusted all rebel forays in the rest of Greece to light forces and, as early as April, he began to gather around him a large number of troops. In the end, Grammos's two lines of defense were manned by more than 12,500 fighters. Further north at Mount Vitsi, the most important natural fortress of the area he chose as his main base, and equally fortified, he had stationed 1,500 men. Lastly, in the mountains of Epirus, he left about 3,000 guerrillas under the command of a daring captain, Yannoulis. These last troops, acting on their own initiative, were to cut the enemy's communications as soon as operations began.

Ten days before D-day, indiscreet interviews in the press by foreign officers, and the even more indiscreet publication of a map, informed Markos of the plan of action and even of the starting date for the attack. Naturally, he took advantage of this to get his last reinforcements to the scene and to see that his units were deployed for action.

In order to occupy the "impregnable fort", the Army General Staff assembled an impressive force. Five entire divisions, 40,000 men in all, supported by air force, artillery, and all the auxiliary services, would undertake the main action. Another 7,500 men of the army and 4,500 of the national guard would block the principal roads of Epirus and would face those bands who, from the Pindos to Mourghana, would try to hinder communications. Better fighting units had been entrusted with the same mission in Thessaly and in Macedonia.

The plan of action foresaw three phases in all: the first one was preparatory and intended to clear out the area around the main base. The second phase should lead, in a few days, to the occupation of several strong positions of the outer defense line. As soon as that was done, even partially, they would undertake the third phase, the success of which depended on the result of an extremely daring maneuver. One entire division starting from Nestorion in the north, and another one, from Konitsa to the south, would advance along different stream beds so as to take control, in two or three days, of all of the Albanian frontier and cut communications between Grammos and Albania. After that, the offensive would be generalized; the army would attack from all sides in order to occupy their "impregnable fort". But planning is one thing and realization of that plan quite another.

The offensive began with great enthusiasm following heavy bombardment of the area by both planes and artillery. On June 14, 1948, two divisions launched an attack with a south-southwest axis, and on the 16th, two others attacked from the opposite side in an east-northeast direction. Combat without let-up continued until the 20th of the month and, in certain areas, until the 25th. These battles were murderous. Nevertheless, though the positions around the "fort" had been cleared out, and though some "impregnable" positions had been captured (e.g., Great Ondria, which controlled two narrow valleys), the army did not open a real breach in the outer defense line. Ten days had gone by, everything had been tried, the third phase of the plan had even begun, but there were still no decisive results.

The reasons for this were many. Firstly, the underground batteries of DAG had hardly been touched by the bombing and shelling. Secondly, the rebels were for the first time, using ammunition at will for their artillery, mortar, and machine-guns. Thirdly, the mine-fields were more widespread, more numerous and denser than had been suspected. Lastly, and mainly, the toughness of the defenders—a fundamental factor—could not have been greater.

Finally, to complete the misfortunes of this great offensive, the two divisions that were to encircle the Fort along the Albanian border, could advance only three to five kilometers. They came under heavy fire from machine-guns and artillery. One of the two spearheads of these advances, the 41st Brigade, suffered particularly heavy losses.

In addition, the rebel bands in action along the fringe of the battle had performed feats of valor. Yannoulis, the lawyer turned guerrilla leader, and who took part in the battle against Grevena, had done everything possible to relieve pressure on the threatened Fort.

As soon as the big offensive got under way, Yannoulis and his men, demonstrating great mobility and unbelievable endurance, threatened almost all the communication and all of the bases of Epirus. Some strong units of about 400 men occupied a group of villages well to the south of Ioannina, and so imperiled the communications of Epirus with Missolonghi and Patras. Other stronger bands harassed 75 kilometers of the Ioannina-Konitsa road and, one night, took a village scarcely 20 kilometers from the capital of Epirus. For ten days Yannoulis' forces were everywhere, even managing to penetrate army positions.

It became clear that the Greek General Staff and the American Mission, who both favored this operation, had underestimated many factors. Changes in the plan of operation "Coronis" had to be made. Although it is considered unwise to change a plan in the midst of the battle, it is equally disastrous not to do so if this is deemed absolutely necessary. The murderous fighting abated and, for five days, officers of the Army General Staff, headed by the director of operations during the Greek-Italian war, General Kitrilakis, studied the situation together with commanders of the fighting units. The new plan differed greatly from the old one. The two advances from opposite directions along the Albanian frontier were cancelled. Strong frontal attacks, combined with artful maneuvers on the most inaccessible terrain, as well as surprise night attacks, would open the way to the Fort. Large herds of animals, led in the right places, would be used to neutralize the mine fields just ahead of each main assault.

The "new first phase" began on June 28   and lasted until July 7   and in certain sectors until July 14th. At the price of great sacrifices from gaining and losing positions two or three times in succession, from falling on unexpected minefields, from changing plans according to circumstances, from overcoming an unprecedented resistance, the army managed to smash part of the outer defense line on July 7th. It is true that at several points the attack had made very little progress. But in the southeast sector, for about 25 kilometers as the crow flies, the outer line of defense had been broken and its positions had been captured to a depth of about ten kilometers. All of the ridges north and south of Eptachori, as well as the village itself and the valley of the small Zouzouliotiko River were in the hands of the army. To the west, the army was now in contact with the "inner defense" (see Map no. 7). Losses were heavy on both sides and efforts considerable, a fact that made for low morale as much on one side as on the other. The army had anticipated spectacular results in a few days. Now, one month had gone by an only partial results had been obtained.

The guerrillas waited in vain for the arrival of international brigades, similar to those that had fought in Spain, and about which they had talked for some time, especially since the battle of Konitsa. And here, they were having to face such a strong offensive by themselves. Finally, and above all, they had believed that they would not yield an inch of the "impregnable fort", which they had defended so obstinately.

Among the guerrillas, disappointment turned into violent decisions. Leaders of units were blamed, or even punished. Sentenced by the Supreme Council, Captain Apostolis was executed for having lost a high crest of strategic importance. However, even more serious was the fact that "General" Bartzotas, a member of the Central Committee of the KKE and of the Provisional Government, and "Lieutenant Colonel" Venetsanopoulos (an ex-officer of the regular army), in their criticism published in the monthly review of DAG, *Democratic Army* (September 1948 issue), attributed the losses in the battle for Grammos to the fall of the mountains around Eptachori. Their capture was due, according to them, to underestimation of the importance of positions, to poor preparation of fortifications, and to mistakes committed by the command during the assault by the national army. In fact, without mentioning names, they cast the blame on Markos. Now, this was serious. It was also basically unjust. Markos Vafiades, the apostle of the pure guerrilla war, who openly disapproved of big battles and of a war of positions, was the chief artisan of this brilliant defense. Now, he was doing his utmost to respect a recent decision of the Supreme Council—fight no matter what the cost, to save a part of the Fort. In particular, he asked for the maximum performance from his forces, active throughout Greece, to do whatever they could to relieve Grammos. On the other hand, Markos carefully organized local defense. In addition to the reinforcements mentioned above, he brought six companies by forced marches from neighboring mountains—a true feat considering that he was under siege—and a brigade from mountains near the Yugoslav-Bulgarian border, plus another from Olympus, even farther away. These reinforcements were to cover the losses sustained and to bring the total number of fighters defending Grammos from the beginning to more than 16,000 men.

The army too was getting very seriously ready for the "new second phase". Besides supplying front line units, the engineers, working night and day, began to open up certain dirt roads. The air force bombed enemy positions daily using large incendiary bombs for the first time.

The preparation of the army also took another form. A radical change was effected in the command structure. The troops which led the offensive comprised until then the Second Army Corps which was very large for such rugged terrain and such great distances, as well as to meet the daily vicissitudes and unexpected events of battle. So the troops of the north and northeast sectors by themselves were to form the Second Army Corps and were placed under the command of an excellent officer, General Kitrilakis. General Thrasyvoulos Tsakalotos, the liberator of Rimini during the 1943 campaign in Italy, was named to command the troops of the south and southwest sectors, and of all Epirus. He had proved himself on many battlefields and was a real leader of fighting men.

Tsakalotos arrived with a small group of officers and immediately, the atmosphere changed in his sector. For ten days he pursued the rebel bands of Captain Yannoulis in a bloody and unceasing chase. Finally, the bands were forced to disperse or to take refuge on the fortified mountain of Mourghana. In this way, the western flank of the Grammos fort was completely covered.

Thus, on the entire periphery of Grammos, the army was in a position to move forward. On July 15, the new attack got under way from the northeast (from Macedonia) and on the 25th, from the southwest (from Epirus). It was immediately blocked from the north by the very rugged positions of Alevitsa-Amouda, of Goupata-Pyrgos and others nearby (See Map No. 7). Continuous strong pressure was necessary even to slowly achieve secondary objectives. To make up for it, the attack was developing well from the southwest, though there were intervals of cruel struggle.

Thus, by July 26, at dawn, after a heavy artillery barrage, forces of the regular army were able to take a natural stronghold, well fortified by the guerrillas, known as Kleftis. With an altitude of 1,850 meters Kleftis was as difficult to seize as it was important for the offensive, being the gate to the western side of Grammos. Then, two hours later withering fire coming from the highest summits and a daring counter-attack by the guerrillas allowed them to reoccupy this strategic position. Nevertheless, not wishing to accept defeat, the men of the army clung to the rocks about two hundred meters below the top of the summit.

For four days and five nights the battle raged. Replenished only during the night with ammunition, food and water brought up on the backs of men, soldiers and guerrillas contested each rock, fighting desperately with guns, hand grenades and bayonets. In response to a proposal to withdraw to a nearby ridge, Tsakalotos answered from Profitis Elias where he was directing operations: "Don't withdraw even half a meter! Stay where you are! Kleftis will be captured even if it takes the whole First Army Corps."

Finally, at 04:30 on August 1, battalion 583 under Major G. Koumanakos[6] launched a sudden assault against Kleftis, spearheaded by a group of selected officers and men. The first squads literally jumped into the trenches of the guerrillas and, after a brief hand-to-hand struggle, they completed the takeover of the position. Immediately afterwards, these units were reinforced by Battalion 584 and two companies of 527 and, still under the command of Koumanakos, undertook other assaults along the wild summit of Smolinghas (2,221 meters). After murderous battles and several lightning actions these forces occupied the summit at 19:45; thus, to the southwest the whole guerrilla line of defense on impregnable Smolikas had crumbled.

On August 7, after much bloody fighting, almost all of the outer defense line had been captured by by the army, as well as many small villages in the narrow valleys. Alone, the imposing positions of Alevitsa and Goupata on the northeast of the perimeter still held. The rebels continued to resist there even when the army was already attacking the inner defense positions. For, it must be noted, from the 7th until the 21st of August, with a six weeks' delay on the initial plan, the third phase of operation "Coronis" got under way.

It would take too long to describe the relentless battles that took place in the next two weeks. On both sides they fought furiously on terrain where the men felt lost and often could not comprehend how the battle was developing. Many acts of bravery and great exploits took place during this passionate confrontation. Let us mention one which is typical of this struggle. On the evening of August 16, an important summit had been taken by Battalion 592 after hard fighting. During the night of the 17th, Markos's men made a lightning counter-attack. In one very densely wooded place, the darkness was such that combat became a game of "hide and seek", played with bayonets and hand grenades. At one moment, the commander of the company in the forest, Lieutenant G. Papadoyiannis, came to grips with a big hefty chap. Fate had chosen well. It was the commander of the enemy battalion, who had one of the most pretentious nicknames among the guerrillas; he was called "captain Aris", the Greek name for Mars, the god of war. A furious hand-to-hand fight ensued. It was a dance of death. For then, the two men—embraced as they were in a mortal struggle—suddenly realized that they were beginning to slide down a steep slope. Moments after they reached the bottom of the ravine they renewed their fight, this time with knives. Captain Aris died on the spot with a knife in his chest. He was buried that way. But neither had his adversary come out ahead in that fierce struggle. Papadoyiannis had received a fatal wound in the neck. He was picked up the next day by the men of another company, but died in a field hospital the same day. It would seem that the gods were thirsty!

Fierce combat continued to rage until August 20th. In the last days blood ran profusely. The guerrillas defended with particular stubbornness the center of their "impregnable fort" here the villages of Aetomilitsa and Grammos lay, the seat of the Provisional Government. But they were now outflanked by the enemy on both sides and, though they expended all their efforts, they could not reverse the tide. Soon they would no longer be able to defend themselves. Markos alone understood this, and on the 18th, he ordered a general retreat.

The Provisional Government and certain of its auxiliary services were withdrawn to Albania in time. Markos, a staunch opponent of stationary battles, but a good strategist and at the same time—from the Communist point of view—a good political tactician, did not believe that he must follow them with the remnants of his army. The only passes which remained open were those of Slimnitsa and Monopylon (Single door) and the army was about to take them. By means of a fierce attack on August 20, Markos cleared the vicinity of the passes towards Albania, and especially towards Vitsi. He immediately sent towards Albania all those who could not be saved otherwise, about 1,500 fighters, more than 3,000 wounded and almost all of his artillery—about fifty pieces. This brilliant retreat was not the only one undertaken by Markos, the former tobacco worker from Kavalla turned general, at the end of August 1948. The rest of his forces, about 8,000 men, were directed further north towards Vitsi, still on Greek territory.

So, that group of nine mountains known as Vitsi, equally well fortified, which touches on the Albanian border and Lake Prespa, was now provided with a considerable garrison, one might even say, an impressive one. Counting the men who were already there plus those who went through Albania from Grammos, as well as some fresh troops from Yugoslav bases, the Mount Vitsi garrison totalled nearly 13,000 fighters. This was dangerous and could soon become disastrous. Ioannis Kitrilakis, commander of the Second Army Corps, had foreseen these two maneuvers of Markos. As early as August 10, he had requested substantial reinforcements from the G G S in order to occupy Vitsi and to bar the routes that he believed DAG would follow. But, due to the lack of available reserves, no reinforcements were sent to him. Moreover, this brilliant staff officer was not an equally able field commander, capable of inspiring his men, or of taking the initiative on the battlefield. He tried to close the passes on the 20th and 21st, but in vain. It was too late! The consequences of this mistake would be ominous. In any case, at the end of August the army had won the battle of Grammos. The "impregnable fort" plus the whole mountain range, were occupied. Booty which fell into the hands of the army was considerable: 85 heavy machine-guns, 326 light machine-guns, 1,480 rifles, 94 mortars and large quantities of food and ammunition.

The dead guerrillas found on the battlefields numbered about 2,500 with 1,053 prisoners and deserters. Estimated wounded evacuated to Albania must have been over 3,000 bringing total casualties to about 6,500. The drain on the national army, nevertheless, had been equally heavy. And this was even more significant when we consider that DAG's artillery was rather weak, and that it had no air force. This meant that the losses were almost exclusively due to small arms and mines. Army losses during the three phases of the battles for Grammos reached 792 dead, 5,085 wounded and 70 missing, or a total of 5,947. According to some military analysts, the rebels often formed a bare wall of rigid resistance...the regular troops put up a marvelous fight. The losses represented a total, for both sides, of more than 12,000 men out of combat.

What was most disatrous for the government side, however, was the realization by the troops that, although they had made an enormous effort and had suffered tremendous losses, the result was not decisive.

The guerrilla war was in full swing again all over Greece, though less intense than before. Most of the frontier had remained open—except the one with Turkey, of course—and the observers of the Balkan Commission had seen with their own eyes flagrant frontier violations both during and after battles. The Provisional Government of the rebels was again established on Greek soil at the village of Pyxos, near the lake of Prespa. They still had an "impregnable fort", but in another place a little to the north, and it was very well fortified and strongly garrisoned. In addition, there was the vague expectation that, during the coming winter, the army would have to evacuate those wild, inhospitable and very exposed mountains for which so much blood had been shed. Lastly, the men of the army understood more than ever before that their adversary fought with incredible obstinacy and that he often had better intelligence than the Greek General Staff.

Certainly, those on the government side also saw the good side of the coin. They counted on an eventual closing of the Yugoslav border. They noted a considerable improvement in their own logistics. They were satisfied with the fighting spirit of all their forces and admired especially the prowess of their raiding forces (LOK).

But the soldier who is continually in the field for more than two years does not find this sufficient; he needs tangible results, at least enough for him to be able to say to himself that the end is in sight.

Now, nobody could say this after Grammos. That is one of the reasons why, one month later victory seemed to be turning into a dangerous defeat.

Fearing Disaster, in Spite of Victory. Soon after the bloody victory of Grammos, the Greek General Staff took the following decisions: one division of the southwest sector would stay on Grammos so that the DAG could not reoccupy it. Two divisions from the same sector would attack the notorious Mourghana further west. All three divisions of the northeast region would attack the Mount Vitsi fort. The overall objective would be to clear the guerrillas out of all the mountains near the frontiers. The idea was good and in harmony with the old tactic of continually pursuing and harassing the enemy. Still, with exhausted men and decimated divisions, the army was preparing an assault against extremely strong positions.

As for Mourghana, it had been the scene of three failures by the army. In the writings and songs of DAG it was called the "guerrilla castle", and the orders of the day reiterated daily that it would be defended like Stalingrad and that the "monarchofascists would be defeated there." This long rocky Stalingrad, half of which belonged to Albania, was particularly harmful because it enormously facilitated forays in depth and thus, could threaten all the communications of Epirus at any moment. Exactly for this reason it was also very carefully fortified. The Greek General Staff later on counted over 2,500 fortification works—minor or major—on the mountain. Mine-fields were also extensive.

The offensive began on September 10, but it was not launched with all of the troops foreseen for the operation because part of them, and later a whole division, was sent to Vitsi where—as we shall see—things took a turn for the worse. Even so, Tsakalotos had at his disposal one division and a brigade with which to attack Mourghana.

The army captured with great difficulty some outposts of the "guerrilla castle" but, after the second day, further advance was impossible. A ferocious defense held in check the most persistent assaults. Then, suddenly, on the 18th, the government announced that, owing to a good maneuver from the northeast side, resistance had been crushed and the whole of Mourghana was in the hands of the national army. At that time everyone was so preoccupied with what was happening on the other side of the Pindos range that no one asked himself what was the secret of this effective maneuver. Later on, no one talked about it, so few indeed are those who knew what really hapened. Perhaps it is time to give the facts.

The headquarters of the Army Corps, as well as Tsakalotos who obstinately insisted on directing the offensive in person, were soon convinced that nothing could be done. The plans of attack were therefore changed. All the command posts of the brigade took up positions near the line of fire in order to follow the action directly and to be personally responsible for it. Four battalions of elite troops, commanded by officers who have become famous (Koumanakos, Peridis, Calogeropoulos, Kolonias), took up positions east of the mountain of a front only a few kilometers long, where the slopes were steepest. That was precisely where the Greek-Albanian border was located. All maneuvers were impossible for Albanian detachments were patrolling the area.

At dawn of the 14th, after an artillery and mortar

barrage during which every piece available was utilized, all the troops—to the last unit—launched the attack. The mountain summit with an altitude of 1,806 meters, dominates the area. Calogeropoulos's battalion was to take it by "passing through a place not only dangerous for goats, but even for smugglers". The battalion advanced with great strides, overthrowing rather weak resistance, for the enemy believed that on such steep land strong forces were not needed. Besides, the enemy had counted on another kind of protection that soon made its presence felt; dense artillery fire against Calogeropoulos's battalion came from the Greek village of Sotira in Northern Epirus on the Albanian side of the frontier. From the same direction, the battalion also drew small arms fire.

General Tsakalotos, who was at that place with his staff, then took personal responsibility for a daring action: the Greek artillery put the Albanian artillery out of action, also destroying some houses in the village. At the same time, an infantry company charged into Albanian territory and overwhelmed the Albanian detachments which, in all certainty, took part in the battle. It was the first and only time that the Greek side returned the compliment for the thousands of raids across the border.

The intensity of the battle did not decrease; on the contrary, defense hardened. But from that time onwards, the defenders and their lines of communications were under fire from the heights which, up to then, had protected them. In fact, on the morning of the 16th, after a short but fierce struggle, that key defense point, summit 1806, was occupied by Calogeropoulos's men.[7]

Twenty-four hours later fighting ceased. The rebels withdrew into Albania, except for a part of them who crossed the national lines and lost themselves in the forests of Pindos. The operation had cost the army 577 officers and men in casualties. But nobody cared about that then. What was of primary importance was that Albania could no longer put at the disposition of the guerrillas this long stepping-stone to Greek territory. This was perhaps the only fortunate consequence of the Grammos victory. For, elsewhere at that moment the situation bordered on disaster.

A large force of rebels, entrenched in the mountains of Vitsi, up against the Albanian and Yugoslav borders and strongly fortified, repulsed all attacks against them by Greek troops from August 22 until September 14.

If there were—during the first four days—some small successes, such as the capturing of a few outposts, later on each position was fought over in deadly battles, being taken one day and lost the next. Now the army found itself literally in front of the guerrilla castle, the "impregnable fort" of Vitsi. Awe-inspiring positions, such as Mali-Mathi and Voutsi on the upper reaches of the Aliakmon River, cost torrents of blood, but still held. For twenty-three days the army fought in every way possible, but the guerrilla positions remained intact. After occupying Grammos, it was believed, everything would be better. Unfortunately, it was not so.

On the contrary, things became much worse. Sometimes at night in the barracks, the soldiers would say: "We chase them here, they reappear there; we push them into Albania, they return through Yugoslavia. The Americans who are helping us are at the other side of the world. The Slavs who are helping them are next door. We have been pursuing them for two and a half years, with what success?" Doubt, disappointment, fatigue, the death of a close comrade, the impossibility of breaking through the new line of DAG—all sapped morale.

On September 14, two entire battalions refused to defend their positions, even though they were not under very strong pressure. Devotion to duty on the part of the officers and some soldiers could not change the situation. Throwing away their weapons, panic-stricken, the men deserted their positions and fled to Kastoria. Met at the outskirts of town by more courageous units which, in the meantime, had been alerted, the deserters found the road barred. They were arrested by the military police and were arraigned immediately before a special court martial, that is, a court composed principally of officers in the field. At least 78 deserters in those days faced the firing squad. All of them were fighters from Grammos.

Then, all of these details were not known to the general public. Nevertheless, they became known to some members of the government, to the Greek General Staff and to the leaders of the Democratic Army.

The first measure taken by the G G S was to withdraw, in effect, to shorten its lines. They were too advanced, being aimed at offensive operations; the breach was dangerous and the morale of the army did not allow attack. All contingents thus took up defensive positions with their main objective being to cover Kastoria, an important army base in northwest Macedonia.

The G G S had acted correctly and in time. For Markos, who realized at once the significance of the September 14 flight, began to prepare for a strong attack against Kastoria, the seat of the Second Army Corps. His preparations lasted until the 19th. During the day there was an exchange of fire, as is customary between enemy armies that retain contact. But, during the night, important troop movements took place in the area controlled by DAG. Such strict security measures were enforced that nothing was evident outside the lines of contact and nothing seemed abnormal to air force reconnaissance on the next day.

Then, on the night of the 19th, there was a general attack along the whole front of Kastoria. Forceful and fierce, the assault lasted without any let-up until the morning of the 21st. For thirty-six hours, Markos, who personally took charge of the operation, threw his best brigades into the battle. They captured important positions and, at many points, penetrated the government lines for three or four kilometers. The low morale and fatigue of the army could not be concealed.

If there was no longer the question of occupying Vitsi, at least there was no striking defeat, and one could count on the line being stabilized. DAG could nevertheless be satisfied. Beaten on its own territory and cut to pieces only one month ago, it now appeared victorious and menacing. The rebels took courage again.

Zachariadis, very skillfully exonerating himself for the Grammos defeat, wrote in the monthly military magazine *Democratic Army* November 1948): *"For the DAG Command,"* he said, *"the operations in Grammos and Vitsi were part of one big plan aimed at diminishing the offensive potential of monarcho-fascism. Grammos did not become the grave of monarcho-fascism, but there its grave was dug. Owing to our maneuver in Grammos, monarcho-fascist strategy has wavered over a vacuum and believed that DAG left Grammos to avoid complete defeat."*

Here perhaps, we should publish some of the 190 photographs from a commemorative album on DAG's second anniversary. It was printed at that time in DAG's own printing shop which was found later in a village near Lake Prespa. The author possesses one certainly rare copy, perhaps the only one.

The Communists may have been satisifed about things and had reason to boast in the village of Pyxos, the new center of the Provisional Government, but the mood in Athens was different. There everyone was very uneasy, for the morale of the troops had been shaken.

Sofoulis, in spite of his age, flew to Kastoria, visited the troops, and talked to the soldiers. Minister of Defense George Stratos, one of the best MP's of the Populists, and the chief of the G G S did likewise. The chief of the American Mission, General Van Fleet, who had observed all the battles from an advance post, followed their example. However, the general was almost the cause of a serious incident. During a meeting of high-ranking officers in Kastoria, he accused the army of having wasted American aid without having crushed the enemy, and wondered whether it was not time for Americans to leave. Showing an unawareness of the difficulties these men faced, he was above all, placing an equal value on money and blood. He had forgotten too that, of the two partners, it was the Greek army which was paying the highest price. Calmly, this challenge was accepted by the Greek officers present. They proved to his satisfaction that all operations had been approved, and sometimes even suggested, by American military advisers. Van Fleet, annoyed perhaps by the fact that he was gambling a successful career, but who was actually both an honest man and a good soldier, did not insist. The affair was closed and the American Mission continued to support the Greek army logistically.

Fortunately for the army, general concern went much further than General Van Fleet. In mid-October the prestigious U.S. Secretary of State, George Marshall, arrived in Athens with the American Secretary of Defense and other personalities to look into the unfavorable turn of events. The author has reason to believe that certain prominent Americans, though it displeased them, had posed to themselves the question, "Must we leave?" But Marshall's answer was definite, and in the negative.

Then again, Sofoulis himself was not satisfied. Discouraged by the outcome and under the influence of old, retired officers who were his friends and had some prestige, he cast the blame upon the military leaders, which did not help matters at all, except on one point. The great old man was more persuaded that Papagos should be placed at the head of the army and invested with full powers.

From the government's point of view, this was perhaps the darkest hour of the guerrilla war. It is not exaggerating at all to say that at the beginning of autumn in 1948, one had the impression that the iron curtain was falling on Greece as well. The bell did not seem to ring the alarm any longer, but rather to toll the loss of freedom and of hope.

Yet, the people on the whole, and the army, more particularly, still had—in spite of everything—great resources of will. To a people eminently attached to freedom, courage and the stubborness of despair played a decisive role. Abundant American material was there only to be put to use.

A renewal of guerrilla activity which then appeared everywhere in Greece, especially in the central and southern regions, was counter-balanced by a rekindled fighting spirit in the armed forces. Certainly, the old successful tactics were still employed, but counter-measures by the army were undiminished.

In mid-September, a naval incident allowed a better undertanding of what was happening in the Peloponnesus and of what was to be done about it. There, the guerrilla war had acquired dimensions equal to those it previously had only in the northern regions. This was disastrous to morale because the population was known for its anti-communist and conservative tendencies. Where, then, did the guerrilla bands find so many men, all those weapons and quantities of ammunition?

In the early morning hours of September 6, as a corvette of the fleet, the "POLEMISTIS", was patrolling the eastern coasts of the Peloponnesus, its crew made out a small caique[8] speeding along the coast. It ignored the corvette's frantic signals to stop. Instead, at full speed the caique entered the deserted bay of Fokianos, (southeast of the town of Leonidion) the narrow entrance of which was flanked by two steep hills. As soon as the navy ship approached and was close enough to let down a launch preparatory to boarding the caique, a hail of fire poured down from the hills. Although an isolated and unimportant bay, it was strongly guarded by a group of guerrillas in naturally fortified positions.

But the unexpected reaction did not deter the stubborn young captain, Pyrros Spyromilios—a sea dog from Chimarra of Northern Epirus—from charging towards the narrow entrance of the bay and firing back with all the weapons of his ship. The guerrilla caique and the surrounding positions responded with heavy fire. But this was a one-sided duel. Suddenly, all firing ceased for the caique had received a fatal hit and blew up.

No prisoners were taken, but a detailed search of the area revealed that the caique had a 250-ton capacity and had departed from the port of Dyrrachion in Albania. It was carrying 2,000 German rifles, 100 machine-guns, 3,000 mines, and large quantities of ammunition, hand grenades, and KKE propaganda material (books, newspapers, printing paper, etc.). The log of the boat recovered nearby, showed that its captain was an Albanian, Hasan Moustafa, and that is crew consisted of Greek guerrillas.

A wide investigation carried out after this incident, proved that members of the KKE[9] had dispatched from Albanian and other Mediterranean ports a substantial number of guerrillas and quantities of war material to the Peloponnesus. This information was extremely useful for the twin purposes of lifting morale and of organizing a better watch on the coasts of southern Greece.

In October, the First Army Corps, freer now in Epirus, could send a large number of its units towards the Grammos-Vitsi line. This fact allowed the Greek General Staff to attempt a new offensive against Vitsi with larger forces all placed under the command of General Tsakalotos. When the latter assumed his command at the end of October, several engagements had already eased the positions of the national forces. Two impregnable heights had been taken by LOK battalions, commanded by Major Christos Papadatos and Ioannis Manetas, with Colonel Kyriakos Papageorgopoulos as co-ordinator of operations.

But on November 10, the pace of combat changed and a

general attack against all positions that were of any strategic importance began. It lasted for five days and five nights without let-up. On the entire front to the north of Kastoria, there was a series of attacks followed by murderous counter-attacks. Key mountain positions were captured and lost, then re-captured, sometimes changing hands three times.

Fate wished all these key positions to be in the hands of the national army when a deep layer of snow blanketed the whole area, from the plains to the mountain heights. Other snowfalls would follow, for the winter was early and very heavy. Thus, it was impossible for any widespread operations to take place in the vicinity of Vitsi until spring. Casualties on both sides were again counted by the hundreds. Bloodshed was to continue but, for the time being, only in regions that were far from the border. In Vitsi that would come much later, when the streams would run red again with the same intensity. Now, the thunder of cannons would be heard elsewhere, and events of a different nature would change the course of this savage war.

Chapter XI

Toward a Final Settlement

In the Diplomatic Sphere. The guerrilla war was in full swing in Greece when this local conflict was made the object of a spectacular diplomatic confrontation between East and West. This confrontation occurred in the General Assembly of the United Nations and was exceptionally long, blustery, and acrimonious. Everyone was expecting as much, for it had been seen coming long before.

On September 16, 1948, the Balkan Committee announced that it was in agreement with a proposal by the Secretary General of the United Nations, one which was unknown until then and which constituted a daring innovation for that period: the creation of an international force which would supervise the Greek frontiers.

On the 17th, the newspapers of the Free World published information which had originated from certain eastern capitals, according to which the "Provisional Government of the Mountains" was requesting authorization to send a representative to the U.N. General Assembly in order to explain its position and to submit proposals for a settlement.

On September 18, the United States of America, France and Great Britain revealed that a few days earlier, on the 13th, the three governments had addressed a very strong protest to Albania concerning its role in the Greek civil war. Some days later, that country—one of the smallest in Europe and not yet a member of the U.N. due to its alignment with fascism—had disdainfully rejected the warning by the three Great Powers.

Lastly, and perhaps most important of all, the precise and documented reports of the Balkan Committee, which attested to the fact that the Democratic Army of Greece had received effective foreign assistance, was continually irritating to the Eastern Bloc. At the opening of the U.N. General Assembly this irritation reached a peak when the numerous and flagrant violations of the Greek frontier during the battle of Grammos were pointed out by this committee.

At that time the U.N. General Assembly was not what it is today. Then, it had no members of insignificant international weight. Not even one seat was occupied by a country whose influence in world affairs was almost uniquely that of its one vote at the United Nations. The General Assembly with 58 members then against its 132 of today—was for a blood-stained humanity just emerging from World War II, the hope of all mankind. Member countries were represented by men who, for good reasons or bad, had already achieved international reputations.

Autumn 1948 marked a turning point in the history of the General Assembly. It would become obvious thereafter, that among other more proper functions of the General Assembly, it would also become one of the greatest rostrums of demagogy in the world. There, in that arena under the gaze of the whole civilized world, interest, passions, and sometimes vulgarity would be given full play.

303

The Third General Assembly opened in Paris on September 22, 1948. The Greek question was raised early in the session although the agenda included many other important matters. And this question immediately became the big subject of discord there.[1] Minister of Foreign Affairs Robert Schuman of France, Ernest Bevin of Great Britain, George Marshall of the U.S.A., and others spoke successively from the rostrum of the enormous auditorium condemning the violations of the Greek frontiers, recalling that Greece was a rare case where legality had been restored under international control, and finally, demanding that peace be re-established there also.

For the others, in return, led by Andrei Vishinsky—the great prosecutor of the famous Moscow trials—maintained the opposite view: what was happening in Greece was due to imperialist and fascist machinations.

For several days invectives followed by equally sharp retorts succeeded one another. Wonderful speeches were made and the prestigious orators used blunt words.

Basically, the main object of the confrontation was not the Greek question itself, but the Balkan Committee. Some considered it indispensable and maintained that it should continue its activities, while others believed it should be dissolved. Vishinsky led the round to the second tune. Although Stalin had told his Yugoslav comrades ten months earlier that the rebellion in Greece should cease, the Soviet Union still appeared at the U.N. as the great protector of the KKE and of its revolutionary struggle. According to Vishinsky, the formation of the Balkan Committee was illegal; it served the interests of certain imperialist powers, not of peace—its mission being to put the blame where it did not belong.

Kardelj, the distinguished Yugoslav delegate, isolated and accused of being a renegade, began bargaining in the hope that he could gain lost ground, or at least make a good impression on his former patrons. According to him, the

Greek question should simply not be discussed by the General Assembly. "New chains," he said, "have been forged for the Greek people"; the Balkan Committee had been created in violation of the U.N. Charter and its activities poisoned relations between the Balkan countries and Greece. The totalitarian regimes referred to the elections held under international control as "new chains". Thus, it was difficult to go any further.

The ripostes were extremely sharp. The plea of Bevin in favor of Greece, "a country which had courageously served the Allied cause", ended with a clear but hard indictment: "*We know the wishes of Greece's northern neighbors,*" he said, "*to extend their territory at her expense. This should not be allowed to pass in silence and do not think that we shall forget this fact . . . . We are participating in the cold war only to defend ourselves, and those who have started it have only to raise their finger, give an order and everything is going to come to a stop in Greece.*"

The debate was not easy. It was complicated even more by the fact that the KKE repeatedly attempted to get a hearing for a representative of "Free Greece" before the Assembly. The Communists tried to do this both by direct appeals from the Provisional Government and by proposals of friendly countries. All these appeals and proposals were rejected by a large majority.

Nevertheless, the forum where this diplomatic confrontation became most acute was in the Political Commission itself. Here debate was heated. The continuity of daily meetings by this Commission, its less rigid procedure, the fact that it prepares the final work of the Assembly in full session, the more detailed arguments presented to a smaller, less-restrained audience where the intervention of orators is more like a discussion than a grand discourse —all this makes the atmosphere in the Commission entirely different from that of the Assembly. Also debate can be much more passionate.

The debates in the General Assembly, in which delegation chiefs, like Vishinsky, often themselves took part, were interrupted by many ballots on questions of procedure, on drafts of resolutions or on amendments of same. The predominant position of the U.S.A. within the United Nations at that time determined beforehand the result of the polls, but did not lessen the aggressiveness of the debates nor the sharpness of the exchanges.

The president of the Political Commission—none other than Paul-Henri Spaak himself—had to intervene continuously, exhibiting not only his oratorical skill, but sometimes, his impetuous character. Thus, on November 3 , when Vishinsky called Minister of Foreign Affairs Carlos Romulo of the Philippines, who supported the Greek position, an "empty barrel" (! . .), Spaak did not merely call him severely to order. He added: "the great actor on the international stage has descended to the level of an unimportant comedian." This was not at all, for that period, the usual language of the United Nations. What caused it and gave vent to unbridled passions was here also, the activity of the Balkan Committee; its reports were disastrous for the communist position. The precise facts which were cited in these reports constituted irrefutable proof of the enormous assistance DAG was receiving from abroad and destroyed the arguments which maintained that this was a civil war pure and simple. The representatives of the communist countries worked unceasingly to counteract the reports of the Committee, concocting all kinds of arguments.

Couve de Murville, then a young and brilliant career diplomat who later became French minister of foreign affairs, observed, not without humor, that Greece's neighbors had an excellent way of proving that the charges against them were false. They had simply to cooperate with the Balkan Committee so that the latter could observe what was happening on the other side of the frontier.

Perhaps, this was what induced Yugoslav representative Bebler to attack the representative of France to the Committee and his assistant as men of Vichy.

Something more must be said about this Yugoslav delegate because he was the precursor at the U.N. of the detractors of these meetings and, besides, helped to undermine the feeling of friendship that the Greeks have always retained towards the Yugoslavs. To support his position this strange delegate made many personal and venomous attacks against several Greek personalities. Then, in order to back up his accusations, he fabricated facts and figures out of nothing. He assured everyone, for example, that one of the reasons for the "rescue" of the Greek children—meaning the abduction—was that the national army used them during the battles to clear the minefields. Insult and impudence were the essential characteristics of his language. So as not to dwell on his serious offenses, we shall mention one of a general nature: Bebler was able to make a speech on the Greek question lasting four hours—a record that has never been broken in any other U.N. hall. Even Fidel Castro himself, when participating in the proceedings of the United Nations, only spoke for three and a half hours.

Therefore, after fifteen days of such debate the Political Commission decided, by a majority of 41 votes to 8, to set a time limit of ten minutes for each speaker. The picturesque Bebler, who did not wish to accept the decision and proposed that it not be applied to those who had voted against it, then received a bitter lesson. It was bitter for it was administered in public by the one whom he had most wished to please. Immediately afterwards, the Soviet representative stated in a glacial tone that Minister Bebler had not been authorized to speak for other countries. Even that did not calm the strange Yugoslav, but the Commission could, finally, get on with its work.

In spite of systematic obstruction which persisted until

the end, in spite of the many proposals that had to be put to a vote, the work of the Political Commission was finally completed on November 9   with an evening session. A long resolution was affirmed by a large majority. In this, the conclusions of the Balkan Committee were accepted, the aid offered to DAG by neighboring countries was condemned and—to mention only the most important point— the mandate of the Balkan Commission was renewed. Finally, on the same evening, the West found itself in agreement with the East for the first time in relation to this subject. The Political Commission unanimously voted for a draft resolution, according to which the president of the Third General Assembly—Minister of Foreign Affairs Herbert Evatt of Australia—was instructed to invite the representatives of Albania, Bulgaria, Yugoslavia and Greece to do their utmost to find a solution to the differences that separated their countries. Spaak, Trygve-Lie, Secretary General of the U.N., and later Selim Sarper, permanent representative of Turkey, were to assist Evatt as mediators.

On November 26, the General Assembly in plenum, again resumed discussion on the Greek question. It began badly. Vishinsky, ardently supported by all of his allies, submitted a resolution according to which all foreign troops in Greece must depart at once. This resolution was rejected after an extremely lively debate.

Then, the atmosphere returned to one of calm again and the draft resolution prepared by the Political Commission —that concerning the abducted children[2]—was accepted. Thus ended a great diplomatic battle which had lasted for more than two months. If in many ways it seemed discouraging, it had not been in vain. Public opinion throughout the world now could understand better the seriousness of the Greek affair. An international committee would be able to continue to keep a close watch on the Greek frontiers, and a serious conciliation procedure had been set in motion. Unfortunately, this last point—one of the most important—did not go a long way!

The efforts of the mediators lasted for about twenty days. On December 14 Evatt announced that there had been agreement on many points, but on others—notably the definite recognition of the Greek-Albanian frontier—there had been no agreement. The mediators would resume their efforts toward conciliation later and Evatt expressed the hope that the results then would be good. This hope was most certainly stated merely for form. Only much later were relations with the Balkan states reestablished and, first of all, those between Yugoslavia and Greece. But, at the end of 1948, circumstances did not yet allow this.

Bloody Interlude. One of the most daring and shocking incursions of DAG was enacted during this period: the raid on Karditsa, a town swollen to a population of around 50,000 with a majority of these being refugees. Small but prosperous, this town lies on the plain of Thessaly hardly twenty-six kilometers from an important military center at Trikkala. During the night of the 11th and 12th of December, four DAG infantry brigades and a cavalry regiment attacked Karditsa. Resistance by defense positions kept up until the end, but the town was entirely taken over that same night.

An unprecedented carnage followed. Altogether there were 37 civilians killed, 105 wounded, and 980 persons abducted. Among the last were men and women, doctors, lawyers, civil servants, and merchants, some from each profession. Besides that, the railway station, two flour mills, and about forty houses were set afire; four hundred stores and the hospital were sacked. Plunder and hostages were sent without delay to the west, to the wild mountains of the Pindos range.

The regular forces were unable to intervene before late afternoon of the next day. The roads had been mined, sabotaged, and destroyed in some places. Besides, the Trikkala garrison did not know that this daring incursion had not been undertaken by an exceptional concentration of rebel forces. So, now it had to be ready to oppose the enemy there, to launch a powerful counter-attack and not to risk falling into any disastrous ambushes on the way. Thus, the rebels remained the uncontested masters of the town for eighteen hours. After that, a ten-hour battle was required to dislodge them.

The psychological blow was a terrible one. It was the first time that a big town, situated in the middle of a plain, was overrun and sacked by the partisans. And what is more, all this took place after the victorious offensive of the previous summer and after the dangerous failure of autumn.

Karditsa would not be the only warning of this kind. On December 23 around midnight, even better armed DAG units attacked simultaneously the towns of Edessa and Naoussa. But this time the national forces had followed the movements of these groups which had left the area of Vitsi on the 18th of the month. So, Edessa and Naoussa were not captured, but tough combat lasting twenty-four hours was necessary to force the assailants to retire.

On the night of the 27th, DAG forces attempted a much more ambitious offensive: they made a surprise attack against Bikovik and Pascovo, two key positions in the defense line of Kastoria, the seat of a national army division. Almost all the rebel forces on Vitsi had taken up positions so as to descend on the plain and capture the town as soon as a breach was opened. However, all were forced to withdraw, together with the units that had led the assault, because the entire line held fast. These three operations alone had cost DAG more than five hundred dead and over one thousand wounded.

On the night of December 28 it was the turn of another small town in Macedonia, named Ardea, against

310

which—as well as against Edessa—artillery was used. There, likewise, the town managed to defend itself.

Public opinion was consoled, but this was scarcely sufficient. After so much bloodshed DAG was showing an increased aggressiveness and, for the first time, attacks on towns were a reality. This fact was both impressive and frightening. What was it all about? How did DAG dare to undertake these operations and why did it accept such heavy losses for them? Pessimistic interpretations were numerous and completely justified. Besides, the activities of DAG were not restricted to these attacks alone. Old habits were not outgrown so quickly.

The list would be long if we were to cite all the raids made by guerrilla groups during the last two months of 1948, for they occurred all over continental Greece and on some islands. Sometimes, they concerned important towns which were occupied for one or two days, as in the case of Siatista in Macedonia and Voulgareli, the birthplace of Napoleon Zervas in Epirus.

In the Peloponnesus old tactics were applied, those of small bands of thirty to one hundred men, each of which always refused to fight openly, but were present everywhere.

Morale was weakened. It suffered most where the action was and indirectly throughout the country. For this reason, the Greek General Staff decided to seriouly tackle the four thousand guerrillas who, divided into around fifty bands, harrassed the whole of the Peloponnesus from the Ionian Sea to the Aegean. One entire army division, small units of LOK, pack and field artillery and all local forces, totalling approximately 11,000 men plus aircraft, were placed at the disposal of the First Army Corps.

General Tsakalotos began with a policing operation which, although causing a strong reaction, proved very beneficial in the long run. On the nights of December 28 and 29, without informing either the government or his superiors, he arrested all those who were thought to be collaborating with the guerrillas. Altogether, some 4,500 persons were arrested. Then, before the government could intervene, he had more than half of them deported to various islands.

This certainly was the fatal blow for the rebels. With the dissolution of the network which was their lifeline, the bands were totally deprived of information and supplies. Further on, it will be explained why operations in the Peloponnesus, though developing more slowly than certain others, were disastrous for DAG.

As a counter-balance, in the central and northern regions of the country DAG retained the initiative and its efforts brought success.

In mid-January DAG had even a greater success. On the evening of January 9, a series of attacks began that lasted the whole night and all the next day. They took place in northwestern Macedonia against the small village of Edessa and other localties nearby. However, forty-eight hours later it became evident that these were diversionary operations. On the night of the 11th, further south in the same district, four brigades of DAG supported by artillery and anti-tank guns, hemmed in the industrial town of Naoussa. The town's garrison of about five hundred men put up a fight but was quickly annihilated. Scenes from the sack of Karditsa were repeated: public buildings, banks, two factories and many houses were either blown up or burned. In addition, shops were plundered and 409 men and 210 women were obliged to make their way to the mountains. Before the rebels departed, a tragic episode was staged in the central square. The mayor of the town, Nikolaos Theofilou, a fifty-year old merchant, was insulted by the invaders as "an enemy of the people" and "a lackey of the Americans" for having earlier organized a reception for General Van Fleet. "I am not the servant of anyone," he replied simply and calmly. "I am a Greek patriot and my compatriots have elected me their mayor. It was then, my duty to officially receive the chief of the American military mission." He was executed then and there.

The reign of terror lasted for four days. Though the army's counter-attack was powerful, it was not able to dislodge the guerrillas without fierce combat lasting over the next five days and nights. Rarely had the guerrillas fought with such obstinancy, whether at their positions around Naoussa, or at the outskirts of the town. They gave the impression that they were battling in order to remain masters of those places. And again, this concerned a town. One had the impression that, as the poet says:

> There was no step lower
> To descend yet deeper
> Toward the abyss of Evil.[3]

In the Political Sphere. This descent toward the abyss could not remain without political consequences. It caused numerous disagreements, justified or not, and some serious friction, ending in a feeling of general anxiety.

The Liberals, in misalliance with the Populists, suffered the most from it. The Liberal Party, founded by Eleftherios Venizelos, had split into two parts on the eve of the 1946 elections. One, with old Sofoulis as its leader; the other, with Sophoclis Venizelos, the son of the Party's great founder. A little after the forming of the first Sofoulis government the two branches had united in order to better combat the communist uprising. Now, along with general pessimism, a series of disagreements on the measures to take and participation in a government under which things had become much worse caused a new division among the Liberals.

Sophoclis Venizelos and his friends left the government in the first days of November, as the battle was raging in Kastoria and in the mountain of Vitsi. A new government was formed, still under the premiership of Sofoulis, but on

313

a narrower base. On the next day, November 19, 54 out of 83 Liberal members of parliament submitted a statement to Parliament through which they recognized Sophoclis Venizelos as the leader of the Party. The old man, unperturbed by this move, countered by explaining that he had been elected party leader by the people, not by the members of parliament. And since he was there, he had to stay where he was. Still, the government had lost some ministers in whom the people had confidence and, more serious yet, it had just won an insignificant majority of only one vote.

To complicate matters further, on November 24, the nearly ninety-year-old prime minister suffered a rather serious pulmonary swelling. He had to remain in bed, even in his office. For some days, many considered him to be at death's door. But the astonishing old man, who had not stopped teasing his doctors during his illness,[4] recovered his health and again took in hand the affairs of state.

Sofoulis regained power so substantially that, on January 9, when King Paul sent an invitation to party leaders to form "a Government of National Salvation", he immediately began negotiations. His efforts were successful and a broad coalition was formed.

The new government was sworn in on January 20. The majority it obtained in Parliament was overwhelming: 223 votes in favor, 54 against—all the latter from the Extreme Right. The small party (22 votes) of George Papandreou, who did not want the premiership of Sofoulis, cast a vote of "tolerance". This was the best government Greece could secure in order to climb up again "from the abyss of Evil".

A very respected economist and a former Liberal, Alexandros Diomidis, was named deputy premier, while Sophoclis Venizelos and Spyros Markezinis—leader of a small progressive party of the Right—entered the government without portfolios. All three of these men were to lighten the burden which weighed down the shoulders of the aged Prime Minister. Constantine Tsaldaris remained in the Ministry of Foreign Affairs; Canellopoulos took National Defense; Constantine Caramanlis, Social Welfare; Constantine Tsatsos, a brilliant professor of philosophy, the Ministry of Education and George Mavros, leader of the Center Union Party, the Ministry of National Economy. The author of this book was placed in charge of the Ministry of Supply.

To complete the good impression which the new government made, on the day after it took office, the 21st, all the formalities were fulfilled so that Papagos could be recalled to active service. The same day he was sworn in as commander-in-chief of the armed forces. Papagos had set certain conditions, as previously mentioned; he wished to have the same powers as those he had assumed during the Greek-Italian war of 1940-41—those of an omnipotent leader. Now, actually, his powers would be even broader since the role of the American Mission would be controlled automatically. Once more, he set the condition of an increase in ground forces. He was fully satisfied on the first point; he was nonetheless, deceived on the second. From one day to the next, all the armed forces of the nation were put under the orders of only one man. He came at the right time. Thirty-six hours earlier, one of the most spectacular battles of the entire guerrilla war had begun; that of Karpenissi in central Greece. This event will be described in a paragraph below. Moreover, before the end of that battle very serious developments had occurred on the other side of the barricade.

On January 27, 1949 the Provisional Government of Free Greece broadcast new peace proposals as follows: *"We propose that 1) All foreign military forces and all foreign missions should depart from Greece immediately, all foreign imperialist interference in our country should stop, and all contracts and agreements which violate the principles of equality and the independence of our country should be cancelled.*

315

2) A ceasefire shall go into effect at once and the opposing armies shall maintain their present positions. 3) An immediate general amnesty shall be declared; all political and trade union freedoms shall be immediately restored, and true equality granted to all national minorities. 4) Negotiations shall begin at once for the formation of a government acceptable to both sides. This government shall apply the agreement and, within two months, shall hold free elections through which the people will decide finally and irrevocably how and by whom they wish to be governed. These are our proposals."

Only indirectly did the new Sofoulis government reply through the program it outlined in Parliament on February 2. It stood for peace, tranquility and understanding between all Greeks. That, however, could only be attained through the final victory of the forces of legality. "The national struggle against the rebel bands will be led with maximum energy and with confidence in a final victory that will restore peace, tranquility and harmony among all Greek people."

Minister of Defense Canellopoulos explained in Parliament a particular aspect of this that was curiously enough contested then by the international donquixotism of democracy: "I declare official'y that all those who are participating in this government have an undying faith in democratic and parliamentary institutions and they will raise this faith as a banner against the communist bands until the final victory."

But what sense can be made out of these new proposals of Markos? In Greece and abroad, the usual explanations were given (weakness, a trap, etc.) but one variation was added. Moscow, worried about the Atlantic Alliance then being prepared (it was to be formed on April 4) intervened to restore peace in Greece in order to keep that country outside the great alliance of the West. Even if all these interpretations were partially true, they seemed inapplicable and utterly useless a few days later.

The End of Markos. On February 4, 1949, the radio station of the Provisional Government read out the decisions that had been taken on January 30 and 31 by the Central Committee of the KKE. It had met in plenum—the 5th—at Mount Grammos, a part of which near the border had been reoccupied by DAG. Now, by this communique the Party announced that: *"taking into consideration that for several months comrades Chrissa Hatzivassiliou and Markos Vafiadis were gravely ill and therefore, could not fulfill the duties assigned to them by the Central Committee, it has decided unanimously to relieve them of all Party jobs."*

Three days later, the Provisional Government accused six of the best known leaders of DAG of "opportunism" and announced their removal. Among them was "lieutenant general" Kikitsas, a former reserve officer of the Greek army, who was then Military Commander of Western Macedonia, that is the district that included Vitsi and the towns of Edessa, Naoussa, Kastoria and Kozani. Also included was "brigadier" Yannoulis,[5] who had fought so well in Epirus in 1948, when Grammos was strongly attacked. But a more tragic fate was reserved for him alone: after a parody of a trial, he was to face a firing squad.

As for Chrissa and Markos, it was neither a matter of illness nor of opportunism. Chrissa Hatzivassiliou, wife of Minister of Foreign Affairs Roussos of the Provisional Government, headed the feminine clandestine network. She had headed again toward the mountains a little while before; she was not seriously ill as she had just taken an active part in the Anti-Fascist Congress of Women in Budapest (Later she did become very ill.) The reasons for her dismissal were different: on November 15, 1948, during a meeting of the Politburo, there was a very tough confrontation—perhaps the last one—between Zachariadis and Markos. Chrissa was the only one present who openly sided with Markos. That was her crime. In fact, it was the crime of many other DAG military leaders who were dismissed in those days; they had remained loyal to their general.

Again, it is indeed interesting to learn the reasons for which Markos was removed. Various explanations were given which were often confused, sometimes contradictory and nearly always incomplete. Without being able to specify with certainty the real reasons for it—something that will never be possible—it seems that behind Markos's disgrace there were two principal explanations completely different in nature from one another. Markos had a great respect for Tito. He thought along similar lines, mainly because he was also a nationalist communist. Recently, Markos had declared himself in favor of the territorial integrity of Greece, something which had cost him the animosity of Georghi Dimitrov—Secretary General of the Bulgarian Communist Party and leader of the Comintern.

Markos had only one serious disagreement with the Yugoslavs concerning the unwarranted interference of their military mission in his affairs and, particularly, that of its chief, General Popovic..."who wants to cover Greece with ruins which is neither good for the struggle nor for the future of the Movement". Lastly, Markos, as a good communist, also believed that Russia was the "Motherland of Socialism", but maintained that the KKE should keep out of the conflict between Stalin and Tito. Furthermore, he believed that if the latter ceased aiding DAG, the struggle would be much more difficult.

On the other hand, the Yugoslavs were always on very good terms with Markos. He was the master at Bulkes; he was treated well and was generously assisted. A minor fact, but very typical and little noted up to the present: Vishinsky and his friends at the U.N. always spoke of the "healthy vigour of the Greek people", of the "true democratic forces", etc. Bebler nearly always spoke of DAG, the Provisional Government and Markos.

So, it seems almost certain that the Cominform, that is to say, Moscow, asked the KKE to remove all those who were not prepared to declare themselves against Belgrade. This would explain, besides, certain acts that took place immediately before these events: the participation in the Fifth Congress of the Communist Party of Bulgaria of Zachariadis and two of his most important friends, Ioannidis and Vlantas and the visit of a Soviet mission to Albania and Bulgaria which aimed at the organization of better logistical support for DAG through these two countries. Lastly, there was the removal—at the time of Markos's dismissal—of General Popovic from the headquarters of DAG. What is certain is that such purges while the army was in the field and the enemy was becoming more aggressive, were absolutely inconceivable and can only be explained if Moscow was behind it.

That said, it must be added equally that just the advice of Moscow, or even something more than that, would not have been enough if there had not been a favorable atmosphere for these purges in the first place. Now, this atmosphere did exist. For, even if Markos had some prestige and was well liked, he also had powerful rivals, one of whom was Zachariadis himself. Disagreement between the two men was substantial and of long standing. Failures and the lack of definite results could only poison their relations and diminish the prestige of the General. Several signs lead one to the conclusion that after Grammos and Vitsi, Markos lost ground to such an extent that Zachariadis became the true commander of DAG. Between November 1948 and February 1949 there were several massive attacks against towns requiring enormous sacrifices in order to prolong an occupation which, objectively, could not last. All this was alien to the spirit of Markos, the capable old guerrilla. Today it is known that he did not even approve of certain battles that he himself had directed. Thus, the political and military leaders had a common aim—the conquest of power—but their tactics to achieve this differed. Perhaps, their final orientation differed also.

These deep disagreements of an objective nature seemed to have been reinforced by others which arose from personal motives. The two men were of different character and were, so to speak, poured out of different moulds. The former Kutvist was dogmatic, fanatic, autocratic, and easily offended. From his early days of Party leadership he had struck hard against his ex-comrades who had not followed Moscow's line or who had had moments of weakness. Typical of this mentality is a signed letter of Zachariadis, unpublished until today, which came into the hands of the army together with other documents. It shows also how strict and tough the Party cadres were and partly explains the execution of Yannoulis. This is why some parts of it are worth quoting here.

On July 26, 1948, in the midst of battle, Zachariadis addressed himself to one of his most loyal followers, Belogiannis,[6] then political commissar of Captain Yannoulis's brigade. This brigade had performed feats of valor in Epirus in order to relieve the Grammos fort when the national army was attacking DAG on all sides.

Now the chief wrote to his faithful commissar that he had learned from two members of the Provisional Government that the brigade was in a bad state, that a fighter had said of his leaders, "If they can, why do they not give us one kilo of bread a day?" Another went even further saying: "Zachariadis must obtain a compromise so that we won't be killed needlessly". "*Such fighters,*" continued Zachariadis in his letter, speaking of those guerrillas who had terrified Epirus for a long time, "*show that they have been broken. They assist monarcho-fascism, are useless and dangerous for they are traitors to the people's struggle.*" And he continued, "*those who are guilty of such treachery must be arrested, condemned by public outcry, and executed in the presence of their comrades.*" This fate was reserved for Captain Yannoulis himself.

320

Lastly, it must be pointed out that, besides disagreements between the two leaders, there were also rivalries among the people that surrounded them. Certain individuals considered themselves more able than their leader. Let us not forget the criticism leveled against Markos in the DAG magazine concerning the battle of Grammos by Lieutenant Colonel Venetsanopoulos.[7]

So, when Moscow "advised" the liquidation of Markos and his friends for reasons related to the confrontation with Belgrade, many leading KKE officers had their own motives to move in this direction. It is reasonable to presume that Markos and his highly-placed comrades got wind of these plans. In this case, the peace proposals transmitted by Radio Belgrade could very well have been a desperate effort to resolve the whole problem by a compromise.

Let us point out in favor of this interpretation that the proposals were not repeated nor supported, as in other cases, by Zachariadis and that, besides, the broadcast took place on the 27th of the month and the dismissal of Markos dated from the 29th or 30th. Lastly, that during the meeting of the Fifth Plenum—this became known later—Markos was accused by Zachariadis of considering the struggle doomed to failure if it was not assisted by foreign military forces.

In any case, the sequence of events was such that the founder and prime mover of the Democratic Army of Greece could only submit, without even the possibility of reacting. He put a brave face on things. On February 8, 1949, the DAG radio station broadcast an announcement by Markos dated February 4 and addressed to "the Greek people, to DAG, and to all my comrades in this struggle". In the first sentence, which was, however, that of a disciplined communist, he indirectly cleared himself of all responsibility for the recent attacks against towns. His health, he said, had worsened from day to day after the battle of

Grammos and had not allowed him to fulfill his duties. The announcement was short and sober; he greeted his comrades, eulogized the War Council and stated that, until a new decision was made, Ioannidis would act as president of the Council. He also warned everyone that the enemy would try to take advantage of his removal and finally, he stated that he was certain of victory. He called "everyone to arms" and acclaimed the Provisional Government, DAG and the Greek people. One must note only that he did not acclaim the KKE. A little later there were rumors that Markos was dead, or even that he had been shot. This was untrue, but today it is known that only his prestige saved him from death then. For the time being, as a good communist and a good soldier, he disappeared from the scene. We shall meet him later behind the Iron Curtain, trying sometimes to justify his actions and those of his comrades.

One should not ignore completely a quite different version of the disappearance of Markos. Although seemingly improbable, left-wing author D. Eudes states that many parts of his book are based on conversations he had had abroad with former guerrilla chieftains whose names, naturally, he cannot mention. According to him, during the night of August 20 to 21, 1948, when Markos managed to bring his troops across from Grammos to Vitsi and beyond the frontier, Zachariadis planned to get rid of him in Albania. On the way, Markos, escorted by about ten of his men, felt that he was being followed by Polydoras, a Communist known for his services" in purges of the hardcore". The General quickened his pace and fire was exchanged on Albanian territory. An Albanian patrol in the vicinity intervened and finally, placed the group under the protection of the Soviet military mission.

One cannot categorically reject this view. But one must also note that it leaves many questions unanswered. In this case, how was Zachariadis able to praise the strategy used in Grammos, which was established and applied by

322

Markos? Why in the commemorative album "on the second anniversary of the Democratic Army of Greece", published in November 1948, was Markos given a place of honor much higher than that of all other officers, almost equal to Zachariadis himself? Why also did Bebler single him out in his speech at the U.N., and why were many documents and proclamations reputed to bear his signature? Why was he allowed to remain in the spotlight for more than four months if he had already been purged, since it was impossible to delay the announcement of his removal from office? If this last were true, how could the confrontation between Zachariadis and Markos take place on November 15, during which the latter was supported by Chryssa Hatzivassiliou? Lastly, why did not even one prisoner out of the hundreds that had been arrested between September 1948 and January 1949 speak of Markos's eclipse?

This was the end of a chapter, but it did not end with the removal of the man who was commander-in-chief of DAG and president of the Provisional Government. In fact, the Fifth Plenum made another spectacular decision at the same time, that of restoring the Party to its initial position on the Macedonian question. The line imposed on the KKE by the Comintern since 1935, as previously stated, was that calling for the creation of an "Independent Macedonian State", which would include regions belonging to Bulgaria, Greece and Yugoslavia; sometimes Greek Thrace had also been added. Since 1935, for reasons already mentioned (see above, Chapter II), the KKE had altered its position and had adopted the principle of "equal rights for minorities". This position had not been changed during the guerrilla war. Perhaps certain minor concessions had been made towards Tito, but the official line of the Party remained unchanged. Now, the Fifth Plenum at the end of February unanimously declared itself in favor of an independent Macedonia. This meant that Greece would have to cede to the new state one of its richest regions inhabited by over one and a half million souls, out of which only one in a hundred spoke a Slavic dialect. As if to seal the agreement, by this same decision from then on the KKE agreed to include in the leadership of the struggle a member of NOF, the Slavo-Macedonian National Liberation Front. How exactly the participation of NOF was officially expressed in this alleged "civil war" will be described below. But already, this sole resolution of the Fifth Plenum was heavy with meaning. Beyond anything else, it meant that in spite of grandiloquent declarations, the KKE was beginning to realize that it was in danger of losing this terrible struggle. Now it was playing a last dangerous trump card. It was aligning itself with Bulgarian claims on the Macedonian question and was utilizing this ace against Yugoslavia.

Indeed, the new state would come in large part, from Yugoslavia and, in addition, would be a satellite of Bulgaria for it would be communist and would have a Bulgarian majority. At that period, Tito's team had not yet had time to create and to cultivate Macedonian nationalism, and everyone knew that Bulgarian influence extended as far as Skopje. As a stab in the back at Yugoslavia and as a service towards Bulgaria, this was perfect. There are reasons to believe that a change of attitude towards the Macedonian question was a condition laid down to the delegation which, under Zachariadis, participated in the congress of the Communist Party of Bulgaria held in Sofia in November 1948.

This important step, naturally, did not remain without compensation: the material assistance offered by Bulgaria to DAG swelled substantially. Nevertheless, these were a series of desperate acts. For even this strategem could not save a truly hopeless situation: on the other side of the barricade, the regular army was now better armed, better commanded, and still determined to fight to the bitter end if necessary.

In the Military Sphere. In the meantime, the battle of Karpenissi unfolded. Situated in a wooded area west of Lamia at an altitude of almost one thousand meters, the town was overwhelmed from all sides by five hundred guerrillas on the night of January 19. They were well armed, had a good fighting spirit, and were commanded by two of DAG's best brigade chiefs, Diamantis and Yiotis. The latter's true name is Charilaos Florakis, present leader of the KKE and a member of the Greek parliament. One of the greatest names in the KKE, Karageorghis, a good doctor turned publicist, directed the total operation as Military Commandant of all Roumeli, that is to say, of central Greece—the region south of the Pindos Mountains.

Fourteen hundred lightly armed men made up the Karpenissi garrison which resisted until the morning of the 21st when it was almost completely annihilated. The small city, or rather the large market-town, was pillaged and partly burned, the loot being particularly abundant. The population suffered large losses: 1,300 men and women in the community were "mobilized" and sent immediately into the mountains nearby. Fifty of the most respected civilians followed them, never to return. The success of this "mobilization"—as of those of Karditsa and Naoussa—was of great importance because, in those days, young volunteers were almost non-existent and losses were heavy.

This was not the only favorable side of the Karpenissi operation for DAG. Of even greater value was the psychological impact, for this important settlement remained in guerrilla hands from January 20 until February 9. During the entire guerrilla war, no other town was held for such a long period.

All efforts by the national army to liberate Karpenissi in the next fifteen days were unavailing. The region is mountainous; all bridges, even the smallest ones, had been

325

blown up; all of the approach roads were mined and were obstinately defended by groups that Karageorghis had moved in from other mountain areas. Towards the end, a thick layer of snow covered the whole district almost to the sea. Opening a breach would be very difficult.

In Athens it was quickly understood that the aim of such a pretentious defense was neither booty nor "recruitment" for both had been realized in the first day: it was mainly a strategic one, the urgent transfer to Karpenissi and central Greece of a part of the regular forces which were exerting such strong pressure on the guerrillas in the Peloponnesus.

Papagos did not fall into the trap. On the contrary, under these difficult circumstances, he immediately showed his qualities as a leader and a general. From the first days of his command, he kept everyone at a distance even those attached to foreign military missions. He surrounded himself with a small group of elite officers with whom he had carried out operations in the Greek-Italian war. Then, without delay, he took some decisions which were far from what was expected.

The military governor of Roumeli, a royalist, an excellent officer and a friend of long standing, was relieved of his command and summoned before a military tribunal. He was charged with leaving unguarded the passes through which the assailants had penetrated into Karpenissi.

On the other hand, Papagos recalled to active service a general—then a member of parliament—who was a republican and a mediocre commander, but a good soldier and known for his animosity toward Papagos. To this man he entrusted the military command of Roumeli.

Orders were given to push to the maximum the dispatch of troops to the Peloponnesus, withdrawing units even from far away and exposed Epirus. Papagos felt that it was necessary to gather a large number of forces in the far south, and then to advance slowly northward spreading out across the entire width of the Peloponnesus in a mopping-up operation. He wished to achieve total pacification of the peninsula because it was important for him to have his hands free in the south. Moreover, the people's confidence had to be restored by actual proof that a peaceful life could begin once again.

From the Peloponnesus Papagos removed only one man, General Tsakalotos, and a few of his collaborators. He was no longer on the best of terms with him, but the Karpenissi affair, with its demoralizing effect on the population, was lasting too long. So Tsakalotos was assigned the task of leading a tough counter-attack. That offensive continued unabated for four days and nights and went forward even during a heavy snowstorm. On February 9, the national army occupied Karpenissi once more, but it was unable to pursue the enemy owing to a thick mantle of snow that covered the countryside, especially the mountains.

The government did not have time to enjoy this success however; two days later the siege of Florina started, an isolated town among the mountains near the Yugoslav border and about forty kilometers from Albania.

Zachariadis was personally interested in this operation and had assigned to it DAG's best units which had fought both at Grammos and at Vitsi. These forces consisted of five brigades and included the officers' school, companies of saboteurs, cavalry, bazooka carriers and artillery which included twenty 75 mm. and 105 mm. guns.

Command of the Florina operation was entrusted to General Goussias, and whose true name was George Vrontissios, a cobbler from the pretty village of Syrako high in the mountains of Epirus, a man who hated Markos. He was a close friend of Zachariadis and had been distinguished in minor operations, primarily for his daring strategy and her ferocious courage.

Zachariadis had inspected all units before the attack and

had explained to the guerrillas the meaning of the recent decisions of the Fifth Plenum. He had then asked them to back up these decisions by occupying Florina so that the Provisional Government could immediately be established there. He himself, with all the KKE leaders accompanying him, would follow the battle from an observation post on a nearby hill.

According to Goussias's orders,[8] the attack which had been launched from all sides the night before should have ended in the capture of the town by eight o'clock on the morning of February 12. But, even at this hour, Zacharia-dis could see through his binoculars only a raging battle. Being so close to Yugoslavia, Florina was defended by a division of the national army, well-armed, but very weakened by the last months of combat. It was com-manded by an excellent soldier, General Nicolaos Papadopoulos, who carried the nickname of "grandfather", probably because of his long grizzled moustache. "Grand-father" had carefully organized his defense. On the morning of the 12th, three outposts of Florina to the north and two to the southwest were lost; some enemy infiltra-tion into the town itself occurred. Early in the afternoon more than two hundred prisoners had been locked up in a building.

The rebel offensive soon resumed, becoming relentless, even reckless. Resistance by the garrison at certain points passed to a daring counterattack that weakened the morale of Goussias's men. Besides, they now had to face other difficulties.

On the 12th and 13th, clearing weather allowed the air force to intervene. And, on the second day, DAG forces guarding the approach routes to Florina came under the first pressure exerted by units of the regular army which had been rushed to the besieged town from all directions. This pressure soon increased and became more persistent. The situation improved for the defenders and "grandfather" then made a strong attack on the 14th. On the 13th and 14th, fairly strong units of the national army had undertaken an offensive against the bases on Vitsi as a diversionary action. But nothing is ever certain in a battle, and the diversionary action appeared to be a main attack. For the rebels, the situation was untenable in spots and particularly dangerous.

The battle for Florina ended on the night of the 15th. The troops of the cobbler-general, defeated and harassed, withdrew over difficult snow-covered terrain to escape complete annihilation. Either they went across the Greek-Yugoslav frontier, or withdrew to the Vitsi fort.

Total dead counted for the rebels during these two operations are estimated to have exceeded one thousand, since 783 were found on the battlefield. Some 350 prisoners were taken, while the wounded who were easily carried away because of the closeness of the Albanian and Yugoslav frontiers, amounted to more than 1,500. Besides, instead of taking the usual loot, DAG abandoned in Florina a considerable number of shiny new weapons. The tactic of massive attacks against towns clearly was becoming too costly. Florina was to be the last operation of this kind.

Omens were not good in so far as Zachariadis's strategy was concerned. Things were soon to become much worse.

In the Peloponnesus, an improvement in the situation for the nationalist side came rapidly. The Greek armed forces, and especially the LOK, brought successes daily. At the end of January one of the greatest efforts of the rebels ended in disaster. Several bands had united to attack the town of Leonidion at the foot of Mount Parnon for the purpose of taking provisions that were necessary to them. The operation succeeded, but on the very next day, the same bands were so hotly pursued that, within a single day, they lost more than 250 out of almost 1,000 men. This was the largest engagement of the campaign in the Peloponnesus. But its true success resulted from numerous small skirmishes.

After the mass arrests of December and complete surveillance of the coasts, rebel forces in the Peloponnesus were deprived of both information and supplies. On the other hand, the population regained its courage and helped the regular forces more, mainly by providing valuable information. Thus, it was now no longer the guerrillas who laid ambushes, but the army; it was no longer they who led the raids, but the soldiers who pursued them to their most remote hideouts.

After the attack against Leonidion, the leaders of DAG in the Peloponnesus realized that they could not conduct widespread operations any longer. When they saw that there was no way for them to receive assistance by sea and that the large-scale attack against Karpenissi had not relieved them, they divided their forces into very small groups. These men were ordered then to remain exclusively in the mountains in an attempt to survive until the time when conditions would have changed. But in Athens, the new tactics were understood at once and so new measures were taken to counteract them: national army units were likewise, divided into small detachments and those units, informed by the population, hunted the guerrillas night and day.

The results were soon apparent. At the beginning of April, from Corinth to Sparta, there were 2,040 dead guerrillas counted and 1,799 prisoners and deserters. All the leaders of the bands were found among the dead. Some guerrillas had vanished completely, having taken refuge in the homes of relatives. Only a few very small bands remained which were easy to hunt down. So easy that in the first fifteen days of April, a whole army division, as well as all of the KKE forces, were transferred to central Greece. There a second mopping-up operation was being prepared which would sweep northward until it reached the boundaries of Macedonia. This operation had the code name "Pyravlos" (Rocket). But before giving a brief account of this operation, it is necessary to take a look at the general military situation and to note an important change in the Provisional Government.

Total pacification of the Peloponnesus henceforth influenced the overall struggle; from that moment on, there was a change of attitude by the rural population. It now had proof that victory was possible and that peace would prevail once again. In these last days the villagers' hatred for the guerrillas had reached a peak; but it was they who contributed to that feeling by the terror they were spreading throughout the countryside. They were punishing with death those who, they said, were their enemies and the members of their families. They were burning houses and carrying off animals.[9] All this was seen and lived through daily by the people in each village the guerrillas entered. Nothing was more poignant than the wiping out of entire families—for "supporting freedom", some were thinking, for "being enemies of the people", others were proclaiming.

On the other hand, the soldier had the right to act against his adversary only as an officer of the law. This meant that the adversary of the soldier, or the civilian forced to oppose him, was protected by a clearly defined legal procedure and, at worst, he would end up in prison. There was one exception to this: the arrests made by General Tsakalotos in the Peloponnesus, and they had not resulted in death, but in exile. Consequently, the punishment inflicted by the army was scarcely comparable to that inflicted by the rebels. So, the rural population—primarily, out of fear but also to survive—was concealing its growing hatred and aiding those who could so easily annihilate it. This disadvantage appears and undoubtedly plays a role in all guerrilla wars of this type. Being both a disadvantage and a weakness, it is at the same time, the beauty of the best political system known up to the present: that of democracy.

Owing to the complete pacification of the Peloponnesus, this disadvantage gradually began to diminish throughout the country. The peasant slowly began to rid himself of his terror and fear.

Nevertheless, the uprising had not yet ended. At the end of April, Papagos submitted a report to the government on the events that had occurred during the three months he had been commander-in-chief. He was optimistic, but it was a very restrained optimism. In Roumeli, two divisions of DAG under Diamantis and Yiotis who had led the attack on Karpenissi, had been hunted for forty days non-stop in mid-winter. However, the rebels had penetrated deep into the Pindos range and had managed to lose their pursuers. In less than three months, all the bands on the plain of Thessaly had been dispersed. Nor were the famous rebel cavalry units spared a similar fate. On March 6, near Karditsa, the best of these units lost almost all of its men, a total of 250.

With unremitting will, Karageorghis tried to regroup his forces and invade central Greece once more. They were attacked by the army during the regrouping operation and had to withdraw with all possible speed towards the north. Only Captain Diamantis's division managed to pass through the government lines and settle down again in the mountains of central Greece. Nevertheless, during these operations DAG losses were considerable.

Lastly, to mention only the most important engagements during the three months covered in the Papagos report, DAG had one worthwhile success. A strong division, recently trained and equipped with "entirely up-to-date Soviet materiel", attacked Grammos in April. It was during this attack that French poet Paul Eluard, from an advance observation post on Grammos, made an appeal to the government troops which "reverberated from two hundred loud-speakers". He spoke, he said, to those who "were coerced to serve a government that did not represent them", to those who "were on the side of the jailers and the executioners". He invited them to cross over to the other side of the barricade and reassured them that they would be free and treated well because, as he said, "for the first time in modern history an army felt itself so strong and so sure of victory that it could show like confidence in man". It was a sad adventure in candor and good faith. The author is in a position to assure his readers that no one who heard this appeal and its translation in the nationalist trenches really believed for a moment that a well-known French poet was speaking in such a manner. Everyone thought that it was a ridiculous political trick and they were amused.

But, as a major part of the regular forces was occupied with the mopping up operation moving from south to north, the great mountain region was, at that moment, poorly defended. One battle-tested division, the Ninth, which had held the most important bastions of the region, had been moved to the Peloponnesus at the beginning of the year to assist in that operation. So, despite a stubborn initial defense and several counterattacks later on, DAG managed to retain nearly all the positions it had occupied on Grammos during its first sweeping April offensive. The enormous sacrifices made in summer 1948 had been all in vain. The Grammos fort, though somewhat less extensive than before, had been restored to its former might. It may be added that the raiding of villages continued, though these were now less numerous, less daring and restricted to certain regions. All this meant that the struggle was not yet over, but that the situation was improving for the nationalists. Moreover, the performance of the national army was exemplary and its effectiveness showed. All the missions assigned to it had been carried out with vigor. Squabbling among the generals had ceased; now each had the assignment for which he had been trained. Foreign officers had been restricted to the role of observers, the only role that suited them. Besides, they had every reason to be satisfied for Papagos had recreated the army of Albania. As sad proof, unfortunately, his losses also testified to it: from January 20 until April 20, 1949, casualties rose to a total of 4,332 officers and men. The losses of DAG, including those in the Peloponnesus, were much heavier: 6,225 dead, some 8,011 prisoners and deserters among whom were many wounded, and 1,559 prisoners from the armed auxiliary services. In all, this made a grand total of 14,237 which, given the circumstances, was enormous.

The Greco-Bulgarian Government. At the top of the revolutionary hierarchy the repercussions of these failures and losses were strongly felt. After the dismissal of Markos Vafiadis, the post of president had been taken over for a few days by Vice-president Ioannis Ioannidis, then by Zachariadis himself. Between March 30 and April 5, the latter had radically reshaped the Provisional Government, at the same time remaining very powerful since he retained the presidency of the War Council and the post of General Secretary of the Party. The presidency of the government was entrusted to Dimitri Partsalidis, general secretary of EAM and one of the oldest members of the KKE, who had escaped with about ten other leading Communist officials on December 25, 1947 from an Aegean island to which he had been exiled.[10] Nearly all the old ministers participated in the new government, but their small group had curiously widened. In fact, besides Karageorghis, who became minister of military supply, four members of the Agrarian Party and Apostolos Grozos, a representative of leftist trade unions (ERGAS), entered the cabinet. But the surprising fact was that three Bulgarians were given top positions: Paskal Mitrofsky, president of NOF, assumed the post of minister of supply; Stavro Gotsev, a member of NOF, became under-secretary of minorities in the ministry of interior affairs and Vangelis Kotsiev became a regular member of the Supreme War Council. In this way, since Tito now had decreased his aid, the assistance of Bulgaria, which had become more valuable, would be secured. But, from another point of view, in this way the KKE became completely isolated in Greece.

In fact, many former officials of EAM had already severed their ties with the Party. One group of EAM leaders had done so in February 1949 by denouncing various errors of the KKE. At about the same time, the small socialist party of Greece (ELD), under the leadership of Ilias Tsirimokos, the future vice-president of the Socialist International, had strongly denounced the resolution by the Fifth Plenum of the Central Committee of the KKE. He stated that he *"unreservedly condemns inexorable sectarianism as put forth by the Central Committee of the KKE, the seizure of power and the imposition of a communist regime through force of arms"*. Furthermore, he *"condemned absolutely and unreservedly the position taken in the resolution concerning a Slavo-Macedonian people by which it avoids the problem of the recognition of universally recognized rights of minorities and comes back to the slogan of a United and Independent Macedonia and Thrace, which injures the common national feeling of the Greek people"*.

So, already with the entrance of two members of NOF into the Provisional Democratic Government, the KKE proved that it was applying its new principles regarding the "Macedonian question" and that, indeed, it intended to detach from the country that precious and eminently Greek province, Macedonia. This policy was to lose for the KKE all of its followers, except those who would blindly obey Moscow's orders. It was to increase the will of the nationalists to crush the rebels as well.

So when, on May 3, foreseeing the strong squall ahead,

335

the Provisional Government announced its most moderate proposals yet for an agreement,[11] Athens, widely supported by public opinion, rejected them despite pressure from Moscow. For the Greek government there was only one condition that must be met for talks to begin with the KKE: DAG must lay down all its arms. This condition—considered indispensable for a feeling of security—the government now felt it could impose more than ever. Events were to prove it.

Last Pursuits and Last Battles. With plans well prepared, on May 5 General Tsakalotos, commander of the First Army Corps, launched the offensive in central Greece foreseen by operation "Pyravlos". His adversary was the young Koliyannis, future general secretary of the KKE in exile, who had just replaced Karageorghis as DAG Commander of southern Greece. Tsakalotos had his two divisions plus all the garrisons of the area, some groups of commandos (LOK), and four units of armored cars and tanks, a total of nearly 50,000 men. Koliyannis had his two divisions of about 6,000 men which were commanded by two of the bravest and boldest generals of DAG: Captain Diamantis and young Captain Yiotis. The rebels also had one cavalry brigade and other local forces, altogether numbering about 6,000 men and making a total of 12,000 fighters.

On April 25, the national army began to seal the principal passes leading to the north of the area held by Koliyannis's forces. Ten days later, all of Tsakalotos's forces began their simultaneous attack. Both experienced guerrilla chiefs—Captains Diamantis and Yiotis—had sensed the danger of the situation. So they had advised Koliyannis to distribute his units in groups of eighty to one hundred and twenty men each. These groups were ordered to avoid, as much as possible, coming into contact with the national forces and to hide in the area so as to enable them to resume their activities when the army had advanced to the north.

According to prisoners arrested during this operation, the guerrilla chiefs were hoping that the regular forces, tired out from continuous combat and now even more exhausted from the long marches, would not give chase for long, especially into inaccessible places.

However, the officers of the national army had received strict orders never to stop their manhunt. Even the smallest guerrilla band was to be hunted until it was annihilated. No excuse was valid for stopping the pursuit, except perhaps, loss of contact. In addition, every unit was to make sure before advancing that it had left no guerrillas behind. These tactics, as well as those of classical warfare, were applied to the guerrilla war. Under these conditions no battles actually took place. There were numerous skirmishes, so many that operation "Pyravlos" lasted about three months. But before the end of July, the mopping up operation had almost cleared central Greece, the plain and the mountains of Thessaly and in general, all the southern end of the Pindos range. In all this vast region only a few small rebel bands remained; they were completely demoralized, weak and disunited. They could in no way be compared with the strong bands so well organized by Markos. Moreover, as soon as they appeared anywhere, they were betrayed by the population and then were pursued by the gendarmerie and local militia. One after another they surrendered or were annihilated.

A small part of the rebel force—probably about 250 to 300 men—under Koliyannis and Yiotis, commander of the First DAG Division of Thessaly, managed, after exhausting marches, to reach the Grammos fort. Another more sizeable part of the rebel force laid down its weapons and disappeared, most often hiding in the homes of relatives. Most of the true fighters of Koliyannis had been killed. The "Pyravlos" operation had cost DAG 1,059 dead, 2,558 prisoners and 1,021 deserters. Among the dead was

Captain Diamantis, commander of the second division of Roumeli who had been cornered on June 21 on a high ridge of 1,150 meters. There were also three brigadiers, nine lieutenant colonels, 18 battalion commanders, 40 company commanders, 51 other officers and four doctors. Among the latter was the chief medical officer of Diamantis's division.

For all those who maintained at that time that the war in Greece was being carried out by bands of brigands which included a few Communists, the number and nature of these sacrifices should offer much food for thought.

A quite characteristic proof of DAG's efficient organization was that among the considerable war materiel abandoned by the guerrillas there was an impressive number of wireless sets.

The guerrilla war was coming to an end. It would soon become a war of positions. Nevertheless, before expiring, it went through some last convulsions. Before summer Zachariadis had closed down the eight training centers for rebel troops in the mountains and all these men with the exception of cadets from the officers' school who were called to Grammos, were ordered to form bands and to go back to guerrilla warfare "in the old style". Their main concerns would be to influence enemy morale, to mobilize both men and women, and to broadcast information. The supply problem was secondary for Albania and Bulgaria fully compensated for Yugoslav assistance which, by that time, had almost ceased. "Noblesse oblige": the minister of supply of Free Greece was named Pascal Mitrofski . . .[12]

However, in spite of a few incursions which had some success—all in the northern part of the country (at Neo Petritsi near the Bulgarian border on May 5, at Metaxades near the Turkish frontier on May 15, and others)—these "last-minute" bands were not able to do much. Hated and informed upon by the population, hunted by the local militia, the rebel bands now sacrificed themselves or surrendered without having fulfilled their mission. The situation was grave, for recruitment also was becoming more difficult every day and events were overwhelming them.

Towards the end of July, more than half the forces of the national army—the best ones, which had participated in operation "Pyravlos"—were moved as speedily as possible toward the regions of Grammos and Vitsi. Only two lightly-armed units remained behind; they were entrusted with a different kind of mission: the repatriation before autumn of all the villagers who had taken refuge in towns —a difficult task, but certainly, both a necessary and an urgent one.

Thus, following government orders, the national army began to organize the peacetime life of rural Greece, while preparing itself, at the same time, for the last great offensive of the civil war against the strong positions along the border.

The Battle of the Frontiers. Papagos had intended to take advantage of the army's success without losing momentum. Already, at the beginning of August, from Florina to Kastoria and from Kozani to Ioannina, almost two-thirds of the Greek army was in battle position. Seven infantry divisions and an entire LOK division were deployed in the area. All were newly equipped with the most modern weapons plus the latest means of transport and communications. Further east, along the Bulgarian border, two additional divisions plus two independent brigades formed the Third Army Corps. Behind this line were airstrips which served an air force of small size but very experienced in mountain warfare.

All of these forces now organized into the "First Army", had been placed under the command of General Constantinos Ventiris. The three army corps were led by generals Tsakalotos, Maniadakis and Grigoropoulos—all three field commanders with considerable experience. The command of divisions and brigades had also been assigned to senior officers who had distinguished themselves during the guerrilla war. Naturally, all this increased the efficiency of the army. Papagos was the right man to make these assignments for he was known to have the talent of selecting good collaborators.

So, "the battle of the frontiers", known under the code name of "Pyrsos" (Torch), augured well for the government forces. General conditions were so favorable that one might have expected DAG to withdraw in time across the frontiers. But this did not happen. On the contrary, the rebel War Council had just decided unanimously to hold the two mountain bastions at all costs. The order was "to resist without any thought of withdrawal".

Today it is known that the Provisional Government was hoping that their defense could last until winter and then, weather conditions in the area would make further operations impossible. Thus they had thought that, after winter, DAG would face a demoralized army and would be able for this reason to resume its nocturnal incursions against well chosen positions. Eventually, it would be able "to carry out a general counter-offensive, to overthrow the enemy, occupy towns and slowly increase the area of Free Greece.

These false hopes seemed to have been equally divided between DAG leaders and fighters. The latter were now less in number and the proportion of women had reached twenty-five percent. They were all resolved to defend these mountain bastions which were their last hope; they knew their terrain perfectly and considered it impregnable. Certainly, these rebel positions were not impregnable, but they were fortified better than ever. Their underground gun emplacements were more numerous than before and for each of the two bastions, prisoners said, there were sixteen field guns and fifteen anti-aircraft guns.

The number of defenders is not definite as it varied according to the source. The figures which seem most probable are the following: 7,000 men on Vitsi and 5,000 on Grammos, some 2,500 rehabilitated wounded distributed in reserve brigades nearby and on Albanian territory. More to the east there were other rebels on two mountains—1,300 men on Kaimaktsalan and 1,500 on Beles, next to the Yugoslav and Bulgarian frontiers. The rebel forces on these mountains could not be considered as defenders of the two forts, but they were, just the same, to undertake diversionary operations. One thousand guerrillas scattered throughout the rest of Greece, could not in any way aid in the defense of the frontier regions.

Papagos decided to postpone the clearing out of Beles, the mountain furthest east on the frontier. Instead, the national army was to occupy Kaimaktsalan which is nearer to Vitsi. This was accomplished at the beginning of July through a series of battles lasting a week. Most of the defenders of that mountain fled into Yugoslavia where they were then disarmed. The others—about one-third— chose to make a stand and so were either killed on the spot or taken prisoner.

As during the 1940 Albanian campaign, General Ioannis Kitrilakis—Papagos's first deputy and operations officer— had prepared a most detailed plan of attack against Grammos and Vitsi. Its main characteristic was to mislead the enemy as to its intentions.

The complex of Vitsi, which had been occupied all along by the guerrillas, was less known, better fortified and had better defenders than Grammos; so the enemy had to be made to believe that the attack against this mountain, as in 1948, would come last. Furthermore, on August 2, after a heavy pounding by artillery and aerial bombardment of enemy positions on Grammos, a powerful attack was un- leashed. This diversionary occupation was led with such spirit that it clearly gave the impression of being the main offensive. Zachariadis's reaction was to rush all his reserves into Grammos. Supported often by a murderous fire originating from Albanian territory, the rebels continued to defend their mountains with ardor and even undertook several counter-attacks. Nevertheless, in five days the troops to the west of Grammos managed to threaten several lines of communication and to take and keep many key positions, the conquest of which would facilitate the final effort. Koumanakis's battalion (see above, Chapter X) took from the guerrillas a ridge (with an altitude of 1,800 meters) that dominated some important passes along the Greek-Albanian frontier.

The army paid dearly for this operation (583 officers and men out of action), but in the end, it greatly facilitated the operation against Vitsi. In the meantime, all of the national army's artillery used in preparing the first assault on Grammos had been quickly transferred to the proximity of Vitsi.

This entire mountain, covering an area of about three hundred square kilometers, was attacked by the national army on the 10th of August. Battles were raging also on Grammos and this fact did not allow the rebels to suppose that, at the same time, a wider and an even more ambitious attack was beginning elsewhere. However, this assault was launched from five different points and orders were to penetrate in depth at any cost. From two other points at the extremes of the line, attacking troops were to push forward from opposite directions along the Albanian border (see Map No.8) so as to encircle the whole mountain range.

These powerful attacks took the guerrillas by surprise and the army, especially the LOK units which led the offensive, made considerable progress during the first day. On August 11, the second day, defense became more obstinate but it was already too late, for the army had achieved deep penetrations at several points. Still, the guerrillas contested every yard of the advance, but the army with the smell of victory now in the air, fought with undiminished ardor. On the one side, they fought with a spirit which arose from their vision of final victory and the restoration of freedom. On the other both men and women fought with equal courage, but that born of despair and the wreck of the "miracle" they had believed in. They also faced the loss of their native land, together with the prospect of long years in exile after three years of superhuman effort, struggle, and sacrifice.

Each bit of land lost was made the object of desperate counter-attacks. On the 14th, in order to relieve the Vitsi fort, a strong counter-attack was launched from Grammos. It was quickly crushed.

For now the army not only had a good fighting spirit, it was also much stronger and after initial successes, it acquired another tactical advantage. Once breaches were opened (see arrows on Map No. 8),pack artillery moved up and so intervened in a more effective manner against fortified positions that could actually be spotted.

The only attack that did not develop according to plan was the one advancing from the southern end of Vitsi towards the north along the Albanian border. The going was slow. It got under way by day instead of by night as originally planned. Another reason for the delay, besides the unusually difficult terrain and the stubborn defenders, was the deadly fire coming from Albanian territory. This fire was so murderous that, in Athens, it provoked serious disagreement between certain ministers and the prime minister. In fact, some members of Themistoclis Diomidis's government (Sofoulis died on June 24 and had been replaced by his deputy premier) insisted that Greek troops should enter Albania and clear out the positions which were firing on Greek troops. In the end, the views of these ministers were not taken into account as Greek blood was cheap during that time.

Indeed, there was another incident in which Albania

directly intervened during the battle of Vitsi. On a hill situated near the frontier, after a bloody skirmish it was determined that a company of the small Albanian army had courageously aided the guerrillas. Furthermore, the papers of the company commander were found on the battlefield along with twenty Albanian dead; seven others were taken prisoner. It is a curious episode which, nevertheless, we will not dwell on.

The important fact is that the battle of Vitsi, ferocious as it was, for all practical purposes ended on the night of August 15. All resistance ceased on the 16th, even from the highest ridges. Hastily departing from the capital of Pyxos (west of Lake Mikri Prespa), the Provisional Government took refuge in Albania. About 4,000 fighters—among which were an undetermined number of wounded—followed it and were sent immediately to Grammos. About one thousand men fled to Yugoslavia where they were disarmed and sent to internment centers.

The second phase of operation "Pyrsos", the storming of Vitsi, had been bloodier than the first phase against Grammos. Within five days casualties in the national army reached a total of 1,682, while DAG counted 1,182 dead and according to prisoners, about an equal number of wounded were evacuated across the border. If one shows the respect that is due the life of man, this slaughter was shocking. But if one looks at it purely from the military point of view, considering the size of the two armies, DAG losses were comparatively much higher than those of the army. For DAG, it was basically its "old guard" that did the fighting. And like Napoleon's Imperial Guard at Waterloo, they died without hope.

Nevertheless, in spite of the spectacular defeat of Vitsi, the Greek Communists unanimously decided to continue the struggle. An official statement issued by the War Council, the Political Bureau of the KKE's Central Committee, and DAG's High Command, dated August 20, stipulated: *"The enemy is gathering on Grammos for a final battle. On Grammos we have everything that is necessary to deal our enemy a mortal blow. We have enough troops, powerful weapons, and the advantages offered by the terrain. It was at Grammos that monarcho-fascism failed last year. It was at Grammos this year that we struck a hard blow against it through our April operations. And on Grammos the enemy got a bloody nose recently. We have behind us the experience of Vitsi and the deep wound we caused the enemy there. Here we can, and we must, bury the monarcho-fascists."* All signed orders found on the dead after the battle were written in the same tone. They insisted: "Grammos would be the unsurpassable mountain for the enemy and its final grave". Whatever the reasons for this decision to defend Grammos, one is horrified to see with what lightheartedness the ideological obstinacy of a few officers can lead men and women to death in the flower of their youth, and with all their illusions.

Through sudden movements of units, a large part of the forces that had taken Vitsi in a few days found themselves before already besieged Grammos. Here, the attack was expected so the element of surprise could only be utilized in local operations. To end the battle quickly and diminish losses, primary importance had to be given to the toughness of the initial blows, which were intended to open some breaches and break enemy morale.

On the 22nd, all was in readiness. King Paul, escorted by General George Ventiris, General Van Fleet and other foreign officers, had arrived that very day at an advanced observation post on Ammouda. The King's arrival would, in a way, give the signal for the attack to begin. But, at the last moment, the offensive was postponed for three days on an order of the Commander-in-Chief.

In delaying the attack, Papagos had a most important reason which was to have terrible consequences for the enemy: fifty "Helldivers" had just been delivered by the Americans. As these fighter-bombers had the ability to dive down on the enemy and rake him with machine-gun fire, as well as to sweep in for accurate low-level bombing attacks, the Commander-in-Chief wanted these planes to be put into action.

And so it was that a little before dawn on August 25, a deluge of fire and steel fell on the mountain positions which defended DAG's last bastion. The key defense position towards the north—a high crest between the First and the Third divisions (see Map No. 9)—was pounded by a hundred pieces of artillery in addition to the air force. The bombardment of the positions that were in front of the 15th Division was also very intensive.

Thus, General Goussias, alias the cobbler Vrontissios, believed that the enemy's plan was to enter the fortified area by breaking through the Tsarno-Pyrgos-Kiafa-Arena line. So, he immediately reinforced it with all his reserves. This facilitated the application of the plan of the Commander-in-Chief for the strong pressure exerted on this line, which toward 06:00 appeared with mass attacks of infantry and at the same time aimed at something else: to render less costly the daring pincers movement along the Albanian frontier. Having been vainly attempted in 1948, this operation would be repeated now; from the north to the south the army would thus encircle the entire mountain complex while, at the same time, it would deliver a strong frontal assault at several points.

Everywhere the defenders fought ferociously. Massive bombardment of rebel positions seemed not to have wrought any serious damage. But it soon became evident that morale had been affected, for at midday, when the threatening and decisive Tsarno (altitude 1,430 m., next to Pyrgos on Map No. 9) was reduced by a bayonet assault, no counter-offensive was attempted. Likewise, important neighboring positions that were occupied an hour or two later, cost much bloodshed but remained permanently in the hands of the regular forces.

346

By that same evening, after very bloody combat, more key positions in the Grammos defense line were captured. With the acquisition of these positions certain army units could penetrate into the mountain fort during the night. In addition, the two thrusts from opposite directions along the frontier, were advancing satisfactorily.

On the morning of the 26th, conditions on the battlefield were generally quite different from what they had been twenty-four hours earlier. Battles were taking place in the middle of the mountain complex. Just beyond and destined to seal the Albanian frontier, the daring pincers movement was beginning to close. Artillery fire was now more effective than previously because it originated from advance positions. The air force too continued its attacks which, in a more limited area, were more frightening and deadlier. On that day, the obstinacy of the resistance began to lessen. In certain positions it was persisting, in others it was weakening and in spots it had ceased completely. The rebel defense was to receive on that same day, another kind of blow, a quite unexpected one.

Until that day, Albania had done everything possible to aid DAG. However, on August 25, the two army thrusts along the Albanian border were no longer troubled by withering fire coming from Albanian territory. By noon it had ceased completely. Enver Hodja, the young Albanian dictator, had suddenly become afraid for he was isolated; Tito was hostile to him. Mountains and sea separated him from his country's protectors who were, at that time, the Russians. If the strong reorganized Greek army—at that moment concentrated on his frontiers—even scratched him, it would occupy without firing a shot all of south Albania, which had a Greek population in the majority. It would come to rest at the strongest positions which it would only have to choose. And once the deed was done . . . Blessed are the possessors.

On August 26, in the midst of the battle, Radio Tirana

hastened to announce that any Greek who crossed the Albanian frontier would be arrested, disarmed and interned. Thus, the Albanian leader stated indirectly to the whole world that the battle was lost. And it was only the second day! In spite of that, several DAG bastions were defended to the last man. But all in vain. Combat continued without let-up on the 26th and 27th, but the progress made by the national army clearly indicated that the outcome of the battle had already been decided. Now it had to end as soon as possible in order to minimize losses.

On the evening of the 27th, all national army division commanders were ordered to continue attacking during the night against positions that still resisted, and especially against those which were along the Albanian frontier. Orders stated that the offensive must continue without intermission.

Some tough combat still occurred during the next two days, but only in isolated cases.

At 19:00 hours on the 28th, the summit of Grammos, with an altitude of 2,520 meters, fell into the hands of the national army. On the 29th, other summits and fortified positions were taken. Then, the morning of the 30th saw the fall of terrible Kamenik, the strongest position on the Albanian border. At 10:00 hours of the same day, all combat ceased. In this last unavailing battle, DAG counted 922 dead and about 1,000 prisoners and deserters. The main rebel army had withdrawn, carrying with it about 1,500 wounded. Suicide had been jointly decided, not for the leaders, but for the others; no member of the War Council, the Politburo or the High Command of DAG was among the dead. The equipment which fell into the hands of the army demonstrated by its volume and variety, on the other hand, the magnitude of the defense. There were six hundred machine-guns, two hundred mortars of various sizes, forty field guns and tons of hand grenades and other ammunition.

During the last phase of operation "Pyrsos", army casualties in only five days, had amounted to 1,795 officers and men. So, in all three phases, the number reached a total of 3,960 casualties. DAG's entire losses during that terrible August, totalled 2,280 dead, about 3,000 wounded and 1,632 prisoners and deserters.

A stone had sealed the tomb about which the entire leadership of DAG had spoken. But, contrary to the hopes of those leaders, the tomb was closing on the bodies of their own children despite their tremendous effort and all their sacrifices. The guerrilla war was essentially over. Finally, the national army had emerged victorious from this terrible unconventional war for which, primarily, it had been quite unsuited.

On the eve of the ninth anniversary of the beginning of the Greek-Italian war, on October 27, 1949, Alexandros Papagos was promoted to Field Marshal, an honor given for the first time ever to a Greek officer.

Among the graves and the ruins, accumulated by nine years of war, occupation and guerrilla warfare (1940-1949), the Greek people at last knew freedom and peace once more. These benefits, so simple and so natural, had long since been forgotten and now seemed so wonderful that one speculated as to how long they would be enjoyed. This last thought was to become an obsession which was going to weigh on the social life and politics of the nation during the months and years to come.

Chapter XII

Retrospectives and Perspectives

Fading Away. The bands that remained behind in Greece after the occupation of the two border fortresses by the national army, did not really make history. Two of them, however, did present some danger for a time. Instead of leaving Grammos for Albania, these rebels had taken a path leading towards the south and with about six hundred fighters, ably commanded by Yiotis, Petritis and Ferraios, they plunged into the Pindos range. Other smaller bands— sometimes under famed leaders like "General" Gouzelis, former commander of DAG in the Peloponnesus—took refuge in other mountainous regions of Greece. But before the end of the year, all of them were exterminated and their leaders—at least those who could not rejoin their colleagues in Albania—were killed. It was not, then, these bands which were the underlying cause of the obsession mentioned at the end of the previous chapter.

One of the causes for this troubled state of mind was more deep-seated. There existed, first of all, the pressure of the Slavic states toward the south, toward the warm seas. This pressure was not at all new. Being an unchanging policy of the Slavic nations, one which had not been denied in recent centuries, it was independent of the social and political regimes of these nations and the alliances that had temporarily united them with Greece and Turkey. Under Communist rule, in which ties of race were reinforced with those of a common political ideology, this pressure had taken a most acute and bloody form. All this had been actively conveyed to the Greek people between 1944 and 1949. Thus, each individual was thinking about it and was seeing that it concerned a historical reality and not simply propaganda. This was the principal reason for general anxiety on the part of the population and made extremely difficult the task of those who wished to cultivate good relations with Greece's northern neighbors.

Another reason for anguish was the certainty that those who wished to realize this pressure had on their side, for the first time in centuries, a considerable number of Greeks ready and willing to aid them. Even after the guerrilla war reserves of this kind still existed in Greece itself and in certain of their own countries. The Communists had a large number of sympathizers in Greece— about ten percent of the population; part of them were prepared to make various concessions, another part was even ready to go into battle and a small nucleus of militants was ready for any sacrifice.

Beyond the frontiers after the great uprising, the Slavic states had at their disposal a sizeable group of Greek nationals, larger than what was at first thought. Civilians who had left Greece—sometimes with their families—and had taken refuge in the neighboring countries to the north, according to officially verified figures, had reached 14,370 in 1947, some 27,450 in 1948, and 35,145 in 1949. Totalling 76,965 persons, the refugees comprised mainly inhabitants of the northern provinces among whom were a good

351

number of "Slav-speaking people", who felt themselves very exposed for having supported the guerrillas. Among them also were quite a number of "recruits" (mobilized by force) who had not inspired sufficient confidence to be enrolled in the Democratic Army, but who dared not return to their homes any more. In addition, there were more than 28,000 abducted children who were to be very well indoctrinated in Communist ideology and would be useful in the near future.[1] Lastly, there were the rugged fighters who had just come from battle and were immediately available. These men, including the wounded and recruits who had not completed their training, totalled an autumn 1949, some 16,000 men and women. They were distributed as follows: 8,000 in Albania, 5,000 in Yugoslavia and 3,000 in Bulgaria.

Should the situation arise, refugees and fighters could constitute a fighting force much stronger than that of the Democratic Army of Greece, especially if one looks back to the beginning of the civil war. The picture looked dark. The only ray of light was the attitude of Yugoslavia, a fact that quickly led Athens to cultivate good relations with Belgrade.

But this was not enough for anxiety to disappear. Besides, the KKE in exile did everything possible to stir up general anxiety. Perhaps these were the last gasps of the struggle, but they very much affected a population which had lived under hellish conditions for years.

Certain studies, otherwise very good, speak of the attitude of the KKE in this period. They cite only one phrase from the proclamation of the Provisional Government of October 15, 1949, broadcast from Radio Sofia the next day, according to which "the guerrilla forces had interrupted their operations in order to prevent the total destruction of Greece". Thus presented, this announcement gives a false picture of reality. The truth is that immediately after the battle of the frontiers, one finds a little of everything in KKE resolutions. So as not to tire the reader, only a few typical ones will be mentioned. First, the Sixth Plenum of the Central Committee of the KKE, on October 9, 1949, declared that it had decided *"to stop the armed struggle leaving only a few guerrilla forces as a kind of pressure. The people's revolutionary movement was obliged to make a temporary withdrawal. Let fascism triumph and celebrate it. History has condemned fascism irrevocably. The Democratic Army of Greece which became the noose around the neck of the enemies of Greece, shall fulfill its historical mission as undertaker of monarcho-fascism"*. Second, this same declaration of the 15th includes the following phrases: *"Those who imagine that DAG does not exist are dead wrong. DAG has not surrendered its arms; it has only put them aside. DAG did not yield, nor has it been crushed; it remains strong in all its might"*. Third, the DAG High Command in its order of the day of October 28, 1949, stressed: *"The main forces of DAG ceased all combat operations. But this doesnot mean surrender and submission. Nor does it mean that they have given up. The war has been stopped, but guerrilla activity will continue"*. Fourth, the Politburo of the KKE Central Committee in a secret resolution on November 14, 1949, which, however, was not long in being published, assigned new active duties for DAG. It stressed that *"DAG forces shall be maintained as long as the period of transition lasts, and their activity will open up new perspectives in the manysided popular struggle for a final victory. The arms shouldered today by young peasants serving in the army will be turned against the exploiters and they will join our forces"*.

When the rebel bands had disappeared completely and all this sounded false, there were other factors which kept alive the painful and shocking experiences of the guerrilla war. There were numerous programs in the Greek language from the radio stations of the Eastern Bloc; they raged and fumed. There were also the passionate militants who, supplied with money and wireless transmitters, infiltrated into Greece in order to reorganize clandestine networks.

Thus, the impression that the armed struggle could be resumed was not fading. The agonizing obsession was persisting. Besides, objectively, this feeling was more than justified during the first years. For, though the outlawed KKE oriented itself after 1950 toward political activity legally disguised, its exiled leadership and a considerable part of its cadres did not seem to have given up the idea of resuming the guerrilla war. This idea was only abandoned several years later. This radical change came about primarily due to the following reasons: first, the liquidation of Zachariadis and a group of his friends which took place between 1955 and 1957. Second, the fact that many of the old fighters of the guerrilla war were aging or were settling down in one way or another. Third, a sudden and pronounced improvement in the standard of living of the Greek people, which had occurred mainly under the strong democratic government of Caramanlis. This fact created unfavorable conditions for a repetition of guerrilla activity. Last, the fact that the armed forces of the nation, as well as the security forces, were more numerous now, well organized, vigilant and carefully purged of all leftist elements.

Besides, and this is perhaps fundamental, conditions in Europe had changed greatly and were no longer favorable for this sort of struggle. In fact, this had led to a definite improvement in relations between Greece and her northern neighbors. These relations were, towards 1960, excellent with Yugoslavia, very good with Romania and good with Bulgaria; they had not yet been restored with Albania. So, the guerrilla war was crushed in 1949, but it gave up the ghost ten years later. Alas! The people do not believe it. The majority of those who lived through the scourge of the guerrilla war, will perhaps never believe it.

354

Losses, Damages and Nature of the Conflict. The guerrilla war of the years 1946-1949 left nothing behind but ruins. Communist dead found on the battlefield, at war's end, rose to 36,839. The total figure must be nearer 50,000 however, since guerrillas always tried to carry their dead away when in retreat. The number of wounded is not known because, whenever possible, they were carried across the frontiers. Anyway, many of them remained in Greece and so are included in the totals for DAG prisoners of war (20,128) and deserters (21,258).

On the side of the nationalists, losses were as follows:

Civilians executed	*4,123*
Priests executed	*165*
Civilians killed by mines	*931*
Gendarmerie officers & men, dead	*1,579*
Gendarmerie officers & men, wounded	*2,329*
Army officers & men, dead	*12,777*
Army officers & men, wounded	*37,732*

As for the operations undertaken by DAG between April 1946 and December 1949, we can mention with certainty as follows:

Raids on population centers	*2,040*
Attacks against posts of the army or gendarmerie	*1,446*
Heavy or small arms attacks against populated settlements, approx.	*3,150*
Cases of heavy or medium arms fire against posts of the army or gendarmerie	*510*
Sabotage of railway lines	*525*
Destruction of railway bridges	*330*
Destruction of road bridges	*476*

The value of the damage caused by the guerrilla war has

been estimated by the Greek Ministry of Economic Co-ordination. In taking into account solely materiel totally destroyed during military operations, the figure of 250 million dollars in 1948 prices is given. If we add the value of the homes that were damaged (about 100,000), the maintenance of the refugees and the working hours lost, this amount rises to one billion dollars, at 1948 prices.

And if we consider that the country had already suffered considerable damage during the war years of 1940 to 1944, and that annual per capita income did not exceed 100 dollars, this figure takes on greater significance. This meant that new capital on which the reconstruction and progress of the country depended was formed very slowly and with great difficulty. In light of these facts, one can see that the additional one billion dollar loss for this country was enormous.

There was also another kind of loss no less important. Because of the guerrilla war, Greece was the only country of the Free World not to benefit from the Marshall Plan, with which Europe was rebuilt within a few years. Actually, except for a few planning studies that afterwards proved very useful, all the credits of the Marshall Plan for Greece were utilized so that the Greek people could survive and rebuild some of the ruins. For a country which was at that time underdeveloped, it was the loss of a unique opportunity.

Freedom was won at a high price; one must not forget that. What is more, with the exception of a small minority, everyone was convinced—justly or not—that this terrible disaster was caused by persons serving foreign interests. That is why in Greece, even today, when referring to this sad period, one can not speak of "civil war" without being considered partial towards the extreme Left.[2]

The truth as to the nature of this war is far from simple. The guerrilla war of the years 1946 to 1949 was certainly a civil war from the point of view that it was fought between

Greeks. But it certainly was not a civil war if we judge it from the point of view of its probable duration without abundant and systematic aid coming from neighboring countries. Without open frontiers and lacking this kind of assistance, the guerrilla war could have been launched, but there is not a shadow of doubt that it would have been crushed in a few weeks, or at most in a few months.

The Causes of DAG's Defeat. These causes have been discussed extensively. The general public and certain publicists believe that there are two main ones: first, the quarrel between Belgrade and Moscow from which the closing of the frontier followed and, second, the material assistance offered by the United States of America to the Greek government. The better informed, add as a third reason, the personal conflict between Markos and Zachariadis which ended in the dismissal of the former and the change in tactics that were introduced by the latter.

But all this is over-simplification and ignorance of the truth. We shall see below just how much truth there is in these ideas that are so widespread. The main reason for the defeat of DAG was the firm determination of the majority of Greeks to fight against it until the bitter end. Prepared by the ordeal of the years 1943-44, the majority of the people knew that, once the guerrilla war had started, the only thing that could be done was to fight back with arms; it did so with persistence, with an incredible spirit of sacrifice, and in spite of certain disappointments and setbacks, in spite of doubt as to the outcome of the struggle. If the people were not resolved to fight, all other factors together would not have been enough to assure victory.

As opposed to the Marxist faith of the minority, the majority held its own beliefs, not always clearly defined, but deep down those of the sanctity of personal liberties and of democracy in the proper sense of the word. Nevertheless, this was not sufficient; one had to defend oneself

357

and to put into practice one's beliefs since the other side was trying to do so through armed force. The majority, misled by sheer size and a sense of well-being, usually does not realize that it must fight and impose its views should the need arise. The majority which, when attacked, is not resolved to act in such a way and in time, is condemned to be subjected to daring minorities. Neither numbers nor abundance of means play the main role; rather it is a question of will, timely action and efficient tactics. History has demonstrated this repeatedly, especially during the twentieth century. The great majority of the Greek people, unfortunately, have lived through one of those demonstrations. That is why, without hesitation, it accepted the challenge.

Another reason for the defeat of the Democratic Army, perhaps second in importance, was the attitude of the minority. For although almost all of the majority was prepared to fight, the largest part of the minority was not. During the first months of the struggle, Markos had estimated that DAG needed 50,000 front-line fighters to completely neutralize the national army and force the government to accept a compromise. However, he was never able to attain this figure. At most, DAG's strength came nearer 30,000 at its peak and this was counting also "forced recruits", both men and women.

One will observe perhaps, that the Democratic Army had 50,000 combatants killed, that it also had over 15,000 who left the country after the war, that there were many armed and unarmed persons in the auxiliary services and lastly, that there were many thousands of informants. All this was true. Nevertheless, if in 1946 and 1947, all those who believed in the KKE had responded to its calls and had joined the Democratic Army, it would quickly have reached a total of 50,000 combatants. Markos would then have been obliged to turn back tens of thousands of volunteers. The auxiliaries and intelligence network members of DAG were useful, but they were a different thing. The auxiliary services utilized inhabitants of villages controlled by DAG, who, for one reason or another, were not going to be good guerrillas. Besides, the intelligence cadres consisted of Party members or "sympathizers" who, in spite of strong pressure by the cadres of the secret network and later, the appeals of the Central Committee, would not take to the mountains. This is the reason why there was a continually increasing need for "forced recruits", who did not fight as well as volunteers and who often performed so poorly that they were sent to work camps in Russia or Poland.

It is now certain that only a small percentage of the party's cadres took to the mountains and gave proof of their unswerving faith and of an extraordinary spirit of sacrifice. Most of them preferred to lose themselves in the comfortable anonymity of the large cities. Perhaps, they had doubts as to the possibility of victory and had retained bad memories of a similar recent experience. Most probably, the blood that had been shed abundantly a short time before influenced both sides, but each in a different way. The fact is that in the ranks of DAG, neither the quantity nor the quality of recruits was satisfactory.

The weakening of an army is never a good thing: DAG dwindled without ever having attained optimum size. We may now state our opinion that if Markos had been able to enroll 50,000 fighting men in 1947, the result of the conflict would have been different. Very probably, a compromise favorable to the KKE would have been necessary. And if that strength had been reached before American war material had been fully put into use, i.e., before the end of 1948, again the outcome would have been more favorable to the Communists.

But the majority of Greek Communists—while remaining true to its beliefs—was not inclined to take to the mountains. This was officially and repeatedly deplored by the KKE. This, then, can be pointed to as being one of the principal causes for DAG's defeat.[3]

Added to the two causes described above, was a third quite different one: the material aid given to Greece first by Great Britain and afterwards by the United States. The British assistance was relatively small, but nevertheless, valuable and decisive. At the time of the country's liberation in 1944, the Greek army—except for some small units —was practically non-existent. It was reorganized with the help of Great Britain and was complemented by the gendarmerie and the national guard which were supplied with old material or weapons already in the country, plus some purchases from abroad. The sum total of these combined forces was small and quite insufficient for the great struggle that was just beginning. Nevertheless, it was thanks to this aid and the material assistance that hundreds of DAG raids were held in check, that a bearable equilibrium could be maintained, and that two critical battles at the end of 1947 in Metsovo and Konitsa could be won.

Certainly, American aid was of a completely different magnitude than that of the British. It allowed the State to survive in spite of the semi-paralysis of the nation's economy; it permitted the spirit of defense to harden and it gave the army time to develop into a modern and important force.

At this point we must mention another related factor to which true significance is not always attributed: the kind of war materiel used by the two rivals. Until autumn of 1947, and perhaps a little later, DAG weapons in general, were not inferior to those of the national army because they were better adapted to the needs of a guerrilla war. These were even some particular items as, for example heavy machine-guns, in which DAG equipment was superior. Besides, a good part of national army materiel which was considered excellent, for example, horse drawn or motorized field artillery, was completely useless in fighting that took place in mountains which usually had no roads at all. As far as overall materiel is concerned, the only advantage the army had over its adversary was the air force which was absent from the other side. From the first months of the guerrilla war, Markos had asked for air cover; he even maintained that he could keep his air force based at small airports he would construct around Little Prespa Lake. But his protectors never dared to fulfil his wish because they feared that such irrefutable proof of intervention on their part would only provoke more direct American retaliation. So the guerrillas had no air force. The psychological effect, especially at the beginning of the conflict, was important. The effect on tactics primarily concerned reconnaissance and transportation, especially the supplying of besieged positions.

But all this was not really decisive during the first part of the war. Although the air force had a few good planes— Spitfires and C-47's—at its disposal, they were scarcely utilized. Most of the planes were slow, heavy DC-3 Dakotas and Ansons which bombed and fired machine guns, but were never intended for such missions, especially as the latter were almost always required in mountainous regions. Under these conditions, the effectiveness of the air force depended more on the daring and ingenuity of the pilots than on the capabilities of the planes themselves. On the other hand, the rebel bands were protected somewhat by their mobility as they usually joined together for an attack, then dispersed immediately afterwards and conducted their operation, as a rule, during the night. The national air force, then, presented for DAG a serious but not insuperable handicap. Naturally, this situation changed as materiel improved.

Anti-aircraft guns and artillery with which certain guerrilla forces were supplied, particularly on the two frontier fortresses, were very successful,[4] but that was meager consolation for DAG. The more experienced pilots, later in the war, flew aircraft with more maneuverability and greater firing precision. Both the psychological effect on the enemy and tactics were enhanced by this.

So, in spite of the incredible spirit of the regular troops in August 1949—and their losses are proof of it—Vitsi and Grammos would not have fallen within a few days if it had not been for the massive intervention of the air force, more particularly the Helldivers, flown by tough, experienced pilots. Backed up against the frontier, these precipitous mountains so strongly defended and fortified, would otherwise certainly have been able to keep up a resistance for at least some weeks.

Yet the benefit from the modernization of the national army's weapons was only extracted at the end of the conflict when American equipment and armament started pouring in. Furthermore, it must be remembered that time was needed to train men in their use. Besides that, the training had to take place while the men were pressed and were continuing to fight the war.

The quarrel between Belgrade and Moscow cannot be considered one of the important reasons for the defeat of DAG. In order for the KKE to justify itself and also to be agreeable to its master, it maintained that the reason for the defeat was the Tito betrayal. This is inaccurate. When Tito first began to reduce aid, defeat was beginning to take form. When Yugoslav aid was seriously diminished in the spring of 1949, defeat was already certain. By the time the Yugoslav frontier was closed in July 1949 it was just around the corner. The rebels had only to pay the price in blood for the last two strongholds to fall. This Yugoslav change of attitude undoubtedly had other consequences for it shortened the struggle and diminished bloodshed on both sides. But it did not alter the fortunes of war.

It is far more difficult to express an opinion on the influence which the quarrel between Nicos Zachariadis and Markos Vafiadis had on the outcome of the conflict. It was certainly extremely damaging for the rebel side, both from the military and the psychological point of view. But it was a long way from there to believing, as is sometimes maintained, that if hit-and-run tactics were continued the war would have ended differently for the rebels.

The tactics of Markos, the great organizer, leader of men, were excellent and were justified until mid-1948. After that, the facts of the matter fundamentally changed. Actually, from 1948 on, in spite of improvement in DAG's armament and organization, the balance of forces was becoming more and more favorable to the national army. This clearly would continue since the nationalists could put a much larger number of fighters in the field than the Communists, moreover, the application of the Truman Doctrine guaranteed nationalist supplies.

In addition, during this period the Party had to bear in mind that sooner or later, it would be obliged to pronounce itself in favor of Moscow and against Belgrade. Considering the ascendancy of communism in the Balkans and the strength and prestige of the Soviet Union, KKE neutrality vis-a-vis Moscow could not last. But a quarrel with Tito would certainly complicate relations with Belgrade and, for those who could look ahead, it would lead one day to the closing of the Yugoslav borders. Now, a guerrilla war on a large scale cannot last if it is not supported by a large part of the rural population or, indeed, if the insurgents are used to crossing frontiers that cannot be guarded. This is an axiom. It is valid for all parts of the world.

Then, there was something else which would change the basic facts of the problem: the lack of new fighters for the rebels. Due to heavy losses the guerrillas were forced to make difficult incursions in order to mobilize men more effectively. This was very costly, and yet they barely managed to fill up the gaps in their forces.

All these factors and others should have led the KKE leaders to the conclusion that time was working against the "Great Uprising". Clearly, the Party had to take radical measures. It was faced with a choice between one, the search for a compromise—good or bad—and two, an all-out war in order to try to attain the impossible before the situation deteriorated further. This seems to be what Zachariadis was trying to do between November 1948 and February 1949, by increasing the aggressiveness of DAG, by trying to occupy towns and by daring to face the national army openly. This was not the old disagreement with Markos any more. Then, was it to augment DAG's light mobile forces, or to try to create a regular army? Was it only a guerrilla war or a guerrilla war and a war of positions at the same time? No, it was neither of these. Rather it was an attempt to play the last card through some daring and very telling strikes against the enemy before it was too late. These tactics failed, it is true, at Florina and elsewhere, but they were spectacularly successful at Karditsa, Naoussa and Karpenissi and, at the same time, shook morale in the entire nationalist camp.

Consequently, it must be said that Markos had estimated the situation very well in the beginning and almost until autumn of 1948, but after that time his tactics were not correct. Defeat could not have been avoided. The results of the mopping up operations in the Peloponnesus and central Greece, where the guerrilla war was still raging, are irrefutable proof of this.

Now, one is also wrong to hold that if Markos's advice had been followed, as to organization and tactics, defeat would have been avoided. However, if he had been given the means he had asked for in time—and we must place stress on the "in time"—the results would have been different, perhaps very different. His tactics were valid for as long a period as it was reasonable to apply them. After that, one must recognize, there was a certain logic in what Zachariadis had tried to do.

What is most difficult to understand is the reasoning of

Zachariadis after the spring of 1949. The outcome of the conflict had been decided. Nothing could save the situation. Why, then, this struggle till the end? Why did he allow so many of his own people to die in vain and among them, the flower of the KKE? There can be only one answer: the Greek Communist leadership, headed by Zachariadis, was grossly mistaken. It had believed that its forces would be able to defend the "impregnable fortresses" of Grammos and Vitsi. In clinging to this belief, the rebels did not hesitate to make any sacrifice.

Several indications offer proof to us that the Bulgarian and Albanian leaders must share responsibility for the decision that was taken. No doubt, they also were fooled as to the possibilities of defense. But they had a special reason for making this decision; for, after the break with Yugoslavia, it was greatly in their interest that a Greek Communist Party hostile to Yugoslavia, exist, even on a small strip of Greek territory. This explains also the tardy participation of two Bulgarians in the Provisional Government. Furthermore, it explains the generous assistance offered to DAG by the two countries until the very last days. And it explains some events of lesser importance, such as the participation of Albanian soldiers in one of the last battles that took place on Greek soil.

Finally, another factor in the defeat of DAG and the victory of the national army was the leadership of Papagos. In order to evaluate the importance of this objectively, one must note that at the time Papagos assumed the responsibility of commander-in-chief, certain very important events transpired, or were going to transpire, in favor of the national army, the experience of the officers obtained from the guerrilla war of 1947-48, the use of increased American war materiel, the decrease in Yugoslav assistance to DAG, and the operations in the Peloponnesus already well advanced. But, given these facts, it must be added at once that much more needed to be done, and it was, above all, thanks to Papagos that it was done. The powers with which he was invested, the prestige he already enjoyed and his personal aptitude permitted him to take all the necessary decisions without losing time, to impose strict discipline on all echelons of the military hierarchy and to give the army maximum effectiveness One must understand that the effectiveness of an army does not depend solely on size, armament and supply; it depends also on the spirit of the troops, the choice of commanders, the distribution of units, the speed of its movements and, lastly, the plan of action. In all these matters Papagos's personal contribution was essential. Without any doubt, Papagos was one of the decisive factors in the defeat of DAG. Most probably he was the unique factor in its defeat during 1949. Without him, it is probable that the guerrilla war would not have ended before spring or summer of 1950.

Naturally, certain other factors contributed to an earlier end to the war. We must mention the effectiveness and spirit of unity of almost all of the politicians, the regular functioning of Parliament during the entire armed struggle, the patriotism and the activities of the King and Queen and still other factors. But before ending this paragraph, we must repeat that all the above-mentioned influences, direct or indirect, would have been inoperative if the first among them had been missing: the resolution of the majority of the Greek people to fight and, if need be, to undergo sacrifices in order to safeguard individual liberties in their native land.

Retrospectives and Perspectives. After the debacle the KKE reorganized itself into three very different branches; one of them was that of the Party abroad and the other two were in Greece. Abroad, those who had left Greece made up the KKE "of the exterior", which rather should be named "the official KKE". This branch had its Central Committee and Politburo, organized congresses, took part in the congresses of other communist parties, published magazines and broadcast in Greek on the radio stations of the eastern bloc. It kept busy looking after the abducted children, saw to the functioning of their schools and directed the Communist movement in Greece. There is no need to mention that it was adequately financed.

Members were scattered among all the Communist countries, but were mainly concentrated in the Soviet Union, Rumania and Hungary. A much smaller number lived in Poland and Bulgaria.[5] The exiles' main center in Russia was Tashkent, the capital of Uzbekistan, an important town near the point where Russia, China and Afghanistan meet.

Those exiles who did not have the privilege of working with the administration of the Party—offices, publications, schools, radio, etc.—usually toiled as ordinary workers and lived a disciplined and rather austere life under the regime for which they had fought so hard.

The administration of the Party was dominated by the Zachariadis group. At all the Party meetings this group praised its General Secretary and demonstrated its loyalty to the Soviet Union and its leaders.[6]

In the first two Party plenums only the last president, Dimitri Partsalides, and Costas Karageorghis, former physician and publicist then general and minister, were present to criticize the General Secretary. Markos was never invited to these gatherings.

At the Third Congress of the KKE in October of 1950, all three of the above-mentioned officials were dismissed from the Party leadership and Siantos was proclaimed posthumously "an agent of the British and an enemy of the working class". According to a French Communist author who conducted an investigation behind the Iron Curtain, Karageorghis died before 1956 "in a cell installed in the basement of Zachariadis's private dwelling".

Only after Stalin's death did Zachariadis's turn come to

be purged. In 1955, a letter signed by four hundred and fifty members of the Greek Communist Party in Tashkent was addressed to Premier Krushchev. This was the first attack. Then, in the Plenum of the Central Committee and in the Politburo, Dimitri Partsalidis, Constantine Koliyannis—the young "lieutenant general" of the Democratic Army—and Apostolos Grozos—representative of the trade unions in the Provisional Government—dethroned the Zachariadis group. Zachariadis, Vassilis Bartzotas and Dimitri Vlantas, all three once very influential in the KKE, as well as other less known leaders, saw their names struck from the Party cadres. Karageorghis and Siantos were restored posthumously and Markos resumed his position in the Central Committee. (He was again excluded from the committee during the Eighth Congress in 1961 "because of the sharpness of his criticism".)

The "dethroned", those who are still alive, do not seem to be living under very good conditions. One of the great men of Greek communism, Andreas Tzimas, is said to have had the good luck towards the end of his life to be appointed concierge of a large building in Prague. Zachariadis, through a letter sent to the Greek embassy in Moscow (at the beginning of 1962), asked to return to Athens to face justice for his actions. This was understood to be a sign of activism. But perhaps it was rather the lack of comforts which induced him to take this step. For even prison or exile on an island in the Aegean Sea would be more agreeable than the life of an unfavored Kutvist in the cold countries of the north. To be precise, in those days Zachariadis lived in a village lost in the Urals, as a clerk of the Department of Waters and Forests. Athens had the snobbishness not to accept his proposal and the cruelty to give the letter publicity.

According to many sources, those who now direct the Party of the exterior are living comfortably. Nevertheless, during the sixties, after various disagreements about which little is known, there was a split within the Party. It took place at the beginning of 1968 after a stormy congress held in a northern Italian town. Those party leaders under Partsalides who lived in Bucharest, supported by the members of parliament who had escaped from Athens after the military coup of April 1967, came into conflict with those members under Koliyannis's leadership who resided in Moscow. As a result of this disagreement, two separate KKE were formed, each one declaring that it was the "Party". The breach was real and very deep. Accusations formulated by each of these parties against the other included the usual arguments that are heard in recent schisms of communist parties elsewhere.

But dogmatic differences do not reveal the deepest reason for this quarrel. In reality, it was simply a difference of opinion on two questions of policy concerning Greece. The first one referred to the recent past: the Central Committee located in Moscow, was accused of having intervened and given very poor direction to the movement in Greece before the coup of April 21, 1967. The other question concerned the tactics to be followed; the Moscow committee was accused of being too obedient to the orders of Eastern Bloc governments and of exercising a rather weak policy toward the new regime established in Greece after April 1967. It was accused thus of betraying the principles of Marxism-Leninism and of discouraging the faithful who were living in Greece. It is useless to add that the Koliyannis group was the one which won out; that group is the only one since then to secure the support of the Eastern Bloc and to be able to use, therefore, all its instruments of propaganda.

Once one of the great men of the KKE and the last president of the Provisional Government, Partsalides, in spite of his sixty-eight years, entered Greece secretly with militants in 1971. He intended to reorganize the Party cadres. After a certain period of time Partsalides was discovered and sent to jail in spite of his false papers and disguise. He was, it seems, betrayed by one of his former comrades to whom he had addressed himself, but who blindly obeyed the leaders of Muscovite tendencies. Perhaps they were afraid—and this is just a supposition—that for him to be active again, the Party of the exterior would lose its hold inside Greece.

Of course, all his in-fighting scarcely strengthens the official Communist Party. Besides, if we recall that among Greek communists Maoist tendencies exist, that several well-known members of the Party have recently declared that they are in favor of a Communist Party that is free from the influence of comrades abroad, we can realize that the old KKE went through, and is still going through, an extremely grave crisis.

To complete this very brief sketch of the KKE of the exterior, let us add two pieces of information: first, those who left Greece before 1950 followed a line of their own. The individuals who spoke a dialect based on a Slavic tongue took refuge or slowly gathered in the town of Skopje in Macedonia which, as is generally known, has some autonomy within the Yugoslav federation.

The number in this group is high; it probably exceeds 35,000. These people are working today in Yugoslavia under the same conditions as the rest of the population. They make their own careers, sometimes they even reach the highest positions; they are assimilated. The guerrilla war finally ended well for them. Unfortunately, this group promotes the propaganda line of Skopje which suggests that there is a Slavic Macedonian national entity in northern Greece. Such propaganda is very harmful to Greek-Yugoslav relations.

The second piece of information is quite different in nature. As of January 1973, an official declaration of the illegal KKE with its seat in Moscow, replaced Party general secretary Koliyannis by Charilaos Florakis. Since Koliyannis enjoyed great prestige among Greek Communists, and as his dismissal occurred some five years after the Party split, it is difficult to find an explanation for this change. What must be particularly noted here is a fact that only the well-informed already know: Charilaos Florakis is the true name of Captain Yiotis, whom we have repeatedly met beteen 1946 and 1949 through his feats of valor for DAG. After the disaster of the Democratic Army at Grammos in 1949, instead of following his comrades and seeking refuge in Albania, he was one of the few who again took to the mountains at the head of a strong band to continue the armed struggle. In order to continue a hopeless struggle after great despair and the loss of all illusions ... Afterwards, his story—unpublished, but absolutely verified—was that of a persistent fighter; he left Greece secretly at the end of 1949 and returned with a forged passport. Arrested and sentenced, he was set free again in 1964, thanks to general clemency measures. Rearrested in April 1967, he was set free in 1971 and left Greece secretly in October 1972. His courage, persistence and loyalty to the official Party and the fact that he was in Greece until the end of 1972 undoubtedly favored his nomination. Nevertheless, the curious fact remains that a man known for his bloody exploits, had been chosen to direct a party that wants the revolutionary periods of the past to be forgotten.

We must mention now a few words about the other two forms under which the KKE survived inside Greece after the debacle. One was the clandestine network, or the Party cadres. As the KKE had a clear revolutionary character around the early 1950's and as memories of the guerrilla war were still very much alive, many of its members were either in prison, in exile, or under police surveillance. Later on, when a repetition of the rebellion did not seem possible any more, the Party cadres became

371

freer and thus more active in the political arena.

In general, the fields of activity in which the Greek Communist Party concentrated its efforts were mainly three: in the first place, there was the development of the network itself in towns and villages. Obviously, these activities were not practiced in broad daylight, especially as the KKE was illegal at that time. But a scrutiny of the cases which the security police uncovered demonstrated that there was a skillful, persistent effort directed primarily at the young.

Another field of action was in the trade unions. For all effort in this sector, KKE's leadership had issued well-defined instructions in October 1950. According to this, the Party was to infiltrate into *every mass organization after a careful examination of that which concerns the masses and without placing a sign on the chest of each member stating that he was a member of the Party . . . no members who had engaged in legal activities should be utilized in the illegal organization; the illegal apparatus must be protected like the apple of one's eye*".

If one did not know these texts at that time, one could still see their practical application. In fact, persons known for their Marxist convictions became very active in trade unionism without ever mentioning the principles or activities of communism. Slowly they achieved success, sometimes by entering the administration of certain trade unions, or sometimes—more rarely—by taking the entire administration into their hands. This was particularly useful to the Party for obvious reasons, but it also helped the activity of the clandestine network in its third field of endeavor: public demonstrations. Needless to say, these were never conducted "with a sign on the demonstrator's chest advertising that he was a member of the Party". Quite to the contrary. They were always made to support in a rowdy way—and bloody at times—the demonstrations of groups with entirely different tendencies. For example, the nationalists were supported in their demonstrations against the West and in favor of the Union of Cyprus with Greece (to which the Soviet Union was opposed as much as certain countries of the West). The workers were supported in their trade union demands, the Center Union party against the National Radical Union, the pacifists in their "marches for peace". But the Communists were lending a hand by always taking the first step in the breaking of windows and even in clashing with the police. No one was fooled by this. Everyone understood who was leading the dance, the dance that seemed to prepare the ground for further developments and which after 1963 had become a dangerous whirl. But nobody understood why this tactic was followed; it played magnificently into the hands of reactionaries. Peace-loving people were becoming afraid. Quite sincerely, they were taking the growing disorder to be the beginning of a new rebellion, or at least, of a situation that soon would be uncontrollable. The results are well known.

The creation of this political climate was greatly encouraged by KKE activity in Greece in another form: that of a leftist party which joined a popular front known by its initials in Greek, EDA (United Democratic Left). Formed after the guerrilla war, EDA was always a small party. With the exception of the special case of 1958,[7] in seven other general elections in the period from 1950 to 1964, EDA received between 10% and 14.5% of the total vote.

In this front there was a little of everything, even politicians of the extreme Right who, otherwise, would never have been elected as members of Parliament. Quite simply, they were a showcase which did not play any role at all and, in this case, did not fool anyone. Almost all of the members of parliament of the EDA were former officials of the KKE who had been in prison or in exile and who had taken advantage of the general amnesty.

We can characterize the activities of the EDA accurately by mentioning two general "directives" which the Party scrupulously respected on every occasion. One is from the Second Congress of the Comintern, the other from Lenin himself. The first states: *"The fact that parliament is an institution of the bourgeois State does not constitute an argument against our participation in parliamentary struggles. The Communist Party does not enter parliament as an organic part of it, but with the intention of acting within parliament in such a manner as to incite the popular masses to destroy the apparatus of the State and parliament itself".* (paragraph 10, Resolution of the Congress). The second, from a text of Lenin: *"From that which precedes springs one part of the provisional character of our position with respect to our common attacks against the bourgeois order; on the other hand, it is our duty to consider the ally[8] as an enemy".* All of EDA's tactics from 1950 to 1967, without exception and concerning any question or any person, could be typified by the above quotes. To give thus in two strokes what all of the tactics of EDA from 1950 to 1967 included, we must add that never on any subject did EDA disagree with Moscow's line.

All these activities of the KKE, naturally, did not assist in the regular functioning of parliamentary democracy, nor in the restoration of a feeling of security and order which was the overwhelming wish of a majority of the people. But now all that is over. Today, as we have seen, the KKE is going through a serious crisis, perhaps the most serious one it has ever gone through.

Besides, the political atmosphere all over the world is changing communism too. On the state level, communism is becoming clearly nationalistic; proof of it is the fact that every communist party, if it does not have to obey another, is little short of being the faithful successor of the principles that geo-political facts have imposed on its predecessors, even those who were tsars or kings. If, now, there are radical changes on the ideological plane, we must not be carried away and lose sight of the geo-political constants. This could be extremely dangerous.

Certainly, the international environment is entirely different in the 1970's from what it was some years ago. Technical progress has altered many things. Due to this fact, the way of tackling problems has changed also. But the problems still exist.

If we let our thoughts dwell a moment on the world chessboard, as the differences between the Soviet Union and China, or if we think of a more local area, such as the Middle East trouble zone, we see that many serious problems exist. We must hope that in the end, realistic solutions will be reached, rather than insistence on the retention of a balance of power.

The two thousand-year-old principle—"If you want peace, prepare for war"—is, unfortunately, still valid. But it is full of immense dangers. By continually preparing for war, one risks going to war, though this has become less likely as there is now the risk of a nuclear war.

Besides, on the ideological plane, communism is not at all what it once was. When it promised a miracle through its theories applied by a scientific State, it found that it had to make important concessions to principle. In spite of that, fifty years later though the progress achieved by communist regimes is not comparable to that of the Free World.

While once communism was united and had only one center, ten years ago it entered a period of "poly-centrism", and is now disunited. The ensuing reactions which are trying to make it turn back by various means, including that of military invasion, may secure local results, but eventually, cause deeper and wider divisions in the Communist world.

These divisions have profoundly influenced the disarray of a large part of the youth. For communism is now out of date. It is no longer a question of knowing whether its means are good or bad; the point is that communism no longer is considered as being in the vanguard for a humanity in search of perfection. It is now more conservative than revolutionary, more nationalist than internationalist; being itself split up, its members quarrel with the Free World and often with the Third World. So it is no longer the avant-garde.

Communism does not any longer attract impetuous youth. And, moreover, this youth which is offered a good life without having done anything yet to justify it, does not even know what it wants. A large part of the younger generation simply seem to want to be different from the previous generation, but without being able to say how, or how much. Another part of it declares itself anarchist without being able to define exactly what the term means. It seems to want to destroy the past without knowing what it is going to build in its place, without caring about the hardships that this destruction will cause. It will think about that after the disaster, sitting among the ruins . . .

In this chaos of ideas and all sorts of conflicts, many are those who opted in favor of a totalitarian regime as a remedy; black, red or white, according to the inclinations of the one who can impose it. What interests people everywhere in the order so visible in the totalitarian state.

This remedy temporarily eases some of the bad symptoms but, in reality, makes the illness graver. In aiming a blow at the freedom and dignity of the individual—virtue that are worth as much as life itself—the disorder goes deep into the body politic and the evil is accentuated to the point that it becomes impossible to control. In this way, one guarantees today's peace at the price of tomorrow's anarchy. But anarchy can not last; it brings suffering and instability with imponderable consequences.

Others choose to maintain or restore pure parliamentary democracy. This option undoubtedly more closely conforms with our desires and is more worthy of a free humanity. But pure parliamentarism—modern democracy in its most advanced form—was born and had been applied in the historical context of the nineteenth century; it conformed to social, moral and economic circumstances entirely different from those of today. These circumstances are the ones that determine the effectiveness of political systems. Especially so as this concerns a political system that offers great privileges to those who want to abolish that system in any way and by any means.

In the last instance, the remedy is easily taken but it does not seem to be effective. The fact that throughout the world the number of countries which have pure parliamentary democracy is continually decreasing, is not due simply to chance. Besides, the fact that it is so often, and so easily, abolished is in itself a major deficiency.

So, the maintenance of the political system under which human life acquires its value—in fact, the survival of the democratic system—does not depend any longer on its ability to face bloody revolutions, such as those unleashed by the KKE between 1943 and 1949. Certainly, one must be able and at the same time be determined to face such rebellions for, otherwise, one invites them.

But the survival of democracy depends, in my opinion, on two significant changes—one relating to international order, and the other to internal order. The first is the effective reinforcement of the methods through which geo-political differences will be peacefully resolved. The other is the better organization of parliamentary forms of government which, although showing full respect for democratic principles, will be adapted to the conditions of our times.

PHOTOGRAPHS

King George II

King George II during army maneuvers

Ioannis Metaxas in 1936.

Alexandros Papagos in 1940, Commander in Chief of the Greek forces during the war in Albania.

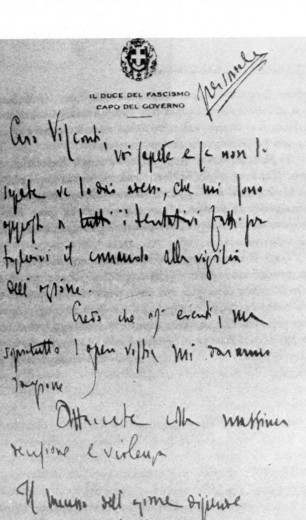

[Translation of the Letter]

THE LEADER OF FASCISM
HEAD OF THE GOVERNMENT

Personal

Dear Visconti,

You know, and if you do not know I am telling you now, that I was opposed to all efforts which were made to deprive you of command on the eve of action.

I believe that events, but most of all your work, will give me reason to justify you.

Attack with as much decisiveness and force as possible. The success of this action depends mainly on its speed.

Mussolini

Rome, 25 October XVIII

Author's notes:

XVIII meant the 18th year of Fascism. It was a necessary addition to the date in the texts and letters of Italian Fascists.

This letter of Mussolini was addressed to General Visconti Prasca three days before the Italian invasion of Greece. If one more proof was necessary that the "serious" border incidents of the last days were false and that the ultimatum was a trick, the date of this letter gives irrefutable proof of it.

383

Mussolini, early in the morning of March 9, 1941. He follows the launching of the great Italian offensive from an advanced observation post. Behind him, Field Marshall Ugo Cavallero, then Commander-in-Chief of the Italian forces in Albania.

Landing of a platoon of the First Regiment of shock troops.

German paratrooper prisoners caged up in a narrow street of Heraklion.

*Colonel Psarros, a perfect and
fearless soldier.*

*Napoleon Zervas, the heroic and fun-loving
patriot.*

(The photographs of Zervas and Sarafis bear their signatures; they are from Woodhouse's
personal album to whom they had been dedicated.)

Colonel Sarafis, the taciturn and thoughtful organizer.

One of the makeshift bridges used very often in those days.

Bridge on one of the rare narrow roads (for cars) of the Greek mountains, in which guerrilla warfare took place during the German occupation. (Photo by Woodhouse)

One of many old bridges in the Greek mountains which were constructed mainly during the 17th and 18th centuries.

Greek guerrilla leader Sarafis, Italian General Infante and British Colonel Chris (Monty) Woodhouse; signing of the agreement between the Greek resistance and the Italian "Pinerolo" division.

The Pinerolo Division arrives in the mountains. In the central group is General Judice (who soon defected to the Germans), commander of the division's infantry units, to the right with his back to the photographer, Infante and Woodhouse. In the group on the right: Colonel Raftopoulos of EDES, General Sarafis, chief commander of ELAS and to the right with beard and black cap, Aris Velouchiotis. In the background, men of the Pinerolo division. (Photo by Woodhouse)

389

Colonel Popoff. To his right, Alexander Svolos, professor of constitutional law at the University of Athens. Second to his left, Lieutenant Colonel Chernitchev who served for many years after the guerrilla war as counsellor of the Soviet Embassy in Athens.

Aris Velouchiotis in the center, to his right, the leader of the American Military Mission, Major G.K. Wines, to his left, Woodhouse and Sarafis. (Photo by Woodhouse)

The Regent, Archbishop Damaskinos, during an official visit to England in September 1945. Behind him, without a beard, Colonel Woodhouse. To his right, Thanassis Agnidis, former assistant General Secretary of the League of Nations then Greek ambassador in London. At the extreme left of the photo, Greek poet George Seferis then Counsellor of Embassy and director of the Regent's diplomatic bureau. To the extreme right, the least popular Englishman in Greece, Ambassador of Great Britain in Athens, Sir Rex Leeper.

391

A committee under the leading official of the British Labour Party, Sir Walter Citrin (left at the back) visits an execution site in Attica. On account of the large number of executions—of both men and women—there had not been enough time for the burial of the dead.

At about the same period in Thrace: The Bulgarian fascists came this way. Death was vertical here, bestiality the same. The priest (to the left) leads the macabre dance. Both the victims and the executioners were Orthodox Christians.

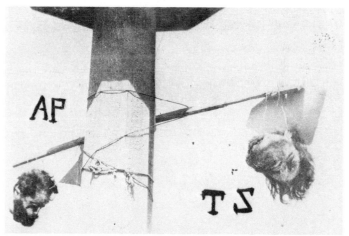

The heads of Aris Velouchiotis (to the left) and his second in command, Tzavellas, hanging on a pole in the central square of Trikkala.

King Paul

King Paul inspecting an infantry battalion.

Themistoclis Sofoulis

The cover of the album commemorating the 2nd anniversary of the foundation of DAG.

Nicos Zachariadis, General Secretary of the KKE

General Markos Vafiadis, commander of the Democratic Army of Greece.

The enlistment.

Training.

Recruits are often almost children.

Women in training.

Preparation for fortifications and a fortified gun emplacement.

Pillbox

Transportation

Telecommunications.

DAG mess.

At the hospital on Mount Grammos

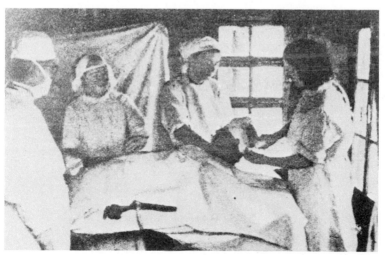

An operating room on Mount Grammos

The cavalry

Machine guns in use.

The artillery.

Infantry in battle

The "Impregnable forts". One slope in the wilderness of Mount Grammos.

SOME OF THOSE WHO WERE REPLACED
(PHOTO ALBUM OF DAG)

Markos Vafiadis.

*Lieutenant General Kikitsas
of DAG, former officer of the
regular army.*

SOME OF THOSE WHO WERE REPLACED
(PHOTO ALBUM OF DAG)

Captain Ypsilantis, major general of DAG.

Captain Yannoulis, standing to the right in uniform among Greek journalists in March 1947. In front, sitting in the center, Vassos Vassiliou, who had asked the Captain about the independence of Macedonia.

Demetrios Vlantas, major-general of DAG and minister of agriculture in the Provisional Government.

Lieutenant General Goussias (pseudonym of the cobbler of Syrako, George Vrontissios.)

411

Ioannis Ioannidis, vice premier of the Provisional Government and minister of interior affairs.

Petros Roussos, minister of foreign affairs (husband of Chryssa Hatzivasiliou)

Vassilis Bartzotas, major-general of DAG as well as minister of finance.

412

Dimitri Partsalidis, before the war. The hour of power Member of the Central Committee of the KKE. Minister of EAM/ELAS and representative of the Party in its most critical negotiations. President of the Provisional Government of DAG in 1949.

Dimitri Partsalidis, 35 years later. The hour of grandeur. Fighting for his beliefs in spite of age and despite lack of means and disapproval of the official KKE, he remains an active fighter. The photo, taken in 1972, is that of a prisoner.

Charilaos Florakis. Known during the guerrilla war as Captain Yiotis, major general of DAG, he was appointed General Secretary of the KKE.

Constantinos Koliyannis. An old offical of the Party, as well as a major general of DAG. He succeeded Zachariadis and remained General Secretary of the KKE abroad with its headquarters in the Soviet Union. Replaced in January 1973, his followers of this strongest branch of te lowers of this strongest branch of the KKE are still called "Koliyannists".

413

The Guerrilla War has just ended. Field Marshall Papagos inspects troops at the front.
Above: In Salonica with an infantry division.
Below: Near the Bulgarian border with an armored division.

414

MAPS

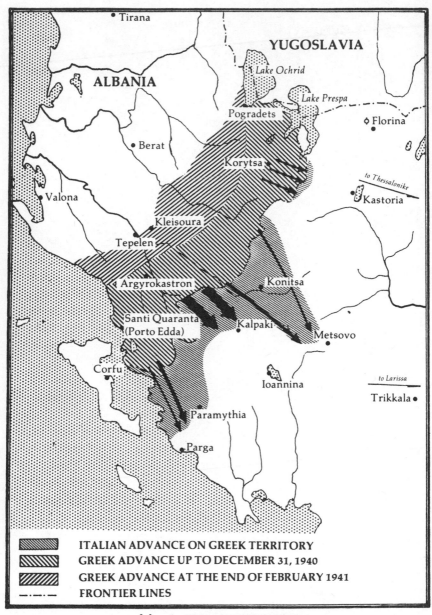

Map 1: **THE ALBANIAN WAR**

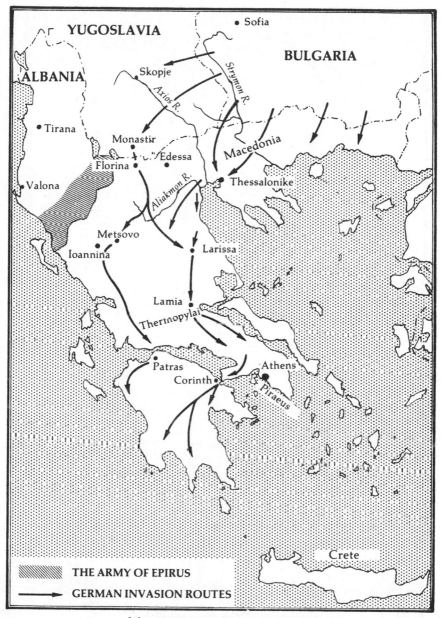

THE ARMY OF EPIRUS

GERMAN INVASION ROUTES

Map 2: **THE GERMAN INVASION**

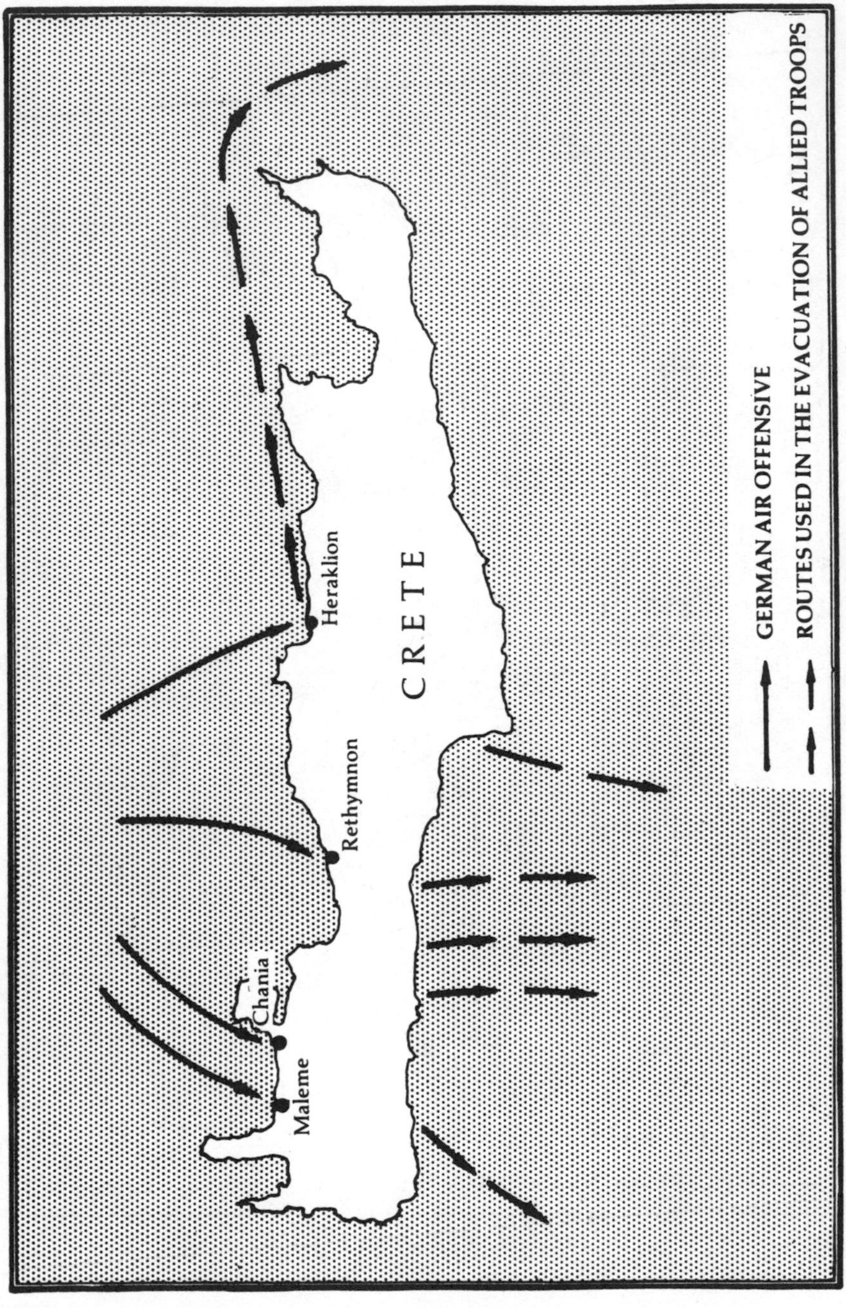

Map 3: THE BATTLE OF CRETE

REST AND TRAINING CAMPS
SUPPLY BASES
ROUTES INTO GREECE

Bulkes

Belgrade

ROMANIA

Bucharest

YUGOSLAVIA

Berkovitsa

BULGARIA

Sofia

ALBANIA   Tetovo   Kumanovo

Rubig   Skopje

Kicevo   Stip   Nevrokop

Tirana   Strumica   Ortakiot
Petrich   Mandritsa

Ochrid   Drama

Korytsa   Serres   Kavalla

Valona   Florina   Thessalonike

Permet   Kastoria

Erseke

Argyrokastron

Ioannina

Map 4: **DAG REST AND TRAINING CAMPS, SUPPLY BASES AND
ROUTES INTO GREECE**

419

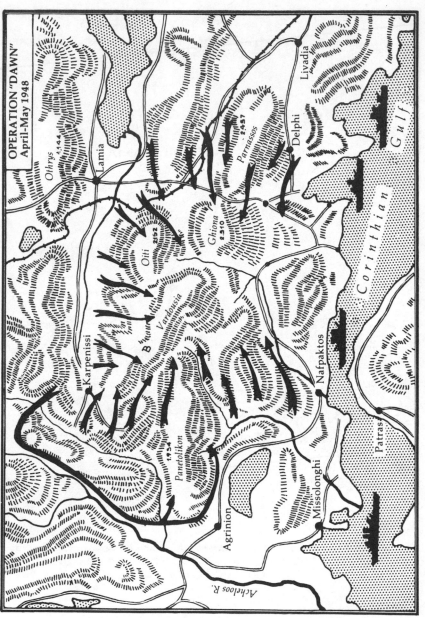

OPERATION "DAWN"
April-May 1948

Ohrys 1,144

Lamia

Karpenissi

Oiti 2152

Vardousia

B

Panetolikon 1,954

Agrinion

Acheloos R.

Parnassos 2,457

Ghiona 2,510

Delphi

Livadia

Nafpaktos

Missolonghi

Patras

Corinthian Gulf

Map 5: OPERATION "DAWN"

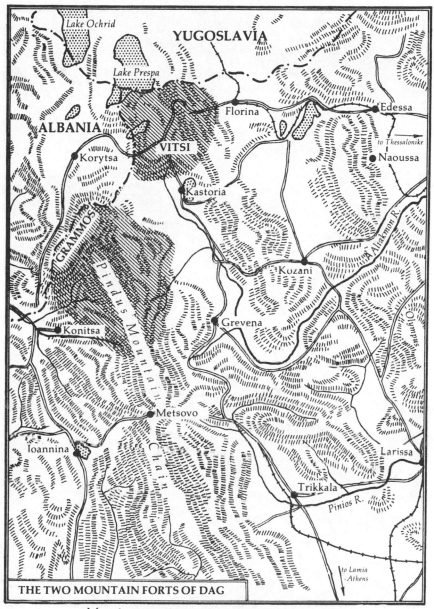

THE TWO MOUNTAIN FORTS OF DAG

Map 6: **THE TWO MOUNTAIN FORTS OF DAG**

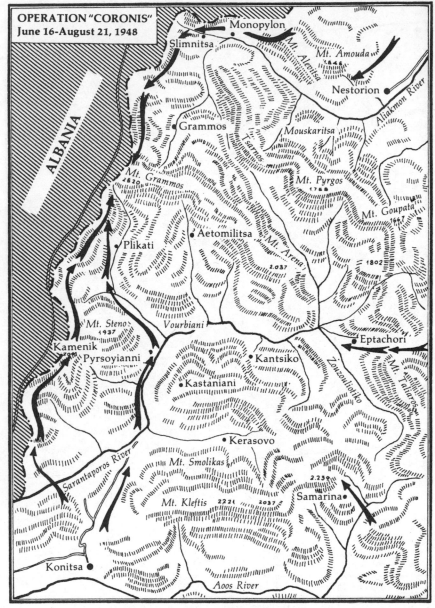

Map 7: **OPERATION "CORONIS"**

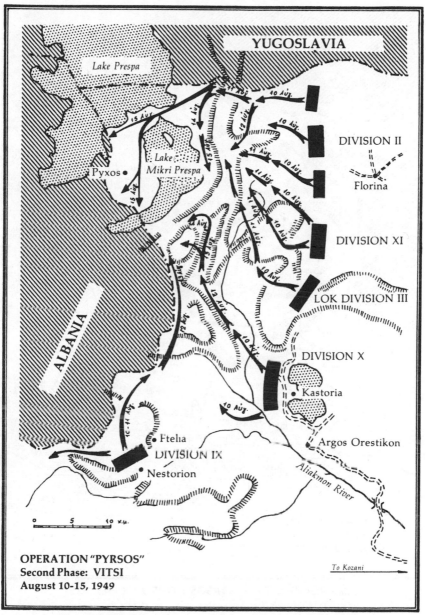

Map 8: OPERATION "PYRSOS"; SECOND PHASE: VITSI

423

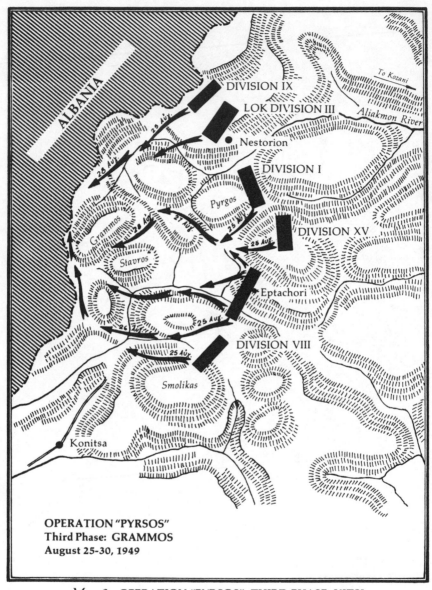

ALBANIA

To Kozani

DIVISION IX

LOK DIVISION III

Aliakmon River

Nestorion

DIVISION I

Pyrgos

DIVISION XV

Grammos

Stavros

Eptachori

DIVISION VIII

Smolikas

Konitsa

OPERATION "PYRSOS"
Third Phase: GRAMMOS
August 25-30, 1949

Map 9: **OPERATION "PYRSOS"; THIRD PHASE: VITSI**

424

FOOTNOTES

Chapter II

[1] For example, as a child the author had seen red paper leaflets stating that the Turkish government had granted a large foreign company the right to use the bones of those who had died during the battle of Sangarius—the most murderous battle of the war—for the production of phosphoric fertilizer.

[7] He died in Paris in 1936.

Chapter III

[1] Mario Cervi, *The Hollow Legions*.

[2] Site of the catastrophic defeat of the Greek army in Asia Minor in 1922. (*Ed. Note*)

Chapter IV

[1] Captain Tsigantes, who was killed later in Athens in an exchange of gunfire with men of the Italian security police who had discovered his hideout.

[2] Upon the arrival of American officers the name of the British Military Mission had changed to Allied Military Mission (A.M.M.).

[3] Dedijer, *Tito parle*.

[4] One of the most bitter complaints of the population of the countryside against ELAS was that it organized ambushes and actions of low military significance without taking into account the reprisals that followed. In order to avenge the death of a German soldier the Wehrmacht usually executed ten to twenty Greeks.

[5] Even today "the well of Meligalas" is an expression of horror in all of Greece.

Chapter V

[1] It is the author's duty for the sake of objectivity to add to the French and Greek edition of this book the following footnote:

Lately I chanced to meet a serious professional who was then a young ELAS guerrilla, one of those who had carried the explosives. According to him, the tiring transportation through the dirty water, using great care to keep the knapsacks of dynamite from getting wet, was done by a group of fifty volunteers to whom the importance of the operation was conveyed only at the last minute. They entered the network of sewers from a "hole" outside the Hatziconsta orphanage at midnight, completed their mission and came out from the same hole at seven in the morning. The young guerrilla does not remember the exact date of his underground walk, neither does he connect it with any holiday. But he does recall that they had waited anxiously to hear the great explosion they were told would take place at ten o'clock that same morning. They had not learned then, nor even later, that the explosives had been discovered by the English. He had attributed the cancelling of the explosion to the various disagreements and conflicts between the leaders of the December revolution, the most conservative of whom (Zevgos, Siantos) may have been influenced by Churchill's visit.

There is no doubt as to the sincerity of the above because of the narrator's character. Neither can the sincerity of the leader of the English patrol be doubted, nor that of the hotel director, who saw for himself the "knapsacks" and the "small boxes" of dynamite.

So the most probable explanation must be that, in order to secure the success of the operation, the ELAS leadership wanted to increase the explosives and the operation was discovered. Let us further note that, according to the opinion of specialists, a large part of the explosive power of the dynamite would have evaporated towards the open sewer.

According to these facts, there does not seem to be any other explanation, especially as the revolution was failing after twenty-three days of bloodshed and terror.

[2] In the official documents on the period this dialogue was expressed in milder terms. I am writing it as Plastiras himself told me and as confirmed by other persons present.

426

Chapter VI

[1] This letter showed that he disagreed with the entry of Greece into the war against Italy.

[2] George Kennan. His long confidential report to the Department of State of February 22, 1946, the major part of which was published in the journal, *Foreign Affairs* (July 1947), signed "X", was the first comprehensive analysis of communist mentality and its effect on the foreign policy of the Soviet Union. Kennan explained in his report why we are faced with a political force fanatically convinced that there could never be a permanent modus vivendi with the United States, and that the Soviet Union—indifferent to the logic of reason—was highly insensitive to the logic of force.

[3] Before the election of Tsaldaris as leader of the Populists another government was formed under the leadership of the president of the Council of State, Poulitsas, which lasted only a fortnight.

Chapter VII

[1] We shall not distinguish between army and national guard as long as there are no true military operations. The national guard was a branch of the army whose men were less trained, lightly armed—often with old weapons—and with officers who largely were army reservists.

Chapter IX

[1] The term designates a person both a member of EAM and associated with the Bulgarians; the extreme Right applied that term even to Liberals.

[2] This Popovic had nothing to do with Koca Popovic (see below). According to reports by certain foreign journalists, the leader of the group was General Petko Dapcevic, "the liberator of Belgrade", who was the Yugoslav ambassador in Athens in 1960. This rumor, which still persists, is completely unfounded.

[3] He is the present editor of the French daily, *Le Monde*.

⁴ Pseudonym of one of the best guerrilla chiefs who had a remarkable record during the occupation as a captain of ELAS in NW Macedonia.

⁵ In the meantime, due to the wounding of Dovas, Lieutenant Colonel G. Palantas had undertaken the command of the brigade.

⁶ We know that the UN Commission of Observers had recommended the formation of a committee that would replace it in a more prmanent way. The proposal had been rejected by the Security Council (4/8/47) because of a veto by the Soviet Union. But, in autumn, the UN General Assembly, by a vote of 40 to 6 with 11 abstentions, had formed an investigative group that was called the "Balkan committee". It was composed of representatives of Australia, Brazil, France, U.S.A., Great Britain, Mexico, Holland and Pakistan. Greece's neighbors had declared that they would not allow the committee to enter their territory, but the committee installed itself in Greece (Thessalonike, Nov. 21, 1947) and immediately undertook a detailed investigation.

Chapter X

¹ Unconfirmed reports said that the 120 prisoners, among whom were four officers and one doctor, had been summarily executed near the village of Tsamanta. In 1971, a mass grave with 120 skeletons was discovered in a stream where the water had washed away the soil. Their hands were tied with wires and many bones were crushed.

² Stratos Moutsoyiannis, the murderer of Christos Ladas, not only was never executed and is now free, but in an inexplicable recent appearance for propaganda purposes, on February 2, 1973 in Athens, he was allowed a press conference, thus causing an unacceptable sensation.

³ Twenty-five years later, one phrase in this discussion makes a special impression: "We do not have a navy". It is interesting to ask oneself where Greece, Turkey and Yugoslavia would be now if Stalin then had the formidable Mediterranean fleet that his successors have today.

⁴ Nevertheless, it is curious that, later on, nobody could find a copy of this interesting book anywhere and it was never republished.

⁵ The Supreme Military Council under the presidency of Zachariadis was comprised of the members of the Politburo of the KKE, Markos

and his faithful chief of staff, and the chief of all political commissars.

6 Major Koumanakos, who also distinguished himself on battlefields in Greece and Korea and who later had a brilliant military career, became a political exile for three years after April 21, 1967.

7 Neither in the memoirs of General Tsakalotos, nor in other attainable sources one can find an explanation for the fall of Mourghana. What has been mentioned above came from individuals who lived through this battle.

8 *Caique* — A small Mediterranean merchant vessel.

9 Among these, one of the most important was the leader of the maritime workers' union, Tony Ambatielos, who was active especially in Genoa and Marseilles. After the guerrilla war he was arrested and sentenced to death but not executed. He remained in prison for many years. His wife, of English nationality, was for years the hysterical heroine of incidents that took place during visits to London by the Greek royal family and other Greek personalities.

Chapter XI

1 The essence of the discussions, as well as extracts of speeches, have been taken from the official minutes of the various U.N. sessions. This applies also to all other appeals on the Greek issue before the United Nations.

2 According to this resolution, the International Red Cross was instructed to search for the abducted children and repatriate them on request of their parents.

3 Free translation from verses written by the Greek poet, Costis Palamas (1859-1943).

4 French doctor Donzelo, who had been urgently summoned from Paris, ordered him to remain flat on his back all the time, even if he found it difficult. Sofoulis answered "It is obvious, doctor, that you are not a Greek. Everybody knows here that this is very easy for me to do because both the Right and the Left are equally disagreeable to me".

⁵ Yannoulis came from the village of Eptachori in Grammos and was one of the original organizers of EAM/ELAS in that area. No one knows why Zachariadis disliked him so much, but this fact eventually led him before a firing squad. The official excuse is not clear. According to D. Eudes (1970), on August 20, 1948, it was recalled that in 1942 he had belonged to a nationalist movement. According to others, Yannoulis was not pardoned for the way in which he answered a question put to him by V. Vasiliou—one of the best-known journalists in Athens today —concerning the autonomy of Macedonia. On that occasion he had categorically stated that the KKE would defend the territorial integrity of Greece. Even that second explanation does not seem plausible. The discussion with V. Vasiliou took place in the Spring of 1947 when a group of Greek journalists, who were trying to see Markos, wandered into the mountains with the representatives of the Balkan Commission and were able to meet captain Yannoulis instead.

⁶ Executed in Athens in March 1952 under a government of the Center presided over by Plastiras, after having been twice condemned to death by two military tribunals; he had returned secretly to Greece in June 1950 across the Bulgarian frontier. He had at his disposal at least two wireless stations and had done some espionage work; the authorities took from him, along with a transmitter some copies of his messages and his cipher code.

⁷ His unusual career began with his graduation from the Army Cadet School of Athens. Between 1936 and 1937, when George II was King of Greece, he served as commander of the Palace Guard. His brother, who also served in the ranks of DAG, was an officer of the gendarmerie and an aide-de-camp of Costas Maniadakis, security chief in the Metaxas regime. This family knew how to disguise itself.

⁸ This order was found in the saddlebag of captain Lefterias, who was killed in the battle.

⁹ Author's note: Let us mention here, in memoriam, the story of my close friend, the late Apostolis Boumbas, or Galanis. Dynamic, clever and patriotic, he dared—though his beliefs were known to all—to come down from the summer meadow near Metsovo in 1947 to spend the winter in Thessaly. He had taken with him two of his younger sons and a young shepherd to guard his flock. Since he had been friendly to the guerrillas who passed by his isolated sheepfold, he thought that he would be safe. But at night, he had gone to the tent of an army captain

and had given him information. One night two soldiers murdered the captain and defected to DAG. Soon after that, a threatening band appeared at Boumbas' sheepfold. The shepherd and the youngest son hid behind some rocks. Boumbas and his elder son were tied with their hands behind their backs and slaughtered. Before he was killed, Apostolis shouted at them: "Slaughter me, dogs! In the end Greece will slaughter you all!" (the boy's testimony) His sheep, about 800 head in all, were carried off by the guerrillas. Of the family, the only remaining members were an old mother, a 20-year-old son and five girls between the ages of two and fifteen.

10 Among others interned there was Andreas Tzimas, a member of the powerful three-member committee of ELAS (with Aris and Sarafis) during the German occupation. He was one of the most capable among the cadres of the KKE. As soon as he arrived at Grammos in April 1948, he was sent on to Belgrade because it seems that he was seriously ill. Later, since he was the enemy of Zachariadis, he was moved from one prison to another in Hungary and elsewhere, until 1956 when, after Stalin's death, the KKE leaders settled matters between themselves. As shall be seen further on, in 1956, Zachariadis was removed and Tzimas and the others were reinstated.

11 Substantially these proposals did not include any particularly awkward conditions. They did not even mention the recall of foreign missions. The Provisional Government declared that it was ready to accept mediation towards a ceasefire with the final aim of holding elections under the supervision of the United Nations.

12 Albania was assisted by shipments across the Black Sea and the Mediterranean and Bulgaria through others from Rumania. Very probably, on the advice of Moscow, Rumania started assisting DAG appreciably from the last months of 1948. It even had placed its hospitals at the disposal of wounded guerrillas from Greece.

Chapter XII

1 During the twenty years following the guerrilla war, some 19,718 expatriates persons, out of which 3,688 were children, have been repatriated.

2 *Editor's Note:* After the fall of the military *junta* that ruled Greece until

1974 the term "Civil War" has supplanted "Bandit War" as the official designation of the conflicts between 1944-1949.

3 For the sake of objectivity the author wishes to add that a) Conditions of mobilization were completely different for the two sides. On the communist side, forced mobilization of followers and non-followers took place in certain areas and often within one or two days of an attack; as for the national army, mobilization was carried out with ease. b) In the communist camp, party leadership for over a year and a half neither adopted DAG officially, nor seriously encouraged followers to enlist. When it did so (1948), the number of volunteers increased, but only a little. c) In practice, the enlistment of volunteers in DAG presented some difficulties which could become very large, especially if they concerned someone in prison or exiled to an island. But, in general, a young man who wished to take to the mountains could do so. d) Although in the national army camp eagerness to get into the fight was a general characteristic, there was also a small percentage of people who played the role of hero after managing to get secure and sometimes profitable positions.

But these facts do not reverse the fundamental one mentioned above; in general, on the one side there was lack of eagerness and hesitation for personal participation in the armed struggle; and on the other, there was great eagerness. Bravery and obstinacy were about equal on both sides of the hill.

4 These successes were greater than is usually believed. Besides the 490 damaged aircraft and 37 injured crewmen—mostly from shrapnel or forced landings but, sometimes, from sabotage—DAG anti-aircraft fire during the guerrilla war brought down 58 planes and caused the deaths of 36 officers and six non-commissioned officers of the air force. Most of these losses were due to the low altitude missions of the aircraft which also drew infantry fire. Bodies of pilots recovered by the national army were always horribly mutilated. This was also true in the case of Lieutenant Colonel Edner of the American Mission who was an observer on a Greek air force plane shot down on January 23, 1949 while flying over the Karpenissi battlefield.

5 For those who took refuge in Yugoslavia, see below.

6 Following are two examples out of many: Ioannis Ioannidis, interim president of the Provisional Government after Markos commented that, "The position of each one of us within the Party is a result of our

432

attitude towards the Soviet Union (Congress of the KKE, 1950), Dimitrios Vlantas, member of the Central Committee and of the Markos government, "We are soldiers of Stalin's great army . . . where Stalin leads, victory is certain" (same Congress as above).

[7] In the elections of 1958, EDA received 24% of the votes. The Cyprus issue was then going through its sharpest and most difficult phase. All of the western countries were opposed to the Greek position and part of the voters, in order to express their reaction, voted for EDA, the only party that was anti-West.

[8] In using the word "ally", Lenin means a "fellow-traveller" of that time, whether the person was a Social Democrat or other.

BIBLIOGRAPHY

Backley, Chris. *Greece and Crete* 1941. London, 1953.

Badoglio, Pietro. *L'Italia nella Seconda Guerra Mondiale*. Milano, 1946.

Capell, R. *Simiomata; A Greek Notebook* 1944-1945. London, 1946.

Cavallero, Carlo. *Il dramma del Maresciallo Cavallero*. Milano, 1952.

Cavallero, Ugo. *Comando Supremo. Diario* 1940-1943. Bologna, 1948.

Cecovini, Manlio. *Ponte Perati—La Julia in Grecia*. Firenze, 1966.

Cervi, Mario. *Storia della Guerra di Grecia*. Milano, 1965.

Chastenet, Jacques. *Winstn Churchill et l'Angleterre du XXe siecle*. Paris, 1956.

Churchill, Winston. *The Second World War*. London, 1948-1953.

Clark, Alan. *The Fall of Crete*. London, 1962.

Dedijer. *Tito parle*. Paris, 1953.

Djilas, Milovan. *Conversations avec Staline*. Paris, 1962.

Erkin, Feridun Cemal. *Les relations Turco-Sovietiques et la Question des Detroits*. Ankara, 1968.

Eudes, Dominique. *Les Capetanios*. Paris, 1970.

Fontaine, Andre. *Histoire de la Guerre Froiden*. Paris, Tome I, 1965. Tome II, 1967.

Freymond, Jacques. *Lenine et l'imperialisme*. Lausanne, 1951.

Kedros, Andre. *La Resistance Grecque* (1940-1944). Paris, 1966.

Koussoulas, George. *Revolution and Defeat*. London, 1965.

Leeper, Reginald. *When Greek Meets Greek*. London, 1950.

Lenin. *Selected Works*. New York, 1946.

Lenine. *Deux tactiques de la social-democratie revolutionnaire*. Moscow, 1948.

Liddel, Hart. *The Other Side of the Hill*. London, 1948.

Long, Gavin. *Australians in the War of 1939-1945*. 2nd vol. Canberra, 1953.

Loverdo, Costa de. *Les Maquis Rouges dans les Balkans.*. Paris, 1967.

Myers, E. C. W. *Greek Entanglement*. London, 1955.

O'Ballance Edgar. *The Greek Civil War 1944-1949*. London, 1966.

Prasca, (Visconti) Sebastiano. *Io ho aggredito la Grecia*. Milano, 1946.

Pricolo Francesco. *Ignavia contro Eroismo*. Roma, 1946.

Roatta. *Il Processo Roatta. Documenti*. Roma, 1945.

Rendel, A. M. *Appointment in Crete*. London, 1953.

Shub, David. *Lenin (Biography)* 9th Edition. New York, 1959.

Stettinius Jr., E. R. *Yalta, Roosevelt et les Russes*. Paris, 1949.

Thayer, Charles. *Guerrilla*. New York, London, 1963.

Tsatsos, Jeanne. *The Sword's Fierce Edge*. Vanderbilt University Press. Nashville, 1969.

Vukmanovic, Svetosar (Tempo). *How and Why the People's Liberation Struggle of Greece Met with Defeat*. London, 1950.

Woodhouse, C. M. *Apple of Discord*. London, 1951.

Woodhouse, C. M. *The Story of Modern Greece*. London, 1968.

Xydis, Stefan. *Greece and the Great Powers 1944-1947*. Thessaloniki, 1963.

Basic monographs and primary sources in Greek.

Ἀρχηγεῖον Στρατοῦ: Ἐκδόσεις Διευθύνσεως Ἱστορίας Στρατοῦ. Ἐχρησιμοποιήθησαν οἱ τόμοι οἱ ἀφορῶντες τὸν Ἑλληνοϊταλικὸν Πόλεμον καὶ τὸν «Ἀντισυμμοριακὸν Ἀγῶνα». (Οἱ τελευταῖοι τόμοι δὲν εἶχον ἐκδοθῆ ὅταν ἐγράφετο ἡ παροῦσα μελέτη, ἀλλὰ τὰ στοιχεῖα των ἦσαν προσιτά.)

Γιαντζῆ Δημητρίου, Ἀντιστρατήγου ἐ.ἀ., Ἀρχηγοῦ ΓΕΣ, Διοικητοῦ Στρατιᾶς: «Τὰ δέκα τελευταῖα μου χρόνια ὡς στρατιώτου εἰς τὴν ὑπηρεσίαν τῆς Πατρίδος» (ἀνέκδοτον).

Γρηγοροπούλου Θεοδώρου, Ἀντιστρατήγου, Ἐπιτίμου Ἀρχηγοῦ Γενικοῦ Ἐπιτελείου Ἐθνικῆς Ἀμύνης: «Ἀπὸ τὴν κορυφὴ τοῦ λόφου (Ἀναμνήσεις καὶ Στοχασμοί, 1914-1952 καὶ 1959-1962)». Ἀθῆναι, 1966.

Γληνοῦ Δημητρίου: «Τί εἶναι καὶ τί θέλει τὸ Ἐθνικὸ Ἀπελευθερωτικὸ Μέτωπο». Ἀθῆναι, 1944.

Δαφνῆ Γρηγορίου: «Ἡ Ἑλλὰς μεταξὺ δύο Πολέμων, 1923-1940». Ἀθῆναι, Ἴκαρος, 1955.

Δαφνῆ Κωνσταντίνου: «Χρόνια Πολέμου καὶ Κατοχῆς. Κέρκυρα 1940-1944». Κέρκυρα, 1966.

«Δημοκρατικὸς Στρατός. Περιοδικὸ μηνιαίας ἐκδόσεως, τοῦ Γενικοῦ Ἀρχηγείου Δημοκρατικοῦ Στρατοῦ»: Τεύχη 3ον (Μάρτιος), 9ον (Σεπτέμβριος), 10ον (Ὀκτώβριος), 12ον (Δεκέμβριος) 1948.

Δρακούλη Μαξίμου: «Τὰ οἰκογενειακὰ τοῦ Κ.Κ.Ε.», Ἀθῆναι, 1949.

Ζαφειροπούλου Δημητρίου, Ὑποστρατήγου ἐ.ἀ.: «Ὁ ἀντισυμμοριακὸς ἀγὼν 1944-1945-1949». Ἀθῆναι, 1956.

Ζαχαριάδη Νίκου: «Θέσεις γιὰ τὴν Ἱστορία τοῦ Κ.Κ.Ε.», Κεντρικὴ Ἐπιτροπὴ τοῦ Κ.Κ.Ε. Ἀθήνα, 1945.

Τοῦ ἰδίου: «Δέκα χρόνια πάλης». Κεντρικὴ Ἐπιτροπὴ τοῦ Κ.Κ.Ε. Ἀθήνα, 1950.

Τοῦ ἰδίου: «Καινούργια κατάσταση, καινούργια καθήκοντα», Λευκωσία, 1950.

Ζέβγου Γιάννη: «Ἡ Λαϊκὴ Ἀντίσταση τοῦ Δεκέμβρη». Ἀθήνα, 1945.

Γ. Π. Κανελλάκη: «Κατηγορῶ τὸ Κ.Κ.Ε. μὲ μάρτυρα τὸ ἴδιο». Ἀθῆναι, 1950.

Καραγεώργη Κωνσταντίνου: «Γύρω ἀπὸ τὸν Δεκέμβρη». Ἀθήνα, 1945.

Κ.Κ.Ε.—Κεντρικὴ Ἐπιτροπή: «Τὸ Κ.Κ.Ε. ἀπὸ τὸ 1918 ὡς τὸ 1931. Μὲ παράρτημα κειμένων τῆς περιόδου 1932-1941». Ἀθήνα, 1947.*

Κ.Κ.Ε.—Κεντρικὴ Ἐπιτροπή: «Δέκα χρόνια ἀγῶνες, 1935-1945». Ἀθήνα, 1948.

Λαζοπούλου Νικολάου: «Ἡ Μάχη τῶν Συνόρων». Ἀθῆναι, 1952.

437

Μαντᾶ Χρήστου, 'Αντιστρατήγου ἐ.ά.: «Πῶς ἐφθάσαμε εἰς τὰς μάχας τοῦ Γράμμου καὶ Βίτσι, 1948 καὶ 1949». ῎Εκδοσις Μαΐου 1950.

Μπαρτζώτα Βασιλείου: «Ἡ Πολιτικὴ Στελεχῶν τοῦ Κ.Κ.Ε. στὰ τελευταῖα δέκα χρόνια». Κεντρικὴ 'Επιτροπὴ τοῦ Κ.Κ.Ε., 1950.

Νάτσινα 'Αλεξάνδρου, 'Αντιστρατήγου Πυροβολικοῦ: «'Ανταρτοπόλεμος». ῎Εκδοσις Γενικοῦ 'Επιτελείου Στρατοῦ. 'Αθῆναι, 1950.

Νάτσινα Θεοδώρου, Γενικοῦ 'Επιθεωρητοῦ Μέσης 'Εκπαιδεύσεως: «Οἱ Μακεδόνες πραμματευτάδες εἰς τὰς χώρας Αὐστρίας καὶ Οὑγγαρίας».

Πανταζῆ Κωνσταντίνου, Ταξιάρχου ἐ.ά.: «Τὰ δύο ῍Οχι». 'Αθῆναι, 1972.

Παπάγου 'Αλεξάνδρου: «Ὁ Πόλεμος τῆς 'Ελλάδος, 1940-1941». 'Αθῆναι, 1945.

Τοῦ ἰδίου: «Ὁ 'Ελληνικὸς Στρατὸς καὶ ἡ πρὸς Πόλεμον προπαρασκευή του ἀπὸ Αὐγούστου 1923 μέχρις 'Οκτωβρίου 1940». 'Αθῆναι, 1945.

Παπακωνσταντίνου Θ.: «Ἡ ἀνατομία τῆς 'Επαναστάσεως». 'Αθῆναι, 1952.

Παπανδρέου Γεωργίου: «Ἡ 'Απελευθέρωσις τῆς 'Ελλάδος». 'Αθῆναι, 1945.

Π⋯λοπούλου Α. 1.: «'Εθνοπροδοσίαι καὶ ψευδολογίαι τοῦ Κ.Κ.Ε.».

Πεντζ⋯ τούλου Θωμᾶ, 'Αντιστρατήγου ἐ.ά.: «1941-1950: Τραγικὴ Πορεία», 'Αθῆναι, 1953.

Πετσοπούλου 'Ιωάννου: «Τὰ ἐθνικὰ ζητήματα καὶ οἱ ῍Ελληνες Κομμουνιστές». 'Αθήνα, 1946.

Τοῦ ἰδίου: «Τὰ αἴτια τῆς διαγραφῆς μου ἀπὸ τὸ Κ.Κ.Ε.». 'Αθῆναι, 1946.

Σαράφη Στεφάνου: «Ὁ ΕΛΑΣ». 'Αθῆναι, 1946.

Σταυρίδη 'Ελευθερίου: «Τὰ παρασκήνια τοῦ Κ.Κ.Ε.». 'Αθῆναι, 1953.

Τσακαλώτου Θρασυβούλου, Στρατηγοῦ, Διοικητοῦ τοῦ Α' Σ. Στρατοῦ, 'Αρχηγοῦ ΓΕΣ: «Σαράντα χρόνια στρατιώτης τῆς 'Ελλάδος. 'Ιστορικαὶ ἀναμνήσεις. Πῶς ἐκερδίσαμε τοὺς ἀγῶνας 1940-1949». 'Αθῆναι, 1960.

Τσάτσου Θεμιστοκλῆ: «Ὁ Δεκέμβριος τοῦ 1944». 'Αθῆναι, 1945.

Τοῦ ἰδίου: «Αἱ παραμοναὶ τῆς 'Απελευθερώσεως». 'Αθῆναι, 1949.

Τσάτσου 'Ιωάννας: «Φύλλα Κατοχῆς». 'Αθῆναι, 1966.

Τυπάλδου Πέτρου, Συνταγματάρχου Πυροβολικοῦ: «Ἡ Μάχη τοῦ Μετσόβου». Γενικὴ Στρατιωτικὴ 'Επιθεώρησις. Μηνιαία ῎Εκδοσις Γενικοῦ 'Επιτελείου Στρατοῦ. Νοέμβριος 1967.

Τοῦ ἰδίου: «Ἡ Μάχη τῆς Κονίτσης». ῍Οπου ἀνωτέρω. 'Ιανουάριος 1968.

Τοῦ ἰδίου: «Ἡ προσβολὴ ὑπὸ τῶν Κομμουνιστῶν τῆς πόλεως τῶν Γρεβενῶν». ῍Οπου ἀνωτέρω. Μάρτιος 1968.

Τοῦ ἰδίου: «Ἡ Μάχη τῆς Φλωρίνης». ῍Οπου ἀνωτέρω. Δεκέμβριος 1967.

'Υφυπουργείου Τύπου καὶ Πληροφοριῶν: «Ἡ ἐναντίον τῆς 'Ελλάδος ἐπιβουλή». 'Αθῆναι, 'Ιούνιος 1947.

438